OBJECTIVE
proficiency

Annette Capel
Wendy Sharp

Self-study Student's Book

D1634504

CAMBRIDGE
UNIVERSITY PRESS

PUBLISHED BY THE PRESS SYNDICATE OF THE UNIVERSITY OF CAMBRIDGE
The Pitt Building, Trumpington Street, Cambridge CB2 1RP, United Kingdom

CAMBRIDGE UNIVERSITY PRESS
The Edinburgh Building, Cambridge CB2 2RU, UK
40 West 20th Street, New York, NY 10011–4211, USA
477 Williamstown Road, Port Melbourne, VIC 3207, Australia
Ruiz de Alarcón 13, 28014 Madrid, Spain
Dock House, The Waterfront, Cape Town 8001, South Africa

http://www.cambridge.org

First published 2002
Reprinted 2004

Printed in Dubai by Oriental Press

Text typeface Minion 11/13.5pt *System* QuarkXpress® [GECKO]

A catalogue for this book is available from the British Library

Library of Congress Cataloguing in Publication data

ISBN 0 521 00031 9 Self-study Student's Book
ISBN 0 521 00030 0 Student's Book
ISBN 0 521 00032 7 Workbook
ISBN 0 521 00033 5 Workbook with Answers
ISBN 0 521 00034 3 Teacher's Book
ISBN 0 521 00035 1 Class Cassette Set

Cover concept by Dale Tomlinson and design by Jo Barker

Produced by Gecko Limited, Bicester, Oxon.

Map of Objective Proficiency Student's Book

TOPIC	LESSON FOCUS	EXAM SKILLS	GRAMMAR	VOCABULARY
Unit 1 Ring the changes 8–13 Talking about change	1.1 Listening and vocabulary 1.2 Grammar 1.3 Summary skills	Paper 4 Listening: 1 Paper 1 Reading: 1 Paper 3 Use of English: 5 (Summary sentences)	Perfect tenses	Introduction to idioms Phrasal verbs Suffix endings
Exam folder 1 14–15		Paper 3 Use of English: 1 Open cloze Paper 3 Use of English: 2 Word formation cloze		
Unit 2 Expectation 16–21 Expectations	1.1 Reading and vocabulary 1.2 Grammar and vocabulary 1.3 Listening and speaking	Paper 1 Reading: 2 Paper 3 Use of English: 2 Listening for details Paper 5 Speaking: 1	Aspects of the future Prepositional phrases *Have no* + noun Pronunciation: homophones	Word formation – noun endings Similes Idioms – nouns used as verbs
Writing folder 1 22–23		Paper 2 Writing: 1 Letter		
Unit 3 Strange behaviour 24–29 Human and animal behaviour	1.1 Listening and vocabulary 1.2 Grammar 1.3 Summary skills	Listening for true/false Paper 3 Use of English: 1 and 5 (Reformulation 1)	Conditional forms	Idioms – order of words *Quite, rather, fairly* Negative adjectives
Exam folder 2 30–31		Paper 3 Use of English: 3 Gapped sentences Paper 3 Use of English: 4 Key word transformations		
Unit 4 Sweet rituals 32–37 Food and ritual	1.1 Reading and vocabulary 1.2 Grammar and vocabulary 1.3 Listening and speaking	Paper 1 Reading: 4 Paper 5 Speaking: 2	Past tenses	Collocation Compound adjectives Adjectives and idioms to do with food
Writing folder 2 38–39		Paper 2 Writing: 2 Review		
Revision Units 1–4 40–41				
Unit 5 The consumer society 42–47 Advertising, shopping	1.1 Listening and vocabulary 1.2 Grammar 1.3 Summary skills	Paper 4 Listening: 2 Paper 1 Reading: 1 Paper 3 Use of English: 5 (Working with two texts)	Countable/uncountable nouns Possession Preposition review Spelling	Idioms with *right* Abstract nouns
Exam folder 3 48–49		Paper 3 Use of English: 5 Comprehension questions and summary writing task		
Unit 6 The sound of music 50–55 Music	1.1 Reading and vocabulary 1.2 Grammar and vocabulary 1.3 Listening and speaking	Paper 1 Reading: 3 Paper 3 Use of English: 1 and 4 Paper 4 Listening: 2 Paper 5 Speaking: 2	Degrees of likelihood Pronunciation: contrastive stress	Phrases with *take* Collocations with adjectives and adverbs Idioms with music words
Writing folder 3 56–57		Paper 2 Writing: 1 Essay		
Unit 7 Vision on 58–63 Art and sight	1.1 Listening and vocabulary 1.2 Grammar 1.3 Summary skills	Paper 4 Listening: 1 Paper 3 Use of English: 2 and 5 (Questions on the texts 1)	Participle clauses	Idioms with *eye* Extended noun phrases

TOPIC	LESSON FOCUS	EXAM SKILLS	GRAMMAR	VOCABULARY
Exam folder 4 64–65		Paper 1 Reading: 1 Lexical cloze		
Unit 8 **Urban jungle** 66–71 City living	1.1 Reading and vocabulary 1.2 Grammar and vocabulary 1.3 Listening and speaking	Paper 1 Reading: 2 Paper 3 Use of English: 3 and 4 Paper 5 Speaking: 3	Inversion	Compound adjectives Words with negative connotation Idioms by key word
Writing folder 4 72–73		Paper 2 Writing: 2 Proposal		
Revision Units 5–8 74–75				
Unit 9 **Fitting in** 76–81 Attitudes	1.1 Listening and vocabulary 1.2 Grammar and vocabulary 1.3 Summary skills	Paper 4 Listening: 4 Paper 3 Use of English: 1 and 5 (Linking 1)	Gerunds and infinitives	Idioms with *come* Prefixes Personal appearance, personality
Exam folder 5 82–83		Paper 1 Reading: 3 Gapped text		
Unit 10 **Globalisation** 84–89 Language and culture	1.1 Reading and vocabulary 1.2 Grammar and vocabulary 1.3 Listening and speaking	Reference devices Paper 1 Reading: 1 Paper 3 Use of English: 4 and 2 Paper 4 Listening: 1 Paper 5 Speaking: 2	Past verb forms Pronunciation: word stress	Expressions with *turn*
Writing folder 5 90–91		Paper 2 Writing: 1 Article		
Unit 11 **For better, for worse** 92–97 Relationships	1.1 Listening and vocabulary 1.2 Grammar 1.3 Summary skills	Paper 4 Listening: 3 Paper 3 Use of English: 1, 2 and 5 (Reformulation 2)	Gradable and ungradable adjectives	Idioms to do with relationships Phrasal verbs
Exam folder 6 98–101		Paper 1 Reading: 2 Themed texts		
Unit 12 **At the cutting edge** 102–107 Scientific advances	1.1 Reading and vocabulary 1.2 Grammar and vocabulary 1.3 Listening and speaking	Paper 1 Reading: 3 Paper 3 Use of English: 4 Paper 5 Speaking: 3	Passive structures Pronunciation: stress and emphasis	Idioms with technical words Idioms with *set*
Writing folder 6 108–109		Paper 2 Writing: 2 Report		
Revision Units 9–12 110–111				
Unit 13 **Save the planet** 112–117 The environment	1.1 Listening and vocabulary 1.2 Grammar 1.3 Summary skills	Paper 4 Listening: 1 Paper 1 Reading: 1 Paper 3 Use of English: 1 and 5 (Questions on the texts 2)	Direct/reported speech	Register Synonyms
Exam folder 7 118–119		Paper 1 Reading: 4 Multiple-choice text		
Unit 14 **Get fit, live longer** 120–125 Sport and health	1.1 Reading and vocabulary 1.2 Grammar and vocabulary 1.3 Listening and speaking	Paper 1 Reading: 2 Paper 3 Use of English: 1 and 4 Listening practice Paper 5 Speaking: 2	Articles review Preposition review Pronunciation: noun/verb/adjective stress	Alliteration Register Expressions with *live* Idioms with nouns and no article

Content of the Proficiency Examination

The Cambridge Proficiency examination consists of five papers, each of which is worth 40 marks. It is not necessary to pass all five papers in order to pass the examination. There are five grades: Pass – A, B, C; Fail – D, E.

As well as being told your grade, you will also be given a graphical profile of your performance, i.e. it will show whether you have done especially well or badly on some of the papers.

Paper 1 Reading 1 hour 30 minutes

There are four parts to this paper and they are always in the same order. Each part contains either one or more texts and a comprehension task. The texts used are from books (fiction and non-fiction), non-specialist articles from journals, magazines and newspapers, promotional and informational materials (e.g. advertisements, guide books, manuals).

Part	Task Type	Number of Questions	Task Format	Objective Exam folder
1	Four-option multiple choice lexical cloze	18	You must choose which word from four answers completes each of the gaps in each of the three texts (375–500 words in total).	**4** (64–65)
2	Four-option multiple choice	8	You must read four themed texts (600–900 words in total) and answer two questions on each.	**6** (98–101)
3	Gapped text	7	You must read a text (800–1100 words) with paragraphs removed. You need to use the missing paragraphs to complete the text.	**5** (82–83)
4	Four-option multiple choice	7	You must read a text (700–850 words) and answer the questions by finding the relevant information in the text.	**7** (118–119)

Paper 2 Writing 2 hours

There are two parts to this paper. Part 1 is compulsory, you have to answer it. In Part 2 there are four questions and you must choose one. Each part carries equal marks and you are expected write between 300–350 words for each task.

Part	Task Type	Number of Tasks	Task Format	Objective Writing folder
1	Question 1 A contextualised writing task within the following formats: • an article • an essay • a letter • a proposal	1 compulsory	You are given material in the form of notes or a short text or an extract from a newspaper. You will have to react to the information, presenting and developing arguments, expressing and supporting opinions, evaluating ideas, etc.	**1** (22–23) **3** (56–57) **5** (90–91) **7** (126–127) **9** (160–161)
2	Questions 2–4 • an article • a letter • a proposal • a report • a review Question 5 Choice of 3 questions on set books: article, essay, letter, review, report	4 choose one	You are given a choice of topics which you have to respond to in the way specified.	Article **10** (176–177) Letter **10** (176–177) Review **2** (38–39) Report **6** (108–109) Set text **8** (142–143)

Paper 3 Use of English 1 hour 30 minutes

There are five parts to this paper, which test your grammar, vocabulary and summary skills.

Part	Task Type	Number of Questions	Task Format	Objective Exam folder
1	Open cloze mainly testing grammar	15	You must complete a text with 15 gaps.	1 (14–15)
2	Word formation	10	You need to use the right form of a given word to fill each of ten gaps in a text.	1 (14–15)
3	Gapped sentences	6 sets of 3 sentences	You must think of a word which would fit into all 3 of the given sentences.	2 (30–31)
4	Key word transformations	8	You must complete a sentence with a given word, so that it means the same as the first sentence.	2 (30–31)
5	Comprehension questions and summary writing task	4 questions on 2 texts and 1 summary writing task	You must first of all answer the four questions and then, using information from both texts, write the required summary in your own words.	3 (48–49)

Paper 4 Listening about 40 minutes

There are four parts to this paper. Each part is heard twice. The texts are a variety of types either with one speaker or more than one.

Part	Task Type	Number of Questions	Task Format	Objective Exam folder
1	Multiple choice	8	You hear four short, unrelated extracts, with either one or two speakers. You must choose an answer from A, B or C.	9 (152–153)
2	Sentence completion	9	You must complete gaps in sentences with information given mainly by one speaker.	8 (134–135)
3	Multiple choice	5	You will hear two speakers interacting. You must choose your answer from A, B, C or D.	9 (152–153)
4	Three-way matching	6	You must match statements about a text to either of two speakers or to both when they express agreement.	8 (134–135)

Paper 5 Speaking about 19 minutes

There are three parts to this paper. There are usually two of you taking the examination and two examiners. This paper tests your accuracy, vocabulary, pronunciation and ability to communicate and complete the tasks.

Part	Task Type	Time	Task Format	Objective Exam folder
1	The interviewer asks each candidate some questions	3 minutes	You will be asked some questions about yourself and asked to express personal opinions.	10 (168–169)
2	Two-way conversation between candidates	4 minutes	You will be given visual and spoken prompts and asked to have a discussion.	see above
3	A long turn for each candidate followed by a discussion on related topics	2 minutes each for the long turn 8 minutes following the long turns	You will be given a written question to respond to. You will then be asked to engage in a discussion on related topics.	see above

UNIT 1 Ring the changes

1 Everyone goes through changes, whether by choice or because of something outside their control. Talk about changes that have happened to you, relating them to these phrases.

- a change for the better
- the earliest change you can remember
- the most unexpected change
- a change involving people
- a change in location
- a change of heart

Which two phrases above are examples of idioms?
Find a third idiom on this page.

2 You will hear six different people (1–6) talking about a key change in their lives. Tick each speaker's life-changing moment. There is one extra that you will not need.

life-changing moment	1	2	3	4	5	6
being made redundant						
gaining media attention						
winning a competition						
meeting 'Mr Right'						
heading the wrong way						
losing something special						
stepping in for someone						

3 Listen again to check your answers. Then describe in detail what happened to each speaker. Try to use some of the phrasal verbs from the recording.

P hrase spot

List phrasal verbs by particle in a notebook and add new ones as you meet them. Remember to revise them from time to time.

4 Match these verbs to the correct particle to form phrasal verbs used in the recordings. For three of them, you will need to use two particles, as they are 'three-part' phrasal verbs.

verbs						
break	catch	cheer	chuck	cut	draw	end
get	hang	jump	look	pay	pick	rabbit
run	settle	stay	take	track	turn	wake

particles			
around	at	back	down
in	off	on	out
up	with		

5 Now complete these sentences with a phrasal verb in a suitable tense, combining one of the verbs in exercise 4 with the particle in brackets. Sometimes a three-part phrasal verb is needed.

EXAMPLE: Let's ...*get down*... *to* business – there's a huge amount to discuss. (down + 1)

a Several of us .... from entering the cave, as we were unsure what we would find in there. (back)

b The radio DJ .... the caller, in a desperate attempt to change the subject. (in + 1)

c Jarvis can no longer afford to heat the flat, and in any case, his electricity .... last Friday. (off)

d Nancy found herself secretly admiring the way Mrs Griffiths simply .... anybody who didn't drive. (down + 1)

e He explained that shortly after they bought the house together, his wife Julia .... a Welsh mechanic. (off + 1)

f Did you know that Samantha .... Martin again – they're spending lots of time together. (up + 1)

g Health authorities have been asked to .... plans to reduce patient waiting lists. (up)

h Molly .... going to visit her ancient relatives by saying she felt violently sick. (out + 1)

E xam spot

Phrasal verbs are tested in both Paper 1 and Paper 3. Remember that they generally belong to an informal style, so should be used with care in Paper 2 Writing, where the tasks mostly require a more neutral or formal register.

E xam spot

Paper 1 Part 1 has three short texts, each with six gaps. Don't panic on finding unfamiliar words in options A–D. Try the other words in the gap first. If you're sure they don't fit, choose the word you don't know.

6 Read the text below, which is from the introduction to a book on *Feng-shui*. Decide which answer (A, B, C or D) best fits each gap.

The ancient Chinese philosophers who considered *feng* (wind or air) and *shui* (water) to be the (1) .... of mankind also understood that these were not the only supportive elements flowing through the landscape. They perceived a subtler (2) ...., calling it *chi* or 'cosmic breath'. This life force is well-known to acupuncturists, who have (3) .... elaborate maps of the 'meridians' or channels it uses to flow through the body. Kung Fu masters believe that *chi* can be concentrated in the body, allowing it to (4) .... almost supernatural feats, such as breaking concrete blocks with the edge of the hand. A real feng-shui master is able to (5) .... the flow of *chi* in a site, and may advise changes to the environment to (6) .... health, wealth and good fortune.

1	A	providers	B	sustainers	C	keepers	D promoters
2	A	vigour	B	weight	C	energy	D stimulus
3	A	shown up	B	built up	C	put up	D laid up
4	A	perform	B	play	C	act	D conduct
5	A	suspect	B	realise	C	sense	D endure
6	A	set about	B	come about	C	go about	D bring about

Grammar clinic

1 Match captions a–d to cartoons 1–4. Which do you think is the funniest? Why?

a 'If you'd been a failure, I often wonder how you would have coped with my resentment.'

b 'When you've been at sea as long as I have, Jenkins, you'll know that an oil slick has many moods.'

c 'You're a hypochondriac, but you've come to the right man. I'm a quack.'

d 'What makes you think your husband's engaged a private detective?'

What grammar area is common to all these captions?

2 This area often continues to cause problems even at Proficiency level. Tick any grammar areas below that you feel you need to work on. Add your main grammar problem if it is not listed.

- ☐ Modal verbs
- ☐ Passives
- ☐ Conditionals
- ☐ Perfect tenses
- ☐ Relative clauses
- ☐ Reported speech
- ☐ Uncountable nouns
- ☐ ....

3 Correct the errors in these sentences, which were written by past Proficiency candidates.

   a Three years ago I have been to Germany on a cultural exchange.
   b Tourism is a word that is being used for the last 50 years.
   c In England last year, I was able to appreciate things I have never seen in my entire life.
   d The noise levels have been measured in our suburb the other day and are twice the acceptable level.
   e All these years I'm practising basketball, I'm trying to become a better player.
   f When you will have bought your train tickets, you should take one each and put it into the machine.
   g Supposing they would have got married, wouldn't the day have come when they got bored with each other?
   h Nowadays, almost every disease has a cure and people have been caring more about their health.

4 Explain how tense choice alters the meaning in these sentences. In which two sentences is there no change in meaning?

   a Mirek *has gone / went* to Gdansk on business.
   b Our society *has been suffering / was suffering* from high unemployment for decades.
   c We *were given / have been given* more time to complete the task.
   d Top government ministers *have been dealing / have dealt* with the problem.
   e Matt and James *have played / have been playing* golf all day.
   f I've *thought / been thinking* about what you said.
   g Is there anything else we *could have done / will have done*?
   h Come October, we *will have lived / will have been living* here for eleven years.

5 Answer these questions so that they are true for you.

   a How long have you been learning English?
   b What have you never done that you would like to do?
   c What change has been made to your town recently that you don't approve of?
   d How many exams will you have taken, including Proficiency?
   e What may have changed in your life by this time next year?

Ⓖ ···⟶ page 180

6 Quickly read the extract below. What type of text is it?

Saturday May 2nd. The Lawns

11.59 I have nothing left. No house, no money, no car, no manuscripts. Eleanor's burned the lot. William's insects. Glenn's trainers. The bloke from the garage apologised for selling her the petrol. He had joined the crowd of excited onlookers as they watched my house burn down.

We stayed and watched until the flames had been extinguished. Then a Chief Inspector Baron told me that Eleanor Flood had been arrested and that in his opinion she should never have been 'let out of that secure unit'. Apparently her career as an arsonist started at teacher training college with a small fire in the bar after she'd been refused a late-night drink.

A fireman came out of the house carrying something carefully in his helmet. I hoped it was some of my fifty-pound notes, but it turned out to be Andrew. He is quite thin when his fur is wet and flattened down.

My father tried to comfort me by saying, 'Houses and   line 17 possessions can tie you down, lad.'

Things are undoubtedly bad. However, I have William and Glenn and Andrew and a smoke-damaged diary that a fireman found under the mattress of Glenn's bed. On the cover are the words: The Top Secret Diary of Glenn Mole (13). On the first page is written: 'When I grow up I wood like to be my dad.'

I have often wondered how I would stand up against fire, flood and tempest. Would I run in panic and try to save my own life? Until tonight I suspected that I would do exactly that. But when I woke to the exploding glass and the choking smoke, I found that my own life was unimportant to me. Nothing else mattered apart from removing my sons from danger.

I expect that by tomorrow I will have embellished the story and given myself a heroic status I do not deserve, but all the same, on this night at this hour, I am pleased to record that I acquitted myself well.

7 The text contains a number of perfect tenses. Underline them, identify them and explain why they have been used.

   Now find seven phrasal verbs and add them to your list.

8 From the text, what have you discovered about

   • the writer?
   • Eleanor Flood?
   • William?
   • Glenn?
   • Andrew?

9 How would you feel if this had happened to you? Is the writer's father right (lines 17–18)?

Summary sentences

1. What changes do you notice in the world around you? Identify the changes shown in the pictures and categorise them, choosing from the adjectives below. Then suggest other changes that could be classified under these categories.

commercial	environmental	physical	political
social	technological		

2. The adjectives above are formed from nouns. Generally, the suffix *-al* is added to the noun, as in *environmental*. Explain the formation rules for *commercial* and *technological*.

   Other common adjectival suffixes to nouns are *-ful* and *-less*. Give examples of such adjectives.

   The suffixes *-able* and *-ive* frequently combine with verbs to form adjectives, for example *enjoyable, supportive*. Explain the formation rules for *creative, desirable* and *variable*.

3. In the Paper 3, Part 5 summary task, you need to say things concisely, using words not present in the texts. For the sentences below, replace the part in italics with a single adjective formed from one of the verbs or nouns given. What adjectives are formed from the remaining words?

admire	alternate	exhaust
experiment	flaw	hope
identify	mass	notice
philosophy	predict	speech
success	understand	

EXAMPLE: I've been given this *very lengthy and complete* list of all the repairs needed in the flat. *exhaustive*

a. My boss's response to my plea for changes in my job description was *exactly what I was expecting.*

b. If it rains, do you have any *other suggestions to replace our original* plans?

c. Both sides in the conflict are *expressing their optimism* about an early ceasefire.

d. Jeremy seems *to have calmly accepted the news* about the break-in.

e. That play I went to see last night was *trying something new* in its use of dialect.

f. I was *incapable of any reply* when Kelly told me she had quit her job.

g. It's *really easy to see* how much fitter Liam has become since he started swimming regularly.

h. Your last piece of writing was *without any mistakes whatsoever.*

4 Extracts A–D show the type of texts used in the summary task.
In A and B, important information has been underlined.
Do the same in C and D. Then answer the questions below.

A

We pick up on <u>health</u> and <u>social status</u> from <u>facial features</u>, as shown by a recent research project where people were <u>unconsciously attracted</u> to healthy females and wealthy men, even when they only had a picture of a face (without make-up or jewellery) to judge them by.

B

It was in 1856, while working is his tiny laboratory at home, that William <u>Perkin</u> <u>produced</u>, quite by <u>chance</u>, the colour <u>mauve</u>, which not only <u>revolutionised the dye industry</u> but also led to important <u>innovations</u> in perfume, photography and, <u>most significantly</u> for modern <u>medicine</u>, to the development of <u>aspirin</u>.

C

Rather than burgers and fries being a product of the social changes seen over the last fifty years in America, the author suggests that fast food brands were to a large extent responsible for these changes, as they profoundly affected both lifestyle and diet.

D

Tiny holes found in human teeth estimated to be over 8000 years old are now believed to be the earliest evidence of dentistry, for when these holes were examined with an electron microscope, researchers found their sides were too perfectly rounded to be caused by bacteria and have therefore proposed that they were drilled by prehistoric dentists.

1 Which information in text A is summarised in the following sentence?
People form opinions of others by looking at their faces.
What has been omitted?

2 Which words in text A could be replaced with *assess* or *evaluate*, instead of the phrase used?

3 Which underlined words in text B could be replaced by others?

5 Choose from a–f the best summary sentence for text B, judging it by the inclusion of information, use of alternative words, choice of register and concision. Say why the remaining sentences are less successful.

a Mauve not only radically changed the dye industry but also led to new discoveries of anything from perfume to aspirin.

b By cooking up mauve in his lab, Perkin pushed the dye industry forward and set the ball rolling in other industries too, such as perfume and photography and aspirin.

c In accidentally discovering mauve, Perkin transformed dyeing and many other areas, notably medicine.

d Perkin discovered a special pale purple colour and this discovery was revolutionary for the dye industry and also for the pharmaceutical industry, since it led to the innovation of aspirin.

e Aspirin owes its development to Perkin, who found mauve by chance in his laboratory at home.

f Commercially-speaking, Perkin's chance discovery was very important, as other innovations followed, for example the development of aspirin.

6 Now write summary sentences for C and D, referring to the parts you have underlined and using between 12 and 20 words for each.

Exam folder 1

Paper 3 Part 1 Open cloze

In this part of the Use of English paper, you will be asked to complete a text which has fifteen numbered spaces. The missing words will have a mainly grammatical focus, although there might be a few vocabulary items. Each space must be filled with **one word only** and must be correctly spelled.

It is very important to read through the whole text carefully before you decide to write anything down. Some answers may be dependent on a sentence which comes later in the text. Awareness of the writer's train of thought and logical argument is often tested at Proficiency level.

The areas which are often tested are:

- fixed phrases
- relative pronouns
- linkers
- prepositional phrases
- phrasal verbs
- prepositions
- collocations
- pronouns
- articles
- comparison

Advice

- First of all read through the whole article carefully and go back and decide which type of word is missing from each space, e.g. a verb, a noun or a preposition, etc.
- Make sure that your word makes sense in the passage and fits grammatically.
- Use only one word in each space.
- Write your answers in CAPITAL LETTERS on your answer sheet.

Example: 0 A S ☐ ☐ ☐ ☐ ☐ ☐

1 Read the text below about French photographer Henri Cartier-Bresson and think of the word which best fits each space. Use only one word in each space. There is an example at the beginning (0).

Henri Cartier-Bresson

Henri Cartier-Bresson helped establish photojournalism **(0)** ...as... an art form. He believed that photography **(1)** .... capture the meaning **(2)** .... outward appearance and so his camera accompanied him **(3)** .... he went in the world. In his twenties, he travelled in Africa, recording his experiences with a miniature camera. Its portability and the ease with **(4)** .... one could record instantaneous impressions **(5)** .... have struck a sympathetic **(6)** .... , and in 1933 he purchased his first 35-millimetre Leica. The use of this type of camera was particularly relevant to Cartier-Bresson. It lent **(7)** .... not only to spontaneity **(8)** .... to anonymity as well. **(9)** .... much did Cartier-Bresson wish to remain a silent, and even unseen, witness, that he covered the bright chromium parts of his camera with black tape to render it **(10)** .... visible. Cartier-Bresson travelled unceasingly, but there was **(11)** .... compulsive or hurried about his travels or his photography, and he explicitly expressed a desire to **(12)** .... his time. One story tells of how Cartier-Bresson was present **(13)** .... the student riots in Paris in 1968. **(14)** .... the explosive nature of the riots, he continued to take photographs at the **(15)** .... of about four per hour.

Paper 3 Part 2 Word formation cloze

In Part 2 of the Use of English paper you will be asked to read a text and complete the ten numbered spaces with a form of the word in capitals at the end of the line.

Here are some examples of the changes you might need to make.

verb to noun: *widen* to *width*
noun to adjective: *information* to *informative*
adjective to negative adverb: *happy* to *unhappily*
verb to adjective: *strike* to *striking*
verb to noun: *act* to *interaction*
compounds: *worth* to *worthwhile*

Advice

- Read through the text carefully and decide which form of the given word you need to use.
- Be careful, as sometimes you will need to use a negative prefix or another form of prefix.
- All the words must be correctly spelled.
- Write your answers in CAPITAL LETTERS on your answer sheet.

2 Below is part of an article about body art. Read the article and use the word given in capitals at the end of some of the lines to form a word that fits in the space on the same line. There is an example at the beginning (0).

It's only skin deep

We are the only animal that chooses what it will
look like. True, the chameleon changes colour –
but not **(0)** .wilfully. . Unlike us, it doesn't get up in the   WILL
morning and ask itself, 'What shall I look like today?',
but we can and do. Indeed, the **(1)** .... of body   ANTIQUE
decoration points to the conclusion that it is a
key factor in our development as the **(2)** ....   DOMINATE
life-form on our planet. No human society
has ever been found where some form of body
decoration is not the norm.
By **(3)** .... their physical appearance, our ancestors   CUSTOM
distanced themselves from the rest of the animal
(4) .... Within each tribe this helped them to   KING
mark out differences of role, status and **(5)** ....   KIN
Our ancestors developed **(6)** .... techniques   ORDINARY
of body decoration for **(7)** .... reasons. How to show   PRACTISE
where one tribe ends and another begins? How to
memorably underline the **(8)** .... of that moment   SIGNIFY
when an individual becomes an adult member of
society? **(9)** .... , without the expressive capabilities   ARGUE
of such 'body language' we would have been
(10) .... less successful as a species.   FINITE

UNIT 2 Expectation

1 Work with a partner. What do the buildings on the right have in common? Have you been to either? If not, would you like to? Why? What would your expectations be?

2 Read the two texts below quickly to get a general idea of what they are about. Were the writers impressed with what they saw or not? What phrases tell you the answer?

A

The Taj Mahal has a great deal to live up to. So much, indeed, that there can be few thoughtful visitors today who, knowing something of its reputation, do not fear the betrayal of expectation. How can anything justify the rhapsodies, the descriptions, the history, the legends, the very photographs? I confirm that it was in such a spirit, almost with fingers crossed behind my back, that I paid my two rupees, passed through the outer arch, and approached the inner, which serves, when you have advanced to the right point, as a frame for the picture before you. They told me that the Taj Mahal is beautiful, and they were right. They also told me that it is white, though here they were wrong, for white is almost the only colour it is not, except for a few minutes immediately after the sun goes down; at that point all the delicate blues and greys and yellows and pinks are drawn from it and leave it like a ghost, until it takes on its evening life and becomes as rich as the moon.

B

I'm perfectly happy to be impressed by New York, but like any other first-time visitor who doesn't have a Venusian passport I can't help but arrive with a record of previous convictions gained from a million TV cop shows, Batman comics, magazines, novels, films, plays and songs. As soon as I arrive, I set out to find the Empire State Building. Suddenly there it is in front of me, disappearing miles up into the sky. It is some sight. I buy a ticket and head for the 86th floor in a lift that goes so fast the passengers have no time to get embarrassed with each others' company. From the top I can see the Chrysler building, the General Electric building and thousands of other buildings I don't know the names of yet, and far below the streets jammed with little winking toy yellow cabs pointlessly swinging out from one slow lane to the next. Over there is the Hudson, the East river, Central Park to the north, the Statue of Liberty, copper green against the bay, welcoming huddled masses on tiny tour boats. I remember someone in my guidebook saying that New York seems like chaos, but to me from the air, it's a work of art.

Exam spot

In Part 2 of Paper 1 read each text carefully and then look through each question. Keep the question firmly in mind when choosing your answer, as some answers may be factually correct but not answer the question. Underline the part of the text where you think the answer is. Some questions may be on the whole text.

3 For questions 1–4, read the two extracts again and choose the best answer, A, B, C or D.

1 What does the writer say about the Taj Mahal?
 A He believed it would surpass his expectations.
 B He had been misinformed about it.
 C It is at its best just after sunset.
 D Its charms had been exaggerated.

2 In describing the Taj Mahal, the writer's tone is
 A lyrical.   C ironic.
 B critical.   C sentimental.

3 What point is the writer making at the beginning of the paragraph on New York?
 A It's good to visit somewhere new.
 B New York is not as dangerous as people think.
 C It's difficult not to have preconceived ideas about New York.
 D Tourists should find out as much as possible in advance.

4 What aspect of the traffic in New York strikes the writer most forcibly?
 A the poor public transport system
 B the width of the streets
 C the low driving standards
 D the number of taxis

4 Work with a partner and discuss the following questions on the texts. The questions are in text order.

1 a Text A: Why would the writer almost have his 'fingers crossed' behind his back?
  b Text B: What do the following all have in common – record, convictions, cop shows?
  c What is the writer implying when he says the Empire State Building is 'some sight'?
  d How does the writer reinforce the fact that the lift is fast?
  e Why does the writer describe the Statue of Liberty as 'copper green'?

S tyle extra

In his description of the Taj Mahal the writer says that it looks 'like a ghost' and then 'becomes as rich as the moon'. These similes are the writer's own. He has used them to make his writing more interesting. You can do the same. Make up similes to describe the following:
  your ideal wife's or husband's hair/eyes
  rain or snow
  a hot/cold day

There are also some similes in English which are fixed expressions. Complete each sentence using one of the similes from the box.

EXAMPLE: The child's behaviour was perfect all weekend.
 She was *as good as gold*.

> like a sieve
> like water off a duck's back
> as clean as a whistle
> as white as a sheet
> as deaf as a post
> like a bat out of hell
> like chalk and cheese
> as warm as toast
> as good as gold

  a Whatever criticism I made was ignored.
    It was ...like water off a duck's back...
  b When he finished washing the car, it was ...as clean as a whistle...
  c My uncle can't hear a thing. He's ...as deaf as a post...
  d My sister and I aren't at all alike. We're ...like chalk and cheese...
  e He drove the car fast to the hospital.
    He went ...like a bat out of hell...
  f My hands aren't cold at all in these gloves.
    They are ...as warm as toast...
  g She went deathly pale when she read the letter.
    She went ...as white as a sheet...
  h I can't remember anything. I have a memory ...like a sieve...

5 What do you know about eco-tourism? If you went on a 'green' holiday what would you expect to find / not expect to find?

Read the text below quickly to get an idea of what it is about. Ignore the words in italics for now.

Jt's Eco-Logical!

If there were awards for phrases that have been misused, then 'eco-tourism' would earn top prize. The term first put in an (1) *appear* in the early 1980s, reflecting a surge in environmental (2) *aware* and a (3) *realise* by tour (4) *operate* that many travellers wanted to believe their (5) *present* abroad would not have a negative impact. It rapidly became the hottest marketing tag a holiday could carry. The bewildering range of 'eco-tours' on offer can be roughly condensed into four (6) *categorise*: nature; culture; (7) *wild* adventure; and personal (8) *grow* or learning.

Nowadays, the eco-tourism label is used to cover almost anything. Doubtless the original motives behind the (9) *moving* led to honourable attempts to provide a way for those who cared to make an informed (10) *choose*. But the lack of (11) *regulate* and a standard industry (12) *define* left many travellers lost in an eco-tourism jungle.

Work with a partner to see how many noun endings you know and then change the words in italics in the text into nouns.

Aspects of the future

1 When we want to talk about the future in English we have to use a variety of tenses, modals and expressions, not just *will do*. The context of the sentence is what tells us which aspect of the future to use.

For example, there are many different variations possible for the verb in brackets here:
What you (do) tonight?

Answers

a What are you doing tonight?

b What will you do tonight?

c What are you going to do tonight? *future intentional*

d What will you be doing tonight? *→future continuous activity is in progress*

e What will you have done tonight? *Future Perfect→an action will have finished*

f What were you going to do tonight? *future in the past — something you're going to do but didn't happen*

Before you can decide which aspect of the future to use, you need to know the context. With a partner, discuss when each of the forms above would be used.

G ⋯⟶page 180

> Note – the present simple is also used to express the future when talking about travel arrangements, e.g. *The ship leaves on Saturdays*, and also about facts that can't be changed, e.g. *Tomorrow is Wednesday*.

---

2 Choose the best alternative in the following sentences.

EXAMPLE: I think *I will* / (*'m going to*) faint – get me a chair!

a Sue *is going to cut* / *is cutting* my hair next week, if she has time.

b That *will be* / *is going to be* the window cleaner – he usually comes round at this time.

c The plane for Zurich *leaves* / *will leave* at 16.00 on Friday.

d He never does any work, I'm sure *he's going to get* / *he's getting* the sack.

e It's a lovely day – I think *I'll go* / *I'll be going* to the beach.

f I rang her up to tell her that *I won't go* / *I'm not going* to the party because I'm already busy that night.

g I'll see you on Saturday. What *will you do* / *will you be doing* in the afternoon?

h By the year 2010 a spaceship *will land* / *will have landed* on Mars.

i The hotel *is not to allow* / *is not allowing* guests to use the car park this week, while building work goes ahead.

j I *will do* / *am doing* the shopping this afternoon, if I have time.

k Peter *will have been painting* / *will have painted* that portrait for three weeks by Saturday.

l This time next year we *will have finished* / *will finish* our exams.

m Don't let him read in the coach – *he'll be* / *he's going to be* sick.

n What *will you be doing* / *will you do* if the flight is delayed tomorrow?

o Tomorrow *is* / *will be* Tuesday.

p I *will have* / *am having* caviar tonight – it's already in my fridge!

q I *will be* / *am going to be* sick – where's the bathroom?

r I'll ring you on my mobile when I *will arrive* / *arrive*.

s Stop worrying – the train *is arriving* / *will be arriving* soon.

t *Will* / *Shall* I help you?

3 With a partner, decide what you would say in the following situations.

EXAMPLE: Your birthday tomorrow.
I'm 30 tomorrow. / *I'll be 30 tomorrow.* (fact/neutral future)

a Your future job in 10 years' time.

b You see dark clouds in the sky.

c The weather next week.

d Your dinner tonight – salmon and salad already in the fridge.

e Your government – a solution to pollution by the year 2030.

f Your intention to clean your car tomorrow.

g An airline timetable – Athens 6.00 Fridays

4 The following expressions are used to express probability:

- *to be bound to* + infinitive
- *to be certain to* + infinitive
- *to be likely/unlikely to* + infinitive

Using a suitable tense or one of the expressions above, talk to your partner about the following:

a The effects the growth in computerisation will have on your life.

b The goals you will have achieved by the middle of the century.

c It's your friend's first day at your college / place of work. Tell him/her what to expect.

5 The following expressions can be used for the very near future.

- *to be about to* + infinitive – more informal use, everyday situations
- *to be on the brink/point/verge of* + gerund/noun – more formal use

EXAMPLE: *The economy is on the brink of collapse.*
She was on the verge of tears.
I'm about to make a cup of coffee.

Make sentences using one of the expressions above and including one of these words or phrases.

disaster	leave home	get married	bed
extinction	a scientific breakthrough	revolution	

Prepositional phrases

6 Complete the sentences below with the following prepositional phrases. (Use each phrase once only.)

on the grounds	in the region of	on the brink/verge of
in vain	in keeping with	on edge
in lieu of	on the fringe of	

a The judge closed the club ...on the grounds... that there was too much noise being made.

b The paintings were given to the state by the millionaire ...in lieu of... taxes.

c The class were ...on edge... the morning before they took the exam.

d The local council believe the new development isn't ...in keeping with... the rest of the town.

e The journalist reported that the city was ...on the brink of... a crisis.

f My brother has always been ...in keeping with / on the fringe of... the Labour party, never at the centre.

g The staff pay rise was ...in the region of... 3%.

h Tom looked ...on the fringe of... for the photos he had put away in the attic. ...in vain...

Have no ...

7 *Have* is often used in expressions with an abstract noun with *no*. It is regularly tested in Paper 3 of the examination.

EXAMPLE: *I have no time to make the dinner this evening.*

Rewrite the sentences below using one of the following expressions.

have no objection to
have no interest in
have no regrets about
have no recollection/memory of
have no hesitation in/about
have no difficulty (in)
have no alternative/choice but to
have no intention of

a She seems to be able to learn foreign languages quite easily.

b I don't mind if you come camping with us.

c I am not going to invite John to the party.

d Sylvia isn't interested in package holidays.

e I'm not sorry I decided to stay at home this summer.

f Some airlines wouldn't hesitate to double book their seats.

g My mother can't remember what she did as a child.

h You have to come with me now.

E xam spot

Paper 3 Use of English tests a broad range of vocabulary, so you should learn vocabulary in an organised way. Write down new words and phrases in your vocabulary notebook under headings such as *prepositional phrases, adjective-noun collocations, phrasal verbs* and so on. Try to include an example sentence to show meaning and usage.

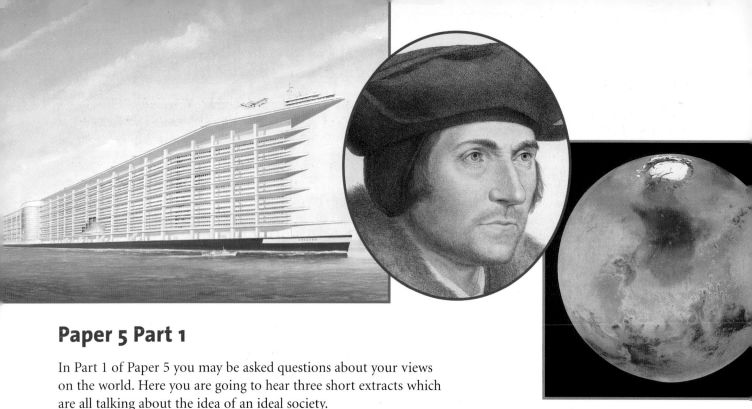

Paper 5 Part 1

In Part 1 of Paper 5 you may be asked questions about your views on the world. Here you are going to hear three short extracts which are all talking about the idea of an ideal society.

Extract 1

1 The words and phrases in italics below all occur in the first extract. Before you listen, work with a partner and explain their meaning.

  a Children *coin* new words to fill gaps in their vocabulary.
  b When I was a teenager, spending the day with my parents held all the *allure* of a wet Sunday afternoon doing homework.
  c The *concept* of a free society is one that many people believe in.
  d You could feel the *tension* in the air when the fans from the opposing teams met.
  e The new plans are *radically* different from the ones before.
  f When I lost the manuscript, there was nothing to be done but to do it again *from scratch*.
  g I've been *plagued* by double-glazing salesmen since I moved into this street.

2 🎧 Now listen to a man talking about the idea of Utopia. What does he say about the following?

  a Sir Thomas More
  b Plato
  c The reason for failure

Extract 2

3 🎧 You will hear a news reporter talking about a ship which has been designed as a 'maritime Utopia'. Complete the gaps with a word or short phrase.

  a The utopian *Freedom Ship* will have room for .... homes.
  b The publicity for the *Freedom Ship* says it is a .... , which is its main attraction.
  c Income to help run the *Freedom Ship* will be raised from a .... on board.
  d The *Freedom Ship* is unlikely to be sunk by a ....
  e The fact that the inhabitants of the *Freedom Ship* are .... will be a problem in integrating the community, according to sociologists.

Extract 3

4 🎧 You will hear a woman talking about a new book about the possibility of people living on Mars. What does the speaker say about the following?

  a the temperature
  b the atmosphere
  c freedom

5 Discuss these questions with a partner.

   a What are your plans for the future?
   b What are the qualities you would look for
      in an ideal partner?
   c What do you think about living in a place
      where you could 'make your own rules'?
   d What would be your priorities if you had
      the opportunity to run an ideal state?
   e Do you think people will colonise Mars?
      Why? / Why not? Would you go if you
      had the opportunity?

Pronunciation

6 A **homophone** is a word which is pronounced in the
   same way as another word but has a different meaning
   or a different spelling or both, for example *warn/worn*.

   Replace the wrong word in each of the sentences with its
   homophone and write a sentence which shows how the
   other word is used.

   EXAMPLE: I don't ~~no~~ *know* what to expect from this
             new government.
             There were no strawberries in the market today.

   a Can you tell me the weigh to the centre of town, please?
   b How many pears of trousers do you own?
   c Let's meat for lunch tomorrow.
   d His new girlfriend is air to a fortune.
   e Walking down the isle was the scariest thing Ellen had
      ever done.
   f The school principle is going to speak to everyone
      at midday.
   g Great the cheese over the vegetables and bake for
      twenty minutes.
   h The horse tossed its main and neighed.
   i This fish bar does the best place and chips in town.

1 Students often try ....
   in order to save money.

2 The sales department ....
   the day after we put the order in.

3 Don't worry about paying – I'll ....
   ....

4 The child had to ....
   for looking after her family when her mother died.

5 We .... when we got
   home so as not to wake anyone up.

6 The woman ....
   the store to grab the first bargains in the sale.

Writing folder 1

Part 1 Letter

Part 1 is the compulsory part of Paper 2, where you will have to write an article, essay, letter or proposal of between 300 and 350 words in length. The letter will usually be formal and may take the form of a letter to a newspaper, reacting to something that has already been printed. Remember that you will only have two hours to complete all of Paper 2, so use your time wisely. It is better to spend some time planning what you are going to write, rather than attempting to do a rough copy of a whole answer.

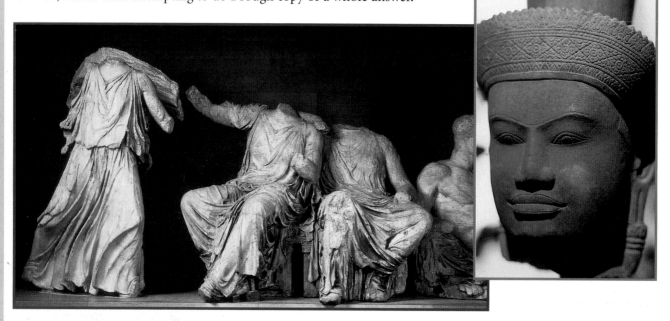

1 Look at these photographs and then read the sample exam task below.

> You have read the paragraph below in a newspaper article, which discussed the sale and exhibition of works of art around the world. You decide to write a **letter** to the editor of the newspaper, commenting on the article and giving your own opinions.

> It is high time that the world's priceless art treasures were returned to the countries they came from. The Elgin Marbles do not belong in the British Museum: their true home is in Greece. Yet this practice of 'theft' continues even in our new century. Ancient sites are vandalised, robbed of their statues, which are quickly sold on to art dealers around the world. The commercial profits are undoubtedly high, but the national loss is impossible to quantify. This cultural barbarism must be stopped.

2 Identify the views expressed and discuss your own opinions, using some of the sentence openers below.

> *The article raises the issue of …*
> *It gives the example of …*
> *It argues that …*
> *According to the writer, …*
> *Some strong language is used, such as …*

3 Read the sample answer and then reorder this paragraph plan.

  – Endorse the condemnation of art theft
  – Give the reason for writing this letter
  – Evaluate the action that could be taken
  – Consider the position of the purchasers

Dear Sir

I have read with interest your strongly-worded article on art 'theft', which appeared in yesterday's edition. I would really like to add my strong views on this subject. I do not wish to comment on the specific case of the Elgin Marbles: that is something for the British and Greek governments to chat about.

What is dead serious is the current practice of stripping ancient temples of their statues, often with disastrous results to both the site and the individual pieces taken. Those who nick these pieces have no understanding of or interest in the pieces as works of art. They merely know that they will be paid good money for producing them, in whatever state. These irreplaceable works of art are often completely trashed: ancient carved faces and limbs are smashed in the rush to remove them. What these people are doing is criminal.

Where does this leave the art dealers? Are they also to be described as thieves, or 'cultural barbarians', to quote from the article? Dealers operate in the commercial world. Most of them are more than willing to buy these artefacts, arguing that if they don't, another guy will. It is a vicious circle. Unless the demand is stopped, the practice will continue.

According to the writer, something must be done. I endorse this view, though it is difficult to see what is practical. One solution might be for governments to band together at international level, to make it a criminal act to purchase ancient works of art from unknown sources – I doubt whether it would ever be possible to police this effectively. It would probably drive the sale and movement of such goods 'underground', for there will always be a demand for these pieces from individuals who are rolling in money. These people are not concerned about the history or origins of these works of art. They only want to display them in their homes.

4 Some of the words and phrases used in the answer are inappropriately informal. Underline them and choose suitable neutral or formal replacements from the words and phrases below.

steal	liaise over	damaged beyond repair
rich	very much	someone else
unite	extremely	

5 The answer could be better linked in places, and the sentence openers more varied. Decide where the following linkers could be used (the ones without a capital letter should not be used as openers). Add any necessary commas.

Paragraph 1: similarly
              At the same time
Paragraph 2: in my view
              Thus
Paragraph 3: However
              therefore
Paragraph 4: Naturally
              nevertheless
              Indeed

6 The answer is 320 words long, but appears unfinished. Write a short paragraph to round off the letter and include an appropriate closing formula.

Advice

- Be accurate in your grammar and spelling.
- Produce consistently appropriate register.
- Show a wide range of vocabulary and collocation.
- Use a variety of linking words and phrases.
- Organise your writing effectively in paragraphs.
- Write relevantly on the given topic.

7 Now answer this exam task, following the advice above.

You have read the reader's letter below in a magazine. You decide to write a **letter** to the editor of the magazine, commenting on the views expressed and giving your own opinions.

Family values have changed – to my mind, for the worse. When I was a teenager, 40 years ago, there was no time to laze around like the present generation do. I had to work in my father's shop after school, then help my mother with the washing up. And I used to spend two hours on homework every night. My own grandchildren don't study at all, they take everything for granted, and expect their parents to run round after them like servants! What do other readers think?

Henry Reid-Streebling

Write your **letter** in 300–350 words. Do not write any postal addresses.

UNIT 3 Strange behaviour

1 Read through the following sayings about the weather and discuss them with a partner. Do you think any of them are true? Do you have similar sayings in your country? Do sayings such as these have any place in our modern world?

- Red sky at night, shepherd's delight,
  Red sky in the morning, shepherd's warning.
- Cows lying in the field means rain is on its way.
- If a cat sneezes, it's a sure sign of rain.

2 🎧 You are going to hear part of a radio programme. A writer called Peter Watkins is being interviewed by the programme presenter, Sue Manchester, about his new book, which discusses the behaviour of animals and birds in relation to the weather.

For questions 1–10 decide whether these statements are true or false.

1 Sue has little faith in the accuracy of sayings about the weather.
2 Peter says that nowadays people are less interested in sayings than in previous times.
3 Peter says that low-flying birds suffer badly in storms.
4 Peter believes that there is a logical explanation for why certain birds change their habits.
5 According to Peter, insects have difficulty in sensing changes in the atmosphere.
6 Sue concludes that the rain goose's behaviour is surprising.
7 Peter says that weather sayings used to be confined to the farming community.
8 Peter says that the sayings fulfilled a basic human need for control.
9 Sue agrees with Peter about the contradictory nature of some of the sayings.
10 Peter says that in the past people relied on animal and bird behaviour to predict the weather.

Idiom spot

In the recording, Peter Watkins uses two common English idioms: *doom and gloom* and *life and death*.

Pairs of nouns are often used and always in the same order. For example, you can't say *gloom and doom* or *death and life*.

Using a dictionary to help you, decide if these pairs of nouns are in the right order and explain how you would use them.

give and take	black and white
again and time	thick and thin
high and dry	go and touch
fortune and fame	sound and safe
blood and flesh	first and foremost
sixes and sevens	soul and life

Complete the sentences below with the correct idiom.

a Jenny promised to live with Nigel through ....
b The house is at .... while it's being decorated.
c When Joe was 18 he left home to find ....
d It was .... whether we would get to the airport in time.
e .... , we need to solve the budget problem and then we can move on to other issues.
f .... , we see this pattern of behaviour repeating itself.
g Mrs Parsons thought she'd lost her cat for good, but then it was returned to her ....
h There needs to be a bit of .... in every relationship.
i My brother James is the .... of any family party.
j My aunt treats her relatives really badly, considering they are her own ....
k When the company closed I was left .... without a job.
l How could you not understand? Look at this letter – it's all there in ....

3 Both speakers in the recording used words such as *quite*, *rather* and *fairly*, which are adverbs of degree, to modify what they were saying.

- *fairly* means 'moderately'
- *rather* can be used before negative adjectives to mean 'moderately'; it can also be used before positive adjectives to mean 'more than expected'
- *quite* has a variety of meanings, ranging from 'moderately' to 'totally', depending on the tone of voice that is used.

Listen to some sentences which include *quite* being read and then match the speakers 1–5 with the appropriate meaning, **a** or **b**.

- **a** totally
- **b** moderately

Note that *quite* means 'fairly' before a gradable adjective. These are adjectives which can be modified, such as *good*, *clever*, *helpful*. *Quite* means 'completely' before an ungradable adjective. Ungradable adjectives are those which can't be modified, such as *fantastic*, *brilliant*, *dreadful*, etc.

G ··· pages 184–5

4 Use the following adjectives and the adverb of degree specified to talk about the sayings below.

- to be dubious of/about; cautious about; sceptical of (use *rather*)
- mystified by/about; annoyed by/about; convinced by/about (use *quite* meaning 'completely')
- certain of/about (use *fairly*)

EXAMPLE: *I'm quite mystified by what is meant by 'Youth is wasted on the young'. After all, young people usually make the most of the time they are young. I think this is just something old people think because they're jealous.*

- **a** Men are what their mothers made them.
- **b** Money is the root of all evil.
- **c** Early to bed, early to rise, makes a man healthy, wealthy and wise.
- **d** If you give a man a fish you feed him for a day, but teach him to fish and you feed him for life.
- **e** Imagination is more important than knowledge.
- **f** Youth is wasted on the young.

E xam spot

In Paper 3 Part 1 make sure you read through the whole text before attempting to fill in the gaps. Quite often the answer to a gap is dependent on information later on in the passage.

5 Read through the article quickly, ignoring the gaps for now. What is the article about?

Natural Forecasters

Reports of unusual animal behaviour prior (0) ......*to*...... the occurrence of earthquakes have been recorded in popular or semi-popular literature dating as (1) .... back as 1784. However, as (2) ......*yet*......, there has been (3) .... in-depth scientific research into the phenomenon and so (4) ......*the*...... scepticism of geophysicists and biologists alike is probably justified. However, (5) ......*given*...... that a geophysical tool has not been designed (6) .... gives advance warning of an impending earthquake, observations of animal behaviour might (7) .... out to be a useful tool.

Animals and birds could act as geosensors. (8) .... is well known that the Earth's electromagnetic field is used by birds and fish as an aid to navigation (9) ......*during*...... migration. Sharks (10) ......*make*...... use of low or high frequency electro-receptors to detect objects (11) ......*and*...... to communicate. Perhaps it is time to (12) ......*put*...... this sensitivity to good use? Animals may have the means to (13) ......*get*...... out and

discriminate the signal that says 'leave this place' or 'fly-away now' or (14) ......*whatever*...... is necessary to survive the coming catastrophe. Animals, therefore, have the potential to act as accurate geosensors, to detect earthquakes (15) ......*whenever*...... they occur.

6 Read the article again and decide where the following words should go.

the	put	little	before	make
far	sort	it	which	yet
given	whatever	and	turn	during

Review of conditional forms

1 How does the weather affect your mood? Do you think people's characters are influenced by where they live and the weather they are used to? Give some examples.

2 Read this article about the effect of the wind on mood.

There's an old English saying: *When the wind is in the east, 'tis good for neither man nor beast.* Whether you believe in folklore or not, this one's got a grain of truth in it. Winds have been associated with a rise in the levels of serotonin, a compound which occurs in the brain and which controls mood, sleep and blood circulation. This rise in serotonin has been found to occur in the Swiss population during a Föhn wind. The Föhn is said to be responsible for traffic accidents rising by fifty per cent and a rise in industrial injuries by twenty per cent.

It's not only the Swiss who suffer. Los Angeles is occasionally buffeted by the Santa Ana, a hot dry wind named after the canyon it sometimes blows through. One study found that murders rose by up to a half during a Santa Ana, no matter if it blew during winter or summer. In California's early days, defendants in crimes of passion were able to plead for leniency, citing the wind as an extenuating circumstance.

The quality of the air can be a force for good, however. The Victorians especially prized sea air for its health-giving properties. Sea air is charged with negative ions which makes it feel invigorating. To get a similar effect you can stand next to a waterfall, or even under a domestic shower.

Now, with a partner, complete the sentences using information from the article.

a When the Föhn blows, …
b If you go to the seaside, …
c Even if the Santa Ana blew at a different time to normal, …
d I wouldn't have murdered my wife …
e You are less likely to have an accident if …
f If I were you, …

3 What kind of conditional is used in each sentence in the exercise above? When do we use these forms?

EXAMPLE: *People can be adversely affected if a certain wind is blowing.* Zero conditional (present tense + present tense). This is used to express a universal truth or habitual action.

G ⋯⋮ page 181

4 There are other forms of the conditional besides the four basic patterns. Look at the following examples and discuss how they are formed and what they express.

EXAMPLE:
But for my father's help, I wouldn't have been able to complete my course.
'But for' is used in third conditional sentences and has the meaning of 'If it hadn't been for'.

a Should you happen to see Lucy, tell her to ring me.
b If you would sit down, I'm sure Mr Peterson will see you soon.
c I'll diet if you will.
d You can borrow the money from me as long as you pay me back.
e Had I known about the weather conditions, I wouldn't have ventured out.
f Provided that you tell the truth, nothing will happen to you.
g You could be a lot thinner now, if you hadn't given up your diet so easily.
h Were the Prime Minister to announce lower tax increases, the country would be delighted.
i You can't come unless you have an invitation.

5   *If* isn't the only conjunction used in conditional sentences. Complete the sentences using the following conjunctions.

given that	on condition that
but for / without	even if
provided that / as long as	suppose/supposing
unless	

a .... lightning tends to strike the nearest high point, you would do well not to stand under a tall tree during a thunderstorm.

b .... you learn to drive better, I won't be getting in your car again.

c .... you use a sun screen, you shouldn't get burnt.

d .... the support of my boss, I wouldn't have been promoted.

e .... you do say you love me, I'm not marrying you.

f I'll give you a lift to school .... you wash the car for me at the weekend.

g .... there was an air traffic controllers' strike, what would you do?

6   Rewrite each sentence, beginning with the words in italics, without changing the meaning.

EXAMPLE: I didn't drown because my instructor knew how to help me.
Had my instructor not known how to help me, I would have drowned.

a Could you tell her my address if, by any chance, you see her.
Should ....

b As people were dependent on farming for their livelihood, it's not surprising that they used animal behaviour to predict the weather.
Given that ....

c You can borrow my bike but you must take care of it.
Provided that ....

d Kindly have a seat as I'm sure Mr Johnson won't be long.
If ....

e My advice to you is to get another job.
If ....

f I'm not earning much money because I didn't work hard enough to pass my diploma.
If ....

g I wouldn't have been able to afford to go to university except that my grandmother left me some money.
But for ....

h Climatic changes may, in due course, render weather lore obsolete.
Were ....

7   In groups, ask and answer these questions.

What will you do if

a someone close to you tells you they are going to marry someone you don't approve of?

b you get an e-mail from someone you fancy?

c there's a power cut tonight?

d your mobile phone is stolen?

What would you do if you

e found yourself in an earthquake?

f found out your best friend had lied to you?

g found some money in the street?

h had the chance to go swimming with sharks?

What would you have done if you'd

i seen a robbery on your way home?

j fallen in love with someone much older?

k been born into a richer family?

l been allowed to do everything you had wanted by your parents?

Reformulation 1

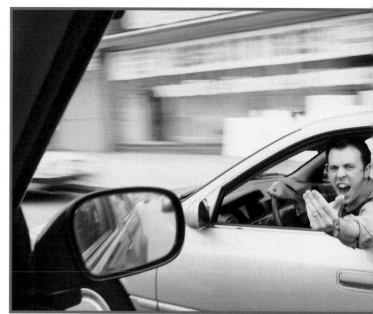

1   Look at the photos and discuss what is happening in them with a partner.
    How do people show that they are angry?

2   Read through the article below on anger and answer the questions that follow.

New psychological research suggests that air rage, road rage and other seemingly irrational outbursts of wild-eyed, foaming–at-the-mouth fury could be extreme reactions to the violation of a set of rules that choreographs our every waking moment: the unwritten unconscious system of personal body space. Apparently, we walk around in a sort of invisible bubble which is egg-shaped – this is because we allow people to come closer from in front than from behind – an entire language is expressed via the amount of distance we choose to keep between each other. In northern Europe and North America (lovers, close friends and wrestling partners aside) the average depth of the bubble is about a metre. When it's intruded upon the physiological responses can range from feelings of mild annoyance and tension to a pounding heart, raised blood pressure, sweating and severe anxiety. Tension levels increase hugely when space is invaded, and responses fall into two categories. The first kind are blocking tactics when you avert your gaze, put your hand up at the side of your head or just make yourself immobile; then there are the tension and anxiety-reduction responses, hair-pulling, foot-tapping, getting red in the face and ultimately leaving the scene.

1   Where do you think you would read this article? What evidence is there to support your decision?
    A in a magazine or newspaper
    B in a psychology textbook
    C in an advertisement
    D in a health awareness leaflet

2   Which of these sentences best summarises the article? Justify your answer with evidence from the text.
    A Some nationalities need more space than others.
    B Everyone succumbs to feelings of anger at one time or another.
    C Anger is a natural reaction in certain circumstances.
    D An invasion of personal space has unpredictable results.

3   Why does the writer describe air and road rage as 'seemingly irrational'?

4   List both the inward and the outward signs which may occur when one's space is invaded.

A good summary will use new language and not incorporate large amounts of the original. This task is also a test of vocabulary. It is important that you can show you are able to manipulate words easily, especially as you have to write a summary within a set word limit. One way of doing this is to use a negative adjective.

3 Complete the second sentence of each pair below with a negative adjective.

EXAMPLE: The driver didn't apologise for his bad behaviour.
The driver was *unapologetic* about his bad behaviour.

a Discretion is not her strong point, I'm afraid.
She is rather ....

b You can't deny that global warming is becoming a real threat.
It is .... that global warming is becoming a real threat.

c Do you find it impossible to write legibly?
Your writing is totally ....

d The damage to the car was of no significance.
There was an .... amount of damage to the car.

e It won't be possible to replace that vase, I'm afraid.
Unfortunately, that vase is ....

f My father never seemed to exhaust his supply of jokes.
My father seemed to have an .... supply of jokes.

g Liz never tries to assert herself in tricky situations.
Liz is a very .... type of person.

h The solicitor's advice led me to the wrong conclusion.
The solicitor's advice was rather ....

4 What makes you angry? Look at this list. With a partner, put them in order with the most infuriating at the top. Justify your decisions.

a Noisy neighbours
b Being overtaken by a sports car
c Rude shop assistants
d Queue jumping
e Unpunctuality
f Poor government decisions
g Being overcharged

Exam folder 2

Paper 3 Part 3
Gapped sentences

This part of Paper 3 mainly tests collocations. There are six questions and each question contains three sentences. In each of the three sentences, one word has been taken out. Only one word will fit all three sentences. The gapped word is always in the same form.

Example:

0 The council's plan may mean demolishing the building or returning it to its original ....

Repeated .... of a hammer on a screw may result in it breaking.

Many cafés and restaurants ban the .... of mobile phones.

Answer: *use* is the only word that can complete all three sentences.

Sentence 1 could be *purpose* or *function* as well as *use*.
Sentence 2 could be *application* or *employment* as well as *use*.
Sentence 3 could be *operation* as well as *use*.

Advice

- Do not attempt an answer until you have read all three sentences very carefully.
- Make sure that your answer will fit in all three sentences. Check that it fits both grammatically and with the sense of the sentences.
- Make sure you spell your answer correctly.
- Write your answer in CAPITAL LETTERS on your answer sheet.

1 For questions 1–6, think of one word only which can be used appropriately in all three sentences.

1 Students are advised to keep their options .... and not to take the first offer of a university place they get.

It is also important to find a doctor who is prepared to be frank and .... with you and answer all your questions.

His interpretation is .... to criticism on two main grounds.

2 Jane didn't relish the .... of telling the class they would have to miss the match.

Being a working mother is often a thankless ....

The policeman took his son to .... for throwing the stone through the window.

3 Politicians seem able to .... with every available tide, depending on what suits them.

Marilyn Monroe had the ability to make everyone's head ....

I'm not sure how the meeting will .... out, now that our key people won't be there.

4 The press believed his answers to the questions were not .... true.

.... speaking, she is a teaching assistant, not a qualified teacher.

You must act .... in accordance with the wishes of your colleagues in this matter, regardless of what you yourself want.

5 The soldier managed to .... himself in battle, despite his obvious fear beforehand.

Politicians need to .... between ageing as a process and ageing as a social phenomenon.

If you look to the right, you should be able to .... the foothills of the Black Mountains quite clearly.

6 No one takes Mr Potter .... any more, after he disgraced himself at the party.

Teenagers are often .... at risk of getting into trouble with the law.

But .... , don't you feel that hitch-hiking is too risky nowadays?

Paper 3 Part 4 Key word transformations

There are eight key word transformations in Part 4 of Paper 3. There are two sentences, one complete and the other with a gap. You must complete the gapped sentence with the word which is given and up to seven other words, so that it has a similar meaning to the first sentence. (You must use between three and eight words in your answer.)

2 Complete the second sentence so that it has a similar meaning to the first sentence, using the word given. Do not change the word given. You must use between three and eight words, including the word given.

Example:

0   It's unlikely that the product would have taken off, if they hadn't run such a massive TV campaign.

likelihood

Without such a massive TV campaign, there .... the product taking off.

Answer: *would have been little likelihood of*

Advice

- Read both sentences very carefully.
- Make sure that you actually use the word given and that you don't change its form in any way.
- Don't add anything which isn't necessary.
- Make sure your sentence means the same as the first sentence.
- You will often need to use the words in the first sentence in a different form. For example, you may have to change a verb to a noun.

1 The group leader's poor judgement jeopardised the safety of the climbers.

put

The climbers' safety .... was put at risk .... by the poor judgement of the group leader.

2 I'm not sure that I totally agree with his theories, but I'll come to his lecture tonight.

reservations

Although ...... I have some reservations about his ...., I'll come to his lecture tonight.

3 Almost as soon as Pete met Sue he decided to marry her.

sooner

No ...... sooner had he met her than .... he decided to marry her.

4 Paula and I have been friends since 1998.

dates

My ...... friendship with P dates back .... to 1998.

5 'It wasn't my fault that the window got broken,' Gary said.

responsibility

Gary denied ...... any responsibility for breaking .... the window.

6 My grandmother has finally got used to living alone.

come

My grandmother ...... has finally come to terms with .... living alone.

7 I am not expecting an increase in summer sales this year.

upturn

I have ...... no expectation of an upturn .... in summer sales this year.

8 The students were told to either keep quiet or leave the art gallery.

no

The students ...... have no choice but to .... keep quiet or leave the art gallery.

UNIT 4 Sweet rituals

1 Think of examples of ritual behaviour in eating
 and drinking. Describe exactly what is involved.

2 🎧 Listen to a man talking about ritual family
 meals. What happens before and during such a meal?
 Describe a family event you have had to attend.

3 This extract is from the novel *Reef* by Romesh
 Gunesekera, a Sri Lankan author. Read it once to
 form an overall impression. What is the relationship
 between the narrator and Mister Salgado?

Before Miss Nili first came to our house on the *poya*-holiday of
April 1969, Mister Salgado only said to me, 'A lady is coming to
tea.' As if a lady came to tea every week. It had never happened
before in his life, or mine, and yet he acted as if it were the most
5 natural thing in the world. Luckily he gave me some warning. He
was concerned to make sure there was plenty of time to prepare,
even though he acted so nonchalant. I made everything – little
coconut cakes, patties, egg sandwiches, ham sandwiches, cucumber
sandwiches, even *love-cake* ... I made enough for a horse. It was
10 just as well: she ate like a horse. I don't know where she put it;
she was so skinny then. So hungry-looking. I expected her to
bulge out as she ate, like a snake swallowing a bird. But she just
sat there on the cane chair, one leg coiled under her, her back
straight and her face floating happily in the warm afternoon haze
15 while huge chunks of the richest, juiciest love-cake disappeared
into her as into a cavern.
　'You like cake?' he asked her stupidly.
　She made a lowing sound between bites. It made him happy,
and although I didn't approve of her being quite so uninhibited so
20 soon in our house, I was touched too.
　'Where did you get this, this cake?' Her lips glistened with my
butter, and one corner of her mouth had a line of golden semolina
crumbs which smudged into a dimple as she spoke.
　'Triton made it,' my Mister Salgado said. *Triton made it*. It was
25 the one phrase he would say with my name again and again like a
refrain through those months, giving me such happiness. *Triton
made it*. Clear, pure and unstinting. His voice at those moments
would be a channel cut from heaven to earth right through the
petrified morass of all our lives, releasing a blessing like water
30 springing from a river-head, from a god's head. It was bliss. My
coming of age.
　'Your cook? He makes a lovely cake,' she said, endearing herself
to me for the rest of my life.
　After tea she said she had to go. I went to get a taxi for her.
35 She stayed with him alone in the house while I went up to the
main road. It didn't take long. A black tortoise of a taxi with a
butter-coloured top came along, and I rode in it like a prince back
to the house. The driver croaked the old horn warning them of our
approach. We rolled in right up to the porch. I got out and held the
40 door open while Mister Salgado helped her in. 'Bye-bye,' she said
to him and then turned to me. 'That cake was *really* good.'

The taxi rolled down to the gate and veered to the left. The
wheels wobbled, making the whitewalls around the rim go fuzzy.
Mister Salgado watched the vehicle slowly disappear.
　'The lady ate well,' I said brightly.　　　　　　　　　　　45
　'Yes.'
　'Sir, the love-cake was good? *Really* good?'
　'Yes.'
　'And the patties also she liked?'
　'They were good.'　　　　　　　　　　　　　　　　　　50
　They were more than good. I knew, because I can feel it inside
me when I get it right. It's a kind of energy that revitalises every cell
in my body. Suddenly everything becomes possible and the whole
world, that before seemed slowly to be coming apart at the seams,
pulls together. But however confident I was about the perfection of　55
what I produced, like everybody else, I needed praise. I needed his
praise and I needed her praise. I felt stupid to need it, but I did.
　She came again the following *poya*-day and then regularly
almost every weekend after that for months. I made mutton
patties and a small cake every time, and she always said how　　　60
wonderful they were. Mister Salgado ate nothing: he watched her
eat as if he were feeding an exotic bird. He drank tea. He always
drank lots of tea: estate-fresh, up-country broken orange pekoe
tip-top tea. He looked completely content when she was there. His
face would be bright, his mouth slightly open with the tips of his　65
teeth just showing. It was as if he couldn't believe his eyes, seeing
Nili sitting there in front of him. I would bring the patties in four
at a time, fried only after she arrived to ensure they came fresh
and hot-hot, straight from the pan. When she finished the last of
the first batch, I would wait a minute before bringing in a second　70
plate. 'Nice and hot-hot, Missy,' I would say, and she would
murmur her approval. After she finished a couple of the new
patties, I would come again with fresh tea. 'More patties?' She
would shake her head – I would always ask when her mouth was
full. This allowed Mister Salgado to speak on her behalf. 'No,　　75
bring the cake now.' It was our little ritual. I would nod, she
would smile and he would look longingly. I would give her
enough time to savour the aftertaste of the patties and feel the
glow of coriander inside her. Let the tea slip down to cleanse her
palate and subdue the nerves that had been excited by the spice　　80
and fattened by the meat, and only then bring out the cake on a
small salver for Mister Salgado to cut.

Style extra

- The first part of the text associates certain animals with Miss Nili. Find these references and explain their effect.
- Triton describes the taxi as having a *butter-coloured* top. Why has the writer used this adjective instead of *yellow*? How does it tie in with Triton?

4 Now read the text carefully, in order to answer questions 1–6.

1 What was Mister Salgado's state of mind before his first tea-party with Miss Nili?
A He felt confident, as it was a role he was accustomed to performing.
B He appeared relaxed, but inwardly, he was worrying about the event.
C He wished he had told his cook about the visit more in advance.
D He became nervous about his cook's obvious lack of experience.

2 What effect did Miss Nili's large appetite have on the narrator?
A He felt rather sorry for her because she was so hungry.
B He suspected that she was hiding some of the food.
C He had mixed feelings about her unconventional way of eating.
D He thought she should take more care when she ate.

3 Why did the narrator derive so much satisfaction when he heard the phrase 'Triton made it'?
A It gave him a sense of purpose in his life.
B Mister Salgado said the phrase so rarely.
C Miss Nili didn't believe the cake was home-made.
D The words improved the atmosphere at the tea-party.

4 How did the narrator feel about his taxi ride back to the house?
A He was annoyed that it was such a slow vehicle.
B He was concerned about Miss Nili during his absence.
C He appreciated being helped out of the taxi.
D He enjoyed the relative luxury of the experience.

5 What do we learn about the narrator in the penultimate paragraph?
A His successes in the kitchen dictated his general mood.
B He thought it reasonable to expect praise for his cooking.
C He knew he would benefit from some help in preparing the food.
D His feelings had been hurt by Nili and Mister Salgado.

6 Which phrase best describes Mister Salgado's behaviour at subsequent tea-parties?
A feverishly eating and drinking
B full of praise for Triton's wonderful efforts
C slightly incredulous at Nili's regular presence
D nervously monitoring the supply of food

5 Explain the precise meaning of the words in italics below.

I would give her enough time to *savour the aftertaste* of the patties …

Savour is a verb that is used in other contexts. Look at these examples from the *Cambridge International Corpus* and underline the noun collocates.

EXAMPLE: At 37, the Oscar-nominated actress is savouring every <u>moment</u> of her newly-conferred status.

a After years in the wilderness, the band were finally savouring success.
b His father, Pat, should have been savouring freedom alongside them, but had died in prison.
c She has decided to retire at 33 and savour the memories of her career.
d Its more recent past can be savoured just by wandering aimlessly through the streets.
e Laurence was now obviously savouring every word quite as much as the wine.

6 Finish these sentences so that they are true for you.

a I savoured the moment when …
b I don't relish the idea of …
c I found it hard to swallow the news that …
d I absolutely devour things like …

Review of past tenses

1 Read the text, ignoring any underlining. Then explain briefly how the appearance and use of the fork has changed over 400 years.

Fork-like implements for spearing food <u>have been used for over 2000 years</u>. For example, the Ancient Romans <u>used to use special spoons</u> with one prong or two at the end of the handle for winkling out shellfish. The first 'modern' fork is thought to have been used in the eleventh century
5 by the wife of the Venetian Doge. Forks are mentioned again three centuries later, in 1361, in an inventory of the plate owned by the Florentine Commune. However, the first real evidence that forks had spread as eating tools came some two hundred years later, in a 1570 engraving of a knife, fork and spoon. In 1605, King Henri III of France and
10 his companions were satirised for their fork-wielding effeminacy. 'They would rather touch their mouths with their little forked instruments than with their fingers,' wrote Thomas Artus, who claimed that they looked especially silly as they strove to capture the peas and broad beans on their plates – <u>as well they might have done</u>, since early forks had long, widely
15 separate prongs and <u>scooping with them must have been impossible</u>.

On returning home from Italy in 1611, the Englishman Thomas Coryat bore the news that he had seen forks in Italy and had decided to adopt them. The reason for the Italian custom was, he explained, that these extremely fastidious, ultra-modern people considered that any fingering
20 of the meat that was being carved at table was a transgression against the laws of good manners, 'seeing all men's fingers are not alike cleane'. However, even Coryat did not regard forks as being for eating with, but for holding the meat in place while carving.

Although in the course of the seventeenth century there was some use
25 of individual forks, <u>people would more often share forks with others</u>, wiping them carefully on their napkins as they would spoons. It was only in the nineteenth century that eating with a fork truly began to proliferate, and at this time there were important modifications to its basic design. Craftsmen had been making forks with three prongs, but
30 these were now shortened, moved closer together, and a fourth 'tine' commonly added. With the fork's design in transition, one-handed eating was increasingly in vogue: <u>the knife was put down once the food had been cut up</u> and the fork was then used to take the food to the mouth. Diners with yet more elaborate manners sought to perform this
35 manoeuvre for every mouthful consumed. This form of 'zig-zag' eating was still customary among the French bourgeoisie in the 1880s, though the English were successfully introducing a new fashion, where the knife was kept in the right hand and the fork held in the left, much as we have been doing ever since.

2 Find examples of the following ways of talking about the past, choosing from the underlined parts of the text and completing statements a–d.

a reference to an earlier point in past time, using the .... tense

b two ways of referring to habitual past action: .... and ....

c two examples of speculating about the past, using ....

d talking about something that continues to be true today, using the .... tense

Find the following past forms elsewhere in the text and explain the choice of tense.

e one past passive infinitive
f two different past tenses in the passive
g three different continuous tenses
h four irregular past verb forms in the active (name their infinitives)

G ···⫶ page 182

Exam spot

Proficiency texts are bound to contain words you don't know, so you need to develop ways of guessing meaning from context clues.

3 Line 30 contains the technical term *tine*. Work out its meaning by looking at the words around it. Which words help you?

Now explain the meaning of these words and phrases.

a implements (line 1) f transgression (line 20)
b inventory (line 6) g in place (line 23)
c effeminacy (line 10) h proliferate (line 28)
d scooping (line 15) i in transition (line 31)
e fastidious (line 19) j in vogue (line 32)

4 Complete these sentences using the verbs in brackets in a suitable tense. You will need to use a passive (P) or a modal (M) sometimes.

a In seventeenth century France, a nobleman's education .... (think: P) to be incomplete until he .... (master) the art of carving.

b From the sixteenth century, women seem to .... (carve) meat at British tables, though by the mid-nineteenth century, carving at formal meals .... (carry out: P) mainly by servants.

c The French .... (insist + *always*) that salad .... (tear: M + P) rather than cut with a knife, a rule which probably .... (arise) in order to eliminate the taste of metal – lettuce .... (dress: P) with oil and vinegar or lemon, which .... (react: M) with some metals.

d Arriving in Athens pursued by the Furies because he .... (murder) his mother, Orestes .... (give: P) dinner, but so horrified were the other diners that they .... (eat) in silence and .... (drink) from a separate pitcher.

e Although live-in household staff .... (continue) to be the norm in America up until the 1920s, their numbers .... (start) to decline in Europe much earlier.

f For the last hundred years, the separate tiers of a British wedding cake .... (support: P) by pillars, although more recently, upturned champagne glasses .... (choose: P) by some couples as a variant.

5 The text refers to *fork-like* implements and *fork-wielding* effeminacy. Combining words like this helps to show your language range. Answer these questions.

1 Who or what might be *spoon-fed* by
   a a vet?
   b an academic?
   c a manager?

2 Why might the following be on a *knife-edge*?
   a a president
   b the economy
   c a drug addict

3 If a salver is *silver-plated*, name an object that is
   a copper-plated.
   b chrome-plated.
   c gold-plated.

4 Why might each of the following have been *foil-wrapped*?
   a soft cheese
   b cat food
   c baked potatoes

5 Sweets are often *sugar-coated*. Can you name a food that is
   a vanilla-flavoured?
   b vitamin-rich?
   c fat-free?

6 Who or what would you describe as
   a flesh-eating?
   b beer-swilling?
   c blood-sucking?

7 What might be
   a oven-proof?
   b foolproof?
   c tamper-proof?

8 How would someone look or behave if they were
   a clown-like?
   b doll-like?
   c owl-like?

Paper 5 Part 2

1 Identify the fruit below and classify their appearance, flavour and effect on your taste buds according to these adjectives.

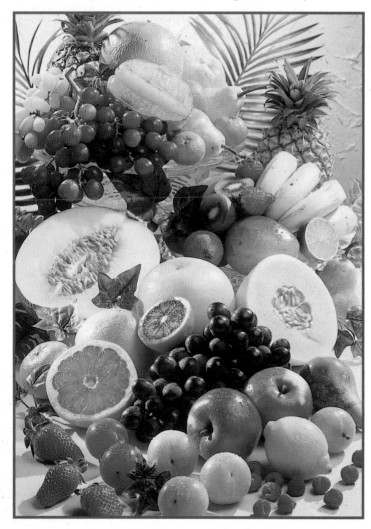

fleshy	tart	luscious
juicy	sour	sensuous
fibrous	bitter	heavenly
chewy	sharp	exquisite
soft	watery	blissful
pulpy	sweet	
tender	sugary	
	overripe	

2 🎧 Now listen to a journalist's report on the growing of mangoes in India. Take notes under these headings and review the main points in pairs.

- Ideal temperature for ripening
- Chief mango-growing area
- Facts about the mango tree
- History of mango-growing in India

3 🎧 Listen again and explain the meaning of these phrases.

a perfect wilting weather
b stacked up according to variety
c exotic foliage
d the Moghul dynasties
e amazing diversity

4 The journalist talks about people in India eating *seasonally* and links this to the lack of supermarkets. Why?

Discuss the following related points.

- Big supermarkets offer maximum diversity, but minimal flavour.
- Local food producers do not get a fair deal from multinational companies.
- There should be larger government subsidies for organic farming.
- People should eat to live and not live to eat.

5 There are many common English idioms to do with food. Use the pictures on the opposite page to complete idioms a–l. Then use some of these idioms in sentences describing the situations in 1–8 opposite.

a the .... on the ....
b the .... of your ....
c put all your .... in one ....
d have bigger .... to fry
e a dog's ....
f take something with a .... of ....
g spill the ....
h sell like ....
i get .... on your ....
j eat humble ....
k forbidden ....
l more .... than Swiss ....

EXAMPLE: Jack told us he had flown to Los Angeles for the weekend and had had dinner with Penelope Cruz, but we didn't believe him.
We took Jack's story about flying to Los Angeles and having dinner with Penelope Cruz with a pinch of salt.

1 This history essay is nowhere near ready to hand in – it is poorly linked and many important points have been omitted.

2 Although I'm freelance, I'm only working for one company – if they closed down, I'd be left high and dry.

3 Not realising that Professor Samuels was in front of him in the canteen queue, Harry started imitating his Australian accent – when the professor turned round, Harry felt really embarrassed.

4 Valentina had decided to stay on as a student, but now she's been invited to set up a new Internet café in Bologna.

5 Liam is Cathy's only child and can do absolutely nothing wrong.

6 I finally managed to persuade Simon to tell me his big secret – he's getting married!

7 Angela adores chocolate but it's the one thing she mustn't have while she's on her diet.

8 The earrings Maria has designed are doing really well on the market stall.

6 Read the task instructions below.

Look at photographs A–D, which show four different fruit desserts. These have been entered in the competition *Forbidden fruits*, where a prize will be awarded for the dessert with the most tempting ingredients and most imaginative presentation.

Shortlist two desserts for the award together and then decide on the winner. Explain your views with reference to all four photographs. You should take about a minute to do this.

Make brief notes about each dessert, using the new vocabulary in exercise 1. Decide which of the idioms in exercise 5 could be used to refer to the desserts.

Writing folder 2

Part 2 Review

In Part 2 of Paper 2, you may be asked to write a review of a book, film, TV programme, concert, or other media event. In addition to reviewing your particular choice, you are likely to have to comment in a more general way, as in the sample task below. Read the question carefully, so you know exactly what is required.

Advice

- When writing a review, provide a balance of information and opinion.
- Do NOT describe the whole plot, as this is inappropriate.
- Introduce your opinions with a variety of linkers.
- Use rhetorical questions to preface opinions and ideas.
- Show your range of vocabulary, including specialist terms.
- Name the film (book, play, etc.) early in the review.

1 Look at the photograph and write three descriptive sentences about the sea.

2 Read this exam task and look at the paragraph plan.

Your college magazine has invited students to contribute a film review to a special feature entitled *Special effects: essential nowadays – or distracting?* Write a review of a film you have seen that uses special effects and say whether you think they are an important aspect of today's films.

- Lead in to review
- Introduce film – 'The Perfect Storm'
- Describe its special effects
- Evaluate importance of special effects in general

3 Decide how well this sample answer follows the plan. What improvements would you make in terms of content and organisation?

This is a very good example to consider. In one way, it is not a typical Hollywood film, as there is no happy ending, but in other ways — the actors used, the money spent, the special effects — it is. Why is it 'perfect'? It is actually a weatherman who uses this word. As he tracks the worsening weather out at sea, we see him getting genuinely excited about the unique set of weather conditions. This was an interesting part for me.

The captain of the fishing boat, acted by George Clooney, does not care about the safety of his men. He only wants to find more fish and make lots of money. So he goes to sea, turning off the weather forecasts and ignoring the sensible advice of another captain (a very attractive woman), who is in love with him and doesn't want him to risk his life. And yes, they catch lots of fish, but then the ice-machine on board breaks down, which means that he needs to return to harbour quickly before the fish go bad, so he decides to go back right through the worst weather.

This is where the special effects start. They are really very good, and include some clever use of computers. You feel as though you are in the boat with them, facing those big waves. * At the end, the ship goes down and we see one of the sailors — the film also has Mark Wahlberg — drifting on an empty sea, thinking beautiful thoughts about his girlfriend. Then the film shows the girlfriend, looking out to sea with an anxious look on her face.

Are special effects an essential part of all films today? ** In this film, the special effects were probably its best thing.

Based on the sentences you wrote earlier about the sea, write a phrase or a sentence to follow the (*), describing the waves.

4 In Part 2, it is important to demonstrate your range of language. Use these words and phrases as replacements in the text. They are in text order.

a blockbuster
b budget
c sub-plot
d portrayed (by)
e heads out
f crew
g eye of the storm
h kick in
i outstanding
j digital imaging
k gigantic
l stars
m cuts to
n scanning the horizon
o prerequisite
p feature

5 The final paragraph contains an example of a rhetorical question. This is a useful stylistic device for introducing opinions and works particularly well in essays and articles – and, as here, in the general comment in reviews.

The writer should have followed up the rhetorical question with some relevant opinions on the use of special effects. For example:

Write about 50 words of your own to follow the rhetorical question (**).

Speak to most Hollywood producers and they would probably argue the case. Yet they are no substitute for an original storyline or engaging dialogue. Used wisely, special effects blend into a film seamlessly, as demonstrated in Ang Lee's Oscar-winning 'Crouching Tiger, Hidden Dragon'. If not, they will only irritate.

6 Now answer this exam task in 300–350 words, following the advice on page 38. Make a paragraph plan and check useful vocabulary in a dictionary before you start writing.

An international film magazine wants readers around the world to contribute a review to a special edition entitled *The Art of Advertising: Selling Products through Film*. Write a review of a memorable advertisement you have seen at the cinema or on television, evaluating its visual impact and its other features. You should also assess how much influence such advertisements have on us.

UNITS 1–4 Revision

Use of English

1 Read this extract from a book by the journalist John Simpson. Use the word given in capitals at the end of some of the lines to form a word that fits in the space in the same line.

In 1997 I went back to Beijing for the first time since the (0) .*disastrous*. events of 1989.	**DISASTER**
The Chinese (1) .... had been reluctant to re-admit foreign journalists who had	**AUTHORISE**
witnessed the Tiananmen Square student protests. Even eight years later, it was still	
(2) .... to get into the Square with a television camera, but we managed it. I looked for	**PROBLEM**
the bullet holes on the steps of the central monument, but they had all been expertly	
filled in; a faint discoloration perhaps, but almost (3) .... The most critical moment	**PERCEIVE**
in Chinese history after Mao Zedong's death seemed to have been entirely forgotten.	
My time in China had given me an (4) .... interest in Chinese art, so I decided to go	**ENDURANCE**
to Liu Li Chang, where for centuries there has been an antiquities market. Unfortunately,	
many things for sale there nowadays are modern (5) .... Empty-handed and	**IMITATE**
somewhat (6) .... , I went into a tea house and sat through the usual ceremony, but	**ILLUSION**
there were (7) .... differences here too: it seemed quicker and the tea lacked that	**IDENTIFY**
extraordinary lingering scent. Thoroughly (8) .... , I returned to my hotel: one of the	**HEART**
enormous, (9) .... places which have sprung up everywhere. Yet here, in a dark shop	**FACE**
tucked away off the lobby, my melancholy mood disappeared, for I met a (10)	**SURVIVE**
from 1989, who remembered me instantly. Not everything had been entirely forgotten.	

2 For questions 1–6, complete the second sentence so that it has a similar meaning to the first sentence, using the word given. Do not change the word given. You must use between three and eight words, including the word given.

1 I'm afraid the only option open to me is to ask you to leave the restaurant.
alternative
I ....*have no alternative but to ask*....
you to leave the restaurant.

2 If I had known the flight was going to be late leaving, I wouldn't have bothered rushing to the airport.
delay
Had I ....*known about the delay*....
to my flight, I wouldn't have bothered rushing to the airport.

3 The authorities made the landlord take on the financial burden of looking after the building.
shoulder
The landlord ....
looking after the building.

4 David looked as if he was about to cry when he saw the damage to his motorbike.
verge
David looked like ....*on the verge of crying*....
when he saw the damage to his motorbike.

5 If you need to contact me urgently, then ring this number.
necessary
Should ....*it be necessary for you to contact me*...... ,
ring this number.

6 I'm sure that the hotel will be good, as it was recommended by Pablo.
bound
The ....*hotel is bound to be good as Pablo*....
recommended it to me.

3 For questions 1–6, think of **one** word only which can be used appropriately in all three sentences.

1 Though well into her 20s by now, Jane's father still .... for her, including buying all her clothes.

Results show that the substance can be handled without adverse health effects, ... that there is adequate ventilation.

Data from other experiments have .... the basis for continuing intensive research on the Martian climate.

2 Over the next seven days, magazines will run awareness-raising .... and many shops will be selling red ribbons.

He was a man of 50, with a shock of grizzled hair, bushy eyebrows, regular .... and the finest forehead I ever saw.

Jackie Kennedy made style and class two distinctive .... of the new American Presidency.

3 You feel bored with your current relationship, but don't give up hope, as someone new is .... to appear on the scene and steal you away.

The men were driven to an isolated area of forest where, still .... and blindfolded, they were released unharmed.

Alyson is now .... for Sydney with three friends, who are keeping her company along the way.

4 I knew there was no alternative but to .... my pride and get on with the job.

In a country where most people live below the poverty line, this year's debt servicing is likely to .... up 28% of export earnings.

You don't have to .... every bit of propaganda – you should make up your own mind.

5 Most of us take an interest in the lives of the famous, but it is usually tempered with a .... of scepticism and a touch of irony.

Her subtle .... on the arm having no effect, Shirley was forced to kick her husband's leg, in order to shut him up.

Even farmers have felt the .... as fuel and fertiliser prices outstrip the price of their crops.

6 At least a size too big, Hannah's straw hat was .... down over her eyes.

He .... a few coins into a fat Coca-Cola machine outside the saloon, but nothing happened.

Roads leading to the sea were reported to be .... by lunchtime, with those inland unusually quiet.

Writing

4 Punctuate the following book review, adding capital letters where necessary. Then divide the review into suitable paragraphs. The first sentence is done for you.

No one has yet written 'Froth: the Trend that Changed History', but *Universal Foam* comes pretty close to being the definitive example of publishing froth. The book blends two recent publishing trends the newer of which is the wacky science subject. If there is a market for books on cryptography chronometry or cod and books on all these subjects have sold well in the last decade then there is no reason why any subject should seem boring. Once you have discovered a subject so obscure that no other publisher has come across it before all that remains is to prove that it holds the key to universal understanding. Cod a biography of the fish that changed the world is a pretty good example but universal foam the story of bubbles from cappuccino to the cosmos outdoes it since it permeates the universe from the smallest to the largest scale. After all there arent any galaxies stretched on the skin of unimaginably vast cod nor do physicists speak of the world arising from fluctuations in the quantum codfish. So the boys bumper book of froth might contain as every best-seller should everything you need to know about the universe. Then again it might contain everything else. Thats pretty frothy too.

In fact universal foam runs into another current publishing style the book of lists. Among the subjects covered here are volcanoes shaving foam champagne fire fighting equipment and meringues. Then you list everything you know about everything in the first list 101 important facts about galaxies 20 things you never knew about the cappuccino and so on. Finally all this is wrapped up in the academic style as old as exams where you simply cram in all the knowledge that you can possibly get hold of and regurgitate it with the echoing solemnity of a tv anchorman on the simpsons suggesting a rhetorical question can everyday foams like milk foam ever be fully understood and controlled. At which point there is foam flecking this reviewers lips. You cant really blame the author sidney perkowitz who has worked hard and writes clearly. It is not his fault that he has nothing particular to say after he has got through the bits that particularly interest him the fairly technical discussions of how to measure foams and describe them mathematically. However the fact is there is no sound reason for this book to have been written in the first place.

····⫶ Crossword page 189

UNIT 5 The consumer society

1 Discuss these topics with a partner.

- What is a shopaholic? Do you think you're one? What percentage of items you buy are things you *want* rather than *need*?
- How often do you buy clothes, CDs, shoes, computer games, books and chocolate?
- How important are designer labels for you?
- Do you think it's necessary to keep in fashion?
- Have you ever had to complain about something you've bought or about malpractice of some kind? What happened?
- Would you prefer a refund or an exchange if you took an item back to the shop?
- Do you know what legal rights you have as a consumer? If not, who would you turn to for advice?

2 You will hear an interview between a radio presenter called Paula and her guest, Mike James, who is the presenter of a programme called *Pricewise*. This is a TV programme which champions consumer rights. For questions 1–9, complete the sentences with a word or short phrase.

1 Mike James was originally a journalist on a .... programme.

2 The majority of stories are kept on a .... for possible use in the future.

3 Mike says it's important for the programme's .... to look through the script when it's written.

4 The land sold to the public was just .... in size.

5 The researcher was given a place to sit .... in the restaurant.

6 If you pay £5, you can order your food .... from the supermarket.

7 One supermarket customer was sent .... instead of apples.

8 When customers wore the trainers they were upset to find that they were ....

9 Mike says that manufacturers and retailers are worried about .... and tend to respond to complaints rapidly.

Exam spot

In Part 2 of the Listening test you need to complete nine sentences with information you hear on the recording. You need to listen for specific information and stated opinions. There is no need to write very much, just **a word or short phrase**. You can simply write down the words you hear – there is no need to use your own words.

3 Listen to the conversation again and write down the phrasal verbs you hear which mean the following. (They are all in the order in which you will hear them.)

a to intend	**f** to discover
b to agree to do	**g** to test
c to investigate	**h** to mention
d to make inquiries	**i** to tolerate
e to be highlighted	**j** to concede

4 The speakers in the recording use the following expressions. What do they mean?

a to read the small print	**d** disgruntled
b a juicy story	**e** teething trouble
c to keep/meet tight deadlines	**f** to take measures

Phrase spot

Mike James talked about *Pricewise* becoming a programme 'in its own right'. *In its own right* means by itself, without being part of another programme.

There are many other expressions that use *right*.

> the right way round
> by rights
> to serve someone right
> in the right
> to be right under your nose
> as right as rain
> to make all the right noises
> right on time
> the film rights
> to be within your rights

Choose one of the above expressions to complete the sentences opposite. (You might need to put it in a different form.)

a .... you should be in bed at 9.00 pm.
b I've had a cold but I'll be .... when I've had a holiday.
c I refused to apologise because I knew I was ....
d The police never found the murder weapon, even though it was ....
e His book has been very successful and it looks like he's all set to sell .... too.
f Helena turned up to the meeting .... for a change.
g You'd be well .... to take that dress back to the shop – it's torn at the collar.
h Dave .... so I expect he'll be promoted ahead of me.
i Turn it the other way, you can't read it if it isn't ....
j It'll .... Michelle .... if no one ever speaks to her again!

5 For questions 1–6, read the text and decide which answer (A, B, C or D) best fits each gap.

Born to shop

Good shoppers may be made in heaven. A scientific study into astrology and lifestyles has shown a remarkable correlation between our star signs and the way we spend money. The research, (1) .... on an analysis of 30,000 people's backgrounds, lifestyles and shopping habits, comes from an impeccable (2) .... . It states that chocolate firms should target those born under Aries, jewellers should (3) .... out Geminis and sports gear manufacturers should focus on Scorpios. All three signs have long been characterised by astrologers as outgoing, sociable and competitive. By (4) .... , those selling more mundane products such as DIY equipment should target Aquarians, while office equipment makers could do no worse than focus on Virgos, who have a (5) .... to be work-obsessed. Taureans, Pisceans and Cancerians are the ideal customer for any company. Their insecurity makes them unusually cautious, meaning they exhibit high levels of brand (6) .... . As for the other signs, well they could be just so mean they're not worth targeting at all!

1	**A** based	**B** derived	**C** deduced	**D** gathered
2	**A** origin	**B** root	**C** foundation	**D** source
3	**A** seek	**B** find	**C** hold	**D** make
4	**A** chance	**B** surprise	**C** contrast	**D** far
5	**A** tendency	**B** direction	**C** trend	**D** drive
6	**A** loyalty	**B** affiliation	**C** fidelity	**D** dependability

Nouns

1 Some of the sentences below, from the *Cambridge Learner Corpus*, contain common mistakes connected with countable and uncountable nouns. Correct the sentences which are wrong and leave the ones which are correct.

EXAMPLE: Information ~~are~~ *is* found on the screens above.
Information is uncountable and the verb should therefore be *is*.

a Put those scissors in the drawer for me, will you?
b How many luggage did you bring with you?
c This lift is for eight persons only.
d The news this morning were terrible – more price rises and a teachers' strike.
e Go out and get a paper for me, will you? I need to see what the news are.
f Marco Polo set off on his travels from Venice.
g Drivers should watch out for roadworks on the M25 this morning.
h Equipments for camping can be found on the ground floor of the building.
i My advice to you is to keep quiet about what is happening in the office.
j Peoples from all over the world are represented at the Games.
k Information about gallery opening times are available on the Internet.
l The fishmonger weighed out three kilos of fishes.
m Look at the dirt on this floor!
n The sceneries in New Zealand are spectacular.
o Traffic is becoming a problem in most cities nowadays.
p The police is aware of the break-in.
q My family live quite a distance away from where I live.

G ···⟶ page 182

2 Some nouns have different meanings according to whether they are used uncountably or with *a* or *an* or in the plural. Write sentences which show the two meanings of the following nouns.

EXAMPLE: damage
The fire did enormous damage to the town.
The judge awarded her £1 million in damages.

a work   f language
b iron   g comfort
c disorder   h experience
d speech   i capital
e room   j coffee

3 Many uncountable nouns can be made singular if they are used with *a bit of* or *a piece of*. They can also be made plural by adding *bits of* or *pieces of*. However, many uncountable nouns have special words to make them singular or plural, for example *a loaf of bread*.

Match the noun with its special word.

a	a burst of	glass
b	a pane of	smoke
c	a stroke of	abuse
d	a grain of	dust
e	a gust of	thunder
f	a speck of	luck
g	a stream of	emergency
h	a ray of	wind
i	a source of	sunshine
j	an item of	applause
k	a rumble of	sand
l	a puff of	amusement
m	a state of	clothing/news

Spelling

4 You must spell correctly in the examination. Read through the following advertisement and find the words which are spelled wrongly. Use your dictionary to help you.

Look around. You're in the midst of a global maelstrom. A swirling mass of converging tecnologies and new business oportunities unleeshed by the Internet. All waiting to be harnesed by companies like Fujitsu – the world's largest IT servises provider. 'We've focussed our energy and resauces on creating technology to solve the unique problems of thousands of individual businesses. Last year aloan we invested £2.5 bilion of our £31.1 bilion global IT and telecomunications revenus on R & D. Innervations that keep your business one step ahead of the Internet. And light years ahead of the competttition.'

Possession review

There are three ways of showing possession in English:

> **A The apostrophe**
> – used with people, e.g. *customers' rights* (NB the customer's rights refers to one customer; the customers' rights refers to more than one.)
> – used with time and distance, e.g. *a day's pay*
>
> **B Using 'of'**
> – usually used with objects, e.g. *the price of petrol*
> – used to talk about position, e.g. *the back of the room*
>
> **C Using a noun as an adjective**
> e.g. *a table leg, a travel agency*

5 Complete the following sentences using one of the forms above, A, B or C.

a (seat, back) Can I sit in the .... on the way home?

b (boss, wife) His .... is in hospital having a baby.

c (room, corner) The boy was sitting in the ....

d (day, pay) When is .... ?

e (week, holiday) Mary only had one .... last year.

f (wine, glass) Would you prefer a .... or a tumbler for your drink?

g (delay, moment) The decision was taken without a ....

h (Anne, best friend) .... has just got a job in Milan.

i (door, handle) Take care with that .... – it's loose.

j (field, sports) The team went out onto the ...., wearing their new strip.

G ⋯⟡ page 182

Preposition review

6 Read the article and fill the gaps with a suitable preposition.

I was (1) .... one (2) .... those sports 'superstores' the other day, hoping to find a pair of trainers. As I faced the giant wall of shoes, each model categorised (3) .... either sports affiliation, basketball star, economic class, racial heritage or consumer niche, I noticed a boy (4) .... to me (5) .... even greater awe (6) .... the towering selection of footwear. He was slack-jawed and his eyes were glazed (7) .... – a psycho-physical response (8) .... the overwhelming sensory data. It's a phenomenon known (9) .... retail architects as 'Gruen Transfer', named (10) .... the man who invented the shopping mall, where this mental paralysis is most commonly observed. Having finished several years (11) .... research (12) .... this exact state (13) .... mind, I knew to proceed (14) .... caution. I slowly made my way (15) .... the boy's side and gently asked him, 'What is going (16) .... your mind right now?' He responded (17) .... hesitation, 'I don't know which (18) .... these trainers is me.'

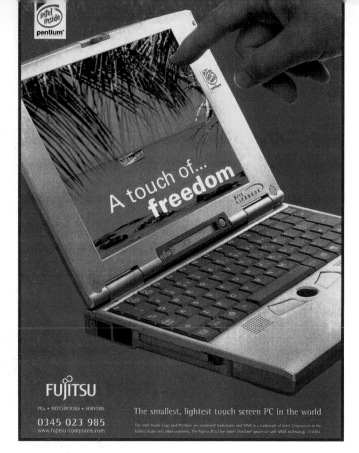

A touch of... freedom

FUJITSU

PCs • NOTEBOOKS • SERVERS

0345 023 985
www.fujitsu-computers.com

The smallest, lightest touch screen PC in the world

The Intel Inside Logo and Pentium are registered trademarks and MMX is a trademark of Intel Corporation in the United States and other countries. The Fujitsu B112 has Intel® Pentium® processor with MMX technology 233MHz.

Working with two texts

1 Discuss these questions in groups.

- What's your favourite advertisement? Why?
- What do you think makes a good advertisement?
- Do you think admen can sell anything? Think of some things that might be difficult to sell.
- Should advertising be curbed in any way? For example, should there be restrictions on cigarettes being advertised on TV?
- Do you think some advertising goes beyond the bounds of good taste?

2 Read the following texts on advertising. Think about:

- where you would find these texts, e.g. in a newspaper, magazine, book, novel, encyclopaedia, leaflet, brochure, etc.
- what style the writer is using, e.g. formal, informal, journalistic, academic, personal, narrative, etc.

A

line 1 Adland is shifting its focus – away from pigeonholing consumers into different age or social groups and towards a better understanding of its audiences' state of mind.

According to new research, consumers have never been more set on individualism and self-expression (there has been an increase in our willingness to complain, for example). And never have they been more set against pigeonholing and rigid classification – long-standing tools integral to the adman's trade.

The demise of job security has rocked the stability of established institutions and trust in them. And the result? A nation of increasingly opinionated individuals who expect the companies they deal with to have as discerning an outlook on the world as they do and to demonstrate a clearly identifiable set of values through
line 16 how they behave.

Advertisers must now target attitudes and aspirations rather than lifestyle – associating their products with a viewpoint or feeling rather than identifying themselves with a particular age or social group. Where once we used brands to help define ourselves, more and more now we are using brands that fit ideas about ourselves that we already have.

This, of course, is making the advertisers' job increasingly difficult. Which is why a growing number of agencies are starting to ask the previously unaskable in an attempt to understand better what we want and how we feel.

B

David Lewis, in his new book, contends that consumers have evolved from being conformist and deferential children, prepared to trust mass advertising, into free-thinking, individualistic adults, who are sceptical of figures of authority and believe in what Freud called 'the narcissism of small differences'.

Reflecting the change from an era of austerity to one of affluence, these consumers have largely exhausted the things they need to purchase and are now concentrating on what they want to buy. For some people consumption – in its widest sense – has even replaced religion as their main source of solace and comfort.

Mass society has shattered and been reduced to a mosaic of minorities. According to the author: 'In a hypercompetitive world of fragmented markets and independently-minded, well-informed individuals, companies that fail to understand and attend to the needs of new consumers are doomed to extinction.'

How is a savvy consumer products manufacturer to confront such a daunting challenge? The first thing to do, says Lewis, is to reconnect with your customers. It is easy to make false assumptions about who these customers are and what they want. One US record company was amazed to discover that the biggest purchasers of rap and techno music were grandparents buying presents for their grandchildren.

3 Find words in the texts which mean the same as the following. (They are in text order.) Use an English–English dictionary to help you.

Text A	Text B
moving	respectful
inflexible	dubious
necessary	condemned
discriminating	clever
hopes	difficult

4 Answer these questions on the texts.

Text A

a What do you think the writer means by 'pigeonholing consumers'?

b Why does the writer use the words 'tools' and 'trade' when talking about the adman?

c How has a decline in job security affected consumers?

d What does 'they' refer to in line 16?

e What are advertisers increasingly doing?

Text B

f What general contrast does the writer make between the past and the present?

g What point is the writer making when he talks about religion?

h What does the writer mean by 'consumption – in its widest sense'?

i Find two other words in paragraph 3 which echo the writer's use of the word 'mosaic'.

j What does the writer see as the solution to understanding changes in buying patterns?

ⓔxam spot

In Paper 3, Part 5 the summary task tests information selection, linking and sentence construction. You will need to pick out at least four points, maybe one or two more – either two from each text or possibly one from one text and three from the other. You must then put the points in your own words as far as possible.

5 Read the two texts again and underline the points which answer this question:

In which ways, according to the writers of both texts, have consumers changed?

Remember to keep the question firmly in mind when re-reading the texts. It's a good idea to use a highlighter pen to underline the points.

6 Now try to express the points you underlined in a different way.

EXAMPLE:
The first point should be:
Consumers have never been more set on individualism and self-expression.
This can be expressed differently by changing it to:
Consumers today have an independent outlook and are keen to assert their point of view.

Now change the other points you have, if possible. (Some words are difficult to find synonyms for.)

Finally, link all your points into a paragraph of 50–70 words which answers the question in exercise 5.

7 Being able to manipulate words will help you with both Part 4 and Part 5 of Paper 3. Complete these sentences by changing the word in brackets into an abstract noun. Use a dictionary to help you.

EXAMPLE: I value her (friend) greatly. *friendship*

a They quarrelled out of sheer (bored).

b Some new products have built-in (obsolete).

c Environmental (aware) has increased dramatically over the last decade.

d He felt great (proud) when his youngest daughter won first prize.

e He's got the (confident) to walk into an interview and get the job.

f The government believes that its (austere) programme will reduce inflation.

g His friends take advantage of his (generous), and borrow his things without asking.

h Now she is 18, she is keen to have her (independent) from her parents.

i He complained that the (inefficient) of the bus service was having an impact on employment.

j His feelings of (insecure) made him desperate to get other people's approval.

k Scrooge is a character in Charles Dickens' book *A Christmas Carol* who is famous for his (mean).

l (Individual) is the idea that freedom of thought and action for each person is the most important quality of a society, rather than shared effort and (responsible).

m Louise's (aspire) to help others come from her own misfortune as a child.

n I think it's important to treat his articles with a degree of (sceptical).

Exam folder 3

Paper 3 Part 5 Comprehension questions and summary writing task

In this part of Paper 3 there are two texts with four comprehension questions and a summary task. There are two marks for each of the four questions and fourteen marks for the summary task. The comprehension questions are testing awareness of the use of language. Sometimes the questions might require you to use information from both texts in your answer.

Here are some examples of questions you might be asked.

Why does the writer use X in paragraph 2?

What image is the writer trying to create in this text?

Which two phrases echo X in the first text?

What is implied by the phrase … ?

What contrast is the writer making in the second half of the text?

In your own words, explain what is meant by X in line 0.

What parallels does the writer draw between … ?

1 Read the two texts, which are on the subject of obsolescence and the arts and answer the questions which follow.

I read that the book is dead. It has fought long and hard against the electronic menace but now faces defeat. I don't believe a word of it. But if the book were truly dead, what an obituary must be written. This towering manifest of the past millennium has outlasted empires, defeated armies, proved more explosive than any weapon, more lethal than any plague, more comforting than any saint. `line 4`

Frantic efforts are now being made to render the book 'obsolete' and small fortunes have been spent putting books on the Internet. All have encountered consumer resistance. People appear to find flickering screens tiring. They make eyes ache since the scanning pulses are in constant movement. Additionally, screens need power, which is costly and weighty.
What these souls are struggling to do is merely to reinvent what Caxton discovered half a millennium ago. It is called a book. Technologists dislike books because they are 'low tech'. Yet the market loves them. They need no power supply and are cheap, small and portable. A row of books is a joy to behold. This object is, in short, a masterpiece. Had the Internet been around for years and had I invented printing on paper, I would be hailed as a millennial genius.

Apart from the art of conversation, culture offers no more complete satisfaction than to read, finish and set down a good book. To read is to tiptoe silently into the realm of another's mind. `line 22`
The book is eternal.

---

1 What is the writer referring to when he talks about 'this towering manifest'? (line 4)
2 Explain in your own words 'to tiptoe silently into the realm of another's mind'. (line 22).

Advice   Comprehension questions

- Read through both texts carefully before attempting to answer the questions.
- If the question says 'Explain in your own words' make sure you do not just repeat what is in the text. You must try to find other words to paraphrase.
- When you are asked what a phrase or word means, read around it to see if there are any clues to help you.

- Make sure you answer the questions fully. If you are asked to find 'words' or 'phrases' in the text, you will only receive a mark if you find all the ones required, i.e. finding only one example receives no marks.
- Write clearly, as you will be penalised for illegible handwriting.
- Don't write too much – you are only asked for a word or short phrase. You don't need to write a full sentence.

How will the dominant medium of the 20th century manage in the 21st? Well, cinema is an art begotten on a technology. And the future of the movies is as bound up with technology as its short past has been.

The century for which cinema has existed has seen innovation and obsolescence at a frantic pace, affecting every element of the medium; sound, colour, 3-D. But movie history is also a graveyard of formats and processes, of treasure mutilated, junked and lost. Film has already outlived a number of death threats, notably from its unruly kid brothers, television and video. Now the threat is from cheaper technologies and strategies that bypass the usual channels.

Film was able to ride out and even profit from the video boom because there have always been films that are worth seeing, but not worth going to see. There are also films that only work in a large and crowded room.

A horror film seen on video is an exercise in masochism if you're on your own, and degenerates into farce if you watch it with friends. There's a communal aspect of film going which can go underground for long periods, but then surfaces with its urgency intact.

Meanwhile televisions grow bigger and cinemas get smaller. At some point cinemas will find themselves duplicating a domestic experience, without its convenience. That's when the pendulum will swing back the other way, and movie theatres will stop trying to compete in terms of choice and offer what they always did best: images projected in their grandeur.

3 Explain in your own words what the writer says happens if you watch a horror film on video.

4 What, according to the writer, will make 'the pendulum swing back'?

2 Read the following exam task.

In a paragraph of between 50 and 70 words, summarise in your own words as far as possible why the writers of both texts believe that books and the cinema will never be defeated by advances in technology.

Below is an answer written by a student. It would receive very low marks. Read the advice at the bottom of the page and then look at the answer carefully and suggest ways of improving it.

> I would like to begin this summary by saying that I totally agree with both writers.
>
> First of all, it is true to say that book are cheap, small and portable. They also look good on a shelf and are enjoyable to read. But the Internet is hard to read and is expensive. Another thing is that films should only be shown in a large room not on video. More people should go to the cinema and not stay at home watching videos. It is good for them to be with other people and share a communal experience.

3 Now write your own summary.

Advice   Summary

- Read the question through carefully and make sure you understand it. Keep it in mind when you look at the texts.
- Don't be tempted to include your own opinion in the summary, even though you may disagree or agree strongly with what is being said.
- You need to find either four or five points over the two texts. Use a highlighter pen to underline the key phrases that answer the summary question.

- Paraphrase the key phrases using your own words as far as possible and link them together so that you have a clear and well-expressed paragraph.
- Count the number of words you have written. You need to write between 50 and 70 words. You will lose marks if you don't keep within the limits.
- Make sure your answer is easy to read – good handwriting and not too many crossings out.

UNIT 6 The sound of music

1 Give your opinion on the following statements.

- Listening to music helps me to concentrate, especially when studying.
- Every child should have the opportunity to learn an instrument.
- Pop music improves my mood.
- Listening to classical music can improve your intelligence.
- I enjoy listening to buskers.

2 You are going to read an extract from a science magazine. Seven paragraphs have been removed from the extract. Choose from the paragraphs A–H the one which fits each gap (1–7). There is one extra paragraph which you do not need to use.

To help you, some of the key words have been highlighted in bold. What do they refer to? When you find the answer to that question you will know which paragraph is the correct one to fill the gap.

Can listening to Mozart boost your brain power? It's a controversial theory that has sent classical 'sharpen your mind' albums to the top of the best-seller charts but divided scientists. The latest research, however, suggests that the so-called 'Mozart Effect' does profoundly affect the human brain.

The excitement started six years ago when researchers reported that people scored better on a standard IQ test after listening to Mozart. But last summer, this 'Mozart Effect' suffered a setback when several sceptics repeated the original study but found no improvement. This is not the end of the story, though. A closer look shows that Mozart's music does have a profound effect on the brain, though no one yet knows why.

1 [ ]

To **their** surprise, the rhythmic patterns sounded like baroque, new age, or Eastern music. If brain activity can sound like music, Shaw wondered, might we learn to understand the neural grammar by working backwards and watching how the brain responds to music?

2 [ ]

After taking **this test**, one group of students sat in silence for 10 minutes. Another group listened to a Mozart piano sonata, while a third group heard either a taped story or minimalist, repetitive music. Then they all took the test again. The Mozart group correctly predicted 62 per cent more shapes on the second test, while the 'silent' group improved by 14 per cent and the third group by just 11 per cent.

3 [ ]

When **he analysed all the studies** as a group, he found no benefit from listening to Mozart. He felt some people did better because of what psychologists call 'enjoyment arousal' – music improves people's mood, so they perform better. But **the critics** are only seeing part of the story says Lois Hetland of Harvard. Chabris summarised only experiments that compared Mozart against silence, not against other compositions. Hetland tested 1,014 subjects. She found that

Mozart listeners outperformed other groups more often than could be explained by chance.

4 [ ]

The milliseconds it takes the subject to make **that judgment** are a precise measure of spatial reasoning. To Seigel's surprise, subjects who took the test after listening to Mozart did significantly better. 'It was as though they had practised the test,' he says. 'Now we have another way to measure the Mozart Effect.'

5 [ ]

The researchers don't know why **it** works or which other pieces might. **They wondered whether the music of Mozart's contemporary Johann Christian Bach would work, or even something by a 20th-century composer such as Igor Stravinsky.**

6 [ ]

Studies yet to be published may shed some light on the subject. At the University of Illinois Medical Center, neurologist John Hughes and a musicologist colleague have analysed hundreds of compositions by Mozart, Chopin and 55 other composers. They devised a scale that scores how often the music's loudness rises and falls in **sequences** of 10 seconds or longer. Minimalist music by the composer Philip Glass and pop tunes scored among the lowest, with Mozart scoring two to three times higher.

7 [ ]

However, a more important **finding** is that, in a five-year study with children, it was found that keyboard music training improves skills that require mental imagery – and after two years of lessons, the effect doesn't wear off. In other words, a childhood rich in music may have lasting benefits.

Read the introduction to get an idea of what the text is going to be about. Then read the text and the missing paragraphs.

Read through the paragraphs on either side of the gap very carefully. Don't just read the paragraph before the gap as this might not give you any clues to the missing text. This part of the exam is testing understanding of content as well as reference devices.

A It is **this experiment** which has drawn so much criticism. Harvard psychologist **Christopher Chabris** looked at results from 16 studies hunting for the Mozart Effect, involving 714 subjects.

B The **sequences** repeating regularly every 20 to 30 seconds may trigger the strongest response in the brain. And of all the music analysed, Mozart most often peaks every 30 seconds. **Results** such as these may help predict which pieces of music have the strongest effect.

C The first hint of the Mozart Effect emerged more than a decade ago. In simulations by neurobiologist Gordon Shaw at the University of California at Irvine, the way nerve cells were connected to one another predisposed groups of cells to adopt certain specific firing patterns and rhythms. These natural patterns, he believes, form the basics of mental activity. In 1988, **Shaw and a student** turned the output of their simulations into sounds instead of a conventional printout.

D Even stronger support for Mozart's effect on the brain comes from other studies. He subjected 30 rats to 12 hours of the *Sonata in D* daily for over two months. These rats ran a maze an average of 27 per cent faster and with 37 per cent fewer errors than 80 others. The study suggests a neurological basis for the Mozart Effect. Some are still not convinced.

E Another **detractor** was psychologist Ed Seigel at Elmhurst College, Illinois, who set out to disprove the Mozart Effect. In his test, a subject looks at two letter Es, with one at a skewed angle to the other. The greater the angle, the harder it is to decide whether the letters are the same or different.

F **So he** and his colleague Frances Rauscher used **part of a standard IQ test** to see whether Mozart's music could temporarily boost people's ability to visualise shapes. In a 1995 study, they asked 79 students to work out what a paper would look like if folded and then cut like a paper doily.

G For consistency almost all studies have used ***The Sonata for Two Pianos in D Major (K 448)***, though some have measured the effect from other music as well. 'It can't be just this composition, and not just Mozart,' says Rauscher.

H Critics take issue with **this vagueness about which type of music is best**. They say that someone has to define what specific musical elements are required.

3 Summarise in your own words what the following scientists concluded about the Mozart Effect. What is your opinion of the Mozart Effect? Do you think it may work?

Gordon Shaw	Christopher Chabris	Ed Seigel
Frances Rauscher	Lois Hetland	John Hughes

There are a number of phrases with the verb *take*. In the text on the Mozart Effect there was *take issue*, which means *to disagree*, and also *taking this test*.

Complete the gaps with one of the following words or phrases:

part	exception to
the view	for granted
place	seriously
a stand	by surprise
issue	advantage
notice	into account/consideration
account of	second place

a The police have to take any terrorist threat ....

b Don't take any .... of what Sue says – she's just in a bad mood.

c The seminar will take .... in the new lecture room on the fourth floor.

d He rarely took .... in proceedings, preferring rather to have a backseat role.

e This institution takes .... that all employees should be treated fairly.

f When you add up your business expenses don't forget to take .... hotel tips.

g The Minister took .... with the interviewer over whether the government was sticking to its manifesto pledges.

h Peter took .... of the breeze and went windsurfing.

i His sudden appearance took me ....

j Fathers tend to have to take .... when a new baby comes along.

k We need to take .... the neighbours if we're going to have a party.

l Louise was fed up with being taken .... and decided to leave both her husband and family.

m The teacher decided it was time to take .... on school uniform and not allow the children to wear trainers in class.

n Linda took great .... the fact that her name had been left off the guest list.

Modals 1: Degrees of likelihood

1 Read this extract from the text on page 50.

Can here means *the idea is possible* rather than *it's definite*. You can substitute *sometimes sounds* here for *can sound*.

> If brain activity can sound like music, Shaw wondered, might we learn to understand the neural grammar by working backwards and watching how the brain responds to music?

Might expresses a more tentative possibility, i.e. that something is less likely.

Likelihood ranges from absolute certainty to complete impossibility and can be expressed in a number of ways:

- with modal auxiliaries *can, may, could, might, should, ought to, must be, can't be* in the present and with a perfect infinitive in the past
- with a sentence beginning with *It* and followed by a *that*-clause
- by an adverbial such as *perhaps, without a doubt*, etc.

G····; page 183

2 Which of the sentences below express the following?

A I think it's likely.
B I'm not sure.
C I think it's impossible.

a The chances are it will rain tonight.
b He can't have got home already, the train won't have arrived yet.
c You could look more enthusiastic if you tried.
d Caroline will probably pass her violin exam.
e You shouldn't have gone swimming off the rocks, you might have had an accident.
f There shouldn't be a problem with your application.
g The package ought to arrive in a couple of days.
h The postman must've already called – look there's a letter on the table.
i I may see you on Saturday.
j There's every likelihood of rain this afternoon.
k It can be quite interesting to re-read books you read as a child.
l She's bound to get lost when she goes to Tokyo.
m The government may have made a bad decision building the Millennium Dome.
n There's a faint chance I'll get a car for my birthday.

3 What do you think is the likelihood of the following happening?

a The birth of another Mozart.
b An asteroid hitting Earth.
c People having brain transplants.
d English losing its world dominance of pop music.
e New Zealand winning the football World Cup.
f Electric cars taking over from petrol-driven ones.

4 In groups decide what person or event the speaker might be talking about in these extracts from radio news bulletins.

EXAMPLE: '… and as the car slows down for him to wave to the crowds a shot is heard …'
It may be a movie star.
The chances are it's a politician.
It's bound to be someone famous because he's waving at the crowds.

a '… he's coming down the steps slowly, and with a final movement that looks like a small jump because of the atmosphere, he …'
b '… and it's believed the first place to see it will be the small Pacific island of …'
c '… a fashion designer who made many women look beautiful, but who tragically was murdered …'
d '… although this invention has very quickly become a necessity, with even young children demanding one, some authorities still believe it to have some risk to health …'
e '… and it's a very exciting night, as the crowds gather, and some people have started climbing onto it, and others have begun to knock holes through it, in the effort to join the people on the other side …'

In the Paper 3 Part 4 transformations, you must use between three and eight words including the key word. Contractions (*can't, won't,* etc.) count as two words. Check your answers for length and accuracy before transferring them to the answer sheet.

5 Complete the second sentence so that it has a similar meaning to the first sentence, using the word given. Do not change the word given. You must use between three and eight words, including the word given.

1 In all probability Alan will get a place to study music at Oxford.
   chances
   The ....
   accepted to study music at Oxford.

2 Professor Potts is unlikely to retire before she has to.
   doubtful
   It ....
   early retirement.

3 Unless there is a last-minute hitch, the Head's job is his for the taking.
   bound
   He's ....
   there isn't a last-minute hitch.

4 It's possible that the fire was caused by an electrical fault in the gym.
   likelihood
   In ....
   of the fire in the gym was an electrical fault.

5 It's pretty certain that we'll win a gold medal this year in the 100 metres.
   foregone
   It's ....
   we'll win a gold medal this year in the 100 metres.

6 Quickly read through this extract from an article about pop music to get some idea of what it is about. Don't fill in any gaps at this stage. When you've read it, answer the questions below.

Band manufacture

The fate of any pop band is a question that (0) ......*no*...... longer is of interest to its fans alone. (1) ......*Not*...... only has the Prime Minister himself recognised pop music's importance (2) .... a business, pointing (3) ......*out*...... that it contributes more (4) ......*to*...... export earnings than the steel industry, but strange as it (5) .... seem, British people spend more on pop than they do on fruit and vegetables.

(6) .... such serious money washing around, the question of (7) .... will be the next big thing is (8) .... too important to be left to random factors such as chance and talent. (9) .... the great names of British rock in the 60s and 70s formed bands spontaneously (10) .... they were discovered and then marketed, their new millennium successors are increasingly (11) ......*likely*...... to be brought (12) .... by marketing men. The Spice Girls, sold as a group of young girls in (13) ......*charge*...... of their own destiny, were in (14) ......*fact*...... dreamed up and promoted by middle-aged men. Designing a band is much the same as designing (15) ......*any*...... other product: take a basic, successful model and adapt it. The challenge, when everything has been tried already, is to persuade consumers that what you are doing is in some way innovative.

a What is the writer's attitude to the pop industry?
b What comparison does the writer make in the article?
c What conclusion does the writer draw?

Now fill the gaps with one word only.

Paper 5 Part 2

1 Link the following instruments with the category they belong in. There is one instrument for each category.

violin	brass
piano	keyboard
drum	electronic
flute	percussion
synthesizer	string
trumpet	woodwind

2 Do you play or would you like to play an instrument? Why? Why not? Do you think some instruments are much easier to play than others?

3 🎧 You are going to hear an interview with Sue Pearson, who teaches violin making at a college in Wales. For questions 1–10 opposite, complete the sentences with a word or short phrase.

Steps to making a violin

1 The interviewer describes string players as very .... about their violins.

2 Sue prefers to have wood which has grown on quite .... in northern Europe.

3 It's important for the grain to be uniform so that the violin will have .... and ....

4 Sue explains that there is a great deal of .... when she makes a violin.

5 The ribs of the violin will be about .... thick when they are finished.

6 The ribs are .... initially to make them more pliable.

7 The top and bottom of the violin are .... by hand.

8 Students find the .... the hardest part of the violin to make.

9 Sue believes the varnish helps to make a violin sound more .... in tone.

10 Sue hopes that in .... time her violins will still be played.

S tyle extra

In the interview you've just heard, wood was described as

finely grained   intricately carved

This kind of adverb–adjective and adverb–participle collocation is fairly common in English and you should try to familiarise yourself with them. Below are some more common collocations.

seriously ill	widely believed
strenuously worded	carefully chosen
singularly unsuccessful	staggeringly expensive
keenly priced	

Write a sentence which includes the following words and one of the collocations above.

EXAMPLE: sister / food poisoning
My sister is seriously ill with food poisoning.
My sister sent a strongly worded letter to the restaurant when she got food poisoning.

a Michael Jackson / plastic surgery
b birthday present / boyfriend
c CDs / retail outlets
d seats / rock concert
e New album / number one

I diom spot

Complete the following sentences using one of these words:

tune	chord	song	string
fiddle	note	score	

a The sales manager was fed up with playing second .... to the marketing manager so she walked out.

b The present government would appear to be out of .... with most young people.

c I put in a bid for that old piano because it was going for a ....

d Sheila did a word-processing course before she went to university, to make sure she had a second .... to her bow.

e The fight occurred when the youths decided they needed to settle the .... with the other gang.

f The speech seemed to strike the right .... with the crowd and they clapped loudly.

g Her biography struck a .... with quite a few elderly people who had had a similar experience.

4 Look at photographs A–D, which show four different ways of appreciating music. Decide the relative merits of each and pick the one you think is most representative of how young people enjoy music today. You have about three minutes to talk about this.

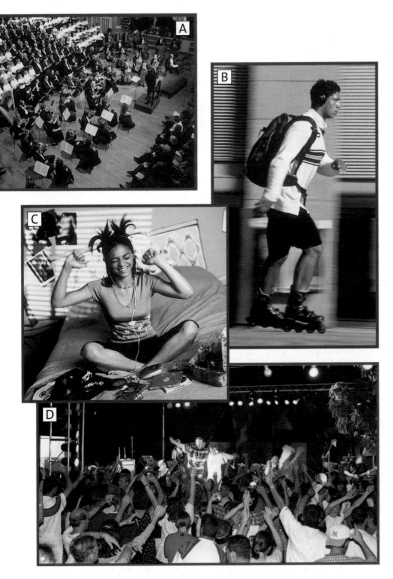

Talk about:
the atmosphere – hushed / electric / expectant / conducive / free and easy / rarefied
sound quality – decibels / interference / poor / excellent
value for money – a rip off / extortionate / a bargain

Pronunciation

5 🎧 In the Grammar section of this unit you looked at modals. The tone of voice that is used with certain modal auxiliaries can change the meaning. Listen to these sentences. What feeling is the speaker expressing? For example, irritation, anger, surprise, being reproachful, etc.

a You could have rung me from the station.
b You could have rung me from the station.
c You might ask before you borrow the car!
d You might ask Pete if you can borrow his car.
e Liz should have got here an hour ago.
f Liz should have got here an hour ago.

6 🎧 You are going to hear other examples of contrastive stress. Underline the word which is stressed in the sentence you hear and answer the question that follows.

EXAMPLE: I wanted <u>white</u> wine with the meal.
Did she get white wine? No.

a I thought you'd gone home.
Is the person at home?
b I thought you'd gone home.
Is the person at home?
c She's an English teacher.
Does she teach English?
d She's an English teacher.
Does she teach English?
e I'm not buying a car.
Is he buying a car?
f I'm not buying a car.
Is she buying a car?
g She's not pretty.
Is she pretty?
h I had wanted to see the paintings.
Did she see the paintings?
i I had wanted to see the paintings.
Did he see the paintings?

Writing folder 3

Part 1 Essay

Part 1 of Paper 2 may be an essay task. You will be given material in the form of notes or a short text on a topic and asked to include this information in your essay, along with your own ideas. This is a discursive task, where you have to present an argument, requiring clear organisation and a logical sequence of ideas.

1 Look at this exam task. Then read the opening paragraph below, which is a competent and clear introduction to the essay required.

You have been investigating the status of music in society and have asked professional musicians and music teachers for their views. Now your tutor has asked you to write an essay assessing the importance of music nowadays, using your notes and giving your own opinions on this subject.

Professionals
1 Local rock bands – lots of live gigs (small venues e.g. parties), CD sales small
2 Classical orchestra – v. tough to find work, low pay
3 Big money for top performers

Music teachers
Music less important than e.g. maths at school – but important from early age
Benefits of playing – creative, brings new friendships
Benefits of listening – relaxing, fun!

Write your **essay**.

Music is something that we perhaps take for granted in our daily lives, particularly when it exists in the form of background music, from advertising jingles to MTV. However, do we as a society take music as seriously as we should? In this essay, I will examine this subject from the perspectives of the professional musician and the music teacher, giving my own views on the status of music today.

2 Even if the notes presented on the question paper are sometimes informal, your essay needs to be written in a neutral register. Think of neutral equivalents for the following words and phrases from the notes.

   a lots of live gigs
   b tough
   c big money
   d fun

3 When writing an essay, there are various ways of introducing an argument. Read these sentence openers. Then choose appropriate ones to insert in a–h below, paying attention both to the ideas expressed and the grammar used.

Generalising
It is often said that …
It is usually the case that …
People tend to regard …
The reality is that …

Specifying
From the classical performer's point of view, …
Professional musicians are seen as …
For rock musicians …

Raising an argument
Considering / Looking at / Taking the example of …
On the question of …
No one would dispute …

Giving one side
One argument in favour of this is …
In support of …
It is true that …

Giving the other side
At the same time …
In actual fact …
On the other hand, …
In contrast to …
Set/Weighed against this is …
This is not to say that …

a … highly-skilled individuals, yet their earnings don't always reflect their talent.
b … teaching music in school, not enough is done.
c … children who learn music at a young age benefit academically.
d … the fact that it is easier to make your own CD these days.
e … everyone should be able to read music, as it is not a fundamental lifeskill.
f … music is more available to us than ever before.
g … the many benefits of listening to music.
h … this it should be added that the best-known performers earn a great deal.

Now write four more sentences based on the content in the notes, with any openers you haven't used.

4 Insert all twelve sentences into this paragraph plan. Make notes on what else needs to be said in each paragraph.

(1 Opening paragraph)

2 General perceptions of the role of music in society

3 Performers

4 Music in schools

5 Benefits of music (playing and listening)

(6 Concluding paragraph)

Advice

- Introduce the essay in the first paragraph.
- Refer to all the major points given in the question.
- Add relevant opinions of your own.
- Make sure your argument is logical and coherent.
- Include an effective conclusion.
- Choose a suitably neutral register.
- Use a variety of sentence openers and linkers.
- Paragraph your answer clearly.

5 Now write an essay based on what is in the plan, being careful to reorder the sentences where necessary and adding appropriate linkers. Write your own opening paragraph and conclusion. You should write 300–350 words.

UNIT 7 Vision on

1 Look at the pictures opposite and decide what they have in common.

2 🎧 You will hear four different extracts. First, read the questions and check any difficult words in your dictionary.

For questions 1–8, choose the answer (A, B or C) which fits best according to what you hear. There are two questions for each extract.

Extract 1 You hear a woman talking about when her son was very young.

1 Why did the woman choose not to tell her son off when he drew on the wall?
   A She felt guilty as she had not been keeping an eye on him.
   B She thought his pictures added some much-needed colour.
   C She believed it was wrong to put a stop to his creativity.

2 Now that he is grown up, how does she feel about the action she took?
   A sceptical
   B vindicated
   C embarrassed

Extract 2 You hear a conversation between two friends about art and photography.

3 What do both speakers regard as important in their preferred art form?
   A colour
   B preparation
   C composition

4 What does the man argue about photography?
   A It begs creative decisions at different stages.
   B Choosing which paper to use is the only variable.
   C Selecting the right film can be highly effective.

Extract 3 You hear a man talking on the radio about Percy Shaw, an inventor.

5 What prompted Percy Shaw to work on his invention?
   A He was involved in a serious car accident.
   B Something on which he had relied disappeared.
   C His eyesight was no longer as keen as it once was.

6 Which part of his invention is likened to an eyelid?
   A the pad   B the base   C the assembly

Extract 4 You hear a woman talking about the eye on the radio.

7 What is the woman's profession?
   A zoologist
   B psychologist
   C journalist

8 What point does she make about staring?
   A Animals make eye contact to signal they are about to attack.
   B False eye spots on animals prove that the eye is irreplaceable.
   C Humans have to resort to less direct forms of intimidation.

Idiom spot

Which of these idioms were used in the recordings?
What do the others mean?

catch someone's eye   turn a blind eye to
cast your eye over   see eye to eye with
have an eye for

Use your imagination to the full to finish these sentences.

a The thing that really caught my eye was ...
b I shouldn't have turned a blind eye to ...
c Could you cast your eye over ...
d I've never seen eye to eye with ...
e You definitely have an eye for ...

3 Read this text about the French artist Georges Seurat. Use the word given in capitals at the end of some of the lines to form a word that fits in the space in the same line.

Exam spot

The Paper 3 Part 2 word formation task tests related parts of speech and compound words. Read the text carefully – a gap may require a plural or negative form.

The Pointillist Georges Seurat (1859–1891)

Few artists discover a (0) ......*meaningful*...... direction so young in life. Barely into his twenties, Georges Seurat did just this, developing one of the most lucid (1) .... styles since the fifteenth century, based on the dot. This was a radical departure from the style of Impressionist artists such as Pissarro and Renoir. (2) ...., the unit of Impressionism had been the brush-stroke, always (3) .... in form – fat or thin, clean or smeared, streaky, squidgy or transparent – and (4) .... mixed to conform with the facts of sight. Seurat wanted something with greater (5) .... than that. A child of late nineteenth-century positivism and (6) .... optimism,

MEAN
CLASSICS

HITHER
PREDICT
INTUITION
STABLE
SCIENCE

Seurat drew on studies of visual colour analysis to generate his own (7) .... style. The most (8) .... work of this nature was 'The Law of Simultaneous Colour Contrast', written by Eugène Chevreul. According to Chevreul, colour recognition was a matter of (9) .... – a web of connected events – rather than the simple presentation of one hue after another to the eye. Seurat resolved to make this process explicit on canvas by (10) .... making his colour patches tiny, reducing them to dots: hence the name, 'Pointillism'.

COMPARE
INFLUENCE

ACT

SYSTEM

Style extra

Look at this example from the text above.

A child of late nineteenth-century positivism and scientific optimism, Seurat drew on ...

The use of an extended noun phrase to preface a sentence like this is common in biographical and other academic writing.

Complete the sentences opposite, which start with noun phrases, writing about people of your choice.

EXAMPLE: One of the most creative artists of the 20th century, *Picasso produced many different styles in the course of his working life.*

a A highly-regarded and influential film-maker,
b Best-known for his magnificent novels,
c Undervalued as an actor until very recently,
d The youngest of a large family,
e Young, rich and famous,

Write two more complete sentences on subjects of your choice.

Participles

1 This image, taken by the Hubble Space Telescope, shows an area of star formation in the heart of a distant galaxy. Would you describe the picture as *beautiful*? Why? / Why not?

How else might you describe it? Would you use any of these words?

dazzling   flamboyant   gratuitous   inspiring
sensational   stunning

2 a Identify the part of speech of each underlined word in the following sentence, which is taken from one of the recordings in 7.1.

You may see a pair of <u>dazzling</u> headlights <u>eyeballing</u> you.

  b Identify the participle and say what it refers to in these examples, also taken from 7.1.

   i Driving home through the unlit outskirts of Halifax at night, Percy Shaw would follow the glint of …
   ii His invention, modelled on the eye of a cat, consists of …

  c Sometimes the position of the participle clause in the sentence alters the meaning. Explain the difference in meaning of these two sentences.

   i I saw our cat sitting precariously on the roof.
   ii Sitting precariously on the roof, I saw our cat.

3 Now read the article that accompanies the Hubble image, ignoring the italics. What does it say about art and beauty?

4 Say whether the italicised participles in the article are used actively or passively. Does each one refer to simultaneous action or to previous action? For example, *Gazing* is an active use, referring to the same time as the action in the main clause of the sentence (*we are savouring*).

Ⓖ ⋯⫶ page 183

Beauty written in the stars

Gazing at the smoky, glowing gas clouds of the 'starburst' galaxy shown here, we are savouring a beauty that is the accidental product of events that happened in a distant time and part of the universe. The result looks like a great painting. To be precise, it is reminiscent of the work of Turner, that masterly nineteenth-century British artist. For John Ruskin, Turner's champion and near-contemporary, the object of art was to reveal the divine hand in nature. That was what he meant by beauty. What might he have said today, *having viewed* the pictures *taken* by the Hubble Space Telescope?

Having been launched in 1990 with an inaccurately ground lens, Hubble was initially a huge embarrassment, *sending* back indistinct images that impressed no one. However, the picture changed, quite literally, in 1993. On *being* successfully *repaired* by shuttle astronauts, the telescope proceeded to relay the most spectacular images to us. Hubble is now like an eye with a cataract removed, *seeing* into deep space with a hard, bright precision that is almost uncomfortable.

There has never been a more gratuitous addition to our store of beauty. Ultimately, when we call a work of art beautiful we are comparing it to nature. The underlying structures of nature *imitated* by artists from ancient Greece until the middle of the twentieth century were chosen because nature was perceived as beautiful. If we don't talk much about 'beauty' in contemporary art, it is due to the fact that art is no longer *concerned* with the representation of nature. Arguably, the photographs taken by Hubble are the most flamboyantly beautiful artworks of our time.

5 Join a sentence from 1–6 with one from a–f, starting each new sentence with a participle clause. Think about timing in the two sentences you are joining. An example (0 + g) is given.

EXAMPLE: *Having slashed the half-finished canvas with a knife, the temperamental artist threw his paints out of the seventh-storey window one by one.*

0 The temperamental artist slashed the half-finished canvas with a knife.
1 The exhibition includes some rather shocking images.
2 Andy Goldsworthy's sculptures often occur in open landscape.
3 Physicists want to create order from chaos.
4 The photographer took quite a few warm-up shots.
5 People come in from the street for an hour's rest.
6 I have already bought two previous works by this artist.

a They don't realise that the beds – and they themselves – are part of an installation.
b They are constantly trying to reduce the universe to a set of basic principles.
c It has received mixed reactions from members of the public.
d I am looking out for a third.
e Then he caught the model unawares in a more relaxed pose.
f They are particularly effective during dramatic weather conditions.
g He threw his paints out of the seventh-storey window one by one.

6 Complete the sentences with a suitable passive participle, formed from one of the verbs below.

| announce   choose   damage   make   search   sell   show |

a The sculptures ....(being) chosen.... for the exhibition will all have to travel to New York by sea.

b Many of the images ....shown.... in advertisements at the moment are based on original artists' work.

c The colourful posters ....sold.... at the gallery could themselves become collectors' items one day.

d Jewellery ....made.... from recycled glass and plastic is particularly popular.

e Delays have mainly been caused by visitors' belongings ....being searched.... at the exhibition entrance.

f The shortlist ....announced.... yesterday has already provoked strong criticism.

g The museum basement ....damaged.... by flooding last November will remain closed to visitors.

Questions on the texts 1

1 Read the dictionary definition for the word *cliché*. Decide which of the images shown are the most clichéd, giving your reasons. Then describe something that is a cliché for you.

> **cli·ché** /£ ˈkliː·ʃeɪ, $ -ˈ-/ *n* a form of expression that has been so often used that its original effectiveness has been lost • *Every time I ask my dad for some money, he always comes out with the old cliché, "It doesn't grow on trees, you know."* [C] • *You should always try to avoid the use of cliché.* [U] • *His speeches tend to be boring and cliché-**ridden*** (= contain a lot of clichés).

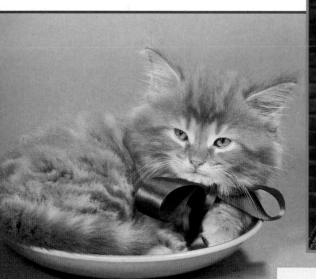

2 Read this text on photographic cliché and identify the main point of each paragraph, choosing from a–d.

   a Images that are now considered clichés were once innovative.

   b Prize-winning photographs are generally not original ideas.

   c Some photographers rely on only one basic idea.

   d Photographers need to look at each other's work for inspiration.

Clichés do little to stimulate photographic expression but much
line 2 to help win dust-collecting pots and medals in competitions. David Johnston shoots environmental portraits using a wide-angle lens with the subject to one side, near the camera, and a second
line 5 person in the background. It's one of my pet hates. I'm not criticising the style of this or any other cliché, it's the continued use of basically the same photograph with different subjects that annoys me.

When does a photographic style become a cliché? There can be little doubt that those images now deemed clichés were once powerful and stimulating photographs, which merited the awards given to them. They influenced many others and so photography could be seen to be moving forward. Such is the way of progress. However, when an innovative winning image is copied by
line 15 numerous others, hell-bent on walking off with the annual club trophy, a cliché is born.

Certainly, photographers with fresh vision should push the boundaries of seeing and style. That's how less gifted photographers move forward. Let's not forget that from time to
line 20 time even the innovators look to others for this. While the slavish copying of any image or existing style is the road to ultimate ruin, we should actively look at those images to find seeds of stimulation.

3   These are some of the types of question that commonly occur in the summary task. Read them carefully but don't answer them yet.

Meaning

a   Why does the writer describe the pots and medals as 'dust-collecting' (line 2)?

b   What is the implication of the term 'hell-bent' (line 15)?

c   Explain in your own words what is meant by the phrase 'the road to ultimate ruin' in the final sentence.

Reference

d   What is the writer referring to when he says: 'It's one of my pet hates.' (line 5)?

e   What does 'this' (line 20) refer to?

Style

f   Explain in your own words why the writer has chosen to use the word 'slavish' (line 20).

4   Look at these answers to question f above. Decide which is the most successful, bearing in mind the advice given in the Exam spot.

a   By choosing to write 'slavish' with reference to the copying of an image or existing style, the writer has reinforced the idea of copying.

b   To show disapproval of those photographers who imitate ideas without adding anything original.

c   'Slavish' supports 'copying'.

5   Answer questions a–e in exercise 3, using no more than 16 words.

6   Now read the second text, which is related in theme to the first. Write a concise sentence (10 words or less), to summarise each paragraph.

Beauty, says the proverb, is in the eye of the beholder. In the way of proverbs, that is a too-easy half-truth. Two people in love may each see in the other a beauty not visible to the eyes of others. It could perhaps be called relative beauty and has only fairly remote kinship to   line 5
authentic beauty, which is not at all relative and is indeed fundamental to the continuance of life on earth.

For beauty is a primary biological factor, even if its importance to every moment of life is greatly obscured by its being so swaddled in cliché and every sort of   line 10
sentimental misunderstanding. For example, unchallengingly, we accept that the rose is beautiful, though it must be said that roses in the wild can make some garden varieties look almost vulgar.

Some of nature's most powerful and remarkable images become clichés through familiarity, thanks to the commercial world we live in. When transferred to a squat   line 17
greetings card or popular poster, the once exceptional image of a many-hued rainbow against dramatic clouds or a florid sunset over tranquil sea is rendered banal and commonplace. Roses fade and sunsets are transient, so let us appreciate them at the height of their beauty and in their natural setting.

7   Answer these questions on the text in 16 words or less.

a   Explain in your own words the meaning of the proverb referred to in the opening sentence.

b   What does the phrase 'remote kinship' (line 5) mean?

c   Why has the writer chosen to use the word 'swaddled' (line 10)?

d   What image does the writer conjure up by using the word 'squat' (line 17)?

e   Which word in the final paragraph means 'ephemeral'?

Exam folder 4

Paper 1 Part 1 Lexical cloze

This part of the Reading paper is composed of three texts from a range of different sources of written English, for example from advertisements, newspaper articles, encyclopaedia entries, literary texts, etc. Each text contains six gaps and is followed by six four-option multiple-choice questions.

The questions test your knowledge of the following.

Idioms

They had a terrible row, all because Mike had got hold of the wrong end of the .... when Sonia was explaining what had happened at the beach.

A line   **B** stick   **C** rope   **D** ruler

The answer is **B**. *To get hold of the wrong end of the stick* means *to misunderstand* something. Idioms are expressions which cannot be changed.

Collocations

Primary education has been .... underfunded in this area of the country for many years now, and it is about time something was done about it.

A seriously **B** deeply   **C** highly   **D** remarkably

The answer is **A**. *Seriously* and *underfunded* are often used together. Words that are often used together in this way are called collocations.

Fixed phrases

Everyone quickly .... their places on the stage in readiness for the curtain to go up.

A made   **B** had   **C** saved   **D** took

The answer is **D**. *To take one's place* is a fixed phrase. This means that it contains elements that can change with the sense of the sentence, e.g. *he took **his** place, they took **their** places.*

Complementation

The menu .... of various starters, main courses and desserts, all, in my opinion, designed to please the eye rather than the palate.

A consisted **B** composed **C** contained **D** comprised

The answer is **A**. *Consist* takes the preposition *of.* Your knowledge of prepositions, reflexives and verb patterns is tested in this type of question.

Phrasal verbs

Pete didn't bother to .... up until nearly the end of the lesson, and then he just slouched into the room and flung himself into a seat with no apology.

A come   **B** show   **C** catch   **D** go

The answer is **B**. *To show up* means *to put in an appearance.*

Semantic precision

The rain .... down slowly under his coat collar, making him feel thoroughly damp and miserable.

A crept   **B** waded   **C** trickled **D** teemed

The answer is **C**. *Trickled* is the only option which refers to slow movement of water. The precise meaning of a word in relation to the whole context, either at sentence or whole text level, is tested.

Advice

- Read the whole text carefully before looking at the options.
- Think carefully about your choice of answer. Remember that you are often being tested not just on choosing a word which is grammatically correct, but also one which best fits the sense or tone of the text.
- Always choose an answer, even if you are not sure you are right. You are not penalised for wrong answers. You have a 25% chance of getting an answer right, even if you really have no idea what the answer is!

The rhythm of life

In all walks of life, music is just what the doctor **(1)** ...., improving the quality of sleep for anxious people, calming overactive children and encouraging and strengthening the sick. Music's healing powers have been noted throughout the ages. Our forebears **(2)** .... use of music to encourage their crops to grow. The ancient Greeks told stories of the power of music in the **(3)** .... of legendary figures such as Orpheus who could charm people with his singing. In our chaotic world, music can **(4)** .... to establish a rhythm in our lives to maintain physical and mental health. So what type of music should we be listening to in order to improve our lives? Bach or Mozart? Heavy metal or Celine Dion? Studies show that the kind of music is irrelevant – it's our right to choose which is the important **(5)** .... In an age of background music, having music which we detest inflicted on us can **(6)** .... out to be a direct cause of discord and potential illness.

1	**A** decreed	**B** ordered	**C** required	**D** specified
2	**A** made	**B** had	**C** got	**D** found
3	**A** bodies	**B** arms	**C** hands	**D** tongues
4	**A** serve	**B** assist	**C** aid	**D** promote
5	**A** matter	**B** subject	**C** topic	**D** issue
6	**A** come	**B** set	**C** turn	**D** stand

The need for aged buildings

Cities need old buildings so **(7)** .... it is probably impossible for vigorous streets and districts to grow without them. By old buildings I mean not museum-piece old buildings, not old buildings in an excellent and expensive **(8)** .... of repair – **(9)** .... these make fine ingredients – but also a good lot of ordinary old buildings, including some **(10)** .... ones. If a city area has only new buildings, the enterprises that can exist there are automatically **(11)** .... to those that can support the high cost of new construction, such as chain stores and restaurants, supermarkets and banks. Neighbourhood bars, small grocery shops, good bookstores and antique shops seldom can. The only harm of aged buildings to a city district is the harm that eventually comes of nothing but old age – the harm that lies in everything being old and everything becoming **(12)** ....

7	**A** seriously	**B** badly	**C** greatly	**D** exceedingly
8	**A** mode	**B** case	**C** state	**D** condition
9	**A** although	**B** let alone	**C** whereas	**D** seeing as
10	**A** overrun	**B** downturned	**C** rundown	**D** upheld
11	**A** limited	**B** curbed	**C** checked	**D** hampered
12	**A** let through	**B** worn out	**C** pulled up	**D** filled in

Merchant@florence

The ubiquitous symbol of Internet era communications, the @ sign used in e-mail addresses is actually a 500-year-old invention of Italian merchants, a Rome academic, Giorgio Stabile, has revealed. He claims to have stumbled on the earliest known example of the symbol's use, as an indication of a measure of weight or volume. He said the @ sign **(13)** .... an amphora, a measure of capacity based on the terracotta jars used to transport grain and liquid in the ancient Mediterranean world. The first known **(14)** .... of its use occurred in a letter written by a Florentine merchant on May 4, 1536. The ancient symbol was **(15)** .... in the course of research for a visual history of the 20th century. **(16)** ...., the sign had made its way along trade routes to northern Europe, where it **(17)** .... its contemporary accountancy meaning: 'at the price of'. According to Professor Stabile, the oldest example could be of great value as it could be used for publicity purposes and to **(18)** .... the prestige of the institution that owned it.

13	**A** substituted	**B** represented	**C** described	**D** expressed
14	**A** instance	**B** remark	**C** notice	**D** illustration
15	**A** exposed	**B** unwrapped	**C** unearthed	**D** located
16	**A** Outwardly	**B** Actually	**C** Logically	**D** Apparently
17	**A** put on	**B** took on	**C** set on	**D** came on
18	**A** enhance	**B** lift	**C** elevate	**D** strengthen

UNIT 8 Urban jungle

1 Would you like to live in any of these cities? Why? / Why not? What are the advantages and disadvantages of living in a big city? What amenities should a city offer its residents and commuters?

2 You are going to read three extracts which are all concerned with city living. First, skim the texts to decide on their style and genre, finding evidence to support your ideas. Do not answer the questions yet.

Cool Brazil

For any urbanist, Curitiba is a place of pilgrimage, thanks largely to Jaime Lerner, the mayor whose initiatives in the 1970s ensured Curitiba would become one of the most prosperous cities in Brazil. Lerner developed a set of solutions that were extraordinarily lateral-thinking, extremely cost-effective, visual in a symbolic way, and politically astute. At that time, Rio and Sao Paulo were planning metro systems, but with a population of just half a million then, this couldn't be justified for Curitiba. Lerner decided that his city would have a 'bus metro' instead, for a fraction of the cost. Twenty bus stations were built at intervals along the main arteries, plus another five in the wider metro area, to allow interchange between express and local services. As traffic built up and the system expanded, the problem of capacity was tackled in two ways. First, express buses were coupled together, and then extended further into *expresso biarticulado* units, to carry a staggering 270 people at peak hours. More significantly, the innovative design of the Curitiba bus shelter – a glass tube entered through a turnstile using a token – means that in a trice, buses empty, fill up and are gone. So popular has the system become that, despite high car ownership, it now carries nearly two million passengers each day.

1 The writer suggests that the mayor's planning decisions
   A derived from obvious ideas.
   B ranked appearance ahead of cost.
   C benefited from external advice.
   D represented shrewd action.

2 According to the writer, what is the main reason for the bus metro's success?
   A extended buses   C quick turnaround
   B lighter traffic   D cheap tickets

English Journey

In the original *English Journey*, the writer J.B. Priestley referred to the young unemployed of England as 'playboys with nothing to play at'. But at least they had a structure of home and chapel to support them, however rigid and wanting. Nothing then could surely ^{5} match the degradation of being out of work and an inhabitant of Castlevale today. The estate is made up of forty or so fifteen-storey blocks dumped in a field outside Birmingham. The police patrol in pairs; the Alsatian dogs run in packs. Very few cars here. And ^{10} not much of a bus service by all accounts. What a farcical piece of planning. Fifty years ago, people migrated to the suburbs because there was a cheap and efficient railway service to transport them to and from work. Not that a railway station in Castlevale ^{15} would be of much use in that respect. Eighteen thousand people, mostly unemployed, living on a square mile of land. Not a cinema or a library to be seen, let alone proper shops, and only one small pub, 'The Artful Dodger', with boarded-up windows ^{20} because they've been smashed so many times.

3 In this paragraph, the writer is
   A arguing for a better rail service
   B contrasting two time periods
   C complaining about city living
   D recommending a writer's work

4 Which of these words is used to convey irritation?
   A wanting (line 5)   C efficient (line 14)
   B farcical (line 12)   D proper (line 19)

A *Magnificent* Failure

Peter Calthorpe invited me to lunch. Together with architect-planners like Andres Duany and Elizabeth Plater-Zyberk, Calthorpe is a founder and passionate advocate of the so-called 'New Urbanism': a search for a return to traditional urban forms and
5 traditional ways of urban life. His most ambitious plan, and the one most often quoted, was for Laguna West, south of Sacramento. Over coffee, he bewailed what had happened to it. During the grim California recession in the early 1990s, the original developer went bust and the entire scheme was taken over by another less
10 visionary one, who completed it in contravention of every New Urbanist principle. Don't go and see it, Calthorpe begged.

I pondered, and finally failed to take his advice – but I was glad I went. The fact is that Laguna West is a catastrophic failure, but a magnificent one, even tragic in the strict sense of that overworked
15 word. For it was an extraordinary concept. Had it been completed as Calthorpe planned it, it would have been one of the great visionary new towns of the 20th century. However, as things have turned out, Laguna West is just another conventional, car-dependent suburb. Only once did I see any evidence of public
20 transport – one solitary bus shelter (later interrogation of the Sacramento transit website revealed a mere four buses out in the morning, four back at night).

5 Why is Peter Calthorpe unhappy with the outcome of Laguna West?
   A The project has suffered due to circumstances beyond his control.
   B His traditional ideas have proved unpopular with residents there.
   C The area has been criticised for its lack of transport provision.
   D His fellow-architects have failed to support his basic principles.

6 Which word is used by the writer to reinforce an earlier statement?
   A so-called (line 3)
   B grim (line 7)
   C overworked (line 14)
   D mere (line 21)

3 For questions 1–6 above, choose the answer (A, B, C or D) which you think fits best according to the text.

4 Explain the meaning of these words and phrases from the texts.

   Cool Brazil a place of pilgrimage; a fraction of; the main arteries; in a trice
   English Journey rigid and wanting; degradation
   A Magnificent Failure passionate advocate; bewailed; in contravention of

Ⓟhrase spot

Several compound adjectives are used in the texts, such as *cost-effective*, *car-dependent*. Compound adjectives are often formed from a present or past participle with a preposition, *boarded*-**up**, another adjective, **lateral**-*thinking* or an adverb, *so*-*called*.

Make compound adjectives using these lists and suggest noun collocations for each one. For example, *well-constructed (house)*; *smashed-up (car)*; *quick-thinking (politician)*.

Adjectives	Adverbs	Participles	Prepositions
quick	well	constructed	down
long	far	smashed	up
short	poorly	sighted	out
		blown	through
		fitting/fitted	
		running/run	
		thinking/thought	

Ⓢtyle extra

The style in *English Journey* resorts almost to note form at times: *Very few cars here. And not much of a bus service by all accounts.* What effect does this have on you? Why do you think the author, Beryl Bainbridge, has chosen to write like this?

Bainbridge describes the blocks of flats as being *dumped* in a field outside Birmingham. What does this suggest to you? Explain how the meaning of the sentence would change if *dumped* was changed to *set* or *landscaped*.

Some words in English, like *dumped*, carry negative connotations. That is, in addition to having a negative meaning, they are used to show disapproval and give extra force to a message, as Bainbridge does. When talking about urban deprivation, words operating in a similar way include ***abject*** *poverty/despair/failure*, *the* ***dregs*** *of society*, ***mob*** *rule/mentality*, *human* ***scum***.

Here are other words used to show disapproval, some of which occurred in earlier units. These criticise unacceptable personal characteristics or views.

chauvinistic *beliefs*
clichéd *images/ideas*
florid *poetry/speeches*
glaring *errors/faults*
a ***vacuous*** *personality*

childish *behaviour*
a ***fatuous*** *remark*
talking ***garbage***
hackneyed *ideas*

Choose five of these words, with different collocations from those given, to use in sentences of your own.

Inversion

1 Look at these examples from the third text in 8.1. What do they have in common?

> Had it been completed as Calthorpe planned it, it would have been one of the great visionary new towns of the 20th century.

> Only once did I see any evidence of public transport.

Inversion is often used in formal English, but in fact also appears in less formal writing and spoken English too, to emphasise or contrast something.

The first example above shows inversion in a conditional sentence, while the second shows inversion after a time adverbial, like the next two examples.

No sooner had we left the building than it started to pour.

Barely had Janie recovered from her operation when she found out she was pregnant.

Sometimes a full time clause precedes the inversion.

Only after a rigorous security check were we allowed to enter the building.

G ···→ page 183

---

2 Finish the sentences using your own ideas and the tenses specified.

a Never before … (present perfect)
b Only once in my life … (present perfect)
c Scarcely … (past perfect) when … (past simple)
d No sooner … (past perfect) than … (past simple)
e Hardly … (past perfect) before … (past simple)
f Not until last month … (past simple)
g Seldom … (present simple)
h Rarely … (future simple)

Inversion also occurs in written description after adverbials of place (usually prepositional phrases).

Opposite the gallery entrance stands an imposing bronze statue.
Under the table sat a tiny mouse with bright, beady eyes.

Notice how the verbs used in these examples are to do with location. Verbs of movement, for example, *come*, *go*, *run*, are also used in this way.

Up the hill crawled the number 77 bus.
Alongside the road runs the River Avon.

---

3 Complete this short description using the verbs below in a suitable past tense. Use each verb once only.

be	do	hang	have
sit	stand	stretch	

At the very end of a dead-end street (1) .... **stood** a rather run-down hotel Jan and I approached it in trepidation in spite of the torrential rain, it looked neither warm nor welcoming. Just inside the door on a rickety bar stool (2) .... **sat** an old man, probably the night porter. Above his head (3) .... **hung** the keys to all the rooms not a single one taken, or so it seemed. We looked at each other, conscious of the rain lashing down outside. Only by chance (4) .... **had** we come this way in the first place, but there was nothing for it: we steeled ourselves and checked in.
At the top of three flights of stairs (no li (5) .... **stretched** a long, dark corridor, tha

---

Here are some other types of inversion:

after prepositional phrases with *no*
On no account should children be left unsupervised in this play area.
In no way can a goalless draw be seen as a good result for United.
Under no circumstances was Sally going to admit defeat.

after *not*
Not only did the team win the county cup, th also came top of their league.
Not one grain of encouragement did she sho him throughout the course.

...ntually led to our room. How could ...y put us so far away when every room ...s vacant? We decided to go down and ... to be moved. However, scarcely ...were.... we back in the lobby when ... or seven taxis drew up outside, ...charging hordes of well-dressed, happy ...ividuals, including a bride and groom. ...eemed the old man's niece had just got ...rried and the entire wedding party was ...ying over at her uncle's hotel. Jan didn't ...ep a wink that night, and neither ...did.... I. It was the best party we'd ...er been to!

...er little

...tle did I think then that I would miss the ...ght lights in years to come.

...tle was she expecting Sam to walk through ...at door.

...th so/such ... that

...popular has the system become that it now ...rries nearly two million passengers each day.

...ch was the outcry that the advertisement ...d to be withdrawn.

...th neither or nor

...smin doesn't relish living in a high-rise ...artment and neither do I.

...any hasn't been asked to work overtime ...d nor should you be.

---

4 For questions 1–8, complete the second sentence so that it has a similar meaning to the first sentence, using the word given. Do not change the word given. You must use between three and eight words, including the word given.

1 That week, the train was late every day except for Friday.
   run once did the train run on time
   Only ...one day the train ran on time...
   that week and that was Friday.

2 Shortly after Sue and Brian met, he announced they were getting married.
   had
   Scarcely ...had Brian met Sue than...
   he announced they were getting married.

3 You are not staying out late tonight!
   no
   Under ...no circumstances you will...
   stay out late tonight!

4 They left their car and almost immediately heard a deafening crash.
   sooner
   No ...sooner had they left their car than...
   they heard a deafening crash.

5 Kerry didn't send us any postcards during her travels through Argentina.
   one
   Not ...even one postcard was sent while...
   she was travelling in Argentina.

6 It wasn't long before the bus company increased their prices for a second time.
   put
   Hardly ...did we put...
   before they increased them again.

7 The demand for tickets is so high that the play has been extended by a month.
   has
   So ...has it been the demand for the...
   the play has been extended by a month.

8 There are beautiful buildings in Barcelona and it has a wonderful climate too.
   only
   In Barcelona, not ...only things have bb but the cl...
   is also wonderful.

Paper 5 Part 3

1   What is the meaning of the idiom below? How might it apply to living in a village as opposed to a city, or vice versa? Suggest some situations relevant to each lifestyle.

The grass is always greener …

2   🎧 You are going to hear three people – Meg, Sally and Kevin – talking about where they live and their new *lifeplan*. As you listen, decide on their relationship and be ready to explain how and why their lives are about to become interlinked.

3   What do you think of their lifeplan? Will it be workable, in your view? What are the pros and cons?

4   🎧 As you listen again, note down the idioms you hear that include these key words. Then match them to explanations 1–6.

a	blue	**1**	only benefits
b	frame	**2**	to summarise
c	roses	**3**	reduce your options
d	burn	**4**	not possible
e	nutshell	**5**	by chance
f	worlds	**6**	things aren't perfect

Ⅰ diom spot

How can idioms be learned most efficiently? They can be grouped in various ways:

- as pairs of words: *high and dry, touch and go*
- by topic: *eat humble pie, spill the beans*
- by form: *out of (the blue/this world), in (a nutshell / the bag)*
- by key word: *strike (it lucky / a chord / gold)*

One of the key words in exercise 4 is used in many other idioms. Which one?
Use it in a suitable form to complete these idioms and then give an example situation to explain the meaning of each.

a   *… a hole in your pocket*
b   *… the midnight oil*
c   *get your fingers …*
d   *someone's ears are …*
e   *have money to …*
f   *… your bridges*

Ⓔ xam spot

In Paper 5 Part 3, each candidate has an individual long turn of two minutes. You will be given a prompt card containing the question you have to speak about. Below the question are three ideas, which you can include or not, as you wish. The emphasis is on your ability to speak fluently and to organise your ideas into a coherent whole. Before you start speaking, use the ten seconds allowed to order your thoughts.

5   Look at the prompt card below. In groups of four, brainstorm and note down possible ideas, starting with the three areas listed but also including other aspects. Remember to think of both positive and negative points.

> **Are there more benefits or drawbacks to living in a city nowadays?**
>
> ➤ jobs
> ➤ transport
> ➤ accommodation

6 Now form two pairs. Each pair should select three of the group's ideas and then decide how to organise these ideas into a short talk.

Things to consider are:

Balance
Both benefits and drawbacks need to be mentioned.

Discourse management
What is the clearest order of ideas?
How will you introduce the topic?
How can you signal a new point?
How will you round off?

Exemplification
Can you give examples to underline your point of view, either personal or general?

Which organisational aspect does each of these phrases relate to? Write **B**, **D** or **E** beside each one.

EXAMPLE: *Speaking personally …*   **E**

a *The question is complex …*
b *All things considered …*
c *… is a separate issue.*
d *One definite disadvantage is …*
e *That is not to say that …*
f *The third and perhaps most important …*
g *Take the area of …*
h *To evaluate this …*
i *By way of illustration …*
j *Moving on to …*
k *Taking everything into account …*
l *More specifically …*

7 One person in each pair should now run through their long turn, with the second person time-keeping and taking notes as to where an idea could be developed or should be cut down. Aim for 30 seconds on each of three ideas, with a short introduction and conclusion.

8 Work in your pair to finalise what you want to say. Then give your two-minute long turn to the rest of the group.

E xam spot

Paper 3 Part 3 tests your awareness of words with different meanings and how these words typically collocate. Read all three sentences first: different words will fit in each gap, but only one word will be possible in all three.

9 For questions 1–5, think of one word only which can be used appropriately in all three sentences.

1 Joe fastened his jacket against the .... air, realising all at once that he was shivering.

With the blockade now lifted, vital medical supplies and .... materials are starting to reach the areas worst affected.

We savoured the rough garlic sausage and .... onion, served with hunks of bread.

2 The curtains were pulled across the windows, allowing only a single .... of light to cut through the gloom.

Staring at the others, Martin secured his hair with a .... at the nape of his neck and then collapsed with laughter.

It is the 40% tax .... which is currently under scrutiny by the government.

3 Brian Yarrow has got money to ...., that's his trouble.

For goodness sake, try not to .... yourself out on this project!

Every night, the lights .... in the window to guide the sailors home.

4 *Grangers*, the restaurant chain, is taking advantage of .... property prices to snap up new outlets in the north-west.

Depression can leave the mother feeling .... for much of the time, often crying for no reason.

That was a rather .... trick you played on me at the company dinner, putting me next to the managing director.

5 Quinn's storyline is too .... for my liking, though there have been several favourable reviews.

The horses broke .... last night and must be halfway to Mexico by now.

I don't suppose you've got any .... change in your pocket, have you?

Writing folder 4

Part 2 Proposal

In Part 2 of Paper 2, you may be able to choose to write a proposal. Proposals can also occur as the compulsory task on Part 1 of the paper.

1   What is a proposal? Who might it be addressed to? Look at the tasks below and decide which ones require a proposal. What is the other text type?

a Your college has received some money from a former student, which must be spent on improvements to college facilities. Others in your class have asked you to argue for the money to be spent on new computers and improved Internet access, putting your case in writing to the Principal.

b You recently returned from an exchange programme in the States and have been asked to write down the benefits and any drawbacks of the programme for the American organiser.

c A television company is running a series on little-known parts of your country and has asked viewers to suggest suitable locations. You decide to put forward your local area and now have to write to the producer.

2   Proposals are designed to be evaluated and usually have to justify a certain course of action. They are forward-looking and tend to outline a set of suggestions and recommendations.

Read the sample task and then look at the writing plan below. Add relevant ideas of your own under the three headings.

An international student organisation is going to hold its annual five-day conference in your country in three years' time. This event regularly attracts over 10,000 students from around the world and requires a city with good transport, sufficient accommodation and varied entertainment possibilities. You decide to propose a city you know well, which you consider ideal for the event.

Write your **proposal**.

Introduction: reason for writing (name city)
Main section: outline city's facilities
1 Transport: international airport, cheap and reliable bus network, ...
2 Accommodation: many hotels plus university accommodation, newly-built conference centre, ...
3 Entertainment: lively city day/night (music, art, cinema, sport ...)
Additional section: relevant additional info – NB special celebration in city in 3 yrs' time
Conclusion: city is ideal because ...

3   A proposal is arguing the case for something, so needs to show conviction. This should be sustained throughout the piece of writing, rather than relegated to the introduction and final sections. Here are some ways of 'selling' the facts to the reader. Can you suggest ways of completing the sentences?

X is of particular relevance/importance because …
Of equal merit is …
Not only can we provide X, but we can also …
Above all …
It is beyond dispute / widely recognised / commonly known that …
The city's good reputation for …
I/We would like to stress/underline/remind …
We believe wholeheartedly in / are convinced / are 100% sure / are totally committed to …

4   The following paragraph undersells the transport facilities of a city. Someone has expanded and rewritten it in a more convincing way below.

As far as transport is concerned, the city has its own airport with a recently-constructed additional terminal. There are regular trains into the city from there. For getting around the city, the bus network is adequate and doesn't cost much.

Our city provides optimum transport facilities, which we are convinced will more than meet your needs. The international airport, conveniently located close to the city, has undergone a major reconstruction programme and now boasts a new state-of-the-art terminal for international flights. Of equal merit is the rapid transit link into the city centre, with trains running every five minutes, 24 hours a day. Above all, we are justly proud of our bus network, which provides a cheap service and reliable connections to all parts of the city and its suburbs.

Now rewrite the next paragraph on accommodation, using some of the language suggested on page 72 and ideas of your own.

There are over 30,000 hotel rooms in the city, in hotels of varying quality. We also have a university with campus accommodation, which could be used. A new conference centre is located on the outskirts.

A range of verbs can be used when making final recommendations. Remember that these are followed by different structures, for example:

argue for; argue that
insist on + -ing; insist that
recommend + -ing; recommend that
suggest + -ing; suggest that
urge … to; urge that

5   Choose the best conclusion from the ones below, giving your reasons why.

a   *This proposal has outlined the many advantages of hosting your event in our city and we look forward to hearing your reactions.*

b   *We would urge you to consider our proposal seriously, for we firmly believe that this city will provide you with an unforgettable conference.*

c   *I hope you have enjoyed reading about our city and look forward to hearing from you soon.*

d   *You can rely on our city's total commitment to your requirements, with high-quality accommodation and amenities guaranteed.*

Advice

- When writing a proposal, remember to be forward-looking.
- Underline any key points given in the question.
- Order the points so as to make the most convincing case.
- Give a succinct introduction.
- Make clear recommendations.
- Write in a neutral or formal register.
- Show conviction throughout.

6   Now complete the task, writing about the city of your choice. Remember to mention the significance of holding the event in three years' time and include any other additional information you think relevant.

Write 300–350 words.

Reading

1 Read this extract from the book *No Logo*. Decide which answer (A, B, C or D) best fits each gap.

1 **A** tokens	**B** emblems	**C** marks	**D** signs
2 **A** scurried into	**B** put onto	**C** tucked into	**D** latched onto
3 **A** caused	**B** kept	**C** served	**D** made
4 **A** flap	**B** bill	**C** note	**D** tag
5 **A** branch	**B** accessory	**C** annexe	**D** extension
6 **A** leading	**B** prevalent	**C** dominant	**D** outstanding

Logos on clothes used to be generally hidden from view, discreetly placed on the inside of the collar. Small designer (1) .... did appear on the outside of shirts, but such sporty attire was pretty much restricted to the golf courses and tennis courts of the rich. In the late 1970s, when the fashion world rebelled against the flamboyance of the hippie era, Lacoste's alligator escaped from the sports club and (2) .... the streets, dragging the logo decisively onto the outside of the shirt. These logos (3) .... the same social function as keeping the item of clothing's price (4) .... on: everyone knew precisely what premium the wearer was willing to pay for style. Gradually, the logo changed from being an ostentatious affectation to an active fashion (5) .... . Most significantly, the logo started to grow in size, a process which continues today. No logo has ballooned more than Tommy Hilfiger's, the brand that has managed to pioneer a clothing style that turns its faithful adherents into walking, talking, life-sized Tommy dolls. Logos have become so (6) .... on the clothing on which they are featured that they have essentially transformed these clothes into empty carriers for the brands represented.

Use of English

2 For questions 1–6, complete the second sentence so that it has a similar meaning to the first sentence, using the word given. Do not change the word given. You must use between three and eight words, including the word given.

1 Many people used to believe that they would lose their soul if their photo was taken.
   widespread
   There was once ....
   taken would mean losing your soul.

2 I'm quite sure that Bill hasn't left yet as I saw him yesterday.
   set
   Bill ....
   as I saw him yesterday.

3 Bridgton is very proud of its new shopping mall.
   takes
   Bridgton ....
   its new shopping mall.

4 We weren't aware at the time that we were making a big mistake.
   know
   Little ....
   big mistake we were making.

5 I had only just come back from the supermarket when I realised I had forgotten to buy any milk.
   returned
   No sooner ....
   I realised I had forgotten to buy any milk.

6 I've often thought of you when listening to that sonata by Barsanti.
   come
   Many's ....
   when I have been listening to that sonata by Barsanti.

3 For questions 1–6, think of one word only which can be used appropriately in all three sentences.

1 The pair collapsed in a .... of giggles as Simon struggled with Sam's bag and pretended to fall over.

Your jacket's a really good .... – is it made-to-measure?

Mayor Winston will have a .... when he reads the taxi drivers' proposals for carving up the city.

2 How much .... do you intend to give of these timetabling changes?

I knew he would take no .... until he'd checked police and security records.

After a week, Maria handed in her .... and booked a flight to Valencia.

3 I've always held her work in .... regard, but I really don't see what she's getting at here.

Temperatures in and around the city have soared to the .... 40s and the humidity is unbearable.

Ben was relishing this quiet stroll through the back streets, his spirits still .... from the way the interview had gone.

4 Older people prefer to travel off ...., when the buses aren't crowded and journeys take less time.

The sun had gone behind a distant ...., leaving streaks of pink and pale yellow in its wake like a glorious memory.

At the .... of their careers, the comedy duo were regularly getting 27 million viewers, including the Queen!

5 I see people struggling to learn the rules of this game, and it .... me that their goal is not to win, but to avoid showing themselves up.

Later in the evening, Connie .... up a conversation in Polish with Andrei from Lvov.

The comedian Harry Enfield's 'Kevin the teenager' character .... an immediate chord with any long-suffering parent of that age group.

6 In this goalless draw with Tottenham, Queens Park Rangers supplied the only chances, Sinton clipping the .... and Barker hitting a post.

Down in Bristol recently, I went to a local .... which offered live jazz and was packed every night.

Interestingly, the wrapped .... of soap came into use only at the beginning of the twentieth century.

Writing

4 Insert rhetorical questions A–E into this essay about modern art and music.

A Is the world of contemporary music any better?
B Yet is there genuine technical skill in Damien Hirst's sheep, pickled in formaldehyde?
C What has happened to good judgement and common sense?
D So should we look again to nature to provide us with the beauty that we crave?
E Have these composers really nowhere left to go?

1 [   ] In my opinion, the art world lacks both. It has, moreover, abandoned its traditional role, that of being pleasing to the senses. Modern artists are merely out to shock, to be sensationalist. Bound up with this ruthless modernism is intense commercialism. Prices are inflated by urban galleries and urbane collectors, whose 'discerning' purchases appreciate by the day, as mediocre artists are successfully hyped as the latest Andy Warhol or Georgia O'Keeffe.

2 [   ] Here, too, we are no longer given works we can enjoy, but 'difficult' music with no discernible melody, that jangles the nerves and leaves us with a dreadful headache. **3** [   ] Yet perhaps I am making the very same mistake as contemporary critics of Georges Seurat's, who shunned his masterpieces and saw him die at the age of 31, poor and unappreciated. Maybe in another twenty years, the music that I personally cannot fathom will be regarded as safe and conventional; the art installations seen as old hat. **4** [   ] The jury's still out.

Living in our post-industrial society, the vast majority of today's artists and musicmakers fail to give us any beauty in their work, exhibiting only their own creative frustration. **5** [   ] Or at least, as Andy Goldsworthy has proved, art could be transported to a more meaningful setting, where commercialism does not hold sway.

····▸ **Crossword page 190**

UNIT 9 Fitting in

1   Discuss the photos opposite with a partner. Why do you think the people have chosen to wear those particular clothes?

2   What would you wear on the following occasions? Make sure you justify your decisions.

- at a friend's birthday party
- on a long-distance plane trip
- on a first date
- at a club
- at a job interview

3   You are going to hear a discussion about what type of dress is most suitable for work. Before listening, complete the sentences below, which contain some of the words and expressions you will hear in the discussion. Choose the word which best fits the meaning of the sentence. Use a dictionary to help you.

a   I try not to make *snap/abrupt* judgements on people when I first meet them.

b   The office manager decided that Friday would be a dress *down/off* day.

c   At most workplaces there is a dress *rule/code* that everyone is supposed to follow.

d   Increasing funding to schools should be of *paramount/capital* importance.

e   The way you dress *tells/speaks* volumes about you as a person.

f   I think that the company has problems, and the complaints we've had are just the *top/tip* of the iceberg.

g   Some companies have a very *lean/laid*-back style of working.

h   Lionel *harboured/fostered* a grudge against the head teacher for many years.

i   They were discussing the best way to *harbour/foster* closer cooperation between departments.

j   The company's progress is being *subdued/constrained* by a chairman who refuses to look forward.

k   He would never wear cheap trainers – too *detrimental/injurious* to his image.

l   Susan went off to the dinner dressed up to the *nines/nose*.

Ⓔxam spot

In Part 4 of Paper 4 you are given a three-way matching exercise. Both the speakers will make some comment on each of the points made, however one speaker may say comparatively little.

4 🎧 Now listen to the discussion between two people talking about suitable clothing for work. Colin works in an advertising agency and Sue is a buyer for a large department store. What is their attitude to wearing a suit at work?

ⓔxam spot

In Paper 4, Part 4 of the exam you are being tested on whether you are aware of how people agree and disagree during a discussion. In the discussion they will rarely say, 'Yes, I agree with you.' Usually the agreement or disagreement will be expressed in a subtler way.

5 Look at the example and the following extract from the discussion.

EXAMPLE: The way you look when you meet someone for the first time is important.

Sue: The effort we take in our own personal appearance and style of dress is, rightly or wrongly, always used by others as an initial indication of our character.

Colin: Well, only fools think that first impressions aren't paramount …

Both Sue and Colin agree that the first time you meet someone it is important to look good.

🎧 Listen again and for questions 1–5, decide whether the opinions are expressed by only one of the speakers, or whether the speakers agree.

Write C for Colin
      S for Sue
or   B for Both, where they agree.

1 Clothes should reflect the personality of the wearer.
2 A suit gives everyone the opportunity to look good, especially if they lack dress sense.
3 People no longer feel the need to dress up if they have little social contact at work.
4 Wearing a suit can make the wearer feel more in control.
5 You can achieve more at work if you feel comfortable.

With a partner, talk about how you made your decisions.

6 What do you think? Should people in a business environment wear serious clothes or are casual clothes acceptable?

ⓟhrase spot

In the discussion you heard two expressions with *come*.

- *Come off it*, you can't really mean you actually like men wearing toupees! – meaning you think what someone has said is stupid or untrue
- *Let me come clean*, I wear trousers because I think my legs look fat. – meaning 'I'll be honest with you'

Expressions with *come* are frequently tested in the Proficiency exam and you should try to familiarise yourself with them.

Complete the sentences below with the right expression, making any other changes you feel are necessary.

come forward	come to blows
come up with the goods	come down in the world
come across	come up with
come out in sympathy with	first come first served
come true	come to terms with

a He has .... losing his job and says he will try to start his own business.
b If you .... my wallet, can you let me have it, please?
c The pilots .... the cabin crew during the one-day strike.
d She's .... a brilliant idea to copy the latest fashions from Paris off the Internet.
e Phil had a huge argument with his girlfriend's father – I think they ....
f Tickets for the concert are free and will be distributed on a .... basis.
g This chairman is good at making promises but he hardly ever ....
h I'd always dreamt of owning my own boat, but I never thought it would ....
i Tony and Lynne have .... – these days they can't even afford proper holidays any more.
j No witnesses to the accident have .... yet, despite the report on the TV.

Gerunds and infinitives

1 It is important to realise that verbs cannot be learnt in isolation. You should always learn what follows a verb in order to use it accurately.

Finish these sentences with the correct form of the words in brackets. There may be more than one answer.

  a I finished (wear) a uniform the day I left school.
  b I used (wear) a grey sweater and black trousers to school.
  c I prefer (you/wear) a suit to work.
  d I prefer (wear) jeans at the weekend.
  e His boss forced (him/shave) his beard off.
  f I saw (her/buy) a new hat.
  g I let (her/wear) the platform shoes to the party.

 G ⋯⟩ **page 184**

2 One of the biggest problems students have when writing compositions at Proficiency level is the use of gerunds and infinitives. Look at the following sentences taken from the *Cambridge Learner Corpus* and correct any mistakes.

  a I would have helped her finding the right wedding dress.
  b We shouldn't spend so much time try to find bargains in the sales.
  c I suggest to use a plaster if you have a blister on your foot.
  d The old uniforms in the museum are worth to be seen.
  e We enjoy ourselves to laugh at the stars at the Oscars.
  f My new glasses enable me to reading more easily.
  g We should let them to enjoy themselves while they are young.
  h I missed to talk to my sister when I was away from home.
  i I convinced him of applying to the Editor of the magazine.
  j You aren't allowed to coming into the hotel without wearing a tie.

3 Some verbs take either a gerund or an infinitive, but change their meaning accordingly. With a partner, discuss the difference in meaning of the following pairs of sentences.

EXAMPLE:
Sheila *stopped having* a break at work. – stopped means *ceased*, i.e. she didn't have a break any more
Sheila *stopped to have* a break before continuing her work. – the reason she stopped was to have a break

  a I mean to mark all these essays before ten o'clock.
  b It will mean having to start earlier.
  c We regret to inform you that you haven't been accepted at fashion college.
  d I regret wearing stiletto heels when I was young.
  e I remember going for long walks in the snow.
  f Remember to buy the milk, will you?
  g I hope you didn't forget to post my letter.
  h I can't forget meeting my first boyfriend.
  i Try to understand my feelings, will you?
  j Try opening the window, if you're feeling sleepy.
  k Professor Winters went on to speak about *Paradise Lost* after he'd introduced everyone present.
  l My mother goes on talking even when no one appears to be listening.
  m Roger came to accept she wouldn't marry him.
  n She came rushing into the room in some alarm.
  o I heard Eminem sing in London.
  p I heard the birds singing in the tree outside my room every morning.

4 Rewrite the following sentences by using the word or words in brackets with a gerund or infinitive. Do not change the meaning of the sentence.

EXAMPLE: (manage) I succeeded in passing my driving test first time.
        I managed to pass my driving test first time.

  a (object)   I don't mind if you leave early.
  b (allow)   Do they let you smoke in that restaurant?
  c (worth)   There's no point asking her out, she's always busy.
  d (forbid)   My father told my sister she mustn't go to the club in town.
  e (avoid)   Book early and you won't have to queue.
  f (recommend) His doctor said, 'You should do more exercise.'
  g (promise)   Don't worry, I'll post that letter for you.
  h (suggest)   I propose we take our bikes with us.
  i (had better) 'Move your car immediately or else I'll call the police!'
  j (deny)   Peter said he hadn't caused the accident.
  k (make)   His mother forced him to apologise.

5 🎧 Listen to this woman talking about her time at school. What does she say about:
- the uniform?
- the teachers?

With a partner, talk about what you remember about the time you were at primary school. Talk about: the teachers, the building, your friends, what you wore, what was popular.

Prefixes

6 Look at the expressions below and decide how the prefix changes the word it is attached to.

EXAMPLE: redo – *to do again*

a self-conscious	e overworked	i pre-arranged
b misheard	f sub-zero	j outdo
c counter-productive	g superhuman	k undervalue
d pro-government	h anti-smoking	

7 Complete the sentences below using a prefix from exercise 6 above and the correct form of the word in brackets. Use your dictionary to check if your word needs a hyphen or not. (NB dictionaries do not always agree on the use of hyphens.)

EXAMPLE: If you leave out your old newspapers they will be (cycle) by the local council.
If you leave out your old newspapers they will be recycled by the local council.

a There's a shortage of (contain) flats in my neighbourhood.
b The local swimming pool is advertising itself as a '(tropic) swimming paradise'!
c I think this printer (live) its usefulness and should be sold.
d Never (estimate) the cunning of a black bear – he is very clever.
e Apparently, it was all a (understand) and they are now good friends.
f Lisa prefers to buy her vegetables (pack) rather than from the market.
g This detergent is (concentrate) so you should use much less than normal.
h My car is fitted with (lock) brakes.
i This meat is (cook) – look it's charred on the outside!
j As I didn't have a suitable (argue) I decided to back down and apologise.
k Their teacher is very (America), and is always praising their educational system.

8 Read this extract from an article about dress quickly to get some idea of what it is about. Don't fill in any gaps at this stage. Answer the following question.

What changes does the writer say have occurred in the way we dress?

Suitably dressed

Today the notion of 'suitable clothing' is dying (0) .out. . It (1)..... now appear that, to all (2)..... and purposes, anything goes. At one (3)..... , it was possible to (4)..... at a glance the difference (5)..... someone dressed for work and someone en route to a nightclub. And, needless to (6)..... , the same clothes would never have been worn to both.

However, in the last thirty years, we have undergone a sea change in (7)..... ideas of what a dress code consists of. Even well (8)..... the 1960s, male air travellers were expected to wear a suit; these days it would (9)..... as no surprise to find them in shorts and trainers.

In fact, (10)..... has been the revolution in our own dress codes that we may find (11)..... dressing down to go to work and dressing up to go (12)..... in the evening. That (13)..... said, there are occasions, a wedding or a funeral, for example, (14)..... only certain clothes will (15)..... .

Now fill in the gaps. Having a good idea of what the text is about will help you.

9 Do you think that clothes are as important as personality? For example, could a scruffy, untidy person ever make a good receptionist? Can you think of other examples of where wearing the right clothes might affect the person's job?

Linking 1

1 How tidy are you? Look at the two photos below. Which one bears similarities to your own room?

2 Decide whether the words and expressions below refer to personal appearance/characteristics or to objects/places or to both. Give an example of how the word is used. Use an English–English dictionary to help you.

EXAMPLE: neat
person – *His hair looks neat, now he has combed it.*
place – *The bedroom looks quite neat when the bed is made.*

immaculate	bedraggled	scruffy
manicured	cluttered	unkempt
houseproud	in disarray	windswept
smart	dishevelled	orderly
spick and span	messy	

3 Read the texts and answer the questions that follow each text.

According to Dr Stephen Driver, people who are excessively tidy often suffer from high levels of stress in an attempt to assert some control over their lives. But, he says, there are ways of changing their behaviour. 'You can teach them to be a flexible tidier along the lines of, "I strongly prefer the room to be neat and tidy but it doesn't have to be." They need to accept that sometimes they haven't got the time or the resources to maintain the standards they set themselves.' He suggests that one way of weaning tidiers off their habit is to encourage them to leave, for example, their clothes on the floor overnight.

But, I hear you say, why do tidy people, and I include myself in this group, have to change? Are we abnormal? No, it's my belief that the rest of the world are bone-idle and don't clear up after themselves. That's why we are so often accused of being obsessively tidy, so idlers feel better. Neat people are neat (in the American sense of the word) and do a great social service by clearing the decks, giving everyone else a clutter-free world to work and live in.

line 18

But as a concession to those who might find it irksome having their worldly belongings continually swept out of sight, here is Dr Driver's solution. 'If someone has to have the room just so, the trick is to move something slightly, a fraction, so the tidier gets used to things changing. Of course, they put things back, but eventually they "habituate" and accept change.' Who's he kidding?

1 Which word in the first paragraph gives the idea of something being done gradually?
2 What defence is given by the writer of people who tidy up excessively?
3 Explain in your own words what two meanings of 'neat' are mentioned by the writer. (line 18)
4 Which word in the third paragraph does the writer use to describe the perceived behaviour of obsessive tidiers?

Over time people have come to regard 'home' as a place that protects them from the elements and acts as a haven of rest and solitude. However, once that has been established, the home becomes a vehicle for personal expression. It is here that we expose aspects of our personality.

Alice Kay is a practising psychotherapist in London who uses home analysis with many of her patients. 'Looking closely at people who hoard things, or conversely people who prefer minimalist living, can be very revealing,' she says. 'Even the state of people's drawers and cupboards tells you a lot about their personality.'

'Problems arise when two different characters live together. Everyone needs to feel in control of his or her life. When one person in a house wants, for example, a painting or a vase to have pride of place this can be a cause of unhappiness. So long as both parties are in agreement, there is no problem. However, if there is strong disagreement there will be a need to talk through the problem. Compromising may mean moving the object to a less prominent position. If the object remains where it is or is thrown out at the first opportunity, then any relationship will be placed in jeopardy.'

5 What do 'haven' and 'vehicle' refer to in the first paragraph?

6 What two contrasting ways of living does the therapist mention?

7 Explain in your own words what might happen if no compromise is reached over an object such as a painting or a vase.

4 Read the following question, which relates to the two texts above, and use the notes below (points 1 to 4) to write the summary.

In a paragraph of between 50 and 70 words, summarise in your own words as far as possible how, according to both texts, people try to control their environment and what can be done to help them become more accommodating.

---

1 Excessive tidiness and putting their things in pride of place.
2 Leave clothes on the floor.
3 Move things slightly every day.
4 More discussion and compromise.

Exam spot

In the summary writing task (Paper 3, Part 5) it is important to use linking devices effectively. This means choosing your words with care. Avoid beginning a sentence with these words – *And, Or, But.*

Link your points together using linking words and phrases, such as the following.

Introducing	**Adding**
First of all,	Besides,
Firstly,	Moreover,
Secondly,	In addition,
In the second place,	Additionally,
Then	Above all,
	Not only, ... but also

Equation	**Summarising**
Equally,	Finally,
Likewise,	In short/brief,
Similarly,	In conclusion,
In the same way,	To conclude,

5 The following are definitions of personality types. With a partner, decide if the definition is correct or not. Use a dictionary to help you. If you think the definition is wrong, write a correct version.

EXAMPLE: An observant person is one who is always interested in everyone else's business. *Wrong. An observant person is one who is good at noticing things.*

a A morbid person is one who is interested in unpleasant subjects, especially death.

b An opinionated person has a lot of excellent suggestions to make when there is a problem.

c A pompous person is one who is full of their own importance.

d A vivacious person is likely to get angry quickly.

e An acquisitive person likes to buy lots of presents for their friends.

f A meticulous person checks everything they do very carefully.

g A discriminating person is racially prejudiced.

h A complacent person is one who is easy going and pleasant to be with.

i An unobtrusive person is one who is shy and introverted.

j A simplistic person likes minimalism and prefers an uncluttered lifestyle.

k A manipulative person likes making things by hand.

l A boastful person is inclined to tell everyone about their possessions and successes.

Exam folder 5

Paper 1 Part 3 Gapped text

This part of the Reading Paper consists of one text, from a range of sources, which has had seven paragraphs removed and placed in jumbled order after the text. You must decide from where in the text the paragraphs have been removed. This part tests knowledge of cohesion (how the text hangs together), text structure and global meaning.

You are going to read an article about telling lies. Seven paragraphs have been removed from the extract. Choose from the paragraphs A–H the one which fits each gap (1–7). There is one extra paragraph which you do not need to use.

Questions 1, 2 and 3 have some clues to help you. Some words have been underlined in both the main article and the missing paragraphs. When you have the answers to questions 1, 2 and 3 do the same with the other questions. Find the words which tell you which paragraph goes where and underline them. Some words will be topic words and others grammatical links.

Would I lie to you?

Blatant dishonesty has invaded our culture. Sue Jackson explains how to spot a liar.

Who hasn't told a lie? Even the most upstanding individual probably utters one occasionally to help the day to run more smoothly. But, according to experts, the extent to which <u>people regularly tell serious untruths has exploded</u>. <u>Lying has pervaded</u> every aspect of our lives.

| 1 |

Research in California reveals that people lie up to 20 times a day, while in a poll last year, a quarter of respondents admitted being untruthful on a daily basis. Only 8 per cent claimed they had never lied – although there is always the chance that even then they weren't being honest. Many of <u>these</u> will be <u>sweet little lies</u>, the type psychologists refer to as 'false positives' and the sort we are all guilty of committing when we want to appear more enthusiastic about something than we really are.

| 2 |

Until recently it was thought that only manipulative and Machiavellian characters were prone to excessive fabrication of <u>this sort</u>, but research has proved otherwise. According to experts, anyone under pressure or with a big enough incentive is prepared to say something that isn't true.

| 3 |

<u>That figure</u> rose to one in three among people with university qualifications. Apparently, this sort of background gives people the vocabulary and the confidence to deceive. The lies are more sophisticated and plausible than you might find elsewhere in society.

| 4 |

The proliferation of lying in corporate culture means that there are huge profits to be gained by companies who can weed out real-life fraudsters before employing them. Numerous studies have been conducted, including some using video cameras, to analyse people who lie. There are two main methods of ousting liars, although one, the mechanical lie detector or polygraph, requires subjects to be trussed up in electrodes, so it hardly lends itself to interviews. That leaves body language and psychological testing.

| 5 |

However, sometimes the subconscious takes over. Liars often start blinking fast, a visual sign that the brain is concentrating hard on the task in hand, and are likely to frequently touch their body and face with their hands. Liars are also more likely to tap or swing a foot as they speak.

| 6 |

Everyone seems to agree that good liars don't show non-verbal signals, so you need to know what to look for. Lying takes a lot of effort, so often they will rely on past experience to see them through and reduce the cognitive load.

| 7 |

Experts, however, agree that the one person you shouldn't deceive is yourself – and that, once you begin to do so, it is a sure sign that your untruthfulness is getting out of hand.

A This makes detecting the charlatan who fibs his way through a CV very difficult. In the film *Liar, Liar* the comedian Jim Carrey played a smooth-talking lawyer and consummate liar who specialises in dealing with untrustworthy clients whom no one else will take on. Only when his young son made a wish to see his father get through an entire day without lying was Carrey's character forced to tell the truth. Mayhem ensued.

B Things like 'That was delicious, thank you', 'You look great in that dress' and 'Of course I want to see you'. <u>They</u> are mostly considered <u>harmless social lubricants</u>. But at the other end of the spectrum are the compulsive liars who are effortlessly dishonest.

C Visual clues are not wholly reliable, as experienced deceivers are aware of the common give-away signs and take calculated measures to avoid them. Shifty eyes, for instance, are traditionally thought to be a sure way to tell whether someone is being dishonest, but experienced fabricators will capitalise on this myth.

D So, for instance, people who are lying about where they have been may declare they were at the cinema or the gym so that their untruth doesn't take too much mental planning. It is easier to make up a story about something they know well and have done many times.

E 'We are experiencing an <u>epidemic</u> of lying,' says Professor Leo Damak, an expert in lie detection at a leading university. 'It has always been around, but we are much more aware of it now.' <u>In one study of college students, 85 per cent of couples reported that one or both of them had lied about past relationships or recent events. In another, it was found that dating partners lie to each other in about a third of their conversations.</u>

F A recent study found that pathological liars are just as likely to be self-confident, attractive and popular as they are introverted and withdrawn. It also seems that the better educated a person is, the higher their level of deceit. It was found that falsehoods typically occurred in <u>one fifth</u> of all ten-minute conversations they have.

G Obviously, many won't stand for ambiguity any more. By being more aware of how and why someone will tell a lie, they have more chance of catching him before he tells another and causes real harm.

H However, vocabulary and sounds are generally considered more reliable indicators than body movements. Liars tend to use fewer words, take longer to start answering a question and pause a lot as if to mentally rehearse what they are about to say. Their voices may adopt a high pitch and they are prone to repetition.

Advice

- Read through the base text for general meaning and then read the removed paragraphs very carefully. Go back and read the base text more carefully.
- Highlight any words which will help you to find which paragraph goes where.
- You need to fully understand what is going on in each paragraph to be able to do this task. However, both subject and grammatical links are important.

- Try to find a suitable paragraph for each gap. Check it fits by reading both the paragraph before and the paragraph after.
- Go back at the end and check that the whole passage makes sense.
- As a last check, make sure the extra paragraph wouldn't fit in any of the gaps. If it would, you will need to check all your answers carefully again to see where you have gone wrong.

您 好 嗎 ?　Merhaba. Nasılsın?

szia! hogy vagy?　Здрасти. Как си?

Γεια σου Τι Κά νεις;　Cześć, co słychać?

1　Before reading the article, talk about these questions with a partner.

- Look at the words above. Can you recognise the languages?
- Roughly how many languages are there in the world?
- Approximately how many languages do you think die out every year?
- Which language is spoken more than any other?
- Do you think your language is worth learning by other people?

2　Read through the article quickly and then answer these questions.

a　Why do you think the writer chose the title *Death sentence* for this article?

b　Do you think the writer is in favour of or against having a world language? Underline the part of the text which gives you the answer.

3　Read the article again more carefully and then answer the questions which follow.

Death sentence

A language dies only when the last person who speaks it dies. One day it's there; the next it is gone. Here is how *it* happens. In late 1995, a linguist, Bruce Connell, was
5　doing some fieldwork in the Mambila region of Cameroon. He found a language called Kasabe, which no westerner had studied before. *It* had just one speaker left, a man called Bogon. Connell had no time
10　on that visit to find out much about the language, so he decided to return to Cameroon a year later. He arrived in mid-November, only to learn that Bogon had died on November 5.
15　On November 4, Kasabe existed as one of the world's languages; on November 6, it did not. The event might have caused a stir in Bogon's village. If you are the last speaker of a language, you are often
20　considered special in your community. You are a living monument to what the community once was. But outside the village, who knew or mourned the passing of what he stood for?
25　There is nothing unusual about a single language dying. Communities have come and gone throughout history, taking their languages with them. But, judged by the standards of the past, what is happening
30　today is extraordinary. It is language extinction on a massive scale. According to the best estimates, there are now about 6,000 languages in the world. Of *these*, about half are going to die out during this
35　century. *This* means that, on average, there is a language dying out somewhere in the world every two weeks or so.

A survey published by the US Summer Institute of Linguistics established that there
40　were 51 languages with only one speaker left – 28 in Australia alone. There are almost 500 languages in the world with fewer than 100 speakers; 1,500 with fewer than 1,000 speakers; more than 3,000 with fewer than
45　10,000 speakers; and a staggering 5,000 languages with fewer than 100,000 speakers. Ninety-six per cent of the world's languages are spoken by only 4% of its people. No wonder so *many* are in danger.
50　Many languages die as a result of cultural assimilation. When one culture assimilates another, the sequence of events affecting the endangered language is usually characterised by three broad stages. The first
55　is immense pressure on the people to speak the dominant language. The second stage is a period of bilingualism; people become increasingly efficient in their new language while still retaining competence in their old.
60　Then, often quickly, bilingualism starts to decline, with the old language giving way to the new. This leads to the third stage, in which the younger generation increasingly finds its old language less relevant.
65　Is language death such a disaster? Surely, you might say, *it* is simply a symptom of more people striving to improve their lives by joining the modern world. So long as a hundred or even a couple of thousand
70　languages survive, that is sufficient. No it is not. We should care about dying languages for the same reason that we care when a species of animal or plant dies. *It* reduces the diversity of our planet. In the case of
75　language we are talking about intellectual and cultural diversity, not biological diversity, but the issues are the same.

Increasing uniformity holds dangers for the long-term survival of a species. The strongest ecosystems are those which are most diverse.　80　If the development of multiple cultures is a prerequisite for successful human development, then the preservation of linguistic diversity is essential, because cultures are chiefly transmitted through　85　spoken and written languages. Encapsulated within a language is most of a community's history and a large part of its cultural identity.

Sometimes what we might learn from a language is eminently practical, as when we　90　discover new medical treatments from the folk medicine of an indigenous people; sometimes *it* is intellectual, as when the links between languages tell us something about the movements of early civilisations.　95　Sometimes it is literary. Every language has its equivalent – even if only in oral form – of Chaucer, Wordsworth and Dickens, and of course, very often it is linguistic: we learn something new about language itself – the　100　behaviour that makes us truly human, and without which there would be no talk at all. Ezra Pound summed up the core intellectual argument: 'The sum of human wisdom is not contained in any one language, and no single　105　language is capable of expressing all forms and degrees of human comprehension.'

Not everyone agrees. Some people believe that the multiplicity of the world's languages is a curse rather than a blessing. If only we　110　had just one language in the world – whether English, Esperanto, or whatever – we would all be better off. World peace would be established. Or so *they* think.

4 What do the words in italics in the article refer to? DEATH OF A LANGUAGE

a Here is how *it* happens. (line 3)

b *It* had just one speaker left (line 8)

c Of *these*, about half are going to die out (line 33)

d *This* means that, on average, (line 35)

e No wonder so *many* are in danger. (line 49)

f Surely, you might say, *it* is simply a symptom (line 66)

g *It* reduces the diversity of our planet. (line 73)

h sometimes *it* is intellectual (line 93)

i Or so *they* think (line 114)

E xam spot

A good understanding of the different reference devices used in texts will help you in Paper 1 Parts 2, 3 and 4.

5 Read the article again and answer these questions.

a What does the writer mean by 'caused a stir' in line 17?

b Explain in your own words what happens during 'cultural assimilation'? (lines 50–51)

c What point is the writer making when he gives a comparison between languages and animals? (lines 71–73)

d Why does the writer believe that 'linguistic diversity' (line 84) is important?

e What examples does the writer give of what we can learn from a language?

f Explain in your own words what Ezra Pound stated. (lines 103–7)

6 Esperanto is an artificial language, based on Western European languages, which was once believed to have a future as a world language. It has never become popular. Why do you think that is? Do you think that your first language could be a world language? Why? / Why not?

7 Read through the text below. Where would you find this type of text? Give your reasons.

Pidgin and Creole

Just as a language may develop varieties in the form of dialects, languages as a whole may change. Sometimes rapid language change occurs as a result of (1) .... between people who each speak a different language. In such circumstances a pidgin language may (2) .... . Pidgins are grammatically (3) .... on one language but are also influenced, especially in vocabulary, by others; they have relatively small sound systems, reduced vocabularies and simplified and altered grammars, and they rely (4) .... on context in order to be understood.

Pidgins are often the result of traders meeting island and coastal peoples. A pidgin has no native speakers: when speakers of a pidgin have children who learn the pidgin as their first language, that language is then called a creole. (5) .... the creole has enough native speakers to form a speech community, the creole may (6) .... into a fuller language.

For questions 1–6, read the text above and decide which answer (A, B, C or D) best fits each gap.

	A	B	C	D
1	approximation	contact	link	acquaintance
2	issue	stem	spring	arise
3	based	derived	built	hinged
4	decisively	thoroughly	closely	heavily
5	Whereas	Promptly	Once	Presently
6	increase	expand	enlarge	swell

Wish and *if only*

1 Read this business anecdote and then answer the question below.

WISE UP, THINK GLOBAL

The British company was chasing a multimillion-pound deal to sell slate from a quarry that it mined to a Spanish customer. The meeting was arranged, the plane arrived and the guests were whisked off to a smart restaurant. Everything was in place – but the interpreter failed to turn up. The directors managed to say the five words of holiday Spanish that they knew between them – several times – but most of the meal passed in embarrassed silence. The guests returned to Spain the next day and, needless to say, there was no deal.

One of the directors might have said to his colleague during the meal 'I wish I had learned Spanish' or 'I wish the customers could speak English'. What else might have been said using *wish*?

2 What verb form do you use after *wish* when you want to talk about

   a the present?
   b the past?
   c something that is annoying you?

3 What difference does it make if you begin a sentence with *If only ...* rather than *I wish*?

> *Hope* and *wish* are often confused. If you want something to be true or to happen in the future and you believe it's possible, then a structure such as *I hope* is required. *Wish* is used for things which you want to happen but think may not happen.

G ···⫶ page 184

4 Look at the following sentences. They are all taken from the *Cambridge Learner Corpus* and contain errors that Proficiency candidates have made in the exam when using *wish*. Work with a partner to correct them.

   a I wish you a nice time when you go to Paris.
   b I wish I will be able to suppress my laughter when he speaks, but I can't.
   c She wishes she would be more positive about the future.
   d I wish you like the present I've got you for your birthday.
   e I wish you to have a pleasant stay.
   f I wish they allowed us to enter the club last night.
   g Ryan wishes he would remember things more easily.
   h I wish me to have some luck.
   i I wish her children can be as well-behaved as yours.
   j I wish they stopped smoking; it's making me cough.
   k I wish there'll always be green hills and rivers.
   l I wish I would live a long time.

5 What do you wish for? Talk with your partner about things that you wish for now, in the past and in the future:

   • your family   • your country
   • your job/studies • the world

Would rather, It's time, etc.

6 With a partner discuss how you would complete these sentences. Give reasons for your choice.

   a It's time (go) home. (said as a general statement)
   b It's time (go) home. (said to a particular person)
   c I'd rather (spend) my money on clothes than cigarettes.
   d I'd rather Michael (leave) his bicycle somewhere else.
   e I'd rather she (give) me some flowers instead of chocolates yesterday.
   f It's high time (do) his own ironing.
   g It's about time (take) a more serious attitude to her job.

G ···⫶ page 184

Sentence transformation

7 For questions 1–8, complete the second sentence so that it has a similar meaning to the first sentence, using the word given. Do not change the word given. You must use between three and eight words, including the word given.

1 I really think you should be more assertive about your rights.
   up
   It's about time .... more.

2 You should really stop behaving like a child.
   though
   It's high time .... a child.

3 They should do a proper review of teachers' salaries.
   out
   It's time ....
   a proper review of teachers' salaries.

4 I think it preferable for all students to write in ink.
   rather
   I .... in ink.

5 I would like to complete a complaint form.
   fill
   I wish ....
   a complaint form.

6 It's a pity that he turned up with no warning.
   let
   I wish ....
   he was coming.

7 It's a shame she wasn't aware how much I cared for her.
   strength
   If only ....
   of my feelings for her.

8 Please don't wear shoes in the house.
   rather
   I ....
   your shoes in the house.

The interpreter failed to turn up to the meal with the British company. *To turn up* is a phrasal verb that means 'to come or arrive rather casually'. *Turn* is often tested at Proficiency, as a phrasal verb, a phrasal noun or in an expression.

The following are all expressions with *turn*. Read the sentences below and rewrite them using one of the expressions in the box.

not to turn a hair	to turn a blind eye
to have a nice turn of phrase	to toss and turn
not to know which way to turn	to take it in turns
to turn as red as a beetroot	a turn-up for the book
to turn the clock back	

a Well, there's a surprise – I never thought he'd get a girlfriend.
b He expresses himself well.
c He went scarlet when she asked him to dance.
d You can't return to the past, however much you may want to.
e I didn't know what to do when the airline told me they'd lost my luggage.
f I couldn't sleep last night for worrying.
g The head teacher decided for once to ignore the fact that the boy was late.
h Muriel wasn't the least bit put out when we told her the awful news.
i Now, everyone must wait to have a go with the new computer game.

Paper 5 Part 2

1 With a partner, look at the photos A–D and talk together about which country you think they were taken in. You have about a minute to do this.

2 Now, you have three minutes to talk together about the aspects of global culture that the photos show.

Things to think about:
- How do you feel about a global culture?
- In what ways do you think it affects culture in your country?
- Does it widen or cross the generation gap?

3 🎧 You will hear three extracts from a lecture on globalisation. For questions 1–6, choose the answer (A, B, or C) which fits best according to what you hear. Read through the questions carefully before you listen. After listening, discuss your answers with your partner.

Extract 1

1 How does the speaker feel about the woman's experience?
   A He is appalled at the loss of tradition.
   B He dismisses it as of little importance.
   C He accepts it without surprise.

2 What point is the speaker making when he talks about sceptics and radicals?
   A To emphasise that globalisation is still a new idea.
   B To show how seriously the concept of globalisation is taken.
   C To warn us of the disagreements globalisation causes.

Extract 2

3 According to the speaker, how has globalisation affected the family?
   A Women's fight for equality has threatened family life.
   B Women have achieved less than they should have done.
   C Women are attempting to rewrite history.

4 What does the speaker say about nation states?
   A They are trying to revive their cultural identity.
   B They are not as powerful economically as they once were.
   C They are being weakened from within.

Extract 3

5 What evidence does the speaker have for the negative effect of globalisation?
   A Rich countries are tampering with statistics.
   B Many goods produced in the Third World are unsafe.
   C Underdeveloped countries are a dumping ground for certain goods.

6 The speaker says that one effect of globalisation is that
   A only Western culture is beginning to dominate the world.
   B the West is at greater risk of pollution.
   C former colonies are beginning to play a greater international role.

Pronunciation

4 In the recording in this unit you heard the word *fieldwork*. Where is the
   main stress in this word? Make as many combinations as you can from
   the following words and say where the main stress should go. Some
   combinations are written as one word, some as two words and others
   take a hyphen. Use a dictionary to check.

   EXAMPLE: *old <u>house</u>*
             <u>boat</u>house

old	seat	back	bench
tea	house	woman	carpet
bag	horse	park	dog
red	boat	wine	sheep
road	sign	glass	race

5 For questions 1–10, read the text below. Use the word given in capitals at the
   end of some of the lines to form a word that fits in the space in the same line.
   There is an example at the beginning (0).

   Remember the words must be spelled correctly. Use your dictionary to check.

Modern culture?

When people talk about contemporary culture they are just as (0) ......*likely*......   LIKE
to be talking about fast cars, trainers or high heels as they are to be talking
about Shostakovich or Shakespeare.

    Goods have become as (1) .... a measure and marker of culture   MEAN
as the Great and the Good. The word 'culture' can now cover just about
anything. Culture is no longer merely the beautiful and (2) ....   SINGLE
It wasn't until the late twentieth century that a (3) .... interest in   SCHOOL
objects began to (4) .... the traditional interest in -isms, with   PLACE
historians, (5) .... critics and philosophers all suddenly becoming   LITERATE
fascinated by the meaning of objects, large and small. Is this a sign, perhaps,
of a society cracking under the strain of too many things?

    Our current (6) .... with material culture, one might argue, is   OBSESSIVE
simply a (7) .... to the Western crisis of abundance. There are   RESPOND
obvious problems with this materialist (8) .... of culture.   CONCEPT
If our experience of everyday life is so (9) ...., then how much   SATISFY
more so is the (10) .... of our everyday things under scrutiny.   SPECTATOR

Writing folder 5

Part 1 Article

For Part 1 of Paper 2, you may have to write an article based on some form of written stimulus, for example a request from a newspaper or magazine editor.

Real-world articles carry an eye-catching title, open with a thought-provoking statement and use stylistic devices to hold the reader's interest throughout.

1 These quotes are all to do with globalisation. Match each one to the organisation to which it refers.

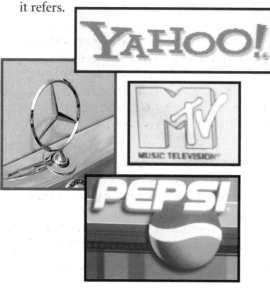

a It can locate thousands of sites on your chosen topic within seconds and operates at country-level now, so you won't need to wade through lots of irrelevant American stuff.

b Name me one bar in the whole world where you can't get this or its local equivalent – they'll be serving it on the moon next!

c Many denigrate it as a 24-hour bombardment of Western pop culture, but to its fans, it's quite simply where life is at.

d The company has a high profile and its logo pops up everywhere, even at sports events – driving one is a real status symbol.

2 Read the article below and choose the best title, a, b or c.

a *GLOBALISATION MEANS STANDARDISATION*

b *LIKE IT OR LUMP IT*

c *DON'T WORRY, BE HAPPY*

Nowadays, we hear a lot about the growing threat of globalisation, accompanied by those dire warnings that the rich pattern of local life is being eroded, and that its many dialects and traditions are on the verge of extinction – but stop and think for a moment about the many positive aspects that globalisation is bringing. Read on and you are bound to feel comforted, ready to face the global future – which is surely inevitable now?

Consider the Internet, that prime example of our shrinking world. Leaving aside the all-too-familiar worries about pornography and political extremism, even the most parochial must admit that the net offers immeasurable benefits, not just in terms of education, the sector for which it was originally designed, but more importantly on a global level, the dissemination of news and comment. It will be increasingly difficult for dictators to maintain their regimes of misinformation, as the oppressed will not only find support and solace, but also be able to organise themselves more effectively.

MTV is another global provider that is often criticised for inflicting popular culture on the unsuspecting millions around the world. Yet the viewers' verdict on MTV is unerringly positive; it is regarded as indispensable by most of the global teenage generation who watch it, a vital part of growing up. And in the final analysis, what harm can a few songs and videos cause? Indeed, they unite rather than divide, console rather than enrage. 22

Is the world dominance of brands like Nike and Coca-Cola so bad for us, when all is said and done? Sportswear and soft drinks are innocuous products when compared to the many other things that have been globally available for a longer period of time – heroin and cocaine, for example. In any case, just because Nike trainers and Coke cans are for sale, it doesn't mean you have to buy them – even globalisation cannot negate the free will of the individual. 26

Critics of globalisation can stop issuing their doom and gloom statements. Life goes on, and has more to offer for many citizens of the world than it did for their parents' generation.

3 Do you agree with the views expressed? Why? / Why not?

4   Look back at the article to find these expressions, which are used to underline a point of view.

in the final analysis (lines 22–23)
when all is said and done (line 26)

Do you know these similar expressions? Fill in the missing words.

a   at the ....END OF.......... of the day
b   ....ALL.......... things considered
c   when you ....COME.......... to think of it
d   in the ....COLD.......... light of day
e   ....ALL.......... in all

5   Read this rhetorical question, which introduces the fourth paragraph of the article.

Is the world dominance of brands like Nike and Coca-Cola so bad for us, when all is said and done?

Turn statements a–c into rhetorical questions, using one of the expressions from exercise 4 and making any changes necessary.

EXAMPLE: The net effect of globalisation is to standardise everything.
Isn't the net effect of globalisation to standardise everything, when you come to think of it?

a   American products impose a way of life that many of us regard as alien.
b   Globalisation could bring more equality to the world.
c   It's very depressing to find a McDonald's in every town.

Write three more rhetorical questions on aspects of globalisation.

Advice

- When writing a Part 1 article, read the question carefully.
- Underline key points to cover.
- Make notes of ideas for each point.
- Order these ideas logically and to best effect.
- Use rhetorical questions to maintain interest.
- Avoid using vocabulary in the question.
- Write in an appropriate register.
- Include a punchy final message.

6   Use the advice above to answer the following Part 1 task. Write 300–350 words.

You read the extract below in an international current affairs magazine in which the editor invites readers to contribute articles entitled 'Globalisation – good news or bad?' Write an article commenting on the issues raised by the editor and giving your own views.

This magazine often features reports from around the world on the recent trend towards globalisation. Is it a menace or a boon? Is local culture really under threat? What first-hand evidence do you see of globalisation and what are your own reactions to it? Write and tell us!

HIGH   LOWS
UPS AND DOWNS
                            OF
BI - NOMIALS
TRI -||-

1 What ups and downs in relationships are suggested by this picture?

2 🎧 You will hear an interview with Steve, who talks about the love of his life, Abby. For questions 1–5, choose the answer (A, B, C or D) which fits best according to what you hear.

1 How did Abby feel about Steve five years ago?
   A She felt the same way as Steve did about her.
   B She was uncertain about starting any relationship.
   C She thought he was fun to be with occasionally.
   D She looked up to Steve, but didn't love him.

2 How did Steve explain Abby's change of heart initially?   *NOT NORMAL BEHAVIOUR*
   A He saw it as an aberration, brought on by boredom.
   B He thought she was having a laugh at his expense.
   C He put it down to her being lonely and unattached.
   D He decided something at work must have upset her.

3 What did Steve's work colleagues suddenly notice about him?
   A He was putting in longer hours than he had done.
   B He was showing more commitment to his work.
   C He seemed preoccupied by a personal problem.
   D He spent less time chatting with them in the office.

4 On hearing Steve's declaration, the first thing Samantha did was to
   A get some flowers for Abby.
   B tell Steve's office he was sick.
   C burst into tears at his news.
   D rush round to Abby's place.

5 At the family wedding, Steve
   A announced his plan to get married to Abby.
   B showed an American how to drive a British car.
   C was given advice by someone he didn't know well.
   D was attacked by his mother for ditching Samantha.

3 Do you think Steve and Abby's marriage will work? Why? / Why not?

4 Steve says Abby has always had *a streak of theatricality*. What does he mean by this?

Many adjectives collocate with *streak*, for example *jealous, nasty, romantic, ruthless, sadistic, vicious*. Are all of these attributes negative?

Fill the gaps in the 'problem page' letter with words from the recording. Then decide what advice you would give Christine.

> **Can too much romance be a bad thing? I'm beginning to think so! I met Max at my local gym seven months ago and it was love at (1)** ....FIRST SIGHT.... **. I soon discovered his deeply romantic (2)** ....STREAK.... **, which I absolutely revelled in to begin with. He would bombard me with chocolates and fluffy toys, turn up on my doorstep with champagne and roses and e-mail me every day with really (3)** ....SLUSHY.... **messages. The trouble is, he still does. I feel our relationship should have moved beyond these excessively romantic (4)** ....DISPLAYS.... **, but he obviously sees it differently. I'm sure Max is the (5)** ....ONE.... **for me, and I'd say 'yes' immediately if he (6)** ....POPS.... **the question. But I really can't take much more romance. It's suffocating! What should I do? I don't want to hurt his feelings.**
>
> *Christine (22)*

Idiom spot

Explain the meaning of these idioms from the recording.

a tying the knot
b cast my net
c bolt from the blue
d time on her hands
e calling the tune
f carrying a torch for
g rolled up her sleeves
h at death's door
i giving me the cold shoulder
j get a grip

Now complete these idioms, four of which contain keywords from a–j.

k The union *has its* ....HANDS.... *tied*, as it can no longer support any form of industrial action.
l The party has been *losing its* ....GRIP.... on those middle class voters who have traditionally been so loyal.
m I've got a cunning plan *up my* ....SLEEVE.... which I think you're going to approve of.
n We're ....CLUTCHING.... *at straws* here – there's no way a deal is going to be struck.
o Once again, it seems that the government has failed to ....GRASP.... *the nettle* on transport.
p I haven't quite *got to* ....GRIPS.... *with* Jack's eccentric behaviour, though I'm learning fast!
q Marion *played right into* management's ....HANDS.... by voicing her concerns so blatantly.
r There are several jobs *up for* ....GRABS.... in the marketing department.

5 What do these two examples have in common?

> *To fend off the problem, I threw myself into my job.*
> *I couldn't keep up the pretence any longer.*

Make similar expressions, choosing from the lists below. Some of the nouns will be used more than once. Suggest other noun collocations for each phrasal verb if you can.

blurt out	an argument
bottle up	a problem
choke back	a secret
fend off	criticism
keep up	appearances
shoot down	emotions
sweep aside	tears
tease out	rage
tone down	blows
whip up	accusations

Now use some of these expressions in sentences of your own based on the following situations.

a You have seen your best friend arm-in-arm with someone other than their partner.

b A publisher doesn't want to hurt a new writer's feelings but thinks their novel is rubbish.

c At a protest rally, a student is giving a passionate speech to the crowd.

d Two teenagers are having an argument which has degenerated into physical violence.

e You had to give some disappointing news to your family and it has affected them, though they don't want to show this.

f A politician is demolishing a member of the opposition party's reasoning in a debate.

Gradable and ungradable adjectives

1 Do you send and receive personal e-mails? Have you ever made new friends on the Internet? Do you ever visit its chat rooms? What are the advantages and disadvantages of long-distance relationships like these?

2 Skim the text below to find out why the Internet was especially important for Richard and Cindy. Ignore the gaps for the moment.

Love on the INTERNET

Richard and his American wife Cindy are extremely affectionate towards (0) ......*each*........ other and talk constantly – using sign language. Cindy has been deaf (1) .....SINCE........ birth, but Richard lost his hearing only recently. He had had problems (2) .....AS........ a child, although doctors failed to find (3) ..ANYTHING... amiss. However, on finishing university, his hearing difficulties became acute and he moved back to his mother's house for (4) ......A....... while. He was so depressed he (5) ....BARELY...... ate and his weight dropped to forty-four kilos. (6) ....HAVING....... been surrounded by sound his whole life, he found living in this new silent world completely devastating.

Richard learnt sign language (7) ....SO....... as to be able to communicate again and it was his audiologist (8) ....WHO..... suggested getting on-line. (9) ..WITHIN.... days, he was surfing the web, (10) ..HAVING.... daily contact with other deaf people in chat rooms. For the (11) ....MOST..... part, he chatted to Americans, finding them particularly upbeat. No (12) ..SOONER.... had he got chatting to Cindy than he was bowled (13) .....OVER....... . Cindy, (14) ..WHOSE....... home was in Louisiana, invited him to America, (15) ......AND...... , on the night of his arrival, he proposed. Their signed wedding took place on a Mississippi riverboat shortly afterwards.

(margin notes: FROM; HARDLY/SCARCELY; IN ORDER TO)

Now fill in the missing words, one word in each gap.

3 Look back at the beginning and end of the first paragraph. Are the adverbs in the adjectival phrases *extremely affectionate* and *completely devastating* interchangeable? Why? / Why not?

Which adverbs can only be combined with the adjectives in column A and which only go with the adjectives in column B? Make two lists. Which three adverbs can be used with both sets of adjectives? Is there any difference in usage across the sets?

entirely
deeply   fairly
absolutely   **A**   **B**   immensely
              angry   awful
              cheerful   broken-hearted
              hurt   impossible   pretty
very   irritable   terrible
              upset   wonderful
                                        quite
utterly
              really   rather

G ···▸ pages 184–5

4 Choose adverb–adjective combinations from the ones below to complete sentences a–e. Use each only once. Make three more sentences with the ones left over.

utterly stubborn	absolutely amazing
rather envious	really dreadful
pretty lonely	deeply disappointed
quite disreputable	fairly laid-back

a It's been .... around here without Tom, but we're all putting on a brave face.

b The guys are .... about their poor performance and hope to play better against Australia next month.

c Sally felt .... at causing the break-up of Ian and Fran's marriage, though didn't regret spilling the beans about his infidelity.

d I find it .... that anyone manages to have a social life outside this workhouse!

e I'm .... of your three-week trip to Mauritius – if only I could come with you.

5 Although adjectives are usually said to be either *gradable* or *ungradable*, in practice many can be both, depending on usage.

*Suspicion is a **natural** reaction in any failing relationship.* (ungradable)

*When he held my hand, it felt like the most **natural** thing in the world.* (gradable)

In these pairs of examples, in which is the adjective being used gradably?

a I felt a real glow of satisfaction in solving the puzzle.

b There's a very real chance that Jo could be back home soon.

c The flower can be up to ten centimetres across and is of the purest blue.

d There is no such thing as pure science in today's world: our lives benefit endlessly from its practical applications.

Based on these examples, what can you say about the differences between gradable and ungradable use?

6 Choose suitable suffixes from the box to make adjectives from these verbs and nouns, making any necessary changes to the base word and being careful with spelling.

EXAMPLE: adore *adorable*

-able	-ary	-ible	-ical	-ive	-ous	-some

a alternate
b caution
c collapse
d detest
e honour
f labour
g loathe
h mendacity
i philosophy
j repel
k tenacity
l theatre
m virtue
n volunteer

7 For questions 1–10, read the text below. Use the word given in capitals at the end of some of the lines to form a word that fits in the space in the same line. There is an example at the beginning (0).

Making contact in tomorrow's world

In a world where everyone has (0) *increasingly* individualised **INCREASE**
interests, it becomes harder to find people who share them.
The *Lovegety*, already a (1) .... hit in Japan, hints at **MASS**
the future for badge technology. It is a pendant-shaped
radio transmitter that sends out simple offers of activities,
from rather (2) .... things such as 'fun' to more **DETERMINE**
specific invitations, like 'movie'. When a pink plastic female
Lovegety approaches a blue one on the same (3) ...., **SET**
green lights flash.
Even as a gimmick, this is an intriguing social experiment.
Regan Gurung, who researches into (4) ...., argues **RELATE**
that badges could (5) .... more significant information **CLOSE**
than hobbies and interests. His work suggests that an
(6) .... based on similar levels of self-esteem is **ALLY**
absolutely (7) .... 'Self-affirming' types have a **CRUX**
natural affinity, while the opposite is true for those with
low self-image. After self-esteem would come extroversion
and neuroticism, leaving other traits, such as reliability,
low in the (8) .... Gurung postulates that **RATE**
well-designed matching software might achieve 60 to 65%
success. (9) .... though this statement may be, social **BULL**
engineering technology looks set to make (10) .... **ROAD**
into our lives.

Reformulation 2

1 You are going to read two texts on the subject of belonging to a group. First, discuss ways in which people conform in society.

- How important is it for an individual to feel part of a group?
- Why might someone join a sports or social club – or a gang?

Groucho Marx once said, 'I wouldn't want to belong to any club that would have me as a member.' What did he mean by this?

2 Read these two texts, which have been taken from books on social psychology. Where do they overlap in subject matter?

A

With the exception of Groucho Marx, people are essentially clubable animals. Whether they sign up for a music society or support a football team, they gather together because they have common interests. Some join a club to further their career, while others merely want to take part in something that involves two or more participants. Group membership brings many benefits – a feeling of belonging, a sense of cohesion and assistance in the pursuit of common goals. It may also enable the individual to reap favours from other members.

People tend to belong to clubs whose attitudes are similar to their own, thus ensuring support for their own beliefs. The individual conforms to the group, but something considerably more surprising happens to the group as a whole. One might expect that the attitude of each member would drift towards the intermediate position held by the rest of the group. In practice, if the members' attitudes are biased in one direction, simply by interacting together their attitudes become accentuated in the same direction.

Membership of a group reduces individual responsibility, leading to greater risk-taking. This is often down to a mistaken belief that the group is invincible, usually coupled with extreme optimism, where inconvenient facts are ignored and any doubts the individual has are suppressed in the desire to conform.

B

A group is a collection of individuals, and the biases and shortcomings of individuals are likely to be found at group level too. However, groups often behave bullishly, reaching more polarized decisions than individuals. Irvin Janis has studied the rationality of group decision-making, using the term 'groupthink' (borrowed from George Orwell) to refer to poor group thinking.

Janis identifies three major symptoms of groupthink. One is the tendency to overestimate the group, line 11 giving rise to the illusion of invulnerability, coupled with belief in the inherent morality of the group. Another is closed-mindedness, with group members disregarding the need to consider additional (outside) information or alternatives when making a decision. Finally, Janis identifies pressures towards uniformity within the group, leading to self-censorship, and, where necessary, direct pressure being exerted on dissenters in the drive towards unanimity.

Janis mentions a number of antecedent conditions that may foster groupthink. These include the cohesiveness of the decision-making group, structural faults within the organization to which the group belongs and, sometimes, a provocative context, such as high stress arising from external threats. The groupthink model can successfully be applied to a wide range of situations, though it has to be stressed that it has a narrow focus, primarily addressing decision fiascos.

3 Which words in text A echo the phrase *illusion of invulnerability* in text B (line 11)?

E xam spot

An important skill in the summary writing task is the ability to reformulate what is said in the two texts. While it is acceptable to use key words, for which there is often no paraphrase, overuse of the actual wording of the texts is penalised. Reformulation will also enable you to show your range of language.

4 Find the following words and phrases in text A. For each one, choose the correct reformulation, a or b.

1 *further their career*
   a advance their professional life
   b apply for a new post

2 *reap favours*
   a receive good turns
   b acknowledge preferences

3 *ensuring support*
   a requesting help
   b guaranteeing backing

4 *drift towards the intermediate position*
   a weaken in ability
   b accept the middle ground

5 *accentuated*
   a exaggerated
   b approved

5 Now reformulate these phrases from text B in as few words as possible, using a dictionary to help you. You do not need to change the key words 'group' and 'groupthink'.

   a groups often behave bullishly
   b identifies three major symptoms
   c the tendency to overestimate the group
   d the inherent morality of the group
   e closed-mindedness
   f self-censorship
   g direct pressure being exerted on dissenters
   h the drive towards unanimity
   i antecedent conditions that may foster groupthink
   j a provocative context

6 In a paragraph of between 50 and 70 words, summarise in your own words as far as possible what, according to the two texts, are the main flaws in group decision-making.

Exam folder 6

Paper 1 Part 2 Themed texts

This part of the Reading paper is composed of four themed texts from a range of sources. There are two four-option multiple-choice questions for each text. The questions have a variety of different testing points – detail, opinion, attitude, tone, purpose, the main idea, implication and text organisation features, such as exemplification, comparison and reference. The questions are in the order in which you will find the answers in the text. Sometimes one question will test global meaning, that is, the overall meaning of the text.

Advice

- Read through the text carefully.
- Try to guess the meaning of unknown words from their context. Don't waste too much time worrying about words you can't guess.
- Read the question carefully and then find the answer in the text.
- Underline your answer in the text and then find the option, A, B, C or D, which best matches your answer.
- Read the text again to check you are right.
- Take care, as sometimes one of the possible answers may look right, but not answer the question.

You are going to read four extracts which are all concerned with the way people behave. For questions 2–8, choose the answer (A, B, C or D) which you think fits best according to the text. Question 1, which follows Comic Relief, has been done for you. Read it through carefully to see how to get the right answer.

Comic Relief

Laughter has always struck people as something deeply mysterious, perhaps even pointless. The writer Arthur Koestler famously dubbed it the luxury reflex: 'unique in that it serves no apparent biological purpose'. When prompted to speculate about what humour is and which area of the brain it occupies, some researchers have followed this general line, suggesting that a sense of humour must be a late evolutionary addition to the brain – an extra module tacked onto all the more sensible bits for some unknown reason. Or perhaps a rogue remnant of circuitry buried deep in the brainstem. Others have busied themselves with trying to construct evolutionary explanations as to why we should take pleasure in the obscure, the ridiculous or the plain risqué.

Theories about humour have an ancient pedigree. One long-running idea expressed by Plato is that humour is no more than a delighted feeling of superiority. We revel in the misfortune of others. The psychoanalysts Kant and Freud felt that joke telling relies on building up a psychic tension which is punctured by the ludicrousness of the punchline. We release pent-up energy safely in a burst of laughter. But most modern humour theories have settled on some version of Aristotle's belief that jokes are based on a reaction to incongruity, when the punchline is nonsense, or to the resolution of incongruity, when we suddenly realise that the silly answer has a clever second meaning.

1 What conclusions have some researchers drawn about humour?

A People often laugh at things for no reason.

B Humour is an emotion created for a purpose.

C Humour originates from a smaller part of the brain than other emotions.

D It isn't a very well-developed emotion.

Read the text and then read the question. Don't look at the answers as yet. Go back to the text and underline the part which gives you the answer. The answer for question 1 is **B**, because 'some researchers' in the question is 'others' in the text. The writer says people think it may be pointless; Koestler also says it seems to be pointless. However, we are looking for 'some researchers'.

A is wrong because in the text it always gives a reason why people laugh – because it's obscure/ridiculous/risqué or because of the ludicrousness or incongruity.

C is wrong because there is no mention of a smaller part, only an 'extra' part. We don't know its size.

D is wrong because there is no mention of how developed it is.

2 Today it is believed that

A we laugh to diffuse tension.

B most jokes depend on absurd endings.

C jokes are a safe way of insulting rivals.

D we shouldn't laugh at other people.

Shaking hands

Is your grip limp and clammy or pulverising and purposeful? Is it accompanied by a vigorous shake or minimal movement? And how long can you keep it going?

Psychologists have concluded that your handshake does indeed reveal the truth about your personality. To the delight of business trainers who have long been urging us to get a grip, a firm handshake seems, well, unshakeably linked to a good first impression. And that first impression is more likely than not to be borne out by personality tests. A team led by an American professor shook the hands of 112 people who did not realise that their greeting was under scrutiny. This was not any old team, but fully trained professionals, schooled in handshaking for months before being let loose on the unsuspecting volunteers. Men's handshakes were found to be generally firmer than women's, and people offering a strong, active, dry handshake together with direct eye contact left an impression of being more expressive and assertive than those with weaker grips.

The only trait that confounded expectation was the finding that men who were more open and liberal tended to have weaker handshakes and so left a lukewarm first impression. Women on the other hand who were more liberal and intellectual tended to have a firmer handshake and therefore were more likely to create a good first impression.

3 In introducing the subject of shaking hands, the writer's tone is

A suspicious.

B humorous.

C disapproving.

D offhand.

4 What are we told about shaking hands?

A Practice is important to making a good impression.

B Clever women make a better first impression than clever men.

C It is not a reliable guide to personality.

D Tolerant and broad-minded men are apt to have an unsatisfactory handshake.

THE PERFECTIONIST

Alexandra, my therapist, says I'm a perfectionist. I demand impossibly high standards from myself, so I'm bound to be disappointed. There may be some truth in that. Most of us in show business are perfectionists. They may be producing rubbish, acting in rubbish, writing rubbish, but they try and make it perfect rubbish. That's the essential difference between us. If you go into the Post Office to buy stamps, the clerk doesn't aim to give you perfect service. Efficient, maybe, if you're lucky, but perfect – no. Why should he try? What's the point? There's no difference between one stamp and another, and there's a very limited number of ways in which you can tear them off the sheets and shove them across the counter. He does the same transactions, day in, day out, year in year out, he's trapped on a treadmill of repetition. But there's something special about every single episode of a sitcom, however trite and formulaic it may be, and that's for two reasons. The first is that nobody needs a sitcom, like they sooner or later need postage stamps, so its only justification for existing is that it gives pleasure, and it won't do that if it's exactly the same as last week's. The second reason is that everyone involved is aware of the first reason, and knows that they'd better make it as good as it possibly can be, or they'll be out of a job.

5   The writer talks about selling stamps to make the point that

   A   it requires similar skills to being in show business.
   B   you should always strive to do your best.
   C   some jobs require a greater degree of thought than others.
   D   it's a tedious job.

6   What does the writer suggest about sitcoms?

   A   They are often uninspired.
   B   They become part of people's daily life.
   C   People enjoy their lack of originality.
   D   Their writers are treated poorly.

The subjectivity of psychology

A great scientist once said, 'When you cannot measure, your knowledge is of a meagre and unsatisfactory kind.' He was of course a physicist. You can be sure he was not a psychoanalyst.

Social science has always been a little defensive about its status, a little sensitive about its claim to be scientific. So when another great physicist announces that measurement is the key to scientific knowledge he is apt to receive more attention than he deserves among social scientists. Psychologists have now got over such feelings of professional inferiority, but there are still a few who believe that good measurement is the highest mark of good science, that deeper understanding lies always in the direction of greater precision. The worship of measurement for its own sake is not, to be sure, a majority view. More common, but equally wrong, is the opposite opinion that measurement violates the dignity of man, that numbers bruise the human spirit. At this extreme there seems to be a fear that the paraphernalia of science will block our view of one another and clutter our channels of direct, intuitive understanding. Wisdom, as usual, lies somewhere between compulsion and revulsion. The first sensible step is to acknowledge that measurement is a means, not an end in itself.

7   What is the writer's attitude to physicists?

   A overawed
   B defensive
   C unimpressed
   D intimidated

8   Which of the following best summarises the writer's argument?

   A It's important to take a scientific approach to psychoanalysis.
   B Intuition is more important than measurement.
   C It's necessary to take a balanced view of measurement.
   D Greater accuracy leads to better results.

1   Discuss these questions on the role of science today.

- How have the lives of ordinary people been affected by recent scientific advances?
- In what areas are scientific discoveries likely to be made in the near future?
- Should scientific research be subject to tighter governmental controls?

2   You are going to read an extract from a 'popular science' book, that gives information about living cells and DNA. This is presented as a gapped text, as in Paper 1, Part 3. First read the text, ignoring the missing paragraphs. How has the writer tried to simplify the subject for the non-scientific reader?

The miracle of life

2 microns

Scientists at Cornell University recently released photographs of a guitar no larger than a human blood cell, its strings just one hundred atoms thick. This Lilliputian instrument was sculpted from crystalline silicon, using an etching technique involving a beam of electrons. The implications of being able to develop machines that are too small to be seen with the naked eye are breathtaking, but we should not lose sight of the fact that nature got there first. The world is already full of nanomachines: they are called living cells. Each cell is packed with tiny structures that might have come straight out of an engineer's manual. Minuscule tweezers, scissors, pumps, motors, levers, valves, pipes, chains and even vehicles abound.

1

Individually, atoms can only jostle their neighbours and bond to them if the circumstances are right. Yet collectively, they accomplish ingenious marvels of construction and control, unmatched by any human engineering. Somehow nature discovered how to build the intricate machine we call the living cell, using only the raw materials to hand, all jumbled up. Even more remarkable is that nature built the first cell from scratch.

2

Like any urban environment, there is much commuting going on. Molecules have to travel across the cell to meet others at the right place and the right time in order to carry out their jobs properly. No overseer supervises their activities – they simply do what they have to do. While at the level of individual atoms life is anarchy, at this higher level, the dance of life is performed with exquisite precision.

3

Even nowadays, some people flatly deny that science alone can give a convincing explanation for the origin of life, believing that the living cell is just too elaborate, too contrived, to be the product of blind physical forces alone. Science may give a good account of this or that individual feature, they say, but it will never explain how the original cell was assembled in the first place.

4

It would be wrong, however, to suppose this is all there is to life. To use the cliché, the whole is more than the sum of its parts. The very word 'organism' implies cooperation at a global level that cannot be captured in the study of the components alone. Without understanding its collective activity, the job of explaining life is only partly done.

5

With the discovery of DNA, however, this mystery was finally solved. Its structure is the famous double helix, discovered by Crick and Watson in the early 1950s. The two helical strands are attached by cross-links and we can imagine the whole shape unwound and laid out to make a ladder, where the handrails are the two unwound helices and the rungs the cross-links.

6

Each rung is actually a pair of bases joined end to end and it is here that geometry comes in. A is tailor-made to butt neatly with T, while C and G similarly slot together snugly, though the forces that bind these base pairs in their lock-and-key fit are in fact rather weak. Imagine the two handrails being pulled apart, breaking all the base pairs, as if the ladder had been sawn up the middle. Each would be left with a row of complementary projecting arms.

7

So long as the base-pairing rules work correctly, this is guaranteed to be identical to the original. However, no copying process is perfect, and it is inevitable that errors will creep in from time to time, altering the sequence of bases – scrambling up the letters. If the message gets a bit garbled during replication, the resulting organism may suffer a mutation. Viewed like this, life is just a string of four-letter words, for we are defined as individuals by these minuscule variations in DNA.

3 Now read paragraphs A–H and use the underlined parts to help you fit them into the text correctly (there is one extra). Remember to look for links before and after a gap.

A Can <u>such</u> a magnificently self-orchestrating <u>process</u> be explained or might the mystery of life be, in the end, impenetrable? <u>In 1933</u>, the physicist Niels Bohr, one of the founders of quantum mechanics, <u>concluded that</u> life hides its secrets from us in the same way as an atom does.

B <u>It is this templating</u> that is the basis for the replication process and ultimately, the recipe for life. If a DNA molecule is pulled apart and if there is a supply of free base molecules – As, Gs, Cs and Ts – floating around, they will tend to slot in and stick to these <u>exposed stumps</u> and thereby automatically reconstruct <u>a new strand</u>.

C <u>Near the top of my list of its defining properties</u> is reproduction. Without it, and in the absence of immortality, all life would sooner or later cease. <u>For a long time</u>, scientists had very little idea how organisms reproduce themselves. Vague notions of invisible genes conveying biological messages from one generation to the next <u>revealed little</u>.

D Of course, <u>there's more to it than</u> just a bag of <u>gadgets</u>. The various components fit together to form a smoothly functioning whole, like an elaborate factory production line. The miracle of life is not that it is made of nanotools, but that these tiny diverse parts <u>are integrated in a highly organised way</u>.

E <u>Boiled down to its essentials</u>, this secret can in fact be explained by molecular replication. The idea of a molecule making a copy of itself may seem rather magical, but it actually turns out to be quite straightforward. The underlying principle is in fact an exercise in <u>elementary geometry</u>.

F <u>I beg to differ</u>. Over the past few decades, molecular biology has made gigantic strides in determining which molecules do what to which. Always it is found that nature's nanomachines operate according to perfectly ordinary physical forces and laws. No weird goings-on have been discovered.

G <u>The former</u> perform a purely scaffolding role, holding the molecule together. The business part of DNA lies with <u>the latter</u>, which are constructed from four different varieties of molecules or *bases*, with the chemical names adenine, guanine, cytosine and thiamine – <u>let's use their initials</u> for simplicity's sake.

H As a simple-minded physicist, when I think about life at the molecular level, the question I keep asking is: How do all these mindless atoms know what to do? The complexity of the living cell is immense, <u>resembling a city</u> in the degree of its elaborate activity. Each molecule has a specified function and a designated place in the overall scheme so that the correct objects get manufactured.

4 At the end of the first paragraph, the writer refers to a set of technical things, from tweezers to chains. Decide which is suitable for these actions.

a The floodwater was extracted by means of ....

b A trumpet is played by shutting off a series of ....

c Julie's hair had been hastily lopped off with ....

d The splinter was finally pulled out with ....

e The bike had been secured to the railings with ....

❶diom spot

Many technical words are used in other contexts, for example, *a negotiating **lever**, a **chain** of super-markets*. They also occur in some idioms. Choose the correct word to complete idioms **a–j** and explain their meanings.

bolt	chain	fuse	gear	knife
nail	spade	strings	tubes	wires

a the final .... in the coffin
b to call a .... a ....
c to go down the ....
d a weak link in the ....
e to blow a ....
f with (no) .... attached
g to get your .... crossed
h to shoot your ....
i to get into ....
j to twist the ....

Passive structures

1 Look at the timeline and make statements about these key events in astronomy, using suitable tenses in the passive. If you are unsure about the formation of passive structures, turn to the Grammar folder first.

G ···⟩ page 185

1997 The *Sojourner* rover vehicle analyses rock on the surface of Mars

1989 *Voyager 2* spacecraft flies past Neptune and transmits photos back to Earth

1929 Edwin Hubble finds proof that the universe is expanding

1900 — 1910 — 1920 — 1930 — 1940 — 1950 — 1960 — 1970 — 1980 — 1990 — 2000

1965 Arno Penzias and Robert Wilson detect cosmic microwave radiation (which supports the Big Bang theory)

1990 Launch of Hubble Space Telescope (named in honour of Edwin Hubble)

2 Scientific texts are often written impersonally using passives, because their focus is on *what* has been discovered or developed, rather than on *who* was responsible (the agent). In this example, from 12.1, it is not important to know who produced the nano-guitar – the emphasis is on the innovation itself.

This Lilliputian instrument was sculpted from crystalline silicon.

Rewrite these sentences in the passive, making the underlined words the subject of each sentence and deciding whether the agent needs to be mentioned.

a They gave the Nobel Prize for Chemistry to <u>Marie Curie</u> for her discovery of radium.

b *Voyager 2* detected <u>ten previously unknown moons</u> as it flew past Uranus in 1986.

c Astronomers have suggested that there is '<u>dark matter</u>' in the universe, but they haven't been able to detect this as yet.

d Scientists have found <u>meteorites</u> in Antarctica which they believe have come from the Moon.

e In 1924, Edwin Hubble proved that <u>other galaxies</u> existed by producing accurate distance calculations for them.

f Earlier astronomers had already observed these '<u>spiral nebulae</u>', but had assumed them to be part of our own Milky Way galaxy.

3 The following examples show other contexts where it is appropriate or necessary to use the passive. Again, the passive reflects the chosen emphasis in the sentence. The passive use also influences the register, producing an official or impersonal tone.

Young children must be supervised on this play equipment at all times.

The rail company concerned has confirmed that all safety checks are to be completed by the year end.

More than a thousand people are thought to have been affected by the recent flooding.

It has often been claimed that chewing gum aids concentration.

Rewrite these sentences using the passive to change their register.

a You mustn't bring your lunch into the lab!

b NASA are going to send more missions to Mars.

c They found that the 'miracle' drug had unpleasant side-effects.

d They are hoping that Bill Gates will open the new building.

e Power cuts have severely affected homes in and around the city.

f Three research students are carrying out further tests.

g You can't take photographs inside this museum.

h They will use infra-red equipment to search for further survivors today.

4 The *Cambridge Learner Corpus* shows that at Proficiency level, candidates sometimes find it difficult to use passive infinitives and participle forms accurately. Correct any errors in these sentences.

a I did not have to be remind of what had happened on that day.
b If your boss doesn't mind you delaying some mornings, public transport could be a solution.
c Protect tender plants from being damage by frost.
d It was strange to been invited by his brother rather than by John himself.
e Despite asked to attend a second interview, I wasn't offered the job.
f Even though it may prove impossible for all the reasons to discover, research continues.
g They were expecting that the hospital would make an announcement the following morning.

5 Complete the text below using suitable passives. Where a modal passive is required, be careful with the tense choice.

THE END OF THE DINOSAURS

In 1990, ten years after Nobel prizewinner Luis Alvarez first suggested a link between the extinction of the dinosaurs and an asteroid collision, a huge impact crater (1) .... (discover) underground, near the village of Chicxulub in the Yucatan, Mexico. Recent research (2) .... (show) that this crater (3) .... (could not + cause) by volcanic activity. This is because a significant quantity of the element iridium, which is extremely rare on earth, (4) .... (detect) at the crater site, supporting the view that the crater (5) .... (must + form) by an asteroid. 65 million years ago, iridium-enriched dust (6) .... (would + throw) up into the atmosphere, causing the sun (7) .... (blot out) for many weeks. As a result, the temperature would have plummeted and the plants which (8) .... (eat) by the dinosaurs (9) .... (would + kill) by the accompanying acid rain. With the removal of their food chain, the dinosaurs could not have survived.

6 For questions 1–6, complete the second sentence so that it has a similar meaning to the first sentence, using the word given. Do not change the word given. You must use between three and eight words, including the word given.

1 The European Space Agency's *Rosetta* mission aims to land a probe on a comet.
for
The aim of the European Space Agency's *Rosetta* mission is .... on a comet.

2 It will be necessary to wear safety gloves throughout this experiment.
duration
Safety gloves .... of this experiment.

3 Using electron beams, it is possible to manufacture machines that are too small to see.
naked
Tiny machines that cannot .... are manufactured by means of electron beams.

4 Recently, astronomers have been finding more and more planets outside our solar system.
increasing
Recently, an .... outside our solar system.

5 Advances in science should soon yield a cure for cancer.
brink
Scientists are thought .... finding a cure for cancer.

6 Although they tried to dissuade Josh from continuing with it, he has opted for physics as a career.
advised
Despite .... Josh has chosen a career in it.

Paper 5 Part 3

1   You are going to listen to a recorded task from Paper 5, Part 3, where one candidate will speak for two minutes and a second candidate will be asked to comment. First, look at the prompt card below and decide what aspects might be covered in the recording.

> **What are the implications of scientific research today?**
>
> ➤ career opportunities
> ➤ commercial interests
> ➤ moral issues

2   🎧 Now listen to the recording. How many of your ideas are covered? Do you agree with the speakers? Why?/Why not?

Pronunciation

3   Check the meaning of these expressions.

   a   in the vanguard of
   b   a double-edged sword
   c   the lay person
   d   for its own sake
   e   subject to enough regulations
   f   the greater good

   🎧 Now listen to Jana using these expressions. Notice how she stresses certain words and slows down or pauses when making an important point. This can be quite effective in a two-minute talk – and will allow you time to think about what you want to say next.

4   🎧 Practise using the following words, building them up into the phrases and sentences you hear on the recording.

   a   concern
   b   duty
   c   repercussions
   d   significance
   e   cusp
   f   reservations

℗ hrase spot

In the recording Jana used the idiom *set the ball rolling*, which means initiate a course of action. Make further idioms and expressions with *set*, choosing from the phrases below.

Which two other common verbs combine with the remaining phrases?

the wheels in motion
your teeth on edge
rings round
a fast one
the scene
in stone
the gauntlet
a tight ship
the strings
(set)   out your stall
the other one
your heart on
a dangerous precedent
your socks up
the world on fire
out all the stops
the record straight

5 Use expressions with *set* to describe the situations below.

EXAMPLE: The investigation has found Peter Gresham to be entirely innocent and will publish their findings. *The investigation will* **set the record straight** *about Peter Gresham.*

a As soon as Jenny spotted the new gadget in the shop window, she was determined to buy it.

b The consultant explained in detail to the whole department how she could help them.

c Allowing her teenage son to stay out late last Wednesday night has given him an argument for doing so again.

d No contract has yet been signed and both sides are keen to be flexible.

e The vivid description of the Martian landscape at the beginning of the book helps the reader to visualise it better.

f The sound of a young child attempting to play the violin never fails to irritate me.

g No sooner had the brilliant young scientist finished his PhD than a leading biotech company took steps to recruit him.

h Carla's a good singer, but she's never going to be outstanding.

6 For questions 1–5, think of one word only which can be used appropriately in all three sentences.

1 Concerned doctors .... him up to a drip immediately and close relatives were called.

By then it was dark, so I found the edge of her coat, ... my finger through a buttonhole and led her across the car park.

It is increasingly common for teenage boys to be .... on steroids in their efforts at bodybuilding.

2 Gerry was seen as a computer wizard, capable of debugging convoluted .... in his sleep.

It was as if the speaker's words contained a concealed .... that only we were picking up.

Remember to dial the area .... if you're phoning from outside Nottingham.

3 They lost badly, even though the match was against a .... team of veterans, including three players who were over forty.

You can do Business Studies from .... in four weeks, providing you already have a good grade in maths or English.

When it came to paying, the store knocked off ninety pounds because there was the tiniest little .... on one of the panels.

4 Customs and Excise say that for every kilo of drugs they ...., ten times that amount gets through.

Rival companies would dearly love to get a bigger slice of the action and will .... any opportunity to do so.

Critics of the scheme will .... on this last point to argue against any further change.

5 As with any complex project, it's a .... of getting the right mix of skills.

In the brain, the cerebral cortex is a layer of grey .... lying above each cerebral hemisphere.

Helping him to escape had not been a minor .... and he knew that if these people were caught they would be punished.

Writing folder 6

Part 2 Report

If you choose to write a report for Part 2 of Paper 2, make sure you use impersonal language and adopt a neutral tone. It is appropriate to include passive structures to achieve this. Sub-headings and other organising devices such as bullets will make your report easier to read.

1 Look at the sub-headings opposite, then read the report below, which is on career opportunities for science graduates. Decide where the sub-headings fit, and suggest where bullets and additional paragraphing would be helpful.

Exciting new opportunities
A more unconventional path
Academic research
Next steps
A broad scope of employment
Education as a career

This report aims to summarise the current career opportunities for new science graduates, drawing largely on the experiences of past and present students. Many final year students have already been invited to interviews and some have even been offered jobs, conditional on their graduation in June.

The first point that should be stressed is that many interesting opportunities exist outside the specialist scientific fields. This is dealt with in the final section of the report.

Returning to pure science, it has been estimated that there will be over a thousand post-graduate posts available for the next academic year, throughout the country. Students should consult their tutor for advice in the first instance. High-achievers should contemplate applying for scholarships to the U.S.A., where much of the research is at the cutting edge. Should students wish to follow up on specific research possibilities in the States, they are advised to consult Professor Grimbleton.

The fast-moving developments in biotechnology and genetics look set to provide many job opportunities for graduates, as many recently-formed companies are being expanded in their bids to become a market leader. Four local companies have specifically requested graduate trainees from this college. They are Bio-futures, Genotech, PJF Seed Research and Railton Systems. Application forms can be obtained from the Administration Secretary.

Many of our past students have opted for jobs in teaching and it is recommended that anyone considering such a career should attend one of the information days planned by this department. At this event, it will not only be possible to meet Head Teachers and Science Coordinators from schools in the region, but also to talk to former college students who are now qualified and practising teachers.

As indicated above, any report on current opportunities would be incomplete without mentioning some of the other non-scientific jobs that past students have taken up with relish. While none of these jobs can be said to demand the recall of actual scientific learning, the generic skills that students have been given through their undergraduate science courses are directly relevant. Here are some of the more unusual career moves: accountancy, stockmarket brokering, counselling, air-traffic control, casino management.

More details on all the areas mentioned in this report can be found on the student website. A booklet is also in preparation.

2 The report contains some 'signposting' devices, for example, *As indicated above.* These are included to help the reader to process the report without undue effort. What other examples of signposting can you find in the report?

Here are some more useful signposting devices. Which are looking forward and which refer back?

a As already discussed …
b Alongside this decision …
c Below is a different interpretation of …
d The previous statement confirms that …
e Further ideas will be elaborated in the next two sections.
f As mentioned at the outset …
g It should now be considered whether …
h It would appear then that …
i The aspects covered earlier suggest …
j This does not necessarily mean that …

3 Find examples of the following in the report opposite.

a compound nouns
b compound adjectives
c prefixes
d suffixes
e topical expressions, e.g. *market leader*

4 Now look at the following exam task.

You belong to an international film club and have been asked to write the club's annual report this year. This report is written for club members and has to include information about the main events held over the last twelve months, to present plans for activities in the coming year and to summarise the current financial position of the club in respect of money received and payments made.

To plan your report, make a spider diagram like the one below. Spend at least five minutes thinking of what to include under each of the three areas, adding to the ideas given. Then draft suitable sub-headings, further dividing the three main sections if necessary.

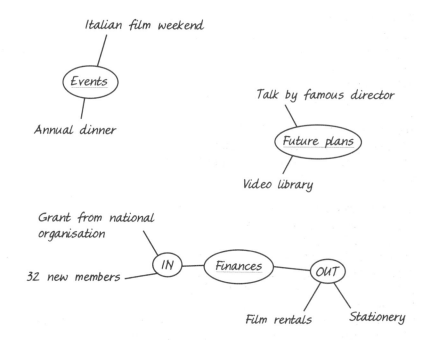

Advice

- When writing a report, make a detailed plan.
- Draft sub-headings for each section.
- Add bullets when listing information.
- Signpost the information clearly.
- Write in a neutral and impersonal style.
- Include passive structures.
- Use a range of relevant vocabulary.

5 Now use this advice to write your report, in 300–350 words.

Use of English

1 Read this extract from an article about socks. For questions 1–15, think of the word which best fits each space. Use only one word in each space.

Socks

Mr Twenty-First Century strikes a pose on (0) .....*the*..... pages of a 1939 issue of British *Vogue* magazine. He wears a jump-suit, belt and waistcoat festooned (1) .... hardware. His hat is 'an antenna snatching radio out of the ether', *Vogue* tells (2) .... (3) .... quite today's mobile-phone man, (4) .... close. However, as we reach his socks, the best *Vogue*'s futurologist can (5) .... up with is 'disposable'. Throwaway insults are (6) .... new for socks. And that's not (7) .... they have to put up with. Over a day, the average human foot (8) .... off at least half a cup of moisture – manna from heaven for those odour-causing micro-organisms.

Yet socks are (9) .... the most ancient of human inventions – an Egyptian mummy's knitted socks are arguably the oldest surviving examples, (10) .... hand-sewn versions may (11) .... back to the Bronze Age. They surely deserve a (12) .... future than consignment to the bin.

Not (13) .... appreciates the sock's versatility, though. Albert Einstein famously eschewed socks altogether, apparently regarding them as an unnecessary luxury. I too go sockless in the summer. (14) .... the frost begins to bite, I can't help wondering, (15) .... Einstein have been wrong?

2 For questions 1–6, think of **one** word only which can be used appropriately in all three sentences.

1 Another .... : never criticise your partner directly.
She slowly stuck the .... of her tongue out at the teacher.
The Pargeters soon reduced the once-tidy flat to a ....

2 I hope your new plan for raising money will .... out better than the last one did.
The amount of money spent on space research is likely to .... public opinion against them.
The children had to .... somersaults and then race up the ladder.

3 Petunia was from a poor Shropshire family, from a less .... background than Patricia.
If the Opposition were .... they would stop being so abusive.
The European market will get through 320 million of the embedded microprocessor .... cards.

4 David set the .... for the evening by appearing in a dinner jacket.
An ideal marriage, he replied, his .... implying there was no such thing.
I'd prefer a .... or two lighter; navy blue is so dark.

5 The subject .... itself demands the applications of thick layers of paint.
However, if a cosmic ray particle collides with .... inside the magnetosphere, neutrons can be ejected.
The forced sale was over in a .... of hours.

6 He had fallen into the .... of having a cup of coffee from the vending machine every time he passed it.
Interrupting his wife is a really bad .... of his.
Mother Benedicta, immaculate in her black .... and white, starched coif, listened carefully to what was being said.

3 For questions 1–6, complete the second sentence so that it has a similar meaning to the first sentence, using the word given. Do not change the word given. You must use between three and eight words, including the word given.

1 The children agreed they would each tidy the playroom on alternate days.
turns
The children ...agreed to take turns in tidy... .... the playroom.

2 Professor Smith talked firstly about living on Mars, and then discussed the Space Lab.
went
After talking about living on Mars, Professor Smith ...went on to talk about... ...to discuss... the Space Lab.

3 It's a shame Peter didn't wear a suit to the wedding.
put
If only ...Peter had put on a suit for... the wedding.

4 Everyone remembers my great-uncle because he was always having arguments with his wife.
having
My great-uncle ...is famous for having had... arguments with his wife.

5 We must always bear in mind that many scientific breakthroughs are due to luck.
sight
We must ...keep in sight that... ...luck... plays a large part in many scientific breakthroughs.

6 When it comes to friendship, I prefer having a few close friends to many acquaintances.
rather
As far ...as I am concerned I rather... ...have... a few close friends than many acquaintances.

Writing

4 Improve this report on an exchange visit by inserting suitable compound adjectives where the symbol * appears, choosing from the list below.

deep-sea   easy-going   glass-bottomed
half-day   inter-continental   long-standing
meticulously-planned   record-breaking
trouble-free   wider-ranging

Here is my report on our club's recent exchange visit to Australia. Without exception, members who participated in this trip were highly appreciative of the * itinerary, not to mention the warm welcome extended by our * Australian hosts. This * relationship continues to flourish and we will be hosting a * number of visitors this summer (see below).

Travel
The * flights went smoothly and we arrived in Melbourne on schedule. A coach had been organised to transport us to the civic reception, where our individual hosts awaited us. Travel within Australia was mostly by plane – unfortunately, our visit coincided with the grounding of much of the Ansett fleet, so our transfers were not entirely *.

Trips
The highpoint was the Great Barrier Reef, where two exhilarating days were spent * diving. Those members who chose not to dive were given the alternative of a * cruise in a * boat, which was said to be very enjoyable for all concerned.
Some members have suggested that the visit to the Kakadu National Park could have been extended, as it was rather rushed. In subsequent years, it might also be more informative to visit during the dry season, which would allow * access to the park.

Return visit
There will be 48 visitors to us in July, including six families with young children. In view of this, it will be necessary to find extra hosts. Strategies for achieving this should be agreed at the next club meeting. In anticipation, could the following suggestions be tabled:
● advertising in relevant journals
● feature in local newspaper
● posters in public places, e.g. library
● mailshot to schools and colleges
● interview on KJY radio
● club website?

Perhaps other members should be asked for further suggestions in advance of the meeting.

····⁝· Crossword page 190

UNIT 13 Save the planet

1 Look at the photos and discuss the problems shown. Try to think of some solutions.

2 Think about your daily routine. Make a list of ten ways in which you could help the environment by making changes to that routine.

3 🎧 You are going to hear four different extracts on subjects related to the environment.

Read through questions 1–8 below. Choose the answer (A, B or C) which fits best according to what you hear. There are two questions for each extract.

Extract 1 You hear a woman talking about her job.

1 How does the woman get her message across to the school children?
   A She helps teachers to make their lessons more relevant.
   B She takes advantage of their interests.
   C She believes in getting them out of the classroom.

2 What does she find frustrating?
   A The lack of time she has in the classroom.
   B That more waste could be recycled.
   C The low prices paid for recycled waste.

Extract 2 You hear part of a radio news programme about a landslide in southern England.

3 What does the man say about the landslide?
   A It is a warning for the future.
   B More could have been done to prevent it.
   C The type of rock is susceptible to landslides.

4 What do the speakers both mention?
   A Sea levels are rising.
   B Heavy rainfall was partly to blame.
   C It's dangerous to go near the cliff.

Extract 3 You hear a man talking about seeing some stags (male deer) in Scotland.

5 When the speaker mentions the fight he tells us how he
   A kept himself hidden from sight.
   B went downwind of the animals.
   C moved quietly nearer them.

6 What does he say about the stags?
   A They are a rare sight.
   B They are keen to prove themselves.
   C They are most frequently seen in the early morning.

Extract 4 You hear two people talking on the radio about a controversial theory.

7 What does the man say about the theory?
   A It was ahead of its time.
   B It wasn't a very scientific theory.
   C It has never been acknowledged by the government.

8 What do the speakers agree about?
   A Lovelock's approach was too amateurish.
   B Lovelock was rather an odd person.
   C Lovelock alienated fellow scientists.

4 🎧 The extracts you heard are in a mixture of different registers. Listen again, and then with a partner decide whether the extract is formal, informal or semi-formal in tone. Give reasons for your decisions.

5 The following are all examples of words which have been used inappropriately by Proficiency candidates. The words are either formal, informal or neutral. Decide when it would be appropriate to use each word.

EXAMPLE: kids/children
'Kids' is informal and used mainly in speaking; 'children' is neutral.

a people / persons
b amelioration / improvement
c bloke / man
d narrate / tell
e frequented / went to
f reckon / think
g boozing / drinking
h mates / friends
i fellow / guy
j snaps / photographs
k pluses / advantages
l lousy / terrible
m prudent / careful
n guts / courage
o becoming / attractive

The words in the exercise above are all synonyms – that is words with the same or similar meaning. Synonyms can rarely be used interchangeably, either because of difference in register (as above), or because of a difference in use. For example, *rife* and *widespread* have a similar meaning – 'existing in many places':

*Many illnesses are **rife** in areas with a poor water supply.*

*There is **widespread** flooding of coastal areas.*

However, *rife* is a formal word which suggests something unpleasant, whereas *widespread* is a neutral word.

6 Decide which of the words in italics in each sentence below fits best. Justify your answers and think of a sentence using the alternative word.

a I can't afford to buy a new car this year – I'm *broke/destitute*.
b Her mother is always telling her she should eat more, as she's much too *slender/skinny*.
c Dr Pitt has made many *opponents/enemies* because of his rudeness.
d I have a feeling my mother's been *sneaking/tiptoeing* into my room and reading my diary while I'm out.
e My sister's baby started *yelling/shouting* in the middle of the night.
f The woodland has been *ravaged/destroyed* by fire and the landscape may never recover.
g Pablo *struck/hit* the castle door forcibly with his fist to make it open.
h I felt the rain *trickling/leaking* slowly down the back of my collar.

7 For questions 1–6, read the text below and decide which answer (A, B, C or D) best fits each gap.

The future

The environmental (1) .... for the future is mixed. In spite of economic and political changes, interest in and (2) .... about the environment remains high. Problems of acid deposition, chlorofluorocarbons and ozone depletion still seek solutions and concerted action. Until acid depositions (3) ...., loss of aquatic life in northern lakes and streams will continue and forest growth may be affected. Water pollution will remain a growing problem as increasing human population puts additional stress on the environment. To reduce environmental degradation and for humanity to save its habitat, societies must recognise that resources are (4) .... . Environmentalists believe that, as populations and their demands increase, the idea of continuous growth must (5) .... way to a more rational use of the environment, but that this can only be brought (6) .... by a dramatic change in the attitude of the human species.

	A		B		C		D	
1	A outline	B outset	C outcome	D outlook
2	A concern	B attention	C responsibility	D consideration
3	A wane	B diminish	C depreciate	D curtail
4	A finite	B restricted	C confined	D bounded
5	A make	B force	C give	D clear
6	A on	B about	C off	D in

8 In pairs or groups, draft a plan, to present to the rest of the class, to make your region more environmentally friendly and attractive for the residents/tourists. You should agree on the register to use – formal or informal, and what vocabulary you will need. Think about:

- rubbish removal / improved recycling
- pedestrianisation / cycle paths
- better and cheaper public transport
- tree planting and more green areas
- the needs and problems of tourists

Reported speech

1 How much do you know about endangered species? The five animals above are examples of animals which are or have been endangered. With a partner, decide which animal you think is no longer endangered.

2 🎧 You will hear part of a radio interview with a woman who helped save the rhino from extinction in the wild. Before you listen, read through the notes below.

Area visited:
.... **1**

Habitat of rhino:
.... **2**

Susan was there to
.... **3**

She found a
.... **4**

People she met:
.... **5**

People who gave her a lot of help:
.... **6**

Condition of rhino today:
.... **7**

Now, listen and complete the notes.

3 With a partner take it in turns to report verbally to each other what you heard in the interview. Try to put in as much detail as possible.

EXAMPLE: *The man said that he had recently been to southern Africa.*

G ⋯⟶ page 185

- When reporting, it's usual to go back one tense. This is called 'backshifting'.
  'I saw her yesterday.'   *She said she had seen her the day before.*

- In conversations, people sometimes don't backshift if what they are reporting happened not long ago.
  'I saw Rachel this morning. She says she'll meet us at the cinema at seven, if that's OK?'
  Backshift also doesn't need to happen if a fact is still true or the speaker believes it is true.
  He said that elephants are still in danger today.

- There are some structures which are more difficult than others when reported because they do not always follow either of the patterns outlined above.

4 Report the following. Begin each sentence with *She said ... .*

EXAMPLE: 'I shall see you at the meeting.'
    She said she would see me at the meeting.

a 'My grandmother could walk to school without worrying about traffic.'
b 'You must come to tea sometime!'
c 'You must remember to recycle the rubbish.'
d 'You mustn't smoke in the restaurant.'
e 'Companies which pollute rivers must be fined.'
f 'If I were mayor, I'd make public transport free.'
g 'If the children picked up the rubbish regularly, I'd pay them.'

When reporting it is often possible to use a verb or a verb plus an adverb which carries much of the meaning of the sentence.

'I hate you! You're scum!' she said to Tom and then she walked out of the door.
She screamed abuse at Tom before walking out of the door.

'Shh! You're not supposed to talk in here!' the librarian scolded us.
The librarian sternly told us off for talking.

5 Use the following verbs to convey the meaning of the sentences below. Take care with these verbs – some are followed by a gerund, others by an infinitive and others by a clause. Sometimes a preposition is required.

object	suggest	sigh	insist
refuse	claim	declare	decide

a 'What about going to Crete this year for our holiday?' Tina said.

b 'I will always love you, Daphne!' Fred said.

c 'I've made up my mind – I'm going to take the job, but I'm not keen!' Colin said.

d 'It can't be helped. I know you didn't mean to drop it,' my mother said.

e 'Leave that window shut. We don't want to catch our death of cold,' the old man said.

f 'That's my book you've got in your school bag!' Rose said.

g 'I'll go out if I want to!' my brother said.

h 'I have no intention of going by train, thank you very much,' Lucy said.

6 Which of the following adverbs would fit with the reporting verbs above? Insert one adverb in each of the sentences you wrote in exercise 5.

passionately	confidently
categorically	peevishly
tentatively	reluctantly
resignedly	stubbornly

7 Write a sentence in direct speech which ends with these adverbs. (Use a dictionary to help you.)

a '...............................' the shopkeeper said angrily.

b '...........................' the policeman said sarcastically.

c '...............................' the teacher said pedantically.

d '................' my grandfather said absent-mindedly.

e '...' Theresa said decisively.

f '.......................................' the doctor said blankly.

g '..................................' my neighbour said rudely.

h '.......................................' his boss said cautiously.

8 For questions 1–15, read the text below and think of the word which best fits each space. Use only one word in each space. There is an example at the beginning.

The first naturalists

There came a time, maybe 20,000 years ago, (0) ....when........ man, instead of being merely a hunter, started to domesticate animals. The dog helped in his hunting activities and geese and ducks were kept and bred (1) ...as............... a source of food, which was easier than (2) ...to harm... to go out and hunt them. Once humans had domesticated animals they (3) ...paid............ their attention to plants. Instead of being nomads, drifting from place to place following the game animals, they began to create farms and thus enter upon a more settled (4) ...way........... of life. Villages and towns sprang (5) ...on.................. in places where previously there had been only a hamlet. Now animals and plants began to be kept (6) ...not............... merely for food but also for interest's (7) .... or for their beauty.

The first writers on animal life were Aristotle, in 335 BC, and Pliny, in 75 AD, but for many hundreds of years after Pliny the subject of natural history, in (8) .... with many other areas of knowledge, (9) ...hardly........... progressed at all. For the most part (10) .... zoos as existed were in the hands of the dilettante nobility and were no (11) ...more............... than second-rate menageries, (12) ...without..... any scientific purpose.

However, in the seventeenth century, naturalists began to realise that they needed a system for classifying living things (13) ...., as more plants and animals were discovered, (14) ...it.............. was difficult to (15) ...keep......... track of them all.

9 In the recorded interview, it was pointed out that biodiversity was important for a healthy planet. In groups, talk about which of the following you think is the best way to maintain biodiversity. Present your ideas to the rest of the class.

- Keep animals in zoos.
- Have more national parks.
- Have egg and sperm banks of endangered species or collect and preserve the DNA of endangered species.

Questions on the texts 2

1 The following texts are on alien species. These are species which are introduced into a non-native habitat. Read text A and then answer the questions opposite.

A

Far off in the South Atlantic, 2500 kilometres from the nearest landmass, Africa, a war is being waged on a lonely spot called Gough Island. One side has suffered heavy casualties: over 1000 dead this year, 63 alone on one particularly bloody night. The outcome of this interspecies warfare is a foregone conclusion. Battered they may be, but the mice remain unbowed.

Out in its isolation, Gough is home to animals found nowhere else. The mice, however, arrived quite recently on sailing ships looking for seals to kill. They now over-run the island, the base camp and the food store of the other newly
line 12 arrived species: the currently ten intrepid scientists and meteorologists who live there for year-long stretches. The humans face long evenings, with limited scope for entertainment. In some ways, here is a microcosm of human
line 16 attitudes towards new alien species. It's a grudge match.

Whether by choice or chance, when humans have gone to new places, other species new to those lands have always journeyed with them. Australia's dingoes were brought in by its aborigines for hunting. Polynesians sailed from island to island with pigs, yams and around 30 different plants. Later, whether as stowaways on ships, planes and trains, or deliberately carried for utility, vanity or idiocy, newly arrived species have delighted and intrigued. Only recently has humankind realised the harm its species-spreading habits might be doing; and, nowadays, gone on, often, to forget the benefits.

1 Apart from a wish to overcome the other, what do the mice and the men have in common?
See paragraph two – think about the island.

2 Why are the scientists referred to as 'intrepid'? (line 12)
Try to guess the meaning from the context here.

3 Explain in your own words what the writer means by 'a grudge match'? (line 16)
You should be able to get an idea of what this phrase means by reading what came before – you can use one or two phrases to try to explain if you can't just think of the perfect one.

4 According to the text, how are alien species introduced into an area?
Remember there might be more than one answer.

2　Read text **B** and answer the questions which follow.

B

Alien species are those moved by humans to areas outside of their native ranges. Once transported in this manner, they become removed from the predators, parasites and diseases that kept them in balance in their native environments. As a result of losing these controls, they often become pests in the areas into which they are introduced. In Hawaii, alien species have caused a tremendous amount of damage to the environment and economy and pose an ever-increasing threat to its natural resources, native species and ecosystems.

Because of its isolation, Hawaii originally had thousands of species found nowhere else on Earth. But it has suffered the highest rates of extinction of any area of the USA and one of the highest rates anywhere in the world, with hundreds or possibly thousands of unique species already extinct.

The primary agent of this remarkable loss of native biodiversity has been the massive introduction by humans of alien species to the Hawaiian Islands. It has been estimated that before the arrival of humans, new species became established in Hawaii (under their own steam or blown by storms) once every 70,000 years. Now Hawaii receives in excess of twenty new species per year.

They arrive in Hawaii in a variety of ways. Many, such as ornamental plants, are legally imported and planted, but then spread to forests when they reproduce and their seeds are blown there by the wind or carried by birds. Others, like agricultural insect pests and a variety of other flying

line 23　insects, arrive as unintentional hitchhikers on agricultural produce, cargo or aeroplanes. Still other species, like reptiles, are smuggled illegally into the state to satisfy their owners' urge to have an exotic pet.

1 What, according to the writer, keep a species under control in its natural habitat?
More than one thing.

2 In your own words, explain how different species got to Hawaii before humans arrived?
Try to paraphrase both elements of the answer.

3 What word in text **A** echoes the phrase 'unintentional hitchhikers' in line 23 of text **B**?
*Go back and read text **A** carefully to find this.*

3　In a paragraph of between 50 and 70 words, summarise in your own words as far as possible the reasons given in both texts why new species have been introduced by humans.

4　The pictures show some animals and plants that have been introduced by humans into a different environment either accidentally or on purpose. In groups talk about any animals or plants which are not native to your country and whether their introduction was a good thing or not.

Exam folder 7

Paper 1 Part 4
Multiple-choice text

This part of the Reading paper consists of a text from a range of sources with seven four-option multiple-choice questions. The questions may test any of the following: content, detail, opinion, attitude, tone, purpose, main idea and implication. They may also test organisational features such as exemplification, comparison and reference.

Advice

- Read through the text carefully.
- Read through the questions very carefully to make sure you really understand what the question is asking. Then find the answer in the text.
- Underline your answer in the text and then find the option, A, B, C or D, which best matches your answer.
- Read the text again to check you are right.
- Don't spend too much time worrying about a word you can't guess the meaning of.

You are going to read an extract from an article about the disposal of old computers. For questions 1–7, choose the answer (A, B, C or D) which you think fits best according to the text.

Into the Silicon Valley of Death

Old computers never die. They just leach heavy metals into our drinking water. That's the worst-case scenario, anyway. Some of them just sit in the loft or the shed, quietly accumulating dust and obsolescence. Others – a very, very few – are refurbished or recycled. Over a million of the things, each year – and that's a conservative estimate. And if you think that's the best place for them, consider this: each desktop PC unit contains up to 9 kilos of lead. Other toxic substances, too – cadmium, mercury, dioxins – but for the moment, let's concentrate on the lead. You may need a computer to do the sum: 8,165 metric tonnes of poisonous residue spread under the topsoil every 12 months, and that's just the British Isles, granulated in a mulch of eggshells, banana skins and mutton bones. Include the lead waste from other dumped electronic equipment, and the total rises to around 27,000 tonnes – sitting below ground upon which new houses may one day be built, and through which water pipes will be laid. Bear in mind that – as even the most casual PC-users will have noticed – each new generation of computers is superseded more swiftly than the last. And you will gather that, while this may seem a slow-burning environmental problem, it is heating up rapidly.

In a steel hangar on an industrial estate in central England, one company is trying to address the problem, and, in the process, doing very nicely out of it. RGA began as a one-room outfit over a sweet shop and now has an annual turnover of £15 m. It offers its clients the safe extraction and disposal of the toxic nasties lurking within their decommissioned computers, and the secure destruction of any sensitive data.

A visit to their warehouse is a surreal experience. It's like paddling in a Sargasso Sea of obsolete technology. You see shoals of keyboards beached on the concrete floor; piles of nicotine-yellowed hard drives, spotted with the stains left by adhesive toys and security tags; pallets of grimy mice; crates stacked with fragments of acid-green circuitry; keyboards filleted from laptops, flimsy and forlorn. Seeing a heap of computers disembowelled by the thousand in a featureless concrete bay exerts a weird kind of culture shock. Of this material 80 per cent can, after a scrub-down, be returned to use, or cannibalised for spare parts. The remainder is exported to plants in France and Mexico which specialise in reclaiming useful chemical and metal elements from technological trash. And what these companies can't use is crunched up and landfilled. ▶

Adapted from an article by Matthew Sweet first published in The Independant 29 October 2000

However, what generates the big bucks for RGA is data destruction. As the complexity of the disposal process indicates, computers aren't a cash-rich scrap purchase. Although PCs contain small amounts of gold and other valuable elements – one US survey estimated that the landfilling of computer equipment resulted in the annual burial of 120,000 tonnes of precious metals – they are difficult to extract profitably. The true cost of disposing of an unwanted PC is around £450 – which may be the reason why the press stories that circulated some years ago about hi-tech rubbish collectors getting rich quick by strip-mining piles of decommissioned computers for their gold content have now ceased.

However, a new law is set to change the way things are done. Manufacturers and retailers might be made responsible for the problem of electric and electronic waste. For every shiny new item neatly packed in a bed of polystyrene and cardboard, they will receive a broken-down model in a plastic bag. And they won't be able to pass the cost on to the consumer – or not in any obvious way, at least.

So, what will happen to the machines? There are several options; you can strip the machines for reusable components or valuable metal elements, extracting and storing the toxic chemicals inside them. That's expensive. There are, however, cheaper and less ethical options. Send the offending material to countries where the rules about what you may or may not stuff in a hole in the ground are non-existent. Or you can donate more recent models to schools or just pile up the PCs in a warehouse. The day of the computer mountain is on its way.

There's a mournful quality about the sea of deconstructed computers lapping around the benches in the RGA warehouse. How, thanks to the dependence that our working lives and our shopping trips and our banking activities have put upon them, have we come to believe that these machines are somehow more than a sum of their parts? Well, they are, not because they might start answering back or take over the world, or offer us lives free of manual labour. There is a chemical ghost in these machines, one which, if ignored for too much longer, will eventually return to haunt us. ■

1   What does the writer say about computers in the first paragraph?
    A   They are best taken away and buried in the earth.
    B   They contain more heavy metals than other electronic equipment.
    C   They may poison drinking water on a number of sites.
    D   They are better stored in the home than recycled.

2   What does the writer say about RGA in the second paragraph?
    A   The company does its job very professionally.
    B   The company is prospering.
    C   The company has had to move premises a number of times.
    D   The company refurbishes computers for clients.

3   How does the writer feel when confronted with the warehouse?
    A   Disconcerted that such useful things have ended up in this way.
    B   Surprised that people have misused the computers.
    C   Annoyed that some machines are being exported.
    D   Anxious about what will happen to the machines.

4   What are we told about the disposal process in paragraph four?
    A   Computer manufacturers no longer use gold in their machines.
    B   Destroying the stored data is a time-consuming business.
    C   Only certain companies are equipped to remove the precious metals.
    D   It is uneconomic to dispose of the actual machines.

5   What does the writer imply about the new law in paragraph five?
    A   That the new law needs to be amended.
    B   That manufacturers and retailers will ignore this law.
    C   That the consumer may pay in the long run.
    D   That more environmentally-friendly materials have to be used.

6   Why does the writer use the phrase 'stuff in a hole in the ground'?
    A   To give an example of what to do with the computers.
    B   To emphasise the fact that no safety precautions will be taken.
    C   To underline the fact that poor countries should have a fair share of this process.
    D   To clarify what most people think should be done with the computers.

7   What point is the writer making in the last paragraph?
    A   New computers are easier to use nowadays than previously.
    B   Computers will be more powerful still in the future.
    C   Old computers require more care and attention than we have previously given them.
    D   Computers make us more dependent than we should be.

UNIT 14 Get fit, live longer!

1 Work with a partner and decide whether the following statements are true or false.

   a Most people get enough exercise from their normal daily routine.
   b The younger you are, the less active you need to be.
   c It's a good idea to eat pasta or a banana before you exercise.
   d It's better to eat a large meal at lunchtime than in the evening.
   e Jogging is the best form of exercise.
   f To live longer you need to give up smoking, drinking alcohol and coffee and become a vegetarian.

2 Read through text A and text B. What impression do you form of Mark Twain in the first text and of the writer in the second?

A

Longer health, not just longer life

The current emphasis in age research is on what experts call 'compression of morbidity': finding ways to ensure that the rising number of people who achieve the apparent maximum lifespan do so in tolerable health, not just after extra years of decrepitude. Much of the advice handed out is simple common sense: adopt a healthy lifestyle, eat and drink in moderation, do not smoke, take regular exercise but don't overdo it. These rules are often flouted, sometimes without apparent ill effect. In a speech at his 70th birthday celebration, Mark Twain outlined his own survival strategy:

> I have made it a rule to go to bed when there wasn't anybody left to sit up with; and I have made it a rule to get up when I had to. In the matter of diet, I have been persistently strict in sticking to the things which didn't agree with me, until one or the other of us got the best of it. I have made it a rule never to smoke more than one cigar at a time. As for drinking, when the others drink I like to help. I have never taken any exercise, except sleeping and resting, and I never intend to take any. Exercise is loathsome.

He lived to 75. In 1910, that was much longer than most Americans. But even for those who stick to the rules, all that a healthy lifestyle can do is to improve their chances of staying in reasonable shape for their age; it will not slow down the ageing process. Nor yet, for all the hype for this hormone treatment, that vitamin supplement and yonder course of injections, would any of the patent remedies so widely and profitably peddled.

B

Diary of a runner

'You've become a terrible bore.' So said a friend last week. I was, naturally, affronted. But, if the truth be known, I've been a terrible bore for more than six months (well, at least I have personally only been aware of it for six months, others may have more uncharitable views). The source of my dullness can be traced back to the day I resolved to run the marathon. Don't get me wrong, I'm not suggesting that marathon runners as a group are dull. No, I stand alone in my dullness for, being so palpably unsuited for such a pursuit, I feel the need to discuss my training regime with anyone who crosses my path. And, sure enough, here I go again. So, what has inspired me to embark on jogging some 2000 km in preparation for a legendary painful five hours of running? Masochism has to be a prime suspect; no one can embark on those wet, windy winter training runs without gaining some weird vicarious pleasure from the sheer ghastliness of it all. But in my case, I suspect the real motivator is the anticipated sense of achievement in finding a whole new facet to my character rather than an innate desire to win or the knowledge that exercise might lengthen my lifespan.

3 Read the texts again and then read each question. Underline the part of the text which answers the question. Then choose the answer (A, B, C or D) which you think fits best according to the texts.

Text A

1 What does the writer say about people's attitudes to their health?
   A They know that it will be difficult to remain in good health until they die.
   B They are often resistant to adopting a healthier lifestyle.
   C They are unsure how to go about changing their lifestyles.
   D They often wrongly think they need to push their bodies too far.

2 What does the writer think about hormone treatments, vitamin supplements and courses of injections?
   A The claims put forward for them have no basis in fact.
   B They are often not medically approved.
   C They have not been adequately tested.
   D He thinks eating a healthy diet is more effective.

Text B

3 What does the writer say about being boring?
   A He thinks it a prerequisite for all marathon runners.
   B His obsession is making him boring.
   C He believes his friends are more boring than he is.
   D Being alone too much is making him boring.

4 The writer says he wanted to run a marathon
   A because he has a competitive nature.
   B to discover for himself whether he had the will to do it.
   C to show everyone he was fit enough to do it.
   D because he enjoys running whatever the weather.

S tyle extra

Which of the texts is more informal in tone? What evidence can you find to support your decision? Things to think about – vocabulary, punctuation, linking and tone.

The writer of the second text used the phrase *wet windy winter*. This use of several words with the same consonant sounds close together is called *alliteration* and is often used in poetry. What effect does this have on the reader?

Make similar phrases with the following nouns.
children   desert   salesman   teacher

4 The choice of verb you make will often change the tone of what you are saying. For example, in the first text, the writer talked about rules being 'flouted'. This is a more emphatic way of saying ignored or defied.

For each sentence, replace the words in italics with one of the verbs in the box and make any other necessary changes. Decide what difference the new verb makes. Use a dictionary to help you.

yank	harangue	resolve	swear	seethe
unearth	crave	loathe	scrounge	

   a She *lectured* me for over an hour about the need to keep fit.
   b Laura *decided* to give up chocolate at New Year.
   c I *promise* I won't use your bike again without asking first.
   d 'Can I *borrow* £5 from you, do you think?'
   e My sister really *wanted to eat* coal when she was pregnant.
   f Jo *was very angry* when his mobile was stolen.
   g Don't *pull* the door open like that – you'll only break it.
   h The boys *found* some interesting old photos.
   i Trevor *doesn't like* what he calls 'fitness freaks'.

P hrase spot

Read the sentences below and replace the words in italics with one of the phrases with *live*. Use an English–English dictionary to help you.

live in clover	live it up	learn to live with
live down	live by your wits	live up to your expectations

   a James really *had a good time* when he was in Ibiza last summer.
   b The neighbours are the original neighbours from hell, but short of moving, we have to *get used to* them.
   c The yoga class was brilliant – it *was everything we wanted*.
   d No one will let me *forget* my tennis skirt falling down.
   e Not all footballers *have a life of wealth and comfort*, you know.
   f Conmen *get by as a result of deceiving people*, rather than by honest work.

Articles review

1 With a partner, do the quiz below to see how much you know about articles. When you have finished, check your answers with the Grammar folder on pages 185–6.

1 Which of the following do not need an article?

the USA, the Indonesia, the Netherlands, the Gambia, the Antarctic, the Hague, the Berlin, the North Pole, the Europe, the European Union, the Oxford University, the Sahara, the Sierra Nevada, the Times, the Olympics

2 Which of these words requires *a* rather than *an*?

European, apple, university, hour, one-day ticket, household, union, MP, hotel

3 Decide which of the sentences below is correct, i) or ii), and say why. If both are correct, then say what the difference in meaning is.

a   i   Ken's a personal trainer.
　　ii   Ken's personal trainer.
b   i   I've been to the gym.
　　ii   I've been to a gym.
c   i   My coach makes a great energy drink.
　　ii   My coach makes great energy drink.
d   i   I love rich food.
　　ii   I love the rich food I had at the festival.
e   i   Japanese enjoy sumo.
　　ii   The Japanese enjoy sumo.
f   i   Come to dinner.
　　ii   I went to the dinner on Saturday.
g   i   I play violin.
　　ii   I play the violin.
h   i   I play tennis.
　　ii   I play the tennis.
i   i   I want a drink of water.
　　ii   I want one drink of water.
j   i   The weather is wet at the moment.
　　ii   Weather is wet at the moment.
k   i   You need to wash the face.
　　ii   You need to wash your face.
l   i   Go to bed!
　　ii   If you look under the bed you might find the book.

2 Read through this article and fill in the gaps with a suitable article: *a, an, the* or – (no article). There is sometimes more than one possibility, depending on meaning.

The perils of keep-fit

(1) .... exercise season is upon us and January is (2) .... busiest time at any gym as (3) .... old members work off (4) .... excesses of (5) .... holiday period and new ones (6) .... excesses of (7) .... past five years. But (8) .... experts warn that we should proceed with (9) .... care; throwing yourself too vigorously into (10) .... new fitness regime can make you vulnerable to (11) .... number of (12) .... health risks.
'(13) .... exercise is (14) .... stress on the body,' says Dr Nick Webborn, (15) .... medical advisor to (16) .... National Sports Medicine Institute. 'That's how it makes you fitter. You stimulate your body and it adapts to this stimulus by building (17) .... muscle and strengthening (18) .... heart and lungs.'
Done correctly, this will be one of (19) .... most potent things you can do for your health – (20) .... moderate exercise has been shown to lower (21) .... risk of (22) .... endless day-to-day ailments.

G ···⟶ pages 185–6

3 Many nouns require no article when used as part of an idiom or expression, for example *to take something to heart*.

Write a sentence to show you know how to use the following idioms or expressions. Use a dictionary to help you.

a   by word of mouth
b   to lie face downwards
c   to set foot on
d   to have a heart to heart
e   to walk hand in hand
f   to stroll arm in arm
g   to be nose to tail
h   to come face to face with
i   to live from hand to mouth
j   to be made by hand
k   to fight tooth and nail
l   to see eye to eye

Prepositions review

4 The prepositions tested below are ones which the *Cambridge Learner Corpus* has shown us commonly cause problems. Complete the sentences with a suitable preposition. There may be more than one possible answer.

  a That bloke over there is well known for dealing .... steroids.

  b We agreed .... the plan to go jogging every morning.

  c You shouldn't laugh .... Tony, he can't help being slow.

  d Melissa shouted .... the player to look behind him.

  e What are you thinking .... at this moment?

  f If I catch you throwing your ball .... my house again, I'll tell your father.

  g I don't object .... you watching the Olympics, as long as you don't stay up all night.

  h His professional approach is typical .... our team.

  i The Sports Council voted .... the amendment late last night.

  j You can't insist .... a refund of your gym membership you know.

  k Let me congratulate you .... your fine achievement.

  l Sal certainly doesn't care .... running, but enjoys long walks.

  m We discussed it for ages before we finally agreed .... a solution.

5 With a partner, ask and answer using the verbs below and the correct preposition. Use an English dictionary if you need help.

  EXAMPLE: apply – *What did he apply for?*
                  He applied for a grant.
              – *Who did he apply to?*
                  He applied to the manager.

a rely	**f** interfere
b take pride	**g** admire
c look forward	**h** apologise
d prohibit	**i** accuse
e consist	**j** believe

Word formation

6 Look at the following words from the texts in 14.1. What part of speech is each word in the text? What other forms of the word are possible?

Text A
apparent tolerable sense moderation regular survival

Text B
bore known personally resolved unsuited suspect

  EXAMPLE: apparent (*adjective*)
              appear, appearance, apparently, apparition, disappear, disappearance

7 Use an appropriate form of one of the words above to complete each sentence below.

  EXAMPLE: ...*Apparently*..., there's a bus strike – that's why the buses aren't running.

  a His .... of the game is limited, to say the least.

  b The referee was the only .... of the plane crash.

  c The supporters need to be more .... of players from different countries.

  d What a lot of .... you talk!

  e We need to have a .... of this problem as soon as possible.

  f He aroused the .... of the police when he bought an expensive sports car.

8 For questions 1–4, complete the second sentence so that it has a similar meaning to the first sentence, using the word given. These all include some type of word formation.

  1 Helen's running style seems to be improving now she has lessons.
    signs
    Helen's running style .... now she has lessons.

  2 I really admire the changes you have made to your diet.
    full
    I .... the changes you have made to your diet.

  3 Sam is reputed to inspire young athletes.
    has
    Sam .... young athletes.

  4 I would have arrived even later at the meeting, if Professor McDougal hadn't kindly assisted me.
    kind
    But ...., I would have arrived even later at the meeting.

The News

Win 100,000 CASH PRIZES TODAY – page 7

ORANGE JUICE CAN TURN CHILDREN ORANGE!

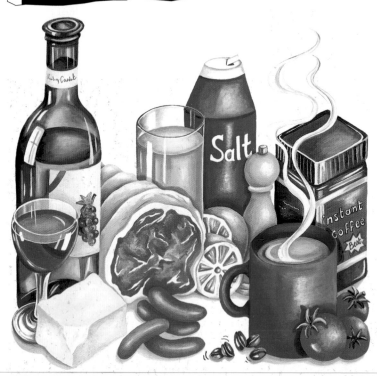

1 Do you know of any health scares in your country about any of the products above?
Do they make you anxious or are you complacent and take no notice of them?

2 You are going to listen to two people, Alice and Robert, discussing health scares on a radio programme. Before you listen, read through the opinions below to check you understand the vocabulary.

a It's good to be aware of potential threats to health.
b The plague was the worst epidemic we have had to date.
c People will be able to live longer in the future.
d People worried more about their health in the past than they do now.
e It's relatively easy to prey on people's preoccupation with their health.
f Doctors can be irresponsible in their actions.
g It's easier to avoid heart disease than many other diseases.

🎧 Now listen to the recording and decide whether these statements are made by the speakers or not. Write *Yes* or *No* after the questions.

Pronunciation

In the recorded interview Alice and Robert used the following words:

object   frequent   discount

Listen to the interview again. How were those words pronounced?

Underline the part of the word which was stressed. Which part of speech are they?

Certain words have a variable stress pattern, depending on whether they are used as a noun, adjective or verb, for example: *object.*

> I don't ob**ject** to your opening the window.
> The boy tripped up over some **ob**ject in his path.

3 Write two sentences for each of the following words, showing how they are used as either a noun, adjective or verb, and then read them aloud. Use an English dictionary to help you.

frequent	entrance	incense	invalid
present	discount	produce	alternate

4 With a partner, look at the photos and talk together about the lifestyles of the people in the photos.

You will need to compare and contrast the photos. Think about the lifestyles of the people represented and any possible implications for their future.

You have about a minute to do this.

5 Work in groups to make a joint presentation about the following topic.

Imagine that there is going to be an advertising campaign to persuade young people to keep fit and healthy.

Decide what form the campaign should take in order to have the greatest impact, e.g. posters/TV/cinema/magazines/talks in schools, colleges, etc.

Also think about what aspect of health and fitness should be highlighted – should it be cigarettes/diet/exercise/drugs, etc?

You will need to give opinions, make decisions and evaluate the potential impact of the advertising campaign.

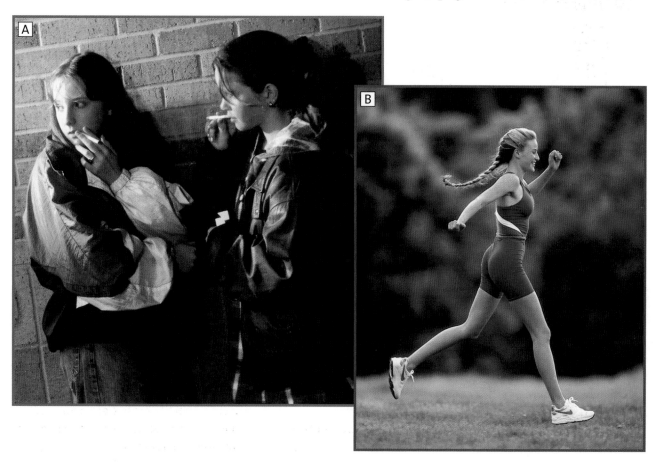

Writing folder 7

Part 1 Proposal

Writing folder 4 looked at a Part 2 proposal. In Part 1 of the paper, the proposal will be a reasoned argument in support of a particular decision or plan. To give the reader the complete picture, it may be necessary to include arguments against such a course of action, in order to refute them. The task is based on input that is sometimes graphic in nature.

1   The following graphs give information about sports activity in a college last year. What do the trends indicate? Choose a suitable course of action (A, B or C) for the college principal to take.

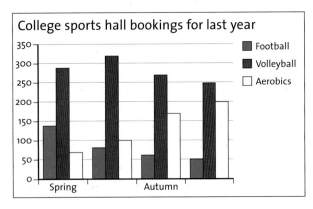

College sports hall bookings for last year

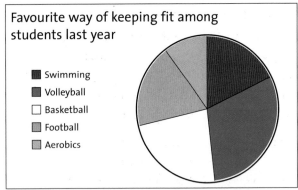

Favourite way of keeping fit among students last year

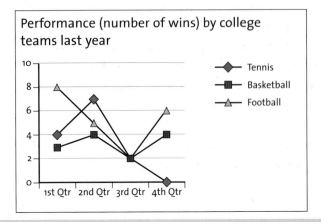

Performance (number of wins) by college teams last year

A To maintain the success of our football team, the sports hall should give priority to team practices, especially given that it has been under-used for other activities, such as aerobics.

B Judging by the popularity of volleyball among our students, we should fund a new college volleyball team and allocate more sports hall time for this.

C The college should take steps to recruit new players for the basketball team, which is under-achieving despite regular practice time being available in the sports hall.

2   Now read this exam task.

Your college has received a critical external report on its sports provision, an extract of which is given below. As a member of the sports committee, you discover that substantial national funding is available for the upgrading and enlargement of facilities. You decide to write a proposal for your principal, outlining why the college should apply for funding and how the money could be spent.

The student demands for sport at the college cannot currently be met, due to the fact that both the sports hall and swimming pool are rented out to the general public at peak times. Moreover, the hall is in a bad state of repair and the limited changing facilities overcrowded. The principal insists that no resources can be allocated for improvements and that the college must continue to encourage outside bookings in order to cover its costs. Members of the student sports committee are very unhappy with this intransigent position, which disregards the health and well-being of students and has affected the performance of college sports teams.

Write your **proposal**.

3 Look back at the advice given for writing a proposal on page 73 before you read the draft answer opposite. An R or T to the right of a line means that the register or tone needs improving. Underline the parts to be edited and then suggest improvements to make the proposal consistently formal in register and less aggressive in tone. An example is given.

4 The following expressions are useful when arguing for or against a course of action. Decide what each refers to, writing

A for high priority
B for low priority
C for no action

a give priority to   A
b take the initiative in
c place less emphasis on
d set in motion immediately
e put on hold (temporarily)
f allocate minimal resources to
g back the establishment of
h freeze the development of
i sanction major investment in
j pull out of

5 Now, using some of the expressions above, answer the task in exercise 2 in 300–350 words. Refer to the graphs in exercise 1 for ideas on what course of action to recommend. Your final paragraph should urge the principal to take action.

rather negative

Following the <u>damning</u> external report on our   T
sports facilities, we demand that you alter your   T
hardline position and give students increased
access. Barring students from using the pool and the
hall at certain times is really mean. And as the   R
report points out, your crazy policy is adversely   T
affecting our basketball and swimming teams, both of
which have hitherto represented the college at the
highest levels of competition and won many events.

It has come to our notice that funding is available
nationally, which we would be in a good position to
apply for. Why haven't you found out about this   T
already? Anyway, our recommendation would be to   R
put in for this money, which would enable the   R
college to carry out much-needed repairs to the
sports hall, such as the replacement of the dodgy   R
flooring and major improvements to the lighting –
you can't even see the ball sometimes! We estimate   R
that the money would also allow for an extension of
the present changing facilities, whereby separate
'wet' and 'dry' areas could be introduced, to
service the pool and hall respectively. This would
be extremely popular with all users of the
facilities, not least the general public, who are
often critical of the present arrangements.

If this work were to go ahead, we believe that the
college could do nicely out of it, by hiking up   R
the fees for external use of the facilities. At the
same time, you'd better reconsider the extent to   T
which these college facilities are out of action for
students and reduce the number of hours allocated to
the public. We are not against public use of the
facilities, which strengthen the links between the
college and the town, but we feel you are totally
out of line in offering them so much time.   T
Why don't you limit it to mornings and restricted   R
evening hours, when students would be less likely
to go there?

UNIT 15 The daily grind

1 Do you think you will stay in the same career throughout your working life? In what ways might the workplace change in the next ten years? What expectations do you have about job security in the long term?

2 You will hear an interview with the head of an employment agency, where she talks about expectations in today's job market. First read questions 1–5 and underline any unfamiliar vocabulary. Check your understanding with another student.

  1 How does Diane Webber view 'jobs for life'?
  A She regrets the fact that this situation is no longer the norm.
  B She feels that many long-serving employees failed to make a useful contribution.
  C She believes that people should have challenged their employers' motives more.
  D She wishes the workplace had been more secure in the past.

  2 According to Diane, younger workers in today's workplace
  A learn all the skills they need early on.
  B accept lateral moves if they are attractive.
  C expect to receive benefits right from the start.
  D change jobs regularly to achieve a higher level.

3 What does Diane say about continuity in companies?
  A It is desirable in both junior and senior management.
  B It is impossible to achieve in today's more competitive environment.
  C It is unimportant, due to the greater emphasis on teamwork.
  D It is necessary, but only up to a point.

4 According to Diane, what is the actual benefit of higher levels of personnel movement?
  A higher levels of output
  B better problem-solving
  C more creativity
  D greater efficiency

5 Diane considers that nowadays, companies are at most risk from
  A run-of-the-mill employees who play safe.
  B successful high-fliers who quickly move on.
  C unreliable staff who lack commitment.
  D external advisors who have undue power.

  Now listen to the recording and, for questions 1–5, choose the answer (A, B, C or D) which fits best according to what you hear.

3 🎧 Listen again and then explain what Diane meant by the following expressions.

a a golden handshake
b cut their teeth
c progress up the rungs
d a mixed blessing
e dog-eat-dog
f the slightest whiff of
g snapped up
h a track record
i mindset
j the jury's still out
k a quantum leap
l quick fixes
m keep their heads down

4 The expressions *quick fix* and *quick exit* were used in the recording. Many other nouns collocate with adjectives describing speed. Explain the meanings of the underlined phrases in a–h.

a Let's get a quick bite before the play starts.
b Life in the fast lane was proving even more hectic than Henry had imagined.
c Benson had a reputation for trying to make a quick buck.
d Travellers in business or first class may use our fast track channel.
e I'm just going to have a quick dip in the pool, to cool down.
f Both companies could end up in the slow lane, due to lack of investment.
g The team pride themselves on their rapid response, generally one to two days maximum.
h After a quick catnap, he was ready to face the press.

❶ diom spot

Neologisms

Many of the expressions in exercise 3 have only entered the language recently and are used particularly in business and in journalism. Complete these examples with one of the expressions (a–m).

1 On the question of the manager's survival, ...
....
2 The spin-off from his success is ....
in attendance and greater commitment all round.
3 It only takes .... lower interest rates for the retail industry to get excited.
4 We live in a solution-hungry time, where people are confused, busy, and anxious to latch on to any ....
they can.
5 The Chancellor can plausibly ask the financial markets for their trust, given his .... of prudent fiscal management.
6 The arrival of the so-called independent advisors was .... for staff, who were asked to produce fresh data almost overnight.

The term *golden handshake* now has its opposite in business, which you can form below. Match the colours to the nouns given (one colour is used twice). Then use the expressions in sentences a–f.

blue	goods
golden	ink
green	chips
red	knight
white	hello
	shoots

a In spite of substantial investment, the company is still bleeding .... and drastic action is likely before the year end.
b Although we cannot report much that is positive, some encouraging .... are starting to appear, particularly in certain export markets.
c Even the .... ICI and Guinness are beginning to suffer reverses of fortune, as the recession bites.
d Sales volumes of .... such as dishwashers and freezers are virtually static.
e It is thought that top executive James Eagleton received a .... of around $2 million on joining the corporation.
f Rumours that a .... was about to step in proved unfounded and the company was taken over within a matter of weeks.

Clauses 1

1 What do the article title and cartoon below suggest to you in terms of gender differences at work? Read the article to see if your ideas are covered. Ignore the spaces for the moment.

The secretarial gender divide

Male PAs are (0) ....*on*........ a fast track to the top. Or (1) ....*So*........ their female counterparts think, according to a new survey by a leading recruitment consultancy. In (2) ....*what*........ is a female-dominated profession, these concerns clearly deserved to (3) ....*be*........ investigated. However, in reality, there is absolutely (4) ....*no*........ truth in them whatsoever. Similar studies carried out (5) ....*since*........ men started entering the profession have all reached the same conclusion.

One careers adviser claims the fear stems (6) ....*from*........ the fact that men increasingly use support roles (7) ....*as*........ a first rung on the career ladder. With nigh (8) ....*on*........ double the number of students in higher education compared to a decade ago, graduates have had to find new ways (9) ....*into*........ professions, and secretarial work has proved a popular route, particularly for men. And (10) ....*although*........ it appears that men are indeed mega-quick in getting promotion, this is fully explained by (11) ....*their*........ active seeking out of higher-status roles, (12) ....*rather*........ than by anything more sinister.

Adam Menzies, (13) ....*whose*........ career proceeded rapidly from PA to successful publicity manager, is a typical case. 'I made (14) ....*up*........ my mind to start in a PA role, in order to learn about the business by working day-to-day with a top manager. Even from Day One, I had access to high-level people and had (15) ....*no*........ intention of landing this job eventually.' This stepping-stone strategy is gaining ground in a number of professions.

2 Now fill in spaces 1–15 with one word only.

3 What other jobs could be seen as stepping stones on a career path and why? Think in terms of hierarchies.

4 Think of other ways to link the clause in the third paragraph that begins *in order to* .... . What type of clause is this?

Ⓖ ⋯⟩ page 186

5 Which two linking phrases below are the most formal? Where might you see them used?

for fear that	in case	in order (not) to
so as (not) to	so that	lest

Join the following clauses with suitable linking phrases, choosing from the ones above. In some cases, more than one choice is possible. Be careful with negatives!

a Ambrose Greene checked everything at least three times .... he would fail to spot an error.

b Buy the relevant magazines every week .... miss any advertisements.

c The company took up both references .... satisfy themselves that he was the right man for the job.

d Always dispatch vital documents by registered mail .... they go astray and you need to trace them.

e It is worth allowing extra time if travelling on public transport .... you won't be in a rush at the other end.

f I used to commute into the office at the crack of dawn .... have to travel in overcrowded trains.

g The clients are being sent a map .... they don't know their way around.

h Elzevir paid great attention to his feet, ... he should slip on the ferns and mosses with which the steps were overgrown.

6 Finish these statements so that they are true for you, including an appropriate linking phrase.

EXAMPLE: I would like to work abroad at some point, …
in order to learn another language.

a I would like to work abroad at some point, …

b When I'm older, I won't stay in the same job for more than two years, …

c I want to continue my English studies, …

d It would be useful for me to have my own website, …

e I want to find work that I can do from home, …

S tyle extra

In English, some words to do with people refer only to men *or* women, either because they are gender-specific, e.g. *maid*, or because usage is just like that. (Corpus evidence suggests that *taciturn* is only used of men.)

Group the nouns and adjectives below under these three headings. Decide also whether they are formal, neutral or informal, and whether there are any further restrictions on their use, e.g. offensive, old-fashioned.

used of men   used of women   used of both

nouns

actor	bag	bimbo	bounder
buffer	chairman	charmer	duchess
freshman	geek	gofer	lout
mate	neanderthal	nerd	partner
patriarch	sibling	spouse	thug
vamp	whizz kid		

adjectives

bullish	chivalrous	doting	effeminate
laddish	lanky	prickly	wimpy

Now combine each adjective with a suitable noun and produce an example sentence to illustrate usage and meaning, using a dictionary if necessary.

EXAMPLE: The bullish whizz kid had a reputation for making wild predictions about the futures market.

Linking 2

1 Which of these leadership qualities are the three most important for each of the following people? What are the other characteristics of a successful leader?

a a company chairman
b an expedition leader
c a military commander

decisiveness	intuition
vision	forthrightness
creativity	specialist knowledge
good humour	approachability
determination	stamina

2 Read the two texts on leadership and answer the questions which follow.

It is only when you become aware of the scope and incredible responsibility of the job of chairman that you truly understand the commitment needed. In such a role, there is an almost limitless opportunity to be ineffective, unless you are totally clear about how you are going to set about it. The problem is not eased by the fact that it is a very fortunate chairman who has any significant handover from his predecessor.

Without the benefit of the full breadth of knowledge, which is only gained by holding the job, you already believe you know what you want to do, and this almost invariably includes putting right past mistakes. You are conscious that you need to 'grasp' the organisation immediately and move quickly to convey the necessary dual image of determination and clarity of vision.

You must be clear in your own mind that there is no way one man can manage an enormous company. The job of the chairman is to 'manage' his colleagues on the board. Board discussions must be useful and conclusive. On a sufficient number of occasions, the conclusions reached have to be different from those anticipated. For, if the board has become nothing more than a rubber stamp, it has ceased to work properly.   line 28

In that situation, nobody is to blame but the chairman, and he alone can rectify it.

1 What do you understand by the phrase 'significant handover' in the first paragraph?
2 Which two leadership qualities are seen as vital for a new chairman in the second paragraph?
3 Explain briefly in your own words what sort of board would be compared to a 'rubber stamp'. (line 28)

Bill Gates and Paul Allen, the co-founders of Microsoft, were very bright computer geeks who could take a computer apart, write software and understand new technology. In the early days, their management style of the fledgling company was 'a little loose', in Allen's words. The partners shared every decision and alternated tasks so often that who did what remained unclear. Allen tended towards the new technology and new products, whereas Gates leaned towards negotiations, contracts and business deals. The

line 12 division of labour is interesting in view of Gates's later reputation as the supreme nerd, the man to whom technology is all.

As the two developed management skills on top of their technical expertise, they sought other technical experts, some of whom, over time, would likewise evolve into managers. This corporate style is unchanged. Microsoft management is highly professional, but is inseparable from other professional skills, much as in the early days.

Two other enduring features of its management style developed early on. Decisions were taken in very long discussions – known as 'marathons' – that lasted for six to eight hours. Secondly, the pair expected others to copy their habit of working extremely hard and long. Gates has never lost his stamina.

4 Explain in your own words why the writer finds the 'division of labour' interesting. (line 12)
5 What is the nature of the 'corporate style' referred to in the second paragraph?

3 In the summary task, you can only write 50–70 words, so economical linkers are useful. Look at Unit 9 for some examples. Which of the following linkers would you use to contrast information from the two texts?

At the same time	Likewise
Conversely	On the contrary
In other words	On the other hand
Instead	Otherwise

4 Read the summary task below.

In a paragraph of between 50 and 70 words, summarise in your own words as far as possible the characteristics of the top jobs referred to in both the texts.

5 Now read this overlength answer.

○ The first text says that you need to learn how to do the job once you have taken over as chairman. The second one refers to how people in charge of a young company had to learn as they went along. The writer of the first text sees strong leadership as essential, while the second shows that a looser partnership worked in a young company. The first text talks about the need for concrete outcomes
○ from discussions with board members. The second describes long meetings where decisions were taken. The first text highlights the enormous amount of responsibility that goes with the job, which demands total commitment. In the second text the individuals had to work long hours and expected this of others.
○

(123 words)

Find sentences in the answer that correspond to A–D below. Then underline the parts of the texts summarised by each sentence. Decide whether the remaining sentence is relevant or not.

A The importance of conclusive discussions with decision-makers is highlighted in both.
(11 words)

B The first argues for strong leadership, the second describes a less-clearly defined partnership.
(13 words)

C Total commitment to the job is taken for granted.
(9 words)

D Both texts refer to top people experiencing a learning curve when running a company.
(14 words)

6 Now place sentences A–D above in a suitable order and edit them as necessary, adding equation or contrastive links to produce a final summary.

Exam folder 8

Paper 4 Part 2
Sentence completion

In Part 2 of Paper 4 you will hear a monologue or prompted monologue (that is someone introducing the main speaker). You will need to listen for specific information in order to complete gaps in sentences. There are nine gaps altogether. You will hear the piece twice and you must write your answer – in the form of a word or short phrase – on an answer sheet. You must spell the word or short phrase correctly.

Advice

- You have 45 seconds to read through the questions before you hear the piece. Make good use of this time.
- Make sure you read ahead or else you will get lost and begin to panic. Always know the topic of the next question.
- You should write what you hear; there is no need to change the words into a different form. Make sure the word or short phrase you write fits the sense of the sentence to be completed.
- Look out for clues – e.g. *an* before the gap; the use of a particular preposition, *in*, *on*, etc; the use of *many* rather than *much* to show a countable noun is needed.
- You shouldn't write a whole sentence.

You will hear a man talking about his job working for a car hire company.
For questions 1–9, complete the sentences with a word or short phrase.

John Farrant says that people doing his job have to act in a **1** [   ] way.

John was asked by an older customer to talk him through a **2** [   ] on the phone.

One tourist from the USA was worried about driving in the UK because he had little or no

experience of **3** [   ]

The car which had been taken to Israel was covered in **4** [   ] when it was returned.

John says that car hire companies like customers who require **5** [   ] because they

make more profit from it.

The customer with the medical condition was given a **6** [   ] near the car hire office.

The manager of the centre needed to use the **7** [   ] to avoid being in a crash.

John Farrant thinks that many customers don't believe that reservations clerks

have the customers' **8** [   ] at heart.

The customer in Miami needed a car which had **9** [   ]

Paper 4 Part 4
Three-way matching

In Part 4 of Paper 4 you will hear two speakers talking about a subject, possibly with a presenter to introduce them. You will need to listen for whether the opinions are expressed by only one of the speakers, or whether the speakers agree. There are six statements altogether. You will hear the piece twice and you must write your answer in the form of a letter on your answer sheet.

Advice

- You have 30 seconds to read the statements before you hear the recording.
- Make good use of this time by reading the statements carefully.
- Always know what the next statement is so that you don't get lost.
- The agreement or disagreement is often quite subtle – don't expect to hear a clear 'Yes' or 'No'. Also beware of an answer which is simply repeating what has just been said – it doesn't mean the speaker agrees with it.

You will hear two people, Monica and Edward, talking about the use of the Internet by businesses. For questions 1–6, decide whether the opinions are expressed by only one of the speakers, or whether the speakers agree.

Write **M** for Monica
       E for Edward
       B for Both, where they agree.

1 Companies want to sell over the Internet because they are worried they might lose business if they don't. | **1** |

2 There are some goods which shouldn't be sold over the Internet. | **2** |

3 There have been problems about paying for goods over the Internet. | **3** |

4 Shopping should have an element of social interaction about it. | **4** |

5 It is hard to get directors of large British companies interested in e-commerce. | **5** |

6 Companies should recruit more e-commerce experts. | **6** |

1 What are the challenges and constraints of writing a short story, as opposed to a novel? Think about characters, chronology, detail and any other points of your own.

2 Read the text below, taken from *An old-fashioned story*, a short story by American writer Laurie Colwin, that was published in 1981. What is the significance of the title, in your opinion?

Nelson Rodker was two years Elizabeth's senior, and was a model child in every way. Elizabeth, on the other hand, began her life as a rebellious, spunky and passionate child, but was extraordinarily pretty, and such children are never
5 called difficult; they are called original. It was their parents' ardent hope that their children might be friends and, when they grew up, like each other well enough to marry.

In order to ensure this, the children were brought together. If Elizabeth looked about to misbehave, her mother placed her
10 hand on Elizabeth's forearm and, with a little squeeze Elizabeth learned to dread, would say in tones of determined sweetness: 'Darling, don't you want to see Nelson's chemistry set?' Elizabeth did not want to see it – or his stamp collection. As she grew older, she did not want to dance with
15 Nelson or go to his school reception. But she did these things. That warm pressure on her forearm was as effective as a slap, although her compliance was not gained only by squeezes and horrified looks. Elizabeth had begun to have a secret life: she hated Nelson and the Rodkers with secret
20 fury. While she was too young to wonder if this loathing included her parents, she felt that if they forced Nelson upon her and chose the Rodkers for their dearest friends, they must in some way be against her. At the same time she realised that they were foolable. If she smiled at Nelson, they
25 were happy and considered her behaviour impeccable. If rude, she spent weeks in the pain of constant lectures. Thus, she learned to turn a cheerful face while keeping the fires of her dislike properly banked. The fact of the matter was that an afternoon of Nelson's stamp collection was good for two
30 afternoons hanging around the park with her real friends.

The beautiful daughters of the nervous well-to-do are tended like orchids, especially in New York. Elizabeth's friends were carefully picked over. The little O'Connor girl was common; that her father had won a Pulitzer prize was of no matter. The
35 one friend her mother approved of was Holly Lukas, whose mother was an old friend. Elizabeth never brought her real friends home, since, with the exception of Holly, they were all wrong: the children of broken homes, of people with odd political or religious preferences or of blacklisted movie
40 producers. Elizabeth learned the hard way that these children would not be made comfortable in her house. This might have put a crimp in Elizabeth's social life except that none of her friends wanted to entertain at home. They knew early on that the best place to conduct a private life was in public.

Like most girls her age, Elizabeth became horse crazy. She 45 did not want to share this passion with her parents, who felt riding once a week was quite enough, so she made a deal with the stable that, in exchange for a free lesson, she would clean out the stalls on Tuesdays. This, however, was not known by her mother, who had her expensively outfitted. These riding 50 clothes Elizabeth carried in a rucksack along with her real riding clothes – an old pair of blue jeans and a ratty sweater. It was soon discovered that Elizabeth was coming home late one extra afternoon a week stinking of horse. She was made to remove her jodhpurs at the service entrance and, when 55 these garments were found to be relatively horseless, a search was made and the offending jeans rooted out. Elizabeth was mute. One word about manure, and her riding days were over. But manure was not on her mother's mind and, in fact, when she learned that Elizabeth spent one day a week in the 60 company of a pitchfork, she was much relieved.

At college, Elizabeth had her first taste of freedom. While similarly restrained girls went wild, she reveled in being left alone and staying up late reading anything she liked. Her parents were not against reading, but Elizabeth's reading 65 habits contributed to eyestrain and bad posture and, besides, all that reading made one lopsided. At home on holidays she was correctness itself. In the middle of her first love affair, she was grown up enough to restrain herself from calling her beloved in Vermont, lest her parents find him on the 70 telephone bill. Elizabeth's parents set great store on adult behavior. Had they known what sort of adult Elizabeth had become, great would have been their dismay.

After graduation, her decision to live in New York was not easily come by, but she loved New York and wanted to enjoy 75 it finally on her own terms. Using as collateral a diamond-and-sapphire bracelet left to her by her grandmother, she borrowed enough money to rent an apartment in Greenwich Village. Through a friend of the O'Connor girl's father, she found a job at a publishing company and went to work. Her 80 parents were puzzled by this. The daughters of their friends were announcing their engagements in the *Times*. Elizabeth further puzzled them by refusing to take a cent of their money, although her mother knew the truth: what you dole out to the young binds them to you. To have Elizabeth owing 85 nothing was disconcerting to say the least.

3 For questions 1–7, choose the answer (A, B, C or D) which you think fits best according to the text.

1 What characterised Elizabeth's treatment as a young child?

  A She was surrounded with children who were older than her.

  B She was regarded by adults as being exceptionally intelligent.

  C She was excused any bad behaviour due to her good looks.

  D She was painstakingly prepared for future relationships.

2 What is implied about Elizabeth's childhood in the second paragraph?

  A She complied with her parents' wishes from a sense of duty.

  B She tolerated her mother's plans in order to achieve her own ends.

  C She spent time with Nelson despite his parents being set against her.

  D She disliked having to hide her true feelings from those around her.

3 What do we learn about Elizabeth's school friends in the third paragraph?

  A They were embarrassed that their parents had successful careers.

  B They were reluctant to invite friends back to their houses.

  C They felt uncomfortable in the presence of Elizabeth's mother.

  D They caused Elizabeth to come into conflict with her parents.

4 When Elizabeth's mother found out about her daughter's work at the riding school, she

  A calmed down, as she had been expecting something else.

  B was angry about the unnecessary purchase she had made.

  C was uninterested in anything to do with the riding school.

  D forced Elizabeth to throw away the old pair of jeans.

5 Why would Elizabeth's parents have been disappointed in her during her college days?

  A Her excessive reading went against how they had brought her up.

  B Her changed appearance would not have been as they wished it.

  C Her wild social life meant she could not be studying hard.

  D Her clandestine relationship would have shocked them.

6 Once she moved back to New York, Elizabeth resolved to

  A sell her grandmother's valuable bracelet.

  B stay a single working woman.

  C exist unsupported by her parents.

  D try to be more positive about the city.

7 What is the main implication of this text?

  A It is inevitable that people make friends within their own social class.

  B It is unnecessary to spend time gaining a good education in life.

  C It is worthwhile for parents to talk to their children's friends.

  D It is unrealistic of parents to expect to influence their children.

4 Explain the meaning of a–e in terms of the characters they relate to.

  a in tones of determined sweetness (lines 11–12)
  b turn a cheerful face (line 27)
  c tended like orchids (lines 31–32)
  d put a crimp in (line 42)
  e set great store on (line 71)

5 Elizabeth is said to have been a *rebellious, spunky* and *passionate* child. Find suitable opposites of these adjectives in the list below to describe Nelson. Then suggest opposites for the remaining words.

apathetic	articulate	brazen
callous	conventional	fickle
flawed	loquacious	spineless
trustworthy	unflappable	

Use some of these adjectives when describing characters in Writing folder 8.

Clauses 2

1   Look at these poems. What images do they create in your mind?

> *Pull the blinds*
> *   on your emotions*
> *Switch off your face.*
> *Put your love into neutral*
> *This way to the human race.*
> **Spike Milligan**

> I rue the day
> She went away
> And left me here
> To sip cold beer.
> **Bud Weiser**

> Once at Cold Mountain, troubles cease –
> No more tangled, hung-up mind.
> I idly scribble poems on the rock cliff
> Taking whatever comes, like a drifting boat.
> Gary Snyder

2   Can poetry be successfully translated? How much freedom should a
    translator have? Which poem would be easiest to translate into your
    language? Think of these aspects:

- rhyme
- rhythm
- idiom
- nuance

3   Read this review of a collection of poetry in translation. Use the
    word given in capitals at the end of some of the lines to form a word
    that fits in the space in the same line.

It's hard to issue (0) .....*predictions*...... on exactly what impact Jonathan Galassi's	**PREDICT**
superb translation and (1) .... of the Italian writer Eugenio Montale's	**ANALYSE**
Collected Poems: 1920-1954 will have on English-speaking (2) .... and,	**SCHOOL**
more importantly, on poets. Translations of poetry are often (3)	**TRUST**
today, not because, as the poet Robert Frost once claimed, 'Poetry is what gets	
lost in translation,' but because, (4) .... , the act of turning writing in	**SUPPOSE**
another language into writing in 'ours' is part of a larger (5)	**EMPIRE**
project. As a result, instead of attempting to feel and think beyond the boundaries	
of any single nation-state, much academic work (6) .... itself	**PRISON**
within a restrictively pure nationalist framework of literatures – 'American',	
'English', 'French'.	
(7) .... as I already was with Montale's poetry, my own reaction	**FAMILY**
has been an (8) .... one. After consuming his three main books in a	**EXPECT**
two-day gulp, I felt stunned by the concentrated power of his language. Without	
my particularly wanting them to, the poetry's cadences have infiltrated my	
memory, and its (9) .... images have invaded my dreams. As remote	**ENIGMA**
as Montale's poetry may be from one's own world view in the twenty-first	
century, it (10) .... has to be accommodated.	**NEVER**

Style extra

Find the five occurrences of *as* in the text in exercise 3. In which one could *though* be substituted?

What effect does the change in word order have in this example?

Though it is unlikely, *Unlikely though it is,*	*an original manuscript* *may still be found.*

Complete these sentences, using *as* or *though*.

a Although greatly acclaimed, I find this novel rather disappointing.
Greatly acclaimed ...

b Despite being entertaining, the play is lightweight in comparison with earlier works.
As ...

c Romano was a painter in addition to being a writer.
As ...

d 'A poem begins in delight and ends in wisdom.' *Robert Frost*
As ...

e Although the novel undoubtedly has a gripping storyline, its characters lack development.
Gripping ...

f I have tried to get into the book, but it remains impenetrable.
Much ...

Which of the sentences above contain concessive clauses? What other conjunctions are used in such clauses? Which are the most formal?

G ···> page 186

4 Even at Proficiency level, conjunctions are often confused or inaccurately used. Correct the errors in a–h.

a Although the nice atmosphere, it's a little bit noisy.

b We got on really well, despite that I only knew a little English.

c However it is not easy, I'm making progress day by day.

d Despite of what she felt towards him, making him wait was a game she truly enjoyed.

e Whereas one could see he was eager to talk, nothing came out of his mouth.

f Although that, I know that I will be a good mother.

g Even I was wrong, it didn't make any difference.

h He never achieved a similar success, in spite of he wrote fourteen more novels.

5 For questions 1–5, complete the second sentence so that it has a similar meaning to the first sentence, using the word given. Do not change the word given. You must use between three and eight words, including the word given.

1 It is permissible to lose rhyme in translation, but it is vital to preserve the cadences of a poem.
even
A translator must preserve a poem's cadences, ... in translation.

2 I've never attempted to write poetry, though I have had a go at short stories.
hand
Despite trying .... something I've never attempted.

3 Although poetry readings are fun, the way in which poems are read sometimes annoys me.
exception
Much as I .... how poems are read.

4 The biographer continued to make progress, albeit more slowly than at the beginning of the project.
initially
Good .... , work was now proceeding more slowly.

5 While most writers earn only modest royalties, a lucky few create a bestseller.
strike
A few writers .... earning only modest royalties is the norm.

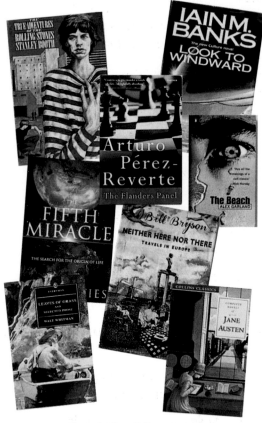

1 Identify the different genres shown in the picture. What kinds of books do you particularly enjoy reading? Say why you are attracted to this genre.

2 🎧 You are going to hear two people talking about books that have impressed them. In each case, name the book, explain what genre it is and summarise its qualities according to the speaker.

3 🎧 Listen again to note down the words which mean the same as a–h.

a engrossed
b overpowering
c take for granted
d conjectures
e classic
f perceptions
g painstaking
h bravery

Pronunciation

4 🎧 The first speaker spoke about the *subtleties* of the plot. Which consonant is silent in this word?

Silent consonants occur for different reasons. Often it is because pronunciation has changed over time without a corresponding change in spelling. Some words have come to English from another language, where they are pronounced differently.

Look at these words and underline any consonants you think are silent. Then listen to the recording to check the pronunciation.

knowledge	heir	dénouement	condemn
wretched	coup	pseudonym	apropos
rustle	indebted	doubt	penchant
rhythm	exhilarating	mnemonic	

5 Check your understanding of the words in exercise 4 by completing the word puzzle. What silent letter is contained in the vertical word that is revealed?

1	_ _ _ _ _ _	with regard to
2	_ _ _ _	a brilliant achievement
3	_ _ _ _ _ _ _ _	a memory aid often using rhyme
4	_ _ _ _ _ _ _	a particular liking for
5	_ _ _ _ _ _ _ _	not a real name
6	_ _ _ _ _ _ _ _	events at the end of a novel
7	_ _ _ _ _ _	very grateful

6 Look at the following Part 3 Speaking task.

> **How important is the printed book in the twenty-first century?**
>
> ➤ technological alternatives
> ➤ practical advantages
> ➤ educational issues

Decide which prompt on the card above each of these statements refers to. Give your own opinion on each one.

a Although I have a computer at home, I would never contemplate downloading a chapter of someone's novel and reading it on screen.

b Powerful though the arguments for the electronic book may be, there are huge development costs and the existing paper product is generally popular.

c Much as I enjoy sitting down with a good novel, I'm intrigued by the possibility of unlimited access on-line, not least the ability to track down obscure works that have been out of print for fifty years.

7 Plan your own talk on the importance of the book in the twenty-first century, working through the checklist below.

Planning stage

- ☐ Which ideas will you concentrate on, or will you touch on all three prompts?
- ☐ What other ideas do you intend to bring in?
- ☐ How will you introduce the talk?
- ☐ How will you move from one idea to another?
- ☐ What will your final point be?

Now record your talk. Stop after exactly three minutes and then analyse your talk, working through the checklist below.

Rehearsal analysis

- ☐ Did you cover all your ideas in the time?
- ☐ Were the ideas logically organised?
- ☐ In which part of the recording were you strongest? Why?
- ☐ Was there any repetition of ideas to cut out?
- ☐ Where could you have elaborated further?
- ☐ Were there any long pauses? How can you minimise these?
- ☐ Did you lack any specialist vocabulary? If so, how did you get round this?
- ☐ How large a variety of structures did you use? For example, did you remember to use concessive clauses?

8 For questions 1–5, think of one word only which can be used appropriately in all three sentences.

1 The director wore himself out trying to persuade the others that there were some fine tragic .... in the rest of the cast list.

Some look-alike .... are even being supplied in similar packaging to that used by the industry leader.

Originating in Spain, merino sheep are now found in many .... of the world, being well adapted to hot climates.

2 In recognition of Trevor's efforts, the company offered him a small .... of its gratitude.

This machine can only be operated by means of a special .... , obtainable from the kiosk opposite.

Residents who rarely exchanged a single word were seated next to each other and by this .... Mrs Thackeray found herself next to Miss Bellamy.

3 Her lawyer insisted she was the victim of a .... concocted by her ex-husband and his brother.

With its stylistic inconsistencies and the many credibility gaps in the .... , this book is a huge disappointment.

Sow lettuce and spinach on the vegetable .... in early March, for cutting in May and June.

4 An interim .... uniting all four committees has just been formed and will meet for the first time next month.

Although it has a black .... and thin black legs, the waitress swears that the fly is a mushroom root and is reluctant to replace the meal.

An increasing .... of evidence points to a definite link with the contaminated water supply.

5 Amaya traced the .... of his finger thoughtfully across his lower lip as he watched the forensics team at work.

The film has received six Oscar nominations and is a hot .... for the Best Director slot – eat your heart out, Spielberg!

People leave the countryside they claim to love looking like a .... and expect the council to foot the bill for cleaning it up.

Writing folder 8

Part 2 Set text question

Question 5 of Paper 2 offers three options, a), b) and c) – one on each of the specified set texts. You may be asked to write a review, article, report, essay or formal letter. It is essential that you refer clearly to the text you have studied, including appropriate detail and possibly brief quotation. Make sure you answer the question: don't just narrate the plot. Every set text question will demand more than narration – for example, description, comparison or evaluation.

1 Read this exam task.

A magazine is producing a special collection of readers' reviews entitled 'The importance of distinct characters in novels'. You decide to send in a review of the set text you have read, in which you give relevant information on the main characters and evaluate how successfully the author differentiates these characters.

Write your **review** in 300–350 words.

---

2 Now read the answer opposite and choose a suitable sentence opener (A–G) to fit the spaces (1–6). There is one extra opener that does not belong anywhere.

English Passengers is a magnificent achievement that, not surprisingly, took its author, Matthew Kneale, seven years to complete. It is a meticulously researched historical novel chronicling an expedition to Tasmania in 1857, where the theories of Darwinian evolution are juxtaposed with the religious beliefs of the day, often in a comical way. **1 [   ]** deals sensitively with the bigger historical picture of the tragic destruction of the Aboriginal islanders' way of life at the hands of white settlers, ex-convicts and religious 'do-gooders', who all in their separate ways contributed to the Aborigines' demise.

2 [   ], events are narrated by a cast of some twenty characters, whose 'first-hand' accounts span fifty years and combine to give the reader a truly epic novel, that is rich in detail and variety. **3 [   ]** largely through the varied use of language itself – from the formality of documents written by the island's governor, where official policy is revealed, to the base and harsh language used by convict Jack Harp. Shifty Captain Kewley incorporates words from his native Manx dialect into his vivid snapshots of the outward voyage, while the Reverend Geoffrey Wilson, the expedition's leader, has a predictably stiff style of narrating.

The pieces contributed by the expedition's doctor are written in scientific note-form, with judicious use of underlining to indicate his sinister concerns. This stylistic device, though hard to process at times, is most effective and develops as we learn more about Dr Potter's nefarious deeds. In the dénouement, the notes become more truncated and you can almost see him underlining in rage. **4 [   ]**, when Wilson goes mad, the author is able to use subtle changes in language to reflect his sorry state.

Perhaps the most difficult character to portray credibly through language is Peevay, the Aboriginal hero. **5 [   ]** even here the author successfully adopts a distinct style, incorporating paradoxical expressions learned from settlers, such as 'tidings of joy'. **6 [   ]**, the third expedition member Timothy Renshaw matures in the course of the novel and becomes the voice of reason and common sense. Helped by Peevay when abandoned in the wilderness, his awakening to the beauty of the land and decision to stay on the island could be seen as a final reconciliation.

A However, it has to be said that
B The author achieves this
C Last but not least
D Similarly
E Much as Kneale has tried
F Throughout the novel
G At the same time, the book

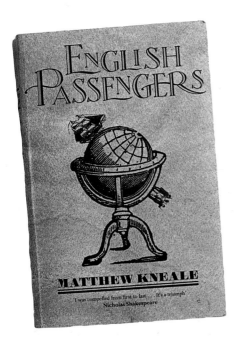

3 In the review, the book is referred to in different ways:

The pieces contributed by
In the dénouement,

Read these sentence openers and decide on their function, writing
B for reference to the book
E for evaluation
C for comparison.

a Up to this point, *B*
b In much the same way,
c Eventually,
d By and large,
e By the same token,
f Subsequent to this,
g To a certain extent,
h Within a matter of hours,
i On balance,
j As it turns out,
k For the most part,

Now write six sentences about the set text you are studying, choosing some of these openers.

EXAMPLE: *Up to this point, very little is known about the main character.*

4 The review refers to the book as a *meticulously researched historical novel*. Using adverb–adjective compounds like this will demonstrate your range of language. Make further adverb–adjective collocations from lists A and B and combine them with a suitable noun from list C. Only the adverbs should be used more than once.

EXAMPLE: *annoyingly paradoxical individual*
annoyingly trivial interpretation

A	**B**	**C**
annoyingly	accurate	characterisation
exquisitely	compelling	chronicle
hauntingly	detailed	depiction
ingeniously	enigmatic	hero
intensely	impressive	images
painstakingly	intricate	individual
subtly	moving	interpretation
utterly	paradoxical	narrative
zealously	pompous	plot
	realistic	portrayal
	trivial	protagonist
	woven	storyline

Advice

- When answering a set text question, decide what language functions the question requires.
- List ideas for each paragraph.
- Decide on key information to include about the book.
- Note down brief quotations (only if they are relevant!).
- Vary your linking devices.
- Introduce the book in different ways.
- Use as wide a range of language as you can.

5 Using the advice above, write the review outlined in exercise 1, referring to the set text you are studying. As a general rule, you should start a new paragraph for each character you introduce, but this will depend on the number of characters and level of detail you go into (see the review in exercise 2 for guidance).

Use of English

1   For questions 1–10, read the text below. Use the word given in capitals at the end of some of the lines to form a word in the space in the same line. There is an example at the beginning (**0**).

Mapping Biodiversity

Preserving (**0**) ....*organisms*....... in museums is one way of retaining them for posterity. But most people agree that it would be nice to keep a few of them alive in the wild, too. At the moment, which survive and which succumb is something of a lottery. WORLDMAP, a computer program, can help by dividing the areas of interest, those which are richest in species, into cells, and then examining the biodiversity of each cell. Planners would then be able to decide which areas are (**1**) .... for development on the grounds that they are areas of special (**2**) .... interest.

ORGAN

ACCEPT
SCIENCE

WORLDMAP can also predict the (**3**) .... of a hitherto (**4**) .... species being found in an area on the basis of its known distribution. Given the (**5**) .... nature of most records, that is a useful trick. And it can select (**6**) .... areas for preservation. These are not (**7**) .... the cells with the highest individual biodiversity, but rather those which, together, (**8**) .... what is preserved by picking places with the least (**9**) .... species.

LIKE
OBSERVE
PATCH
COMPLEMENT
NEED

MAXIMUM
OVERLAP

How much notice the world will actually take of such (**10**) .... is a different question.

RECOMMEND

2   For questions 1–6, think of one word only which can be used appropriately in all three sentences.

1   Make sure you present your information in the right .... when writing a letter of complaint.

To run for the team, simply complete the .... below and send it in by April 13.

At least he is in good .... again.

2   This case would be reported in the next .... of the magazine.

Let me just say that I take .... with the Minister over this question of public health.

Of course I believe he is evading the .... yet again.

3   News of their .... defeat was delayed for over three hours.

Her head swayed like a .... and exotic flower on a delicate stalk.

It was with a .... heart that I said goodbye to George at the station.

4   We will use the most modern technology to .... with the problems of decommissioning and nuclear waste.

Always remember to .... to the person on your right during a bridge competition.

They are the only ones to .... in the futures market and as a result they saw a lot of new work.

5   A confused computer gave the weary couple a .... awakening at one o'clock every morning.

Pietro guessed that the sign was .... , but he was too perturbed to pretend anger.

Amazingly, it was a child playing those haunting notes on a .... instrument.

6   Nick .... his drink down on the wooden seat and rushed indoors to answer the doorbell.

The Robinsons .... off at seven in the morning after a particularly frantic packing session.

If we .... the fire alarm going, we could leave the building in the confusion.

3 For questions 1–6, complete the second sentence so that it has a similar meaning to the first sentence, using the word given. Do not change the word given. You must use between three and eight words, including the word given.

1 'I always said I didn't do anything wrong!' the man said.

outset

From ....
.... doing anything wrong.

2 Luisa and I never agreed on anything to do with the children's education.

eye

Luisa and I ....
.... came to the children's education.

3 Although I am generally sympathetic towards them, I don't usually vote for the Green Party.

line

Much ....
.... taken by the Green Party, I don't usually vote for them.

4 I know you'll find it hard to believe, but I've never read any of Shakespeare's works.

seem

Unlikely ....
..............., I've never read any of Shakespeare's works.

5 Susie believes this job interview is really important.

store

Susie ....
.... this job interview.

6 We were surprised when Daphne made such a rapid recovery.

came

It ....
.... when Daphne made such a rapid recovery.

Writing

4 Improve the register and tone in this proposal, in an attempt to persuade the managing director to take action!

To Andy, our esteemed MD   April 1

We, the hard-working nerds in the IT Department, want to propose some changes to the daily grind. As you know, we're really whizz at sorting out the company's computing problems and, let's face it, you couldn't survive without us. To guarantee a rapid response, we've always been willing to burn the midnight oil when the need arises. But no more, mate! If you want us to slave away like this, you're gonna have to provide us with better conditions, which we demand herewith.

Firstly, it is totally out of order to expect any of us to struggle to work on the bus. Lots of us hit our desks by 6.00 in the morning and most of the guys are still hanging around after the pubs have shut. We therefore insist that you cough up for five stretch limos to provide us with adequate door-to-door transport. The pay-off for you is obvious: increased productivity and goodwill.

And another thing, we are fed up with the rubbish served up in your so-called restaurant downstairs and want our own top-class chef and eatery, to be located on this floor. Give us two hours minimum for lunch, or else – we need a quick catnap before going back to our screens.

Thirdly, to be brutally honest, the money you pay round here is peanuts. How come you've just landed a fat bonus and we've got the big 'O'? Put your money where your mouth is! We're warning you, if you don't do something about it pronto, you won't see us for dust.

We look forward to hearing from you before midday. Get the message, you April fool?

Frank

⋯❯ Crossword page 191

UNIT 17 Defining happiness

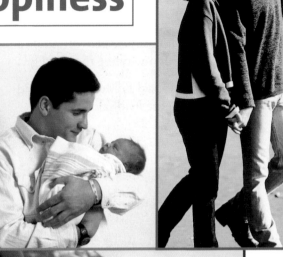

1 Explain the meaning of each of these quotes and say which comes closest to your own views on the nature of happiness.

'Happiness is not being pained in body or troubled in mind.'
'A person is never happy except at the price of some ignorance.'
'Happiness makes up in height for what it lacks in length.'
'All happiness depends on a leisurely breakfast.'

2 Most of these words occur in the recording you are about to hear. Check your understanding by putting them into four meaning groups of three words each.

bliss	contagious	ecstasy	ephemeral
fleeting	foster	idyll	infectious
virulent	nurture	sustain	transient

3 🎧 You will hear two people, Miriam and Ian, discussing their personal views on happiness. For questions 1–6, decide whether the opinions are expressed by only one of the speakers, or whether the speakers agree.

Write   M   for Miriam,
          I   for Ian,
or   B   for Both, where they agree.

1 Happiness is only ever an ephemeral sensation.
2 Domestic harmony is a precondition for happiness.
3 To experience happiness you have to be in a safe environment.
4 Feelings of happiness are usually triggered by something specific.
5 I impose restrictions on my choice of music during times of extreme happiness.
6 Good food is conducive to the experiencing of happiness.

❶diom spot

🎧 Listen again for the following idiomatic expressions and explain their meaning.

a be on cloud nine
b rose-tinted spectacles
c the bee's knees
d put yourself on the line
e tip the balance
f lotus-eating
g in my book
h food for thought

Choose four of the expressions above to use of situations 1–4.

1 In a roomful of people, Jack was the only one to stand up and challenge the speaker.
2 The U2 concert had put Sheena in a really good mood.
3 I think children should show respect for their elders.
4 They were undecided whether to take the day off, but then they saw the sun was shining.

Style extra

Metaphor

In the recording, Ian talks about *infectious* laughter, using the adjective metaphorically. The *Cambridge International Corpus* shows that many words to do with illness and health are used in this way.

4 Form collocates from the adjectives (list A) and nouns / noun phrases (list B) below. There may be more than one possible match.

A	B
bruised	bank balance
contagious	criticism
fatal	dose of scepticism
feverish	egos
healthy	flaw in the argument
jaundiced	loser
sick	sense of humour
sore	state of activity
	turnout of voters

5 Here are some sets of verbs that are often used metaphorically. Give each set a heading to reflect meaning and add any similar verbs. You can check their metaphorical use in a dictionary – or visit an on-line corpus.

EXAMPLE: break out, erupt, hurt, wound – *medical/health*
similar verb: *ache*

a bloom, flourish, mushroom, spring up
b flow, ooze, ripple out, trickle
c burn out, flare up, ignite, smoulder
d blow up, break, rage, sweep
e dazzle, light up, shine, sparkle
f boil, bubble, simmer, stew

6 Make a noun phrase by combining an expression from list A with one from list B. Then use the phrase in your own sentence, continuing the theme with a suitable verb from exercise 5.

EXAMPLE: *A flash of wild inspiration sparkled in her eyes.*

But a word of warning – don't mix your metaphors! For example, it would sound odd to talk about *a wave of sympathy igniting*, because waves are not associated with fire.

A	B
a crop of	critical reviews
an epidemic of	feverish activity
a flash of	minor complaints
a glut of	public sympathy
an outbreak of	pure joy
a plague of	scandalous stories
a storm of	spontaneous laughter
a surge of	unfair publicity
a wave of	violent protests
a whirlwind of	wild inspiration

7 In this extract from *My family and other animals*, the writer and naturalist Gerald Durrell recalls his idyllic childhood on the island of Corfu. For questions 1–6, read the text and decide which answer (A, B, C or D) best fits each gap.

Gradually the magic of the island settled over us as gently and clingingly as pollen. Those were (1) .... days, each with a tranquillity, a timelessness, about it, so that you (2) .... it would never end. But then the dark skin of night would (3) .... and there would be a fresh day waiting for us, glossy and colourful as a child's transfer, and with the same (4) .... of unreality. In the morning, when I woke, the bedroom shutters were luminous and barred with gold from the rising sun. The (5) .... morning air was full of the scent of charcoal from the kitchen fire, full of eager cock-crows, the distant (6) .... of dogs, and the unsteady, melancholy tune of the goat-bells as the flocks were driven out to pasture.

	A	B	C	D
1	elegiac	halcyon	sterile	Elysian
2	yearned	dreamed	wished	aspired
3	hang back	draw in	peel off	spring up
4	stain	shield	fleck	tinge
5	heady	strong	infectious	stimulating
6	bleat	yap	screech	purr

8 Where in the text does Durrell use similes and metaphor?

Think of a particular moment when you were utterly content. Where were you? What was happening around you? Describe the scene and explain how you felt, making use of metaphor.

Comparison

1   The following lists relating to happiness summarise the views of the Greek philosopher Epicurus. How far do they still hold true today, in your opinion? Would you add anything in each column?

WHAT IS AND IS NOT ESSENTIAL FOR HAPPINESS		
Natural and necessary	**Natural but unnecessary**	**Neither natural nor necessary**
Friends	Grand house	Fame
Freedom	Private baths	Power
Thought	Banquets	
Food	Servants	
Shelter	Fish, meat	
Clothes		

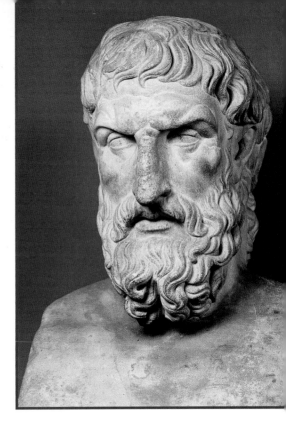

2   Read this text about Epicurus. For questions 1–15, think of the word which best fits each space. Use only one word in each space.

Epicurus, who was born on the verdant island of Samos, took early (0) ....*to*.......... philosophy. When only 14, he started travelling, to learn from the likes (1) .... the Platonist Pamphilus. Finding himself at (2) .... with much of this teaching, he decided to define his own philosophy of life.
(3) .... immediately set this philosophy apart from (4) .... lines of thought was (5) .... emphasis on sensual pleasure. (6) .... , if any, philosophers had ever made admissions of this kind and Epicurus shocked many, (7) .... least when he set up a school (8) .... very aim was to promote happiness. Nevertheless, (9) .... outrage and criticism, his teachings attracted support and spread (10) .... afield, from Syria to Gaul. Even today, Epicurus's name lives on in many languages in adjectival form – in English, 'Epicurean' signifies being dedicated (11) .... the pursuit of pleasure.
In fact, Epicurus drank water (12) .... than wine, and usually dined on bread, vegetables and a palmful of olives. (13) .... were the tastes of the man who, after rational analysis, had (14) .... the striking conclusion that the essential ingredients of happiness were the most inexpensive, (15) .... elusive they might be.

3   What triggers happiness? Compare these pairs of situations and say which would make you happier, explaining why. Use the adjectives given in their comparative forms.

a   – You are offered a free trip to New York.
    – A friend who has been seriously ill makes a complete recovery.
    (glad)

b   – You win some prize money in a competition.
    – You find something special, which you thought you had lost.
    (delighted)

c   – A relation takes you for a meal and pays the bill.
    – You are out on a long walk without any food and someone gives you a big bar of chocolate.
    (content)

4 There are many near synonyms for *happy* in English. Here are definitions for three of them.

exhilarated /ɪgˈzɪləreɪtɪd/ *adj* very excited and happy • *We finally got home at 9 o'clock exhausted but exhilarated.*

for·tu·nate /£ ˈfɔːtʃənət $ ˈfɔːr-/ *adj approving* having good things happen to you • *You're very fortunate to have found such a pleasant house.* [+ *to* infinitive] • *I feel I'm a very fortunate person having so many choices.* [+ v-ing] • *He was fortunate in his choice of assistant.* • *It was fortunate that they had left in plenty of time.* [+ that clause]

ec·sta·tic /£ ɪkˈstæt·ɪk, $ -ˈstæt̬-/ *adj* • *The new president was greeted by an ecstatic crowd.* • *(infml) I wasn't exactly ecstatic (= I was not pleased)* **about/at/over** *being woken up at four o'clock in the morning.*

Now say which of the six situations in exercise 3 above would make you feel

- the most ecstatic
- the most exhilarated
- the most fortunate.

5 Comment on the following statements, which illustrate more ways of making comparisons. You don't have to agree!

a I'm as happy now as I was at the age of 10.
b I'd far rather spend time with close friends at home than be wined and dined at expensive restaurants.
c I'd much sooner be a penniless student than a lonely millionaire.
d Possessing wealth is nowhere near as important as being in good health.
e Listening to CDs of live concerts is nothing like as exhilarating as taking part in an actual live event.
f Watching a football match is not as much fun as playing in one.
g Going on holiday is by far the best remedy for a broken heart.
h Relaxing by a warm fire is a good deal better than being out in a snowstorm.

G ⋯⋗ page 186

6 For questions 1–6, complete the second sentence so that it has a similar meaning to the first sentence, using the word given. Do not change the word given. You must use between three and eight words, including the word given.

1 Our friends in Paris did everything they could in making us feel welcome.
stops
Our friends in Paris ....
.... make us feel welcome.

2 Graham took back his words on noticing there were fresh strawberries on the menu.
tune
Graham ....
when he noticed fresh strawberries were on the menu.

3 We found it difficult not to laugh because the situation was so funny.
keep
We found it difficult to ....
.... a funny situation.

4 Jenny felt elated when she won the regional skating competition.
nine
Jenny was ....
place in the regional skating competition.

5 Reading a thriller is far more enjoyable if you don't know the ending.
nowhere
Reading a thriller is ....
.... fun if you already know the ending.

6 Last year Ralph had a luxurious lifestyle, but since he lost his job, he has had to make a few changes.
clover
Last year Ralph was ....
.... made redundant, he has had to make a few changes.

Full summary task 1

1 Use these pictures to define the term 'quality of life'.

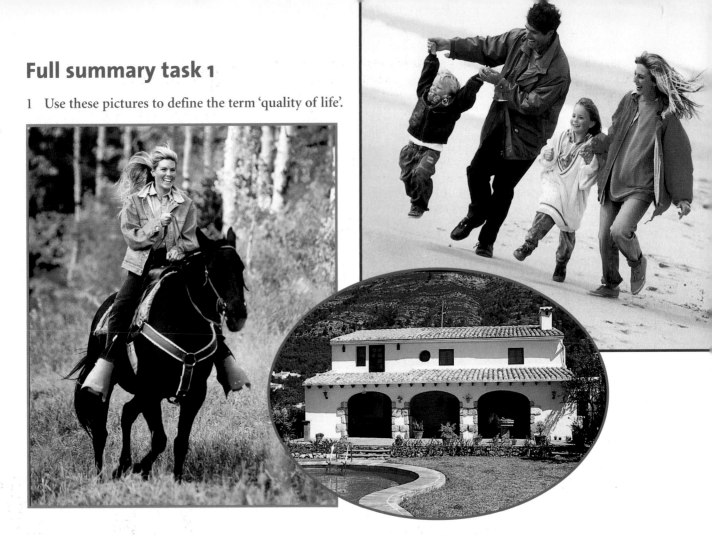

2 For questions 1–5, read the following texts on quality of life. For questions 1–4, answer with a word or short phrase. You do not need to write complete sentences. For question 5, write a summary according to the instructions given.

Quality of life is a broad concept, of which happiness forms only a part. Often the term refers to quality of the living environment. Ecologists employ the phrase when appealing against environmental degradation; sociologists speak of it when evaluating a society. Here, external conditions are equated with the good life itself.

The term also denotes how well people cope, and is commonly used in the therapeutic professions. Medical doctors refer to quality of life as the (restored) ability to work and love, while in psychological discourse, the term refers to mental propensities, such as realism and vitality.

The above two meanings describe preconditions for a good life, rather than the good life itself. A third meaning focuses on the latter connotation and characterises the quality of life in terms of its outcomes: 'products' and 'enjoyment'. Products are what a life leaves behind – in socio-cultural terms, a contribution to the human heritage, but from a
line 15 purely biological perspective, procreation, for otherwise the evolutionary
line 16 mission ends in failure. As for enjoyment, the focus is on personal experience of life, and it is in this sense that happiness is subsumed.

1 Explain in your own words why it might be apt for ecologists to refer to the term 'quality of life'.
2 What is meant by the phrase 'evolutionary mission' in lines 15–16?

E xam spot

Remember the importance of reformulation – you will lose marks if you use words that occur in the texts.

Six months ago, friends we left behind in London expressed envy at our newfound quality of life in the breathtakingly beautiful Lake District.

line 3   Our move was a desperate attempt to redress the balance, abandoning the rat-race in search of a new lifestyle that was admittedly nowhere near as lucrative, but much healthier for all concerned.

We revelled in the sheer novelty of it all: a cosy cottage, enough grazing land for our daughter's newly-acquired pet lamb, and, thanks to a healthy bank balance, a token amount of work, combined with long autumnal walks in the fells. Life was beautiful.

As winter set in, so did reality. Things we had hitherto taken for granted, like access to schools and shops, were now under threat. Now, with spring
line 12   just around the corner, our idyll has finally been shattered by the grim
line 13   reaper: foot and mouth disease. The countryside is dying and hill farmers, who have in any case been struggling to make ends meet, face ruin.

Restrictions on movement have put an end to our hill-walking and yesterday, my daughter watched uncomprehendingly as her pet lamb was led away. Her elder brother accuses us of wrecking their lives. How tenuous happiness is.

3   What is implied by the writer in the words 'a desperate attempt to redress the balance' in line 3?

4   Explain the meaning of 'grim reaper' in lines 12–13.

3   Circle the best synonym for the following words, according to how they are used in the texts.

   a   *environment* – atmosphere, habitat, surroundings
   b   *propensities* – dispositions, susceptibilities, weaknesses
   c   *outcome* – denouement, finale, result
   d   *lucrative* – advantageous, productive, remunerative
   e   *token* – hollow, nominal, superficial
   f   *restrictions* – constraints, inhibitions, stipulations
   g   *tenuous* – doubtful, flimsy, slim

4   Now answer the summary task below, using some of the synonyms from exercise 3.

In a paragraph of between 50 and 70 words, summarise in your own words as far as possible the factors which, according to the two texts, promote happiness and well-being.

Idiom spot

In the second text, the idiom *make ends meet* is used. What does it mean?

Choose suitable idioms to match the cartoons below and then explain the meaning of all eight.

cut corners
down and out
keep your head above water
feel the pinch
in the red
on a shoestring
on your uppers
tighten your belt

Exam folder 9

Paper 4 Part 1
Multiple-choice questions

In Part 1 of Paper 4 you will hear four short extracts. There will be a mixture of monologues – only one person speaking – or a conversation between two, or possibly more, speakers. There are two questions for each extract with a choice of three answers for each question. You will hear each extract twice.

Here are some examples of the types of questions.

What does the speaker say about ...?
What do the speakers agree on?
What is the speaker comparing X to?
Why does the speaker say ...?
What does the speaker think about?
How did the speaker feel about ...?

Advice

- You have 15 seconds to read the questions before you hear each extract. Make good use of this time.
- Use the first hearing to get a general idea of what the extract is about. The questions are in the order in which you will hear the answer on the recording. However, you sometimes need to hear the whole extract to answer some questions.
- Always keep the questions in mind when you answer. Some of the choices for each question may look correct, but not answer the question.
- The second time you hear the extract, mark your answer on your answer sheet.
- Always put an answer, even if you aren't sure. You have a 33% chance of getting it right.
- Points aren't deducted for wrong answers.

Normally in Part 1 there are four different extracts. Only two extracts are included here to give you an idea of what you might expect in the examination.

1 You will hear two different extracts. For questions 1–4, choose the answer (A, B or C) which fits best according to what you hear. There are two questions for each extract.

Extract One

You hear two people talking about a new CD by the singer Ellen Gray.

1 What does the man say about Ellen Gray?
   A She's known to be unconventional.
   B She's uninterested in fame and success.
   C She's not always had an easy singing career.

2 What do the speakers agree about?
   A The CD will be too commercial for some of her fans.
   B The CD is a radical departure from previous work.
   C The CD contains a mixture of musical genres.

Extract Two

You will hear a woman talking about an artist's latest exhibition.

3 What does the speaker say about Kate Schermerhorn?
   A She's at her best portraying working-class people.
   B She insists she prefers working in London to the USA.
   C Her work would appear to contradict what she has said.

4 What is the speaker's opinion of the exhibition?
   A The artist is mocking her subjects.
   B The subject matter is in poor taste.
   C The photos evoke nothing but apathy in the viewer.

Paper 4 Part 3
Multiple-choice questions

In Part 3 of Paper 4 you will hear a conversation between two speakers. In the case of an interview, there might also be a presenter. There are five questions, all in the order in which you hear the information you need to answer them. The five questions each have a choice of four answers. The questions are testing whether you can understand the speaker's opinion, what the speaker is saying generally or in detail and also what you can infer from the conversation. You will hear the conversation twice.

Advice

- You have one minute to read the questions and possible answers.
- Don't get stuck on one question. Make sure you are always reading ahead so that you don't get lost.
- For more advice on how to answer the questions, see the Advice box for Part 1, opposite.

2   You will hear an interview with Darren Roberts, who recently decided to give up his well-paid job in the City of London in order to do voluntary work. For questions 1–5, choose the answer (A, B, C, or D) which fits best according to what you hear.

1   Why did Darren take so long to decide to leave his job in the City?
   A   He thought his lack of motivation was only temporary.
   B   He needed to put in place his financial arrangements.
   C   He enjoyed the atmosphere at work.
   D   He wasn't qualified to do anything else.

   1

2   Why was it so hard for Darren to get a new job?
   A   He had applied to the wrong people.
   B   He gave the impression of being unsuitable.
   C   He was only available for six months.
   D   He was not persistent enough.

   2

3   How did Darren react when he got his new job?
   A   He felt very pessimistic about his abilities.
   B   He felt able to tell ex-colleagues his true feelings.
   C   He suddenly got cold feet.
   D   He decided to accept the challenge.

   3

4   How did Darren get on in his new environment?
   A   The slow pace got on his nerves at first.
   B   He felt rather patronised by some of his workmates.
   C   He fitted into the routine of things quite quickly.
   D   It made him less cynical about people's motives.

   4

5   Darren is planning to continue in the voluntary sector because he believes
   A   he is temperamentally more suited to the work.
   B   he wasn't smart enough to cope with his previous job.
   C   there was no feeling of achievement in his old job.
   D   the shorter hours are better.

   5

1 The statements below form part of the Universal Declaration of Human Rights, adopted
   by the United Nations in 1948. How far are these statements adhered to in today's world?

   • No one shall be held in slavery or servitude.
   • No one shall be subjected to arbitrary arrest, detention or exile.
   • Everyone has the right to a nationality.
   • Everyone has the right to freedom of thought, conscience and religion.

2 You are going to read an extract from a book on human
   rights. Seven paragraphs have been removed from the extract.
   Choose from the paragraphs A–H the one which fits each gap (1–7).
   There is one extra paragraph which you do not need to use.

Values for a godless age

When the Berlin Wall came tumbling down in 1989 so did the plaster cast which had kept the idea of human rights in limbo. It was now free to evolve in response to the changing conditions of the late twentieth century.

 1

Of course, in one sense, the quest for universal human rights standards after the Second World War was an early attempt to communicate across national boundaries, albeit a rather faltering endeavour, with its claims to universality challenged both in terms of authorship and content. More recently, a loosening of the reins of the human rights dialogue has ushered in wider debate.

2

Perhaps the best known of these is Amnesty International, established in 1961. Before Amnesty, there were very few organizations like it, yet now there are thousands operating all over the world. Whether campaigning for the protection of the environment or third-world debt relief, any such organization is engaged in the debate about fundamental human rights. And it is no longer just a soft sideshow.

3

The fact that strangers from different countries can communicate with each other through the worldwide web is having a similar effect in dealing a blow to misinformation. During one recent major human rights trial over sixty websites sprang up to cover the proceedings, while sales of the government-controlled newspaper in that country plummeted.

4

The effect of increased responsibility at this highest level has been to continually extend the consideration of who is legally liable, directly or indirectly, under international human rights law. In part, this is an acknowledgement that even individuals need to be held responsible for flagrant breaches of others' rights, whether these are preventing protesters from peacefully demonstrating or abusing the rights of children.

5

It has been noted that paradoxically, in such circumstances, it may be in the interests of human rights organizations to seek to reinforce the legitimacy and authority of the state, within a regulated global framework.

6

Part of the new trend in human rights thinking is therefore to include powerful private bodies within its remit. The International Commission of Jurists has recently explored ways in which international human rights standards could be directly applied to transnational corporations.

7

Whatever the way ahead, the lessons of the past must be learnt. Any world view or set of values which is presented as self-evident is ultimately doomed to failure. The case for human rights always needs to be made and remade. In a world where globalization too often seems like a modernized version of old-fashioned cultural imperialism, it is important to query the claim that human rights are universally accepted. ◆

A The problem is that the growth of globalization makes the protection of nation states a pointless goal in certain circumstances. Transnational corporations with multiple subsidiaries operating in a number of countries simultaneously wield significant economic and political power and it is often extremely difficult for the state – both home and host governments – to exercise effective legal control over them.

B If the proliferation of pressure groups has raised the profile of the human rights debate, satellite television has reinforced much of the content of their campaigns. The fact that from our armchairs we can all see live what is happening to others around the world has had an enormous impact on the way the struggle for human rights is viewed. It would not be remotely believable to plead ignorance nowadays, for 24-hour news coverage from the world's hotspots reaches us all.

C This is, after all, a uniquely propitious time, as the values and language of human rights are becoming familiar to more and more people, who judge the merits or otherwise of political and economic decisions increasingly in human rights terms. Arguments seem fresh and appealing in many quarters where once they sounded weak and stale.

D On a global scale, it is not strong states that are the problem here but weak ones, as they fail to protect their citizens from private power – whether it is paramilitaries committing murder and torture or transnational corporations spreading contamination and pollution.

E One of the most significant of these is what has come to be called 'globalization', the collapsing of national boundaries in economic, political and cultural life. From the expanding role of the world's financial markets and the spread of transnational corporations to the revolution in communications and information technology, more and more areas of people's lives are affected by regional, international or transnational developments, whether they are aware of this or not.

F Not only must states not infringe rights, and enforce those rights which fall within their direct sphere (like providing a criminal justice system or holding fair elections), but they also have 'positive obligations' to uphold rights enshrined in human rights treaties, even when it is private parties which have violated them.

G The results of its investigations were published in 1999 in a unique pamphlet on *Globalization, Human Rights and the Rule of Law*. The issue to be faced is whether to treat these and other corporations as 'large para-state entities to be held accountable under the same sort of regime as states', or whether to look for different approaches to accountability 'that are promulgated by consumer groups and the corporations themselves'.

H No longer the preserve of representatives of nation states meeting under the auspices of the United Nations, a developing conversation is taking place on a global scale and involving a growing cast of people – for an increasing range of pressure groups now frame their aspirations in human rights terms.

3 How do you view the future for universal human rights? Will increasing globalisation lead to more or less freedom for the individual?

4 Look back at the extract and find words or phrases which mean the same as a–f.

   a caught between two stages of development
   b a relatively weak attempt
   c a relaxing of the rules
   d a less important event
   e causing something or someone great difficulties
   f brief or scope

5 Replace these words and phrases in paragraphs A–H with suitable synonyms or phrases.

   a wield … power (A)
   b proliferation (B)
   c raised the profile (B)
   d propitious (C)
   e infringe (F)
   f enshrined in (F)
   g promulgated by (G)
   h under the auspices of (H)

Modals review

1 Should animals enjoy the same rights as humans? Outline your views with reference to the animal welfare poster shown.

The EU Chemicals Strategy

☠ HARMFUL IF SWALLOWED

100,000 chemicals
10,000,000 dead animals
0 credibility

BUAV
campaigning to end
animal experiments
British Union for the
Abolition of Vivisection   www.StopEUChemicalTests.com

PeTA
People for the Ethical
Treatment of Animals

2 🎧 Listen to this extract about the use of animals in medical research. Is the speaker for or against animal testing? Why?

The speaker used various modal verbs to express different functions. Here are two examples.

Animals must be used in order to trial new drugs and treatments safely. (obligation)
It could in fact be damaging to human health. (speculation)

Before you do exercise 3, turn to the Grammar folder to review the different functions modal verbs have.

G ⋯⋙ pages 186–7

3 As the *Cambridge Learner Corpus* shows, modal verbs often cause problems, even at Proficiency level. Correct any errors in these sentences. One sentence is correct.

  a Animals could be kept in zoos, but they must to have a comfortable place to live in.
  b I've written a few notes about things that may be changed if the campaign is to succeed.
  c His dog ought to be registered because then they might have been able to trace it.
  d Much more should have been done to bring this epidemic under control.
  e You mustn't have been here last summer – the café only opened a month ago.
  f I needn't have bought these batteries if I had known you were going to buy some too.
  g If only we should live our lives again, knowing what we know now!
  h It can't be possible for you to phone back later?

4 Choose the correct modal form in each of these sentences.

  a I *needn't have / shouldn't have* gone out last night as I had so much work to do.
  b You *might have / needed to have* rung me to say you'd missed the bus – I was worried sick.
  c It *must have / could have* been a full three hours later when the ship finally docked.
  d Legally, people *mustn't / needn't* vote in a general election if they don't want to.
  e I'm sure I *don't have to / mustn't* remind you of the need for confidentiality.
  f You really *shouldn't / needn't* cover up for him every time – you'll get yourself into trouble one day.
  g *Need / Ought* I to have let someone know about this earlier?
  h *Would / Might* you mind if I didn't give you a lift all the way home tonight?

5 For questions 1–6, complete the second sentence so that it has a similar meaning to the first sentence, using the word given. Do not change the word given. You must use between three and eight words, including the word given.

1 You didn't spend enough time on this project.
   put
   You ought .... hours on this project.

2 Factory farming was surely less humane before these guidelines were established.
   prior
   Factory farming must .... of these guidelines.

3 I really admire people who are prepared to risk their job for the sake of their principles.
   line
   I really admire people who are prepared .... for the sake of their principles.

4 You should have spilled the beans about Lisa before now.
   let
   If only you could .... secret before now.

5 It's time the organisation told the truth about the misuse of its funds.
   straight
   The organisation should set .... its funds were misused.

6 Would you mind if I asked you to sign this petition?
   raise
   Would you .... asking you to sign this petition?

6 For questions 1–10, read the text below. Use the word given in capitals at the end of some of the lines to form a word that fits in the space in the same line.

Mankind's intuition of freedom, and our (0) _identification_ of freedom with knowledge, sets us apart from animals. The	IDENTIFY
animal's grasp of freedom is (1) .... in comparison, being only the freedom to respond to external stimuli. The	SIGNIFY
nearest creature to us on the (2) .... tree of life, the	EVOLVE
chimpanzee, cannot retain an image for a (3)	SUFFICE
length of time to be able to reflect on it. So animal life is largely a matter of conditioned reflexes, performed in an (4)	TERMINATE
present; in short, animals are little more than machines with	
(5)	CONSCIOUS
While the animal is carried along (6) .... on the stream	SUBMIT
of time, mankind has certain capacities that (7)	POWER
us to resist the current or look into the future. Our (8)	RESOURCE
invention of language was the first step towards this 'conquest of time'. Language 'fixes' experiences, and places the experience of	
the past on an equal (9) .... with that of the present.	FOOT
Imagination was bound to follow, as a (10)	NATURE
progression from 'labelling' a past experience to conjuring up its mental image.	

Paper 5 Part 2

1   Identify what aspect of freedom – or the lack of it – is shown in
    the three pictures A–C, using some of these words and phrases.

civil disobedience   political regime   free speech
sweatshop   child labour

2   🎧 Now listen to the first stage of a Speaking test Part 2 based on these
    pictures. Do both candidates do what is required? Could the discussion
    have been more balanced? If so, how?

3   🎧 Listen to the second stage of the same task. What two additional aspects
    of 'freedom' do the candidates decide to include?

Pronunciation

4 🎧 Read the Exam spot and then listen to utterances a–f taken from the recording. Notice how the speakers stress certain words and vary their intonation.

a Anyway, what about picture A? What might have happened after that photo was taken?

b I didn't say they succeeded.

c Looking at picture B, I suppose it's illustrating the rights of the individual, isn't it?

d Yes, that's an important point, you don't have that freedom of choice everywhere.

e Speaking purely for myself, I'd want to include something on education.

f I'm not sure that's strictly about freedom, though.

Exam spot

Pronunciation, including stress and intonation, is assessed in Paper 5. It is important that what you say has some rhythm and flows as connected speech. Stress important content words and remember to vary your intonation according to whether you are asking a question, agreeing with something or contrasting information. Don't worry if you have problems pronouncing individual sounds – what is important is the overall effect, which must be easy to understand.

5 Now read this task, which is based on the same set of photos.

Imagine that all these photographs have been entered for an award: *Most powerful image in journalism.* Talk about the message that each picture conveys and decide which one should win the award. You have three minutes for this.

Think quickly of one or two points to make about each picture. When you are both ready to start, note the time. Speak for the full three minutes. Remember to give your partner a chance to speak!

6 For questions 1–6, think of one word only which can be used appropriately in all three sentences.

1 Following a strong opening on Wall Street, the market made a modest .... , closing the day up 2.7 at 2030.7.

It would turn into a victory .... if he could go to the conference having won a second term in office.

Undoubtedly this was the best .... of the match, crowned by a brilliantly-disguised forehand down the line.

2 Tony turned up the radio, ... the lights, and sped on through the gloom.

Although I've .... into a lot of his theories, I've never quite got to grips with any of them.

The knife should ideally be .... in boiling water between cutting each slice.

3 The poor man didn't understand more than the general .... of the conversation and looked baffled and tired.

Rural poverty was a problem until the 1970s, when the .... of people to the towns narrowed the gap.

When we looked out the next morning, a .... of snow over a metre high had all but buried the gate.

4 There are fears in some .... that the ending of the scheme could cause recruitment problems for schools.

The house has 25 rooms, including special .... for visiting royals.

The rockface looked much steeper at close .... and the ill-prepared group began to wish they'd stayed in bed.

5 Six massive stone pillars were .... the arches that ran across the top.

How long have you been .... Real Madrid, may I ask?

John and Maryanne are more than capable of .... themselves financially.

6 Males have dark plumage and a golden crest covering head and .... , and utter a call like a bull bellowing.

Both the Senate and the House of Representatives are about to pass a .... that will deal a serious blow to the campaign.

I had a considerable amount of cash on me, but the .... came to a lot more!

Writing folder 9

Part 1 Essay

Writing folder 3 also dealt with the Paper 2 Part 1 essay task. Look back at the advice given. This Writing folder focuses on the range and accuracy of language used.

1 Read this exam task.

You must answer this question. Write your answer in 300–350 words in an appropriate style.

You have had a class discussion on the nature of personal freedom in contemporary society. Now your tutor has asked you to write an essay, using your notes below and giving your own opinions on this subject.

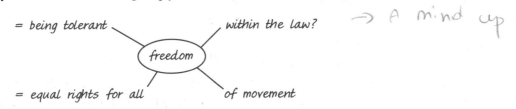

= being tolerant   within the law?   → A mind up

freedom

= equal rights for all   of movement

Write your **essay**.

2 List your own ideas on the diagram. Then read the sample answer below.

To talk about the nature of freedom in contemporary society, you need to think about freedom within the law and freedom outside it for the people. This essay thinks about both sides and also how to be tolerant, equal rights for all and freedom of movement.

According to me, every society it needs to have the law and people all must live within the law. With no law, nobody knows what is right and wrong and someone would get hurt, maybe. Is that freedom? Besides, sometimes people cannot show their religion because they are frightening. This is a problem for those people.

On the other hand I think we must be tolerant of others and what they think and do, but not if they break the law. If I steal your car, you won't have freedom of movement any more, that's what I mean by abiding with the law.

Of course yes, I really think there must be equal rights for all. We do not have this everywhere because in some parts of the world is slavery. Children of four are sold by their families and must work in richer countries, even they don't want. This is not freedom for them. Other countries should think about this so that everyone has freedom.

I think that in contemporary society we think we are free but we all aren't and that's a problem.

3 Tick the boxes that apply to the sample answer. What else do you notice about it?

- ☐ Limited range of vocabulary and expression
- ☐ Reasonably fluent and natural use
- ☐ Evidence of stylistic devices
- ☐ Register and format generally appropriate
- ☐ Adequate range of structures
- ☐ Some attempt at organisation
- ☐ Inadequate development of topic
- ☐ Errors sometimes impede communication

4 To demonstrate your own range of vocabulary and expression, you should avoid using words and phrases from the question if possible.

Underline anything in the first paragraph that comes from the question and then rewrite it, using some of the words and phrases below. Cut any ideas that are unclear, and make any changes and additions necessary to improve it.

human rights civil liberty	
today's world modern life the 21st century	
prejudice broad-minded open-minded	
social code criminal legal system illegal	
confined transfer	

5 The sample answer uses the verb *think* seven times. Replace all these instances with other verbs, for example, *consider, believe, view*, or rewrite them in another way, for example *In my opinion … .*

6 Now work through paragraphs 2 and 4, making improvements to the range of language used. Include the following:

Paragraph 2
it goes without saying that …
the absence of
abide by
worship
multicultural

Paragraph 4
still exists
as young as
forced to
an infringement of their rights
campaign for an end to

7 Paragraph 3 shows some misunderstanding of the question. Explain what this is and comment on the style and register used here.

8 The answer is about 230 words long. Decide how you could expand each of the four sub-topics, using ideas from Units 17 and 18. Draft your own concluding paragraph to replace the final sentence. (40–50 words)

Advice

- Develop all the points given in the question.
- Include relevant ideas of your own.
- Order the paragraphs logically.
- Use synonyms and expressions to paraphrase the wording of the question.
- Choose a suitably neutral register.
- Summarise your main views in a conclusion.

9 Now, using this advice, write your own essay in answer to the exam task in 1. You should write 300–350 words.

UNIT 19 The unexplained

Treasurer's House in York

1 Do you believe in ghosts? Have you ever visited a haunted house? What would you take with you if you did?

2 Work with a partner and look at the adjectives below. Decide which word is the odd one out in each group. Justify your decision.

a naïve   sceptical   ingenuous   simple
b gullible   derisive   credulous   trusting
c cynical   scornful   apathetic   contemptuous
d sensitive sensible   perceptive   impressionable
e shrewd   realistic   pragmatic   temperamental
f upright   immature   irresponsible disrespectful

Which of the words above might you use to describe someone who believes in ghosts? Use an English–English dictionary to help you.

3 🎧 You will hear a radio programme about ghosts. For questions 1–9, complete the sentences with a word or short phrase.

1 Athenodorus was disturbed by the noise made by ......chains...... knocking against each other.
2 Athenodorus was no longer bothered by the ghost after a new .....burial..... took place.
3 The ghost of a loved one in trouble is referred to by the speaker as a '.....crisis apparition.....'.
4 It has often been the case that people mistake .....a patch of mist..... for a ghost.
5 Harry Martindale was .....a plumber..... by trade.
6 Harry had placed .....a ladder..... on the spot where a Roman road used to be.
7 The soldier's head was level with Harry's .....waist...... .
8 Harry said that the soldiers badly needed .....a good wash & shave.....
9 Harry described the soldiers' weapons as looking like .....a sort/roundish dagger.....

4 What do you think about Harry's experience? Do you think it has the ring of truth about it or not? Why? / Why not?

style extra

In the listening passage, what was described as 'rattling' and 'murmuring'?

Words like these are called onomatopoeic words because they seem to sound like their meaning. Opposite are verbs connected with types of sound. Using an English–English dictionary, decide what you would use these words to describe.

EXAMPLE: howl
the noise made by an unhappy dog, also by the wind

creak	rumble	slap
hiss	drip	tinkle
crunch	slam	growl
peal	squelch	slash
click	screech	slither

Complete the sentences below with one of the verbs above.

a The stairs .... as she tiptoed up to her room.

b The policeman's shoe .... as he pulled it out of the mud.

c Hooligans have .... my car tyres with a knife.

d The snake .... across the floor.

e You always know when the postman comes because he .... across the gravel.

f I was kept awake last night by the tap ....

g The glass .... as it broke on the floor.

h Steam .... as it came out of the pipe.

Write a paragraph about one of the following, using some of the verbs above to give a suitable atmosphere.

- Alone in a haunted house
- The Titanic sinking
- Home alone in a storm

---

5 For questions 1–6, read the text below and decide which answer (A, B, C or D) best fits each gap.

Poltergeists

Poltergeists have always been with us; there are (1).... cases as far back as AD 530, and from all parts of the world. The German word poltergeist means (2).... 'noisy spirit', and that describes the behaviour of this phenomenon very well. Among its manifestations are banging noises, things being thrown around, furniture being (3).... and other destructive behaviour; but it also (4).... itself in other, quieter ways, such as hiding things or writing messages. It is seen as a mischievous spirit because that is what the behaviour suggests; a disembodied spirit that enjoys upsetting people. It is clear that many poltergeist activities do not follow the rules (5).... by science; things move without being touched, objects move slowly through the air, solid objects pass through other solid objects, spontaneous fires occur, water appears from nowhere, and so on. It is possible that these paranormal events are (6).... by powers and energies we have not yet recognised, but which everyone has the potential to use.

	A	B	C	D
1	inscribed	recorded	minuted	registered
2	literally	exactly	accurately	plainly
3	loaded up	set in	turned over	stood out
4	intimates	divulges	signifies	reveals
5	brought out	laid down	carried out	put down
6	triggered	derived	evolved	extorted

Word order and adverbs

1 Work in a group. Decide where to put the adverbs or adverbial phrases in the
following sentences.

   a I went home. (yesterday, on foot)
   b She walked to where another coach was waiting. (up the hill, briskly, later, luckily)
   c I was in the mood to go swimming. (hardly, last night)
   d He is lying. (of course, still)
   e Stephen spoke to me. (the other day, in a friendly way, in fact)
   f It rained. (non-stop, all day, heavily, strangely enough)
   g People hide things of value. (apparently, in the attic, rarely)
   h She performed the dance. (far, slowly, too)
   i I think you should get out of the house. (to be honest, more often)
   j I saw the comet. (only, in the sky, yesterday)

 page 187

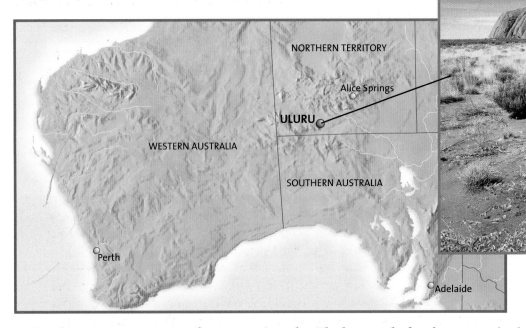

2 Put the sentences, or parts of sentences, in order. The last word of each sentence is given in bold and
capital letters are given. Then put the sentences in order to make an extract from an article about
how Uluru, or Ayers Rock, in Australia came to be created. You will also need to add punctuation.

   EXAMPLE: central a or Ayers huge Uluru mound sandstone Rock is in Australia …
             Uluru, or Ayers Rock, is a huge sandstone mound in central Australia …

   a tells a Another terrible after how battle …
   b originally One Uluru legend that a was states **lake**.
   c that been to the for Aboriginal sacred has hundreds people of **years**.
   d tell Earth paintings Many aboriginal important **stories**.
   e world when the was the time **created**.
   f at to Earth rose up the blood-coloured revolt the form the great bloodshed in **rock**.
   g in that was made They by it spirits the believe 'Dreamtime'…

Adverb or adjective?

- It is possible to change most adjectives into an adverb with the addition of -ly, for example *happy* to *happily*.
- Some adjectives do not have an adverb, for example *friendly*, *lonely*, *silly*. In this case you need to use an adverb phrase, for example *He looked at her in a friendly way*.
- Some adverbs have the same form as the adjective, for example *hard*. *He works hard. He's a hard worker.*
- Some adverbs may have two forms – one which looks like an adjective and the other with -ly. There is usually a difference in meaning.

3 Use one of the words from the box to complete each sentence below.

hard	hardly	short	shortly	right	rightly
high	highly	late	lately	wrong	wrongly

a I .... ever see her nowadays – she's so busy.

b Sally thought very .... indeed of the gypsy's fortune-telling powers.

c The interviewer .... claimed that the house was haunted.

d Sue thought long and .... about whether to take part in the experiment.

e Tell Marje I'll see her ....

f You've done this calculation ....

g They were just saying that they hadn't seen you ....

h The car turned .... round and went back the way it came.

i The article stopped .... of accusing anyone of a hoax.

4 For questions 1–15, read the text below and think of the word which best fits each space. Use only one word in each space.

Carrying out a ghost hunt

(0) ..*Should*.. a visit to a house near you convince you that there may be something worth investigating, follow these simple steps. There is a great (1) ..*deal*.. you can do in the way of preliminary research (2) ..*when*.. you make any attempt to (3) ..*carry*.. out any practical investigation. Maps and early documents devoted to the area can often be (4) ..*of*.. interest and a visit to the local museum or contact with any local archaeological society can produce basic knowledge of the area and its buildings. In (5) ..*addition*.. , maps can provide information on the whereabouts of rivers and streams, pools and lakes. There is a theory that water running underground through streams, old sewers and so (6) ..*on*.. beneath or close to the foundations of (7) ..*a*.. house may subject that property to spasmodic thrusts. (8) ..*When*.. the water builds up, such jolts cause objects in the house to move, (9) ..*while*.. the general strain on the house (10) ..*can*.. produce creaks, cracks and groans that sound eerie (11) ..*at*.. night. Such possibilities have to be (12) ..*taken*.. into account, depending on the reported paranormal activity. At (13) ..*such*.. events, knowledge of previous buildings in the area may produce a clue to any apparitions seen, (14) ..*although*.. unobtrusive personal enquiry in the immediate area may provide a better way of (15) ..*finding*.. out about the background.

Full summary task 2

1 Look at the photos. They are of lucky charms. Do people in your country carry lucky charms? Do you? If not, why not? Do you know of any other lucky charms which are used in different countries?

2 Can you explain the following expressions? Have you any experience of the situations they would be used for?

- Talk of the devil!
- to have a guardian angel
- It's a small world.
- to have second sight
- female intuition
- a feeling of déjà vu

3 For questions 1–5, read the two texts on the paranormal oppposite. For questions 1–4, answer with a word or short phrase. You do not need to write complete sentences. For question 5, write a summary according to the instructions given. Remember the advice you were given in Exam folder 3.

It is in the imagery of sight, hearing, touch, smell, temperature that paranormal cognition, like memory, often emerges into the conscious mind. (Often, though not always. There may be no more than a sudden impression that something has happened, even no more than an unaccountable impulse to act; to cancel a seat on a flight which will shortly crash, for example.)

For this reason I should like to stress the value of spontaneous phenomena to psychical research. Baffling, unrepeatable, uniquely personal as such events may be, the fact that they occur, that certain hallucinations, waking impressions and vivid dreams can be correlated with objective happenings unknown to the person concerned, far way, long ago or not yet enacted, has repeatedly been made plain.   line 12

Even now, of course, such happenings are often dismissed as at best 'anecdotal', or as old wives' tales, or as superstitious nonsense. In the same way, the perfectly accurate report that the inhabitants of the island of St Kilda only got colds when a ship came in was said to be contrary to all common sense by critics in the seventeenth century, only to be accepted as a statement of fact when the germ theory of disease was established in the nineteenth. Many spontaneous instances of the paranormal may eventually turn out to have a scientific explanation. It is vital that people are encouraged to report any instances of psychic phenomena without fear of ridicule or worse.

1 What does the writer imply about someone who cancels a seat on a plane which crashes soon afterwards?
2 What exactly does the expression 'made plain' in line 12 refer to?

An investigation of coincidences should be primarily designed to get at the truth, or at least make progress towards it. The moment that chance ceases to be a convincing explanation, uneasiness sets in. Most people are embarrassed to speak out in case they are thought of as cranks. Their

line 5 experiences may be commonplace enough – the occasional precognitive dream; a feeling of déjà vu or thinking of somebody a moment before they ring up – but they still feel the need for anonymity.

A typical example is Mrs A. As a young child, she had a vision of a boy in a sailor suit, standing on a roof and holding a plant in his hand. He had smiled at her. For years, he always appeared to her at bedtime. In her 20s, Mrs A obtained a job as a receptionist to an optician and, in 1950, she married him. In 1965, after both his parents had died, he brought home with him an album of photographs, some taken of him as a child in the 1920s. At the sight of one of them, 'My heart stopped, and I felt physically ill,' she recalls. 'There in front of me was the little boy from my childhood.' The photo showed her husband as a child in a sailor suit on a roof next to a plant.

line 19 Her coincidence was 'spooky'. But a surprising number of people who clearly regard themselves as free from irrational fears are ready to admit that even mundane coincidences can be disturbing.

3 What word elsewhere in the text echoes the idea of 'commonplace' in line 5?

4 Explain in your own words what the writer means by 'free from irrational fears' in line 19.

5 In a paragraph of between 50 and 70 words, summarise in your own words as far as possible, how, according to both texts, people react to the paranormal.

4 Look at the following words from the texts opposite and above.
   What part of speech is each word in the text? What other forms of the word are possible?

Text 1
imagery
conscious
impression
impulse
psychical
dismissed

Text 2
coincidences
speak out
anonymity
childhood
disturbing

5 Use an appropriate form of the words in capitals to complete the sentences.

a He is an .... critic of what he calls 'paranormal geeks'.   SPEAK
b The newspaper article was .... of the possibility of ESP.   DISMISSED
c Her one wish after her experience was to remain ....   ANONYMITY
d It was very .... of you to bait the poor woman like that.   CHILDHOOD
e There was a rumour of some sort of a .... at the cemetery last night.   DISTURBING
f Children of primary school age are very .... and tend to believe what   IMPRESSION
   they are told.
g .... from all over the world are gathering for the conference on 'Memory'.   PSYCHICAL
h You may not be aware of things happening but your .... probably   CONSCIOUS
   registers events.

Exam folder 10

Paper 5 Speaking

The standard format for Paper 5 is for there to be two candidates and two examiners. It is also possible to have three candidates and two examiners.

One examiner, called the interlocutor, asks the questions while the other only listens. Both examiners will assess you. They are looking for accuracy of grammar, a wide and appropriate range of vocabulary and the ability to express opinions and abstract ideas. Your pronunciation should be clear and you should be able to interact well with your partner(s).

There are three parts to the test and it lasts for nineteen minutes. Part 1 is three minutes, Part 2 is four minutes and Part 3 lasts for twelve minutes.

In Part 1 you will be encouraged by the interlocutor to talk about yourself and give some personal opinions. In Part 2 you have to discuss some form of visual prompt (up to seven pictures or photos) and then have a discussion with the other candidate. In Part 3 you will have the chance to speak for about two minutes on a topic given to you and then have a discussion with the other candidate, developing the topic you have been given.

Advice

- Don't worry if you think you do badly in one part of the test. You are assessed on the complete test.
- If the other candidate is better than you, or not as good, you shouldn't worry. You are assessed on what you do, not in relation to the other candidate.
- It's important to show sensitivity to the other candidate during the test. This means allowing the other candidate to speak and responding to what they say.
- Remember this is your opportunity to show you can speak English – use it!
- Do ask if you are unclear about what you have to do.

Now do this complete Speaking test with a partner, taking it in turns to ask and answer the following typical questions. (Remember that in the exam the interlocutor will be asking the questions.)

Part 1

Ask each other these questions.

Questions for Student A to ask Student B
Are you working or studying at the moment?
How do you spend your leisure time?
What would be your ideal job?

Questions for Student B to ask Student A
How do you travel to work/college every day?
What are your plans for the future?
What is more important to you, to have a well-paid job or to do something to help other people?

Part 2

Here are some photos of useful inventions. Look at pictures A and E and talk together about whether you could live without them. You have about one minute to do this.

A

B

C

D

E

Now look at *all* the pictures. Imagine that an exhibition is going to take place on the theme of 'Essential Inventions'. All these objects are to be included. Talk together about the importance of the inventions shown in the pictures. Then suggest two other inventions you would like to see included in the exhibition.

You have about three minutes to do this.

Part 3

In this part of the test you have to speak by yourself for about two minutes. You should listen carefully while your partner is speaking because you will need to comment afterwards.

Both students should look at the card below. There is a question written on it and Student A has to give his/her opinion on it. There are some ideas on the card for you to use if you like.

Student A

> How has life changed in the past hundred years?
> ➤ work
> ➤ education
> ➤ family life

Student B is then asked to give his/her opinion on what A has said. This should be quite brief.

Both candidates should then talk about the following topic for one minute each. *Do you think marriage is as important today as in the past?*

Now the roles are reversed and Student B has the chance to speak, using the prompts below if he or she wishes.

Student B

> What changes do you foresee in the future?
> ➤ accommodation
> ➤ fashion
> ➤ transport

Student A now has to comment briefly on what B has said.

Both candidates should then talk about the following topic for one minute each.
Does the future worry you at all?

To finish the test both candidates have to talk about changes to our lives in general. This section lasts about four minutes.

Discuss together the following questions.
- What can we do to make the world a better place to live in?
- Are we losing touch with the natural world?
- Are people becoming less important than machines?

1 Read this extract from a book by the American writer Bill Bryson, who is
   renowned for his dry sense of humour. It was written after the writer and his
   family moved back to the USA after living in Great Britain. His wife is English.

   What impression does he give you of life in the USA?

HOW TO HAVE FUN AT HOME

My wife thinks nearly everything about American life is wonderful.
She loves having her groceries bagged for her. She adores free
iced water and book-matches. She thinks home-delivered pizza is
a central hallmark of civilization. I haven't the heart to tell her
5 that waitresses in the States urge everyone to have a nice day.
Personally, while I am fond of America and grateful for its many
conveniences, I am not quite so slavishly uncritical. Take the
matter of having your groceries bagged for you. I appreciate the
gesture, but when you come down to it what does it actually
10 achieve except give you an opportunity to stand there and watch
your groceries being bagged? It's not as if it buys you some
quality time. I don't want to get heavy here, but given the choice
between free iced water at restaurants and, let us say, a national
health service, I have to say my instinct is to go with the latter.

15   However, there are certain things that are so wonderful in
American life that I can hardly stand it myself. Chief among
these, without any doubt, is the garbage disposal. A garbage
disposal is everything a labour-saving device should be and so
seldom is — noisy, fun, extremely hazardous, and so dazzlingly
20 good at what it does that you cannot imagine how you ever
managed without one. If you had asked me eighteen months ago
what the prospects were that shortly my chief hobby would be
placing assorted objects down a hole in the kitchen sink, I
believe I would have laughed in your face, but in fact it is so.

25   I have never had a garbage disposal before, so I have been
learning its tolerances through a process of trial and error.
Chopsticks give perhaps the liveliest response (this is not
recommended, of course, but there comes a time with every piece
of machinery when you just have to see what it can do), but
30 cantaloupe rinds make the richest, throatiest sound and result in
less 'down time'. Coffee grounds in quantity are the most likely to
provide a satisfying 'Vesuvius effect', though for obvious reasons
it is best not to attempt this difficult feat until your wife has gone
out for the day, and to have a mop and stepladder standing by.
35 The most exciting event with a garbage disposal, of course, is

when it jams and you have to reach in and unclog it, knowing
that at any moment it might spring to life and abruptly convert
your arm from a useful grasping tool into a dibber. Don't try to
tell me about living life on the edge.

40   Now basements I know because I grew up with one. Every
American basement is the same. They all have a clothes line that
is rarely used, a trickle of water from an indeterminable source
running diagonally across the floor, and a funny smell — a
combination of old magazines, camping gear that should have
45 been aired and wasn't, and something to do with a guinea pig
named Mr Fluffy that escaped down a central heating grate six
months ago and has not been seen since (and presumably would
now be better called Mr Bones).

   Basements are so monumentally useless, in fact, you seldom
50 go down there, so it always comes as a surprise to remember
that you have one. Every dad who ever goes down in a basement
pauses at some point and thinks: 'Gee, we really ought to do
something with all this space. We could have a cocktail cabinet
and a pool table and maybe a jukebox and a Jacuzzi and a couple
55 of pinball machines...' But of course it's just one of those things
that you intend to do one day, like learn Spanish or take up home
barbering, and never do.

   Oh, occasionally, especially in starter homes, you will find
that some young gung-ho dad has converted the basement into
60 a playroom for the children, but this is always a mistake, as no
child will play in a basement. This is because no matter how
loving your parents, no matter how much you would like to trust
them, there is always the thought that they will quietly lock the
door at the top of the stairs and move to Florida. No, basements
65 are simply and inescapably scary; that's why they always feature
in spooky movies, usually with a shadow of Joan Crawford
carrying an axe thrown on the far wall. That may be why even
dads don't go down there very often.

   I could go on and on cataloguing other small, unsung glories
70 of American household life — refrigerators that dispense iced
water and make their own ice-cubes, walk-in closets, electrical
sockets in bathrooms, but I won't. I'm out of space and anyway
Mrs B has just gone out to do some shopping and it has occurred
to me that I have not yet seen what the disposal can do with a
75 juice carton. I'll get back to you on this one.

2 For questions 1–7, choose the answer (A, B, C or D) which you think fits best according to the text.

1 In the first paragraph, what does Bill Bryson imply about his wife?
A She has very poor taste in food.
B She is only happy so long as she can get things for nothing.
C She is only pretending to be uncritical of the American way of life.
D She is relatively unsophisticated.

2 What is Bill's reaction to having his groceries bagged and getting iced water?
A He feels that the country hasn't quite got its priorities right.
B He would prefer to pay less and pack his own groceries.
C He thinks that service could be even better in American shops and restaurants.
D He is of the opinion that Americans waste a lot of time unnecessarily.

3 Why does Bill enjoy using the garbage disposal?
A It fulfils his notion of what a household gadget should be.
B He has plenty of free time to experiment now he has moved back to the States.
C He is finding it much easier to use than he thought he would.
D It devours anything you put in it without any fuss.

4 What impression do you get of Bill when he talks about the garbage disposal unit?
A He is irritated that the unit is so potentially dangerous.
B He is keen to help around the house and will happily mend the disposal unit for his wife.
C He likes to experiment with it without fear of interruption.
D He thinks the garbage disposal unit should take a wider variety of garbage.

5 What does Bill say in relation to basements?
A He doesn't understand why they are so popular in the States.
B They are under-utilised and he feels they should be better used.
C He thinks that they are generally poorly designed.
D He is confident that his attitude and opinions are shared by other Americans.

6 According to Bill, basements often
A make people feel intimidated.
B remind people of frightening incidents from their childhood.
C make people want to start competing to see who can make the best conversion.
D are a source of argument in families.

7 In describing his current home in the USA, Bill seems
A quite critical.
B fairly effusive.
C sometimes nostalgic.
D quietly indignant.

3 Find these expressions in the article. In your own words, explain what the writer means by each of them. (Sometimes you will need to explain the writer's choice of words.)

a I don't want to get heavy here (line 12)
b a satisfying 'Vesuvius effect' (line 32)
c a trickle of water from an indeterminable source (line 42)
d and presumably would now be better called Mr Bones (lines 47–48)
e so monumentally useless (line 49)
f some young gung-ho dad (line 59)
g other small, unsung glories of American household life (lines 69–70)
h I'll get back to you on this one (line 75)

Expressions with *have*

A man's car had broken down, so he stopped the next car that came down the street.
'What's the problem?' asked the driver of the second car.
'I need some help,' said the driver of the first car. 'My car has broken down and I must get it looked at.'
'I can't help you,' said the driver of the second car. 'I'm not a mechanic. I'm a chiropodist.'
'In that case,' said the first driver, 'you can give me a tow.'

1   The joke above is a play on words. Can you explain it?

The first driver wants to have his car looked at. What does this imply?

2   Read the information about *have* and *get* in the Grammar folder and complete the following sentences.

   a Aunt Paula won't .... her son criticised by anyone.
   b I'll .... the dinner made if you set the table.
   c Trevor .... his clothes covered in oil when he tried to mend his bike.
   d We .... the TV and video stolen in the burglary last month.
   e Mr Johnson always .... his windows cleaned by Jack.
   f I couldn't .... the door unlocked with my key this morning.

G ⋯⋗ page 188

Expressions with *go*

3   In his book, Bill Bryson says he 'could go on and on', meaning he could continue indefinitely. The sentences below all contain a phrasal verb with *go*. Fill in the missing particle or particles in each sentence.

   a Last winter everyone in the house went .... flu.
   b Sue didn't normally go .... competitions but thought she might win this time.
   c At least £500 went .... museum entry fees last time we had a holiday.
   d The police went .... the evidence very carefully.
   e Would you mind going .... some eggs?
   f The boys sat on the beach and watched the tide go ....
   g They timed the fireworks to go .... at midnight.
   h Tamsin's shoes didn't really go .... her jeans.
   i Not many people go .... basic necessities in this country any more.
   j The milk went .... because Tim forgot to put it back in the fridge.

Now match each phrasal verb above with its meaning below.

be spent on =	explode =
ebb =	match =
fetch =	go sour =
enter =	examine =
become ill with =	manage without =

4   Rewrite the following sentences using the word given as part of an expression with *go*. Do not change the word given. You must use between three and eight words, including the word given.

   1 Penny Stone has become really self-important since she was promoted.
   gone
   Getting a .... head.

   2 Paul couldn't stop thinking about the argument he had had with his brother.
   went
   Paul .... the argument he had had with his brother.

3 The manager told the press that his team had played very badly.

record

The manager .... that his team had played very badly.

4 My grandmother would always make us eat everything on our plates when we visited her.

waste

Nothing we were given to eat .... at my grandmother's house.

5 I can never follow what he's saying – he's always changing the subject.

tangent

If he .... I would know what he was talking about.

Grammar review

5 With a partner, correct the mistakes in the following sentences. One sentence is correct. The rest all contain common student errors.

a Being a wet evening, I stayed at home.

b We would like to know all what has happened.

c He already is here.

d Only by listening intently, you will hear it singing.

e It would be easier to decide if my son would be here.

f I have past my exam this summer.

g It's worth to be alive on such a lovely day.

h My family consists in six people.

i That is a mistake I do often.

j Your hair needs cutting badly.

k I suggest to do it immediately.

l This team is the best of the two.

m He is too honest a man to take that.

n My informations aren't up to date.

o I am wanting to meet you for a long time.

p I congratulate you to have got married.

q I wish it stopped raining.

r You can eat as soon as the dinner will be ready.

s It's a five miles journey.

t A man came into the compartment to control the tickets.

6 For questions 1–15, read the text below and think of the word which best fits each space. Use only one word in each space. There is an example at the beginning (**0**).

Making a faux pas

I was staying recently in rather (**0**) ....a............... smart hotel in Melbourne, Australia. No (**1**) .... had I got into bed than I became aware of music coming from the room (**2**) .... to mine. I knocked quite gently on the partition wall to indicate that (**3**) .... was unacceptably loud. I (**4**) ...., nonetheless, have dropped (**5**) .... to sleep. At 2.00 a.m. I was wide awake and the music seemed even louder. I walked out (**6**) .... the corridor to get the room number (**7**) .... telephoning the culprit. A sleepy Australian voice replied and I told him in no uncertain (**8**) .... that his music was disgracefully loud. (**9**) .... ten minutes and the noise was (**10**) .... better. I rang again, even more angry this time. As I appeared to be getting (**11**) .... fast, in desperation I telephoned hotel security. The noise seemed to get even worse. I banged more angrily on the wall. Eventually the hotel security men (**12**) .... up. They entered my room, walked to the side of the bed and pressed a knob. (**13**) .... was silence. (**14**) .... the time it had been my own radio with its loudspeaker by the wall (**15**) .... had been the cause of the trouble.

7 Have you ever had an embarrassing moment when you made a faux pas or put your foot in it? Talk about it with a partner.

Paper 5 Part 3

1 How would you describe someone who is eccentric? Do you know anyone who could be called eccentric?

Eccentrics can be extreme in the exuberance with which they express their sense of humour. The way normal people regard the eccentric often depends upon what they find funny. Read this description of the antics of an eccentric.

> 'His mildest kind of practical joke is to push a dish of meringue trifle into the face of a lady guest at a smart dinner party in his home, having first asked her to smell it to see if it is 'off'. There is an oubliette under one of his dining room chairs, and any boring guest is seated over it and dropped into the wine cellar when he can stand no more. His coup de grâce was the miniature bomb that he planted inside his son's birthday cake, which the boy detonated by blowing on the candles, covering all his little friends with icing. The man's long-suffering wife had to clean them all up, then explain and apologise to their parents after the party.'

Would you find someone like this funny or irritating?

2 🎧 You are going to hear a discussion between Terry Jones, a radio presenter, and Marion Fielding, a psychologist. They are talking about her new book on eccentricity.

For questions 1–7, decide which of the statements are true and which are false.

1 According to Marion, it's unclear how we should define eccentricity.
2 There is more emphasis on conformity in the developed world than in non-industrialised nations.
3 The average person sympathises with eccentric behaviour.
4 Eccentrics tend to disregard other people's feelings.
5 Eccentrics have inquisitive minds.
6 The rats came out when they smelled food.
7 Jack Myers used to frighten his friends by turning loose his animals.

Pronunciation

3 🎧 The woman in the interview talked about a *bizarre or risqué* habit. English has borrowed many words and phrases from other languages. Use a dictionary to find out their English meanings, listen to the recording and then say them aloud.

in lieu of	protégé
ad infinitum	fracas
ad nauseam	cul-de-sac
par excellence	clique
quid pro quo	nom de plume
faux pas	bête noire
prima facie	tête à tête
niche	hoi polloi
risqué	coup de grâce

4   Using the expressions in exercise 3, complete the following sentences.

    a It was such an embarrassing .... when I asked the girl to introduce me to her father and I found out it was her husband!

    b It's possible to give works of art to the government .... of tax.

    c Female writers in the past often used a ....

    d Some of Uncle Thomas's jokes tend to be a bit ....

    e Rosalie and I decided to go to a café for a .... about the office.

    f The boy next door talks about trainspotting ....

    g You are apparently more likely to be burgled in a .... than on a main road.

    h My .... is people smoking in restaurants.

5   For questions 1–4, think of one word which can be used appropriately in all three sentences.

    1 The .... for working-class dissent struck even the least sympathetic observer.

    The late Mr Miles allowed us to use the .... of his house for village fêtes.

    It's not a good idea to pour the coffee .... down the sink.

    2 You need to take your coursework more .... if you want a good grade.

    From the outset, this project was .... flawed.

    You don't .... mean to tell me that you don't want to go to university?

    3 Everyone .... up at the party at exactly eight o'clock.

    I often .... a conversation around to my own interests when I was young.

    His role .... out to be smaller than he had anticipated.

    4 What's the world .... to, when you can't find a taxi after midnight?

    I can't see him .... up with any new terms and conditions.

    The prospect of tougher state censorship is .... nearer day by day.

6   With a partner, look at the Part 3 Speaking tasks below. The prompts are to give you some ideas on the subject. You can use all, one or two or none of the ideas. Student A should look at task A and Student B at task B.

Task A
Is it better to conform or be different from your peers?

➤ Fashion
➤ Relationships
➤ Leisure pursuits

Task B
What makes people in your country laugh?

➤ Popular comedians
➤ Comedy films
➤ Other people's misfortunes

When you are ready, tell your partner your ideas on the subject. You will have about two minutes to speak. When you have finished speaking, ask your partner if he/she agreed or disagreed with what you said. Remember you have to listen carefully to what your partner says as in the exam itself you will be asked questions on it.

Remember it is fine to hesitate in order to gather your thoughts – as long as you don't pause for too long! You can also repeat the question or use phrases such as:

    Umm ...   *Let me see ...*
    Well ...   *I mean ...*
    As I see it ...

You might also want to add something you'd forgotten to mention or return to a previous subject. For this you can use phrases like:

    By the way, ...   *As I was saying, ...*
    Incidentally, ...   *I forgot to say/*
                          mention that ...

It's very likely you will need to generalise during your talk. Use phrases such as:

    Broadly speaking ...   *In general ...*
    To a great extent ...   *On the whole ...*

Writing folder 10

Part 2 Articles and Letters

Writing folder 1 looked at a Part 1 letter. Writing folder 5 looked at a Part 1 article. Both of these task types may also be offered in Part 2 (the essay is only a Part 2 option for the set text questions). The letter will always be formal, while the style of the article will depend on its target readership.

1   Read the Part 2 tasks below and decide what is involved in each one, choosing relevant aspects from the following list.

comparison
evaluation
factual description
narrative
opinion
speculation

A   An in-flight magazine has asked its readers to submit a light-hearted article with the title *Space transport in 2050*. Write an article describing possible future forms of transport and saying how you would take advantage of them.

B   An international ecology magazine has invited readers to contribute an article to a special edition entitled *Ways to save our planet*. Write an article outlining the environmental measures you think should be taken by individuals and by governments and evaluating their chances of success.

C   You see a reader's letter in a general interest magazine which claims that family life is no different nowadays to how it was twenty years ago. You decide to write a letter to the magazine, giving your opinions on the changes in family roles and relationships and suggesting likely future developments.

D   Your school magazine is running a special feature on books students have read, which is entitled *Every good book has a message about life*. Write an article about the set book you are studying, explaining what you feel it has taught you that you can apply to life in general.

E   The publisher of the book you have studied is planning a new edition with pictures and has asked you to suggest which parts of the book would benefit from being illustrated. Write a letter to the publisher, giving your suggestions and justifying them with detailed reference to the book.

What should the style and tone of each task be? Could all three articles (A, B and D) be written in either a light-hearted or more serious tone?
Why? / Why not?

2   Select vocabulary from the pool below that could be used in
    each task. Some words can be used in more than one.

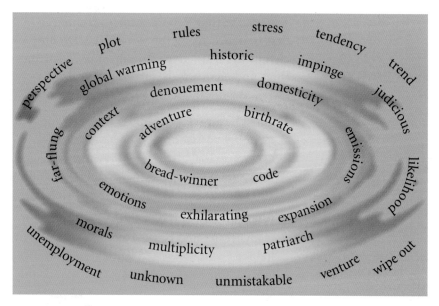

perspective plot rules stress tendency trend
global warming historic impinge judicious
denouement domesticity
context adventure birthrate emissions
far-flung bread-winner code likelihood
emotions exhilarating expansion
morals multiplicity patriarch venture wipe out
unemployment unknown unmistakable

Advice

- Decide on an appropriate style and tone for
  your letter or article.
- Spend a few minutes thinking about the angle
  to take.
- Make a list of possible ideas.
- Order these ideas logically and to best effect.
- Note down relevant vocabulary and expressions.
- Include rhetorical questions to preface opinions.

General advice for Paper 2

- Spend time planning each question.
- Allow equal time for each question (up to
  1 hour).
- Calculate approximately how many words you
  produce.
- Leave time to check your answer for spelling
  and grammar.

3   Don't waste time counting every word of your
    answer. Work out how many words you write on
    average per line and then count the number of
    lines you have written. There are 28 lines per page
    on the exam question paper.

4   Now answer one of the Part 2 tasks on the
    opposite page. Allow yourself 45 minutes and then
    stop writing. Estimate how many words you have
    produced, check what you have written and make
    any improvements within the next 10 minutes.

Reading

1 For questions 1–6, read the text below and decide which answer (A, B, C or D) best fits each gap.

Laughter's geography

Wherever you go, you meet people who think that foreigners have either no sense of humour or at best, a (1) .... one. They are wrong. Humour is universal. But language is not, and neither are frames of reference. Puns that (2) .... on Chinese pictograms and their homophones are hard to render in English. Punchlines that assume an intimate knowledge of Italian politics (3) .... few laughs outside Rome. The comedy that travels easily is often the most obvious: from Britain Mr Bean and Benny Hill; from America, Beavis and Butt-head. Domestic humour is subtler and, generally speaking, more revealing. Take this example from Africa:

A poor beggar is sitting by the side of the road. Suddenly the President's gleaming motorcade (4) .... past. (5) .... afterwards, a plump and ragged man runs sweating by, (6) .... an obviously stolen goat under his arm. A minute later, two policemen come rushing up in pursuit. 'Did you see a fat thief come this way?' they ask. 'Yes', replies the beggar, 'but you'll never catch him on foot.'

1 A crude   B raw   C rude   D clumsy
2 A take   B work   C impose   D play
3 A acquire   B raise   C bring   D make
4 A sweeps   B slides   C tiptoes D flounces
5 A Promptly B Instantly C Shortly D Closely
6 A clutching B retaining C clinging D possessing

Use of English

2 For questions 1–6, complete the second sentence so that it has a similar meaning to the first sentence, using the word given. Do not change the word given. You must use between three and eight words, including the word given.

1 You'll never sell your house if you let the rumours persist of it being haunted.
carry
You .... if you want to sell your house.

2 It was kind of you to help us clean up, but it really wasn't necessary.
helped
You .... the cleaning up.

3 It doesn't matter when he comes, I'm not bothered.
far
He can .... concerned.

4 I asked the press to keep her name a secret so she would remain anonymous.
had
In order .... keep her name a secret.

5 Eliza did better than usual at her début performance, even though she had a sore throat.
excelled
Despite .... at her debut performance.

6 She is unlikely to accept anything except a full apology.
would
It is unlikely that anything .... to her.

3 For questions 1–6, think of one word only which can be used appropriately in all three sentences.

1 It is .... to say that most of the jokes would have bombed, if he hadn't had such a pleasant personality.

There's a .... amount of operatics involved, mostly courtesy of Andrew Tomaz and his orchestra.

And if your skin is .... and sensitive, you shouldn't start off with anything less than a factor 15 sunscreen.

2 They had planned to .... him hostage to secure the resignation of the President.

Pamela fought to .... back the tears which threatened to engulf her.

Tamsin thinks she can .... a party to celebrate, but I think she'll find it difficult to find a venue.

3 By .... at least half that cake should've been mine.

The concept of parental .... is not an unlimited one.

An American network will choose the titles and provide technical help in return for the .... to screen the film.

4 Although Professor Sims would want to return to the .... of poltergeist activity, he said that the report was a very thorough one and well written.

Without .... the most feared of all regimes is a totalitarian one.

The woman in .... was asked whether she had intended to leave without paying for the goods.

5 The comedian was in a sorry .... when he found his programme had been axed.

In this post-welfare ...., travellers need to be reminded of their duty to give up their seat to old ladies.

A .... of emergency in the disputed area has been extended for a further six months.

6 I am indebted to J. Brown for his hair-raising .... of life in jail.

The judge took into .... the family's cramped living conditions and financial difficulties.

Thomas refused to open an .... with the bank, preferring instead to keep his money in a suitcase.

Writing

4 Read this Part 2 letter, written to a magazine on the subject of the supernatural. Add about 100 words to complete the missing narrative, using suitable words and phrases from Unit 19.

Dear Sir

I read the article entitled *Inexplicable Events* in your magazine this month with great interest. As you have asked for anecdotal evidence from your readers, I am writing to share my own story with you.

Before I tell you my own experience, I should stress that, up until last January, I had not been in the least superstitious. Indeed, I have always been very sceptical about the whole area of the supernatural. What I am about to relate has changed my views for good!

I was driving home from a meeting one winter's afternoon and took a country road across the hills to avoid the motorway traffic. As the car snaked its way up the narrow road, the sky darkened around me and it felt quite spooky. I turned up the radio and sang along, in an attempt to raise my flagging spirits. Round the next bend, however, was a sight I never wish to witness again …

Can any of your readers explain my ordeal?

Yours faithfully

Jessica Langley

···❖ Crossword page 191

Grammar folder

Unit 1
Perfect tenses
The perfect tenses are used in English in a number of ways.

Present perfect simple tense
- when talking about events or situations that started in the past and are still true
  Amelia Kenton has lived in the same house all her life.

- when thinking about the present effects of something that happened in the past
  I've lost my purse so I need some money for the bus.

- when talking about a recent event or situation
  Jack has just phoned to wish you good luck.

- when referring to something that will happen at some time in the future
  As soon as I have settled in, come and stay!

Present perfect continuous tense
This can sometimes be used instead of the present perfect simple tense. So, in the first example above, you could also say *Mrs Kenton has been living in the same house all her life.*

Main uses of the present perfect continuous tense are:

- to stress the period of time involved
  I've been sitting at this computer all day!

- to refer to a situation that continues
  Membership numbers at this club have been falling year by year.

- to focus on the present effects of a recent event
  You can tell it's been raining – the seats are still damp.

- to refer to something that has recently stopped
  Have you been crying?

Note that stative verbs such as *be, know, seem* are not usually used in continuous tenses. For example, you would not say *I've been knowing Jim since he was 15*, but *I've known Jim since he was 15.*

Past perfect simple tense
This tense is generally used to clarify the timing of an event. It is used

- to refer to an event which took place before something else
  Sailing towards the harbour, I remembered how it had looked on my first visit, ten years earlier.

  Sometimes this involves using words like *already* or *just*.
  I had just stepped into the bath when the phone rang.

Past perfect continuous tense
This tense is used

- to stress the continuity of an event at an earlier point in time
  Their cat had been missing for over a week when a neighbour spotted it in the local park.

See also above regarding stative verbs.

Future perfect simple tense
This tense is used

- to refer to events which have not yet happened but will definitely do so at a given time in the future
  By the end of September, I will have started that course in London.

Future perfect continuous tense
This tense is used

- to indicate duration at a specified time in the future
  Come next Saturday, we'll have been going out together for a whole year!

Other modal verbs
To express regret about the past, *should* or *ought to* is combined with a perfect tense form.

We should never have bought Alex that drum kit!
I'm sorry, I ought to have remembered that you can't eat strawberries.

Unit 2
Aspects of the future
There are many ways of expressing the future in English depending on meaning. We can use:

Will + infinitive
- to predict what is going to happen based on past experience or opinion
  You must go to India – you'll enjoy it.

- in more formal contexts for arrangements which have been made in some detail
  The tour will begin at 9.30 and all visitors to the site will need to wear good walking shoes.

- for decisions which are made on the spur of the moment
  I think I'll go to Paris next weekend.

Going to + infinitive
- to predict something that you have evidence for
  Look at those clouds – I'm sure it's going to rain.

- to express intentions or decisions
  I'm going to see The Museum of Modern Art when I get to New York.

Shall + infinitive
- to talk about the future instead of *will* with *I* and *we*, although it is used less nowadays than previously
  I shall certainly travel first class next time I go abroad.

- for offers
  Shall I carry your bags?

Present continuous

- to talk about activities or events which have already been arranged or are definite. The future continuous can also be used in this context. It is a little more formal.
I'm travelling on the Orient Express to Venice.
I'll be travelling on the Orient Express to Venice.

- to avoid *going to* + *go* we can use the present continuous form of *go* instead
He's going climbing in the Alps next summer.

- for surprising or unexpected events
Paula is taking her mother on her honeymoon!

Present simple

- to talk about future events such as a timetable or programme
The train for Burnley leaves at 5.00 sharp every Friday evening.

- in temporal clauses after a time conjunction
When you arrive in Beijing, go directly to the hotel and I'll meet you in the lobby.

Future continuous

- to talk about something that is going on at a particular time or over a particular period in the future
The ship will be travelling at 20 knots as it cruises in the Caribbean.

- for something that has been arranged previously
Luisa will be visiting us again in the fall.

- when you want to appear very polite
Will you be needing anything to drink, Sir?

be + infinitive

- for official notices, newspaper reports, formal instructions and to give orders
Passengers are to leave by the rear door of the aircraft.

Future perfect

- to say when something will be completed by
I hope they will have finished the building work on the hotel before we go on holiday.

Future perfect continuous

- to emphasise how long something has been going on for by a particular point in the future
'Air Europe' will have been carrying passengers for fifty years at the end of March.

Note that this tense isn't used with stative verbs, e.g. *see, believe, hear, know, become*, etc.

Expressions

- There are various expressions in English which are used to express future meaning. These include:
to be about to
to be on the verge of
to be bound/likely/unlikely to
to be on the point of

Unit 3
Conditional structures

There are four main types of conditional sentences.

- **Zero conditional** – to express real situations
If/When + present tense | present tense
If I eat too much in the evening, I can't sleep at night.

- **First conditional** – to express real situations
If + present tense | future tense *will*
If you don't apologise, you'll regret it later.

- **Second conditional** – to express unreal situations
If + past tense | *would/could/might*
If I had some money, I would live somewhere warmer.
If I were you, I'd go now before it rains.

- **Third conditional** – to express unreal situations
If + past perfect | *would/could/might* + *have* + past participle
If she hadn't had the chocolate chip ice cream, she would have been in a worse mood.

- **Mixed conditionals**
If + past tense | *might/could/should/would* – for situations in the present which affect the past
If I weren't so untidy, I wouldn't have lost your keys.

 If + past perfect | *would/might/could* + infinitive – for situations in the past which affect the present
If I had moved to California, I would be much richer today.

Inversion and conditionals
Sentences with inversion are more formal than those with 'if'.

- **First conditional**
This often expresses a tentative idea/request/offer, etc.
If you should require more assistance, please telephone.
Should you require more assistance, please telephone.

- **Second conditional**
If you went out in this weather, you'd be thoroughly soaked.
Were you to go out in this weather, you'd be thoroughly soaked.

- **Third conditional**
If I had known there was going to be a storm, I would have stayed indoors.
Had I known there was going to be a storm, I would have stayed indoors.

Other conditional structures

- *If* + *would* | *will*: *If you would take a seat, the doctor will see you shortly.*

- *If* + *will* | *will*: *I'll clean the house, if you'll mow the lawn.*

- Other words and phrases can be used to introduce conditional clauses:

 Providing, provided that, as/so long as are similar to *if*. They are all emphatic forms emphasising a condition.

 Even if introduces an extreme condition.
Well, it's true, even if you refuse to believe me.

 Unless can be replaced by *if ... not* or *providing ... not* but sometimes works better with ***except when***.
I won't give a waiter a tip except when / unless I get excellent service.

 Supposing should be used at the beginning of the sentence and is often not used as a linking word, but rather in the sentence setting up the condition.
Supposing/suppose it rains tomorrow. What will we do?

 Given that is used when some fact is already known.
Given that this area is liable to flood, it would be unwise in the extreme to consider buying a house here.

 But for and ***without*** are often used with third conditional sentences.
But for his help, I would never have managed to survive the ferry crossing.

Unit 4

Talking about the past

There are a number of ways of talking about the past in English.

- To talk about completed actions, the past simple is used.
  Goran Ivanisevic won the 2001 Wimbledon final.

- To talk about events which occurred regularly or habitually in the past, *would* or *used to* can also be used.
  It was our little ritual. I would nod, she would smile and he would look longingly.
  I used to go swimming four or five times a week.
  Every spring, Grant visited his elderly aunts in Maine.

- To talk about something which continued to happen before and after a given event, the past continuous is used.
  While Kevin was visiting friends in Italy, his flat was burgled.

- To talk about a temporary situation in the past, the past continuous is used.
  The two families were eating a meal together for the first time.

For information about the past perfect, see also the section on Perfect tenses on page 180.

Speculating about the past

- To express certainty or near-certainty about something in the past, the modal verb *must* is used with *have* and a past participle.
  Those early settlers must have had access to fresh water.
  You must have seen that Jeff Bridges film at least five times!

- To express uncertainty about something in the past, the modal verbs *could, may, might* are used with *have* and a past participle.
  I suppose it could have been my mistake, though I labelled everything clearly.
  Experts are suggesting that the virus may have been carried long distances on the wind.
  We might have met at that party in 1999?

- To express impossibility about something in the past, the modal verbs *can't* or *couldn't* are used with *have* and a past participle.
  You can't have got to Leeds yet – it's a four-hour drive at least!
  James couldn't have played cricket last week as he was away.

Using the passive in the past

- The passive is formed with the verb *be* and a past participle.
  The telephone was invented by Alexander Graham Bell.
  Repairs were being made to the bridge at first light this morning.
  Fork-like implements have been used for over 2000 years.
  Both sides had been advised to seek fresh legal representation before the trial.

- There are only two passive infinitives that are commonly used in English, the present and the perfect forms.
  This yoghurt needs to be eaten before the 25th.
  Radical cuts to the budget seem to have been made by the Managing Director.

Note that passive infinitives are often used after the verbs *appear, prove* and *seem*, as in the second example above.

Unit 5

Nouns

Nouns can be countable or uncountable.

- **Countable** nouns can:
  use *a/an* or *the* or *some*
  be used in the plural
  take the following determiners: *many, a large number of, several, a few, few, a lot of*

- **Uncountable nouns:**
  can use *the* or *some* or nothing
  are used only in a singular form
  can take the following determiners: *much, a great deal of, a large amount of, little, a little, a lot of*

- Common uncountable nouns include:
  most substances – *coal, china, flour*, etc.
  abstract nouns – *happiness, admiration, freedom*
  all sports
  most nouns ending in -*ing* – *shopping, sightseeing*
  accommodation, information, traffic, advice, luggage, luck, weather, work, homework, furniture, evidence

- Some nouns can be countable and uncountable with a slight change of meaning.
  She has grey hair. There are hairs on your jumper.
  The bridge is built of stone. I've got a stone in my shoe.

- Some nouns can be countable and uncountable but completely change their meaning.
  What's the capital of your country?
  The company has very little capital to work with.

- The majority of uncountable nouns can be made singular or plural by adding a *bit/piece* of or *bits/pieces* of. However, there are sometimes specific words which should be used instead.
  a lump of sugar
  a shaft of sunlight

- Some nouns with a singular form can be treated as singular or plural, depending on whether the noun is seen as a unit or a collection of people.
  The class is/are doing exams at present.
  The committee is/are looking into the matter of vandalism.

- Some nouns look plural but take a singular verb.
  The news is on at 8.00 pm.
  Athletics is an important part of the Olympics.

- Some nouns like *police* look singular but take a plural verb.
  The police are involved in trying to catch the thief.

Possessive forms

Possession can be signalled in English in three different ways – using an apostrophe, using *of* and using a noun as an adjective.

- For people and expressions concerning time and distance an apostrophe is generally used.
  my uncle's sister
  the boy's shoes
  a year's salary

- For objects *of* is generally used.
  the back of the room
  the cover of the book

- A noun is often used as an adjective to indicate kind, use or place.
  a table leg
  a night flight
  a shop window

Unit 6
Degrees of likelihood

- **Can** is used to express possibility without reference to past, present or future.
  He can sound off-key at times when he sings.

- **Could**, **may** and **might** express present possibility with reference to the future, present or past.
  It may/might/could be a good concert/ have been a good concert.

- **May not** and **might not** express possibility negatively.
  Get your ticket for the concert today; there may/might not be many left.
  He may/might not have bought the CD you wanted.

- Deduction is expressed by **must be / must have been**, **will be / will have been** and **should be / should have been**.
  You must be tired after your performance.
  That'll be my guitar teacher; I heard him ring the door bell.
  She should have been able to sing at the concert, her sore throat was much better.

- Impossibility is expressed by **cannot/can't** and **could not**.
  It can't be a flute; it sounds more like a clarinet.
  You couldn't have seen the new video – it hasn't been released yet.

- **Could** and **might** can be used to imply criticism or irritation. Intonation is very important in carrying meaning with these modals.
  You might have told me you'd be coming late.
  You could practise a bit more.

- Various expressions can be used to express likelihood:
  it's a foregone conclusion
  the chances are
  there's every likelihood
  he's bound to
  there's a slim/faint chance
  it's doubtful

Unit 7
Participle clauses

Participle clauses give more information about someone or something. In many ways, their function in a sentence is similar to defining relative clauses.

The man dancing over there is my brother. (The man *who is dancing over there* is my brother.)
The painting sold at auction yesterday has already been shipped to New York. (The painting *that was sold at auction yesterday* has already been shipped to New York.)

- The position of the clause can affect meaning.
  Standing at the top of the hill, I could just see the village. (refers to the subject, 'I')
  I could just see the village standing at the top of the hill. (refers to the object, 'the village')

- **Having** + past participle refers to previous action.
  Having reached the top of the hill, I could just see the village.

- **Being** + past participle is used to express a passive.
  The report being published today will force local governments back to the drawing board.

- Past participle -**ed** clauses are used in a similar way.
  The images provided by the Hubble Space Telescope have given astronomers fresh insights.

Unit 8
Inversion

In the normal word order of a sentence, a subject is followed by a verb.
Madrid offers its visitors an excellent choice of restaurants and some wonderful bars too.

However, sometimes this word order is changed, or inverted. This is usually done to give emphasis within the sentence. For example, the sentence above could be rewritten as:
Not only does Madrid offer its visitors an excellent choice of restaurants, but there are also some wonderful bars.

- The broad negative adverbs **barely**, **hardly**, **rarely**, **scarcely**, **seldom** can be used like this.
  Barely were we into our costumes when it was time to go on stage.
  Seldom does a day go by without someone ringing up to complain about the product.

- **Never** and **nowhere** are used in a similar way.
  Never had I felt more relaxed than that first week on Corsica.
  Nowhere could we find fresh vegetables, and some dairy products were in short supply too.

- Other negative words and expressions like this are **little**, **no sooner**, **not**.
  Little did we realise what we were letting ourselves in for.
  No sooner had Phoebe arrived than she helped herself to a drink without asking.
  Not a single word of thanks did they hear from her.

- Inversion also occurs at the end of sentences with **neither**, **nor** and **so**.
  Tim didn't feel like facing the press and neither did Lucy.
  Students haven't welcomed these new exams and nor have their teachers.
  Karl will be pleased to finish work and so will I.

- Sometimes a time clause precedes inversion.
  Not until two days later did we remember to call the school.
  Only once before have I felt like this about a project.

- Sometimes an adjunct of place precedes inversion.
  At the end of the path lay the meadows.
  In the distance stood the foothills of the Himalayas.

- Inversion occurs with certain prepositional phrases.
  On no account are you to leave this room!
  Under no circumstances can a replacement card be issued.
  In no way does that imply defeat.
  At no time did you give me an accurate picture of what was going on.

- Inversion can occur with **so** + an adjective.
  So loud was the music that we couldn't attempt to chat.
  So consistent has John's performance been that he has earned the nickname 'Strongman'.

- **Such** is used in a similar way to emphasise the extent of something.
  Such is the demand for tickets that they are selling at double their face value.

See also Unit 3 on page 181 for information about inversion in conditional sentences.

Unit 9
Gerunds and infinitives
Verb + object + *to*-infinitive

- Some verbs include an object before a *to*-infinitive: *consider, warn, allow, believe, encourage*, etc.
  I encouraged her to wear her school uniform.

- Some verbs don't require an object: *decide, refuse, hope, fail, agree, start*, etc.
  I decided to throw out all the clothes I hadn't worn for a year.

- Some verbs sometimes take an object and sometimes don't: *hate, help, like, love, want, prefer, need.*
  I like to swim every morning.
  I like you to swim so that you get some exercise.

Verb + (object) + bare infinitive

- Some verbs are followed by a bare infinitive after an object: *hear, feel, make, notice, see, watch, let*, etc.
  I made him shave his beard off.
  Her parents let her choose the shoes she wanted.

Verb + *to*-infinitive or *-ing*?

- Some verbs are followed by a *to*-infinitive: *agree, aim, ask, demand, prepare, hope, manage, wish*, etc.
  I agreed to wear the uniform.

- Some verbs are followed by *-ing*: *consider, avoid, envisage, miss, imagine*, etc. and all phrasal verbs.
  Liz couldn't imagine wearing evening dress.

- Some verbs take either a *to*-infinitive or *-ing* with little or no change in meaning: *begin, start, cease, continue.*
  They began singing/to sing early in the programme.

- Some verbs take a *to*-infinitive or *-ing* but change their meaning: *go on, stop, try, remember, forget, regret, mean, come, hear*, etc.
  They came to accept her opinions. (gradual change)
  He came running into the room. (way of moving)

  He went on to talk about the dress code. (next topic)
  He went on talking even when everyone started yawning. (continue)

  I mean to wear jeans to the barbecue. (intend)
  It means buying a new pair of shoes. (involves)

  I regret to say that you are not properly attired. (present/future)
  I regret telling her that she looked scruffy. (past)

  I remember visiting the Museum of Clothes when I was young. (remember – second action)
  I remembered to post the parcel to her this morning. (remember – first action)

  They stopped dancing when she came into the room. (ceased)
  They stopped to have a cup of coffee halfway through the morning. (reason)

  Try to stand up straight. (attempt)
  If you can't get the car going, try ringing the garage. (experiment)

  I heard Madonna sing in London. (once)
  I hear the birds singing every morning. (repeated action)

Verb + *-ing*

- Some verbs must have an object before an *-ing* when they are in the active: *catch, discover, observe, see, watch*, etc.
  I overheard them talking about the new manager.
  but
  They were overheard talking about the new manager.

- Some verbs don't have an object before *-ing*: *admit, advise, consider, deny, face, finish, suggest*, etc.
  I suggested going to the party early.

Unit 10
Past verb forms
Wish

- To talk about the present a past tense is used.
  I wish I could speak Spanish.

- To talk about the past a past perfect is used.
  If only they had listened to their teacher.

- To express irritation or criticism of something happening now *would* is used.
  I wish he would stop answering me in English when I want to practise French.
  Note: *would* isn't used if the object and subject are the same.

- *If only* is perhaps slightly stronger than *I wish.*

It's (about/high) time / would rather

- are followed by a past tense to express a present idea with an object.
  It's time the government invested in language training.
  I'd rather you learnt Esperanto.

- are followed by an infinitive when making a general statement.
  It's time to leave.
  I'd rather learn Chinese than Russian.

As if/though

- is used with a past tense to suggest an unreal situation.
  He looked as if he had failed the exam. (he hadn't)

Unit 11
Gradable and ungradable adjectives

A gradable adjective can be combined with an adverb like *reasonably* or *extremely* to quantify that adjective. So, for example, you can be *fairly happy* or *very happy*. This cannot happen with an ungradable adjective, as the adjective itself already holds some notion of quantity or degree. These adjectives can be combined with adverbs like *absolutely* or *totally* to add emphasis.
We all feel slightly frustrated by the lack of communication on this project.
Charlotte was absolutely furious when she heard the decision.

adverbs	gradable adjectives
deeply	angry
extremely	cheerful
fairly	happy
immensely	hurt
rather	irritable
very	upset

adverbs	ungradable adjectives
absolutely	awful
completely	broken-hearted
entirely	impossible
totally	terrible
utterly	wonderful

- *Pretty* can be combined with both gradable and ungradable adjectives in informal English.
  Tom finds it pretty quiet around here in the evenings, so he often shoots off to town on his motorbike.
  It's pretty amazing that someone who was at death's door three months ago has just run the London marathon!

- *Really* can also be combined with both types of adjective, though with ungradable adjectives, the use can only be informal.
  For a really comfortable night's sleep, choose Maxton's mattresses every time.
  I've just had a really awful run-in with Duncan over his marketing plan.

- *Quite* can be combined with both gradable and ungradable adjectives, but there is a change of meaning.
  I'm quite busy at work at the moment, but I've known it much worse. (= fairly)
  You're quite impossible at times – sweet wrappers go in the bin not on the floor! (= completely)

Unit 12
Passive structures
Formation

The passive is formed with the verb *be* and a past participle. For modals it is formed with the modal + *be* + past participle.
An unmanned submarine has been developed to automatically track down and follow whales and tuna, alarming many conservationists.
Miniature versions can now be produced at minimal cost.

This table shows the formation of all passive tenses. Those crossed through do not normally occur in English.

Simple present	It is made.
Present continuous	It is being made.
Present perfect	It has been made.
Present perfect continuous	~~It has been being made.~~
Simple past	It was made.
Past continuous	It was being made.
Past perfect	It had been made.
Past perfect continuous	~~It had been being made.~~
Future	It will be made.
Future continuous	~~It will be being made.~~
Future perfect	It will have been made.
Future perfect continuous	~~It will have been being made.~~

Use

The passive is used:

- when the action is more important than the person doing it
  It's going to be quite some time before your car's body panels are cast from titanium.

- when the person who did the action is not known
  In separate incidents across the city, shop windows were smashed and goods looted.

- to produce an official or impersonal tone
  Visitors must be accompanied by a member of staff at all times.

Unit 13
Reported speech

- As reported speech is used to tell someone else of what happened, all pronouns change, almost all verb tenses, except second and third conditionals and past perfects, change and all words referring to a particular time or place change.
  'I saw this film two weeks ago.' → *She said she had seen that film two weeks before.*

- Some changes are not quite so straightforward. *Must* changes to *had to* and *mustn't* becomes *was not to* for obligation. If *must* is used to talk about laws or general truths then it doesn't change.
  'I must buy a new bicycle.' → *She said she had to buy a new bicycle.*
  'You mustn't tell my mother.' → *She said I was not to tell her mother.*
  'You must not go more than 40 kph.' → *He said you mustn't go more than 40 kph.*

- With the first conditional, the verb tenses in the *If* clause backshift in the usual way and *will* changes to *would* in the main clause.
  'If you don't hurry up, you'll miss your flight.' → *She said that if we didn't hurry up, we would miss our flight.*

- As a general rule, the second conditional doesn't change.
  'He would be pleased if you visited him.' → *She said he would be pleased if she visited him.*

- Often a verb or a verb and adverb are used which contain many of the elements of what is being reported.
  'What about picking up the litter?' she said. → *She suggested picking up the litter.*
  'Good Lord! Look at that rubbish tip!' he said. → *He exclaimed in horror when he saw the rubbish tip.*
  'I had absolutely nothing to do with it,' he said. → *He categorically denied having anything to do with it.*

Unit 14
Articles

- Plural, abstract and uncountable nouns do not need an article if they are used to talk about things in general. To limit these nouns a definite article is required.
  Sport is good for you.
  The sport played the most is football.

- Singular, concrete nouns require an article, except for some idioms. The definite article is precise and refers to something, while the indefinite article is vague and more general, or is used when something is mentioned for the first time.
  The runner in first place came from Kenya.
  Steve is going to be a runner in the New York marathon.

- No article is used with: certain countries; names of mountains; meals, unless they are formal ones; *bed, school, hospital, prison* if they are being used for their intended purpose.
  I intend to visit Australia.
  She's in prison for stealing.
  Come down for breakfast!

- The definite article is used with: rivers, seas, oceans, chains of mountains, gulfs and bays; newspapers; before musical instruments; before a superlative adjective; when we know there is only one of something.
  Tessa plays the violin.
  I read the Times.
  The Sierra Nevada is a beautiful mountain range.
  The sky is very blue.

- The indefinite article is used when we mean 'one' of something unless we want to emphasise the amount.
  I'd like a cup of coffee.
  Just one cup, not two.

Unit 15
Purpose and reason clauses

- A purpose clause normally comes after a main clause.
  I keep the answerphone on when I'm working, so as not to be distracted.

- Purpose clauses are introduced by the following conjunctions:
  for fear that (formal)
  lest (formal)
  in order to
  in order not to
  in order that
  so as to
  so as not to
  so that

- A reason clause can come before or after the main clause.
  As it was late, Jenny went straight to bed.
  I'd shut the window in case it rains.

- Reason clauses are introduced by:
  as
  because
  in case
  since

Unit 16
Concessive clauses

These are used to give contrasting information to that given in the rest of the sentence. A concessive clause can come before or after the main clause.
Although Moravia had more than thirty books published in his lifetime, his first novel is undoubtedly the best.
Shakespeare remains on the exam syllabus, even though many British teenagers find his plays inaccessible.

- Concessive clauses are introduced by the following conjunctions:
  although
  despite
  even if
  even though
  in spite of
  much as
  though
  whereas
  while

- *Much as* and *whereas* are less commonly used and occur mainly in formal written English.

- With *though* and *although*, it is possible to omit the verb in the concessive clause.
  Although (we were) exhausted, we stayed up to watch the end of the film.

- *Despite* and *in spite of* cannot be followed by a verb, but take a gerund or noun.
  Despite running all the way to the station, we missed the train.
  In spite of the weather, we had a good time.

  It is possible to add *the fact that* to these conjunctions and then include a verb.
  Despite the fact that Jess had very little money, her trip to Lisbon was a great success.

Unit 17
Comparison

There are various ways of making comparisons in English.

- Using a comparative or superlative adjective
  I'm happier now than I've ever been.
  That is the most outrageous suggestion you've made today!

- Using the structure *not as … as*
  Holly is not as fast on the tennis court as she used to be.
  Note that the variant *not so … as* is less common nowadays.

- Other related expressions are *nowhere near as … as*, *not nearly as … as* and *nothing like as … as*.
  The latest series of Friends *is nowhere near as good as the earlier ones.*
  This CD is not nearly as good as OK Computer.

- Including an adverb of degree gives added emphasis. The nouns *a bit, a good deal, a great deal, a little, a lot* are also used in this way.
  You're by far the cleverest person in this class, you know.
  Sally is a great deal younger than her brother.

Unit 18
Review of modal verbs

Here are further examples of the many different functions of modal verbs. See also Unit 3 Conditional structures and Unit 6 Degrees of likelihood.

Strong obligation

All passengers must observe the no smoking policy on board.
You'll have to wait in line like everyone else, I'm afraid.
I had to walk to school when I was young.

Weak obligation

I ought to save a bit more money each month.
You really should try to keep on top of your homework.

Unfulfilled obligation (past)

George should have gone to visit his parents more often than he did.
We ought to have done more to this house.

Prohibition

Students must not bring any personal belongings into the examination room.
I don't care what you say, you can't stay out later than midnight.

No necessity

We don't need to buy the cinema tickets in advance.
You needn't have bothered to come and see me off at the station.

Speculation

Could it have been the right answer after all?
There might be some money in it for you.

Deduction

That must be the turning just beyond the garage.
It must have been Mike's girlfriend you met.

Ability

I can perform quite well on my forehand, but I can't play a backhand shot to save my life.
Everyone in the class could understand sign language perfectly.

Impossibility

Andrew can't play squash tonight.
There couldn't have been a power failure – the video's still on.

Advice

You should cut down on chocolate if you want to lose weight.
Jerry really ought to see a doctor about his back problem.

Permission

You can have a break now.
You may leave if you wish. (formal)

Unit 19
Word order

There are three normal positions for adverbs:

- at the beginning of a sentence – **Last night** I saw a ghost.
- in the mid-position – I have **never** had a paranormal experience.
- at the end – She left work **in a hurry**.

It is important to remember that there are exceptions to the following general rules regarding the position of adverbs, usually depending on what the speaker is emphasising or sees as most important. Note that some types of adverb can go in more than one position.

Initial position adverbs

- Connecting adverbs – *However, Then*

- Adverbs of time – *Last night, Tomorrow*

- Some adverbs of frequency – *Usually, Once a year, Occasionally*

- Some adverbs of certainty – *Maybe, Perhaps, Naturally*

- Negative adverbials with inversion – *Seldom, Rarely*
  Seldom have I seen him so angry.

- Adverbs of manner, for emphasis –
  Carefully he placed the slide under the microscope.

Mid-position adverbs

The rule here is that these go before a main verb, between an auxiliary and main verb and after the verb *to be*.

- Adverbs of certainty – *definitely, certainly*
  He will definitely win the cup.

- Adverbs of indefinite frequency – *often, seldom, rarely, never, usually, occasionally*
  She often loses her keys.

- Adverbs of manner – *quickly, slowly, carefully*
  He quickly dived into the water.

- Adverbs of completeness –
  I have nearly finished the washing.

- Adverbs of degree – *completely, quite*
  She was quite convinced that she was right.

- Focus adverbs – *just, even*
  He didn't even apologise for forgetting my birthday.
  They just appeared out of nowhere.

End position adverbs

- Adverbs of manner –
  She crossed the lane slowly. He dived into the water quickly.

- Adverbs of place –
  She walked into the park.

- Adverbs of time – *last night, tomorrow, yesterday*
  We saw her only last week.

- Adverbs of definite frequency –
  I go to the gym twice a week.

If there is more than one end position adverb in a sentence or clause, the general rule is to put them in the following order: manner – place – time, though this order can vary for reasons of emphasis.
We were walking peacefully along the beach yesterday, when we got a terrible fright.
She walked hurriedly out of the room.
She ran out of the room in a frenzy.
I met him for the first time at a concert last week.

Any position **adverbs**

- Comment adverbs –
  Personally, I'm very annoyed with him.
  I'm personally very annoyed with him.
  I'm very annoyed with him, personally.

- Sometimes –
  I'm sometimes late with work.
  Sometimes I'm late with work.
  I'm late with work sometimes.

hard/hardly etc.

In some cases there is a difference in the meaning of an adverb which sometimes uses -*ly* and sometimes doesn't. Adverbs that change meanings include: *hard, direct, short, wide, late, free, wrong, right.*
I saw the UFO high over the mountains.
He thinks highly of Aboriginal beliefs.

Unit 20

have and *go*

We use the structure of **have** + **object** + **past participle** when we talk about other people doing things for us, for example *I have my hair cut every three weeks.*

Another use of **have** + **object** + **participle** is of 'experience', for example *I had my car stolen last night.* This is something that happened to me. I didn't organise it. The following are similar examples.
It's good to have the birds singing in the morning now it's spring.
I had a dog follow me home yesterday.

Have + **object** + **infinitive or -ing** form is also quite common.
I won't have you coming home late every night!
Have Mrs Jones sit down please.
The teacher had us all running round the field in the rain.

Look at the following uses of **get** + **object** + **participle**.
I got the car repaired. – This is a more informal way of saying *I had the car repaired.*
She got herself lost on the underground. – It was her own fault.
I'll get the washing done if you do the ironing. – This implies I'll do it myself.
I'll never get this done by tomorrow. – I'll never be able to finish it.

Revision crosswords

These crosswords test the idioms and vocabulary you have learned so far in the units. The number of letters required is given in brackets.

Units 1–4

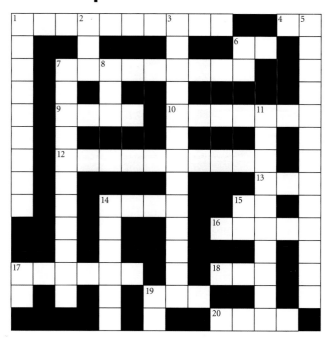

ACROSS
1 do what is expected of you (3,3,4)
4 (and 8, 2 down) .... easy as .... , ... , three (2,3,3)
6 see 19 across
7 cannot go wrong (9)
9 take .... a business (phrasal verb) (4)
10 verb related to 'prevalent' (7)
12 uncertain of a successful outcome (5,3,2)
13 not tell the truth (3)
14 .... chalk and cheese (4)
15 have no objection .... something (2)
16 see 17 down
17 (and 6 down) instead of (2,4,2)
18 see 19 across
19 (and 18, 6 across) manage to avoid (3,3,2)
20 see 19 down

DOWN
1 find with some effort (phrasal verb) (5,4)
2 see 4 across
3 impossible to get another (13)
5 tell a secret (5,3,5)
6 see 17 across
7 pay (4,3,4)
8 see 4 across
11 sorry (10)
14 (and 15 down) be as good as expected (phrasal verb) (4,2,2)
15 see 14 down
17 (and 16 across) fashionable (2,5)
19 (and 20 across) return or retreat (phrasal verb) (2,4)

Units 5–8

Units 9–12

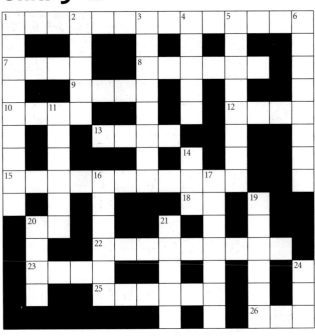

ACROSS

1 ostentatious, stylish (often used of clothes) (10)
5 a .... hate (3)
7 .... close to call; .... hot to handle (3)
8 very bad weather: the eye of the .... (5)
11 very cheap: going for a .... (4)
13 not as good as believed to be (9)
14 a grain of .... (4)
15 someone who can't stop making purchases (10)
18 having respect for: in .... of (3)
19 briefly (2,1,8)
22 on .... account (2)
24 inflexible (5)
28 see 19 down
29 origin (6)
30 (and 3 down) leave (phrasal verb) (3,3)

DOWN

1 moronic, stupid (7)
2 certain to happen: .... conclusion (1,8)
3 see 30 across (3)
4 compare: liken .... (2)
6 little time to complete tasks or projects (5,9)
8 a .... of abuse (6)
9 (and 16 down) .... the blue (3,2)
10 (and 23 down) stay up late working: burn the .... (8,3)
11 ....-called (2)
12 a stroke .... luck (2)
16 see 9 down
17 turn a blind .... to someone's faults (3)
19 (and 28 across) morally justified (2,3,5)
20 under ...... circumstances (2)
21 a loud or unpleasant sound (5)
23 see 10 down
25 the grass ...... always greener (2)
26 promptly: on the ...... (3)
27 leave someone high and .... (3)

ACROSS

1 able to recognise things of good quality (14)
7 say no: .... a proposal (4)
8 a .... of hair, thread, DNA, etc. (6)
9 ready money (4)
10 danger; also verb (4)
12 calm .... (phrasal verb) (4)
13 spick and .... (4)
15 not sleep properly (4,3,4)
18 Thanks! (informal) (2)
20 bit .... bit; minute .... minute (2)
22 not definite (9)
23 between two states: on the .... (4)
25 puzzle, such as a crossword: brain .... (6)
26 eat humble .... (3)

DOWN

1 variety (used especially of species) (9)
2 see 24 down
3 didn't catch exactly what was said (8)
4 standard ways of behaving in society (5)
5 make less flamboyant or less offensive (phrasal verb) (4,4)
6 enormous (8)
11 sentimental; also used of weather conditions (6)
14 see 21 down
16 rather rude or short with someone (6)
17 ecstasy or extreme joy – a literary word (7)
19 deliberately incite an emotion (phrasal verb) (4,2)
20 see 24 down
21 (and 14 down) .... a solution; extract (phrasal verb) (5,3)
24 (and 2, 20 down) return to the past: turn .... (3,5,4)

Units 13–16

Units 17–20

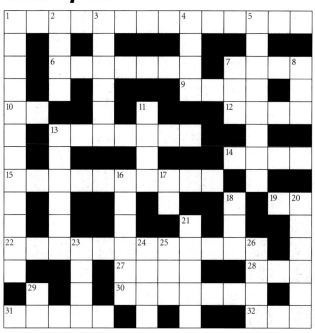

ACROSS

1 gripping; urgent (10)
6 regular; with a beat (8)
10 describes heavy traffic (4,2,4)
13 successor (starts with a silent letter) (4)
14 fast .... ; .... record (5)
17 close down: .... up shop (4)
18 desire; want very much (5)
19 the .... of the problem (3)
20 forgetful (6-6)
23 exclamation (2)
24 become unable to deal with things (4,4,4)

DOWN

1 opt for something unsuitable, in desperation (6,2,6)
2 large and unruly crowd (3)
3 deal with things as they happen : play it by .... (3)
4 blame: .... someone's door (3,2)
5 good to chew (3)
7 ignore: give someone the .... (4,8)
8 neither… .... (3)
9 huge advance or improvement (7,4)
10 zero; the big 'O' (3)
11 .... your heart out! (3)
12 quiet or monosyllabic (8)
15 (and 21, 16 down) regret (a literary phrase) (3,3,3)
16 see 15 down
18 losses or reductions (4)
19 see 11 down
21 see 15 down
22 polite modal verb (3)

ACROSS

1 something to think about (4,3,7)
6 supporting a cause or ideal passionately (7)
7 an advantage or benefit; the opposite of 'minus' (4)
9 keep body and .... together (4)
10 see 29 down
12 be on cloud .... (4)
13 fate; what will happen (7)
14 mistake: a .... in the argument: (4)
15 good at noticing or realising things (10)
19 word used in similes (2)
22 scornful (12)
27 noise made by a contented cat (4)
28 have a debt (3)
30 cause to happen; also noun: pull the .... (7)
31 call a .... a .... (5)
32 the very last clue: the .... (3)

DOWN

1 not have as much money as you used to (4,3,5)
2 verb used to describe the movement of mud, oil, etc. (4)
3 noisy quarrel or fight: originally a French word (6)
4 make a sound like a snake; also noun (4)
5 naïve (8)
7 play on words: noun and verb (3)
8 take legal action for damages (3)
11 clenched hand (4)
13 Never .... my door again! (6)
16 on time; without delay (6)
17 set the wheels .... motion (2)
18 see 29 down
20 cunning; astute (6)
21 a .... of joy; also verb: increase suddenly (5)
23 dull sound; also verb (4)
24 unadulterated, not mixed with anything (4)
25 prefix meaning 'three' (3)
26 a ...... loser (4)
29 (and 10 across, 18 down) It's your decision: It's ....
.... (2,2,3)

Self-study folder

The following pages contain all the answers to the exercises, sample answers for the writing tasks, the tapescripts, and lots of additional notes, including useful background information on the texts and topics. The *Map of Objective Proficiency Student's Book* on pages 3–5 gives full details of the language and exam skills covered in each unit. The *Content of the Proficiency Examination* on pages 6–7 provides information about the exam, with links to the relevant Exam folder or Writing folder.

Unit 1

1.1 pages 8–9

1 The two idioms are *a change for the better* and *a change of heart. Ring the changes,* the unit title, is also an idiom. Note that you can also say *a change for the worse.*

> **Possible answers**
> The earliest change I can remember is when my family moved to a new house. It was definitely a change for the better, as I had my own large bedroom and the house had a much bigger garden.
> The most unexpected change in my life took place when I won a substantial amount of money in a competition, which allowed me to take a break from work.
> The biggest change in my life involving people came about when my father remarried, and, overnight, the number of children in our family grew from two to six.
> When I left home and went to university, I moved to the opposite side of the country, which was very different from where I had grown up.
> I found some old letters the other day, which I had kept for more than twenty years – but I had a sudden change of heart and burnt the lot!

2 The underlined parts of the tapescript confirm the answers.

> **Answers**
> 1 gaining media attention   4 being made redundant
> 2 stepping in for someone   5 meeting 'Mr Right'
> 3 heading the wrong way   6 winning a competition

Speaker 1: I've had a really fantastic year. It all started last November, when I was dragged along to a party by a friend. I was in a terrible mood, I remember, and nearly didn't go. Anyway, I was wearing an outfit I'd made myself – in soft black leather and antique lace, quite an unusual combination! Kelly Johns, the presenter of a big daytime TV show, was there and my little number caught her eye. She came over and we got chatting. She asked whether I could run her up something to wear on the show and I jumped at the chance. That was a real turning point for me. I was soon able to chuck in my day job and concentrate on the clothes side full-time. Through Kelly's show, I've had lots of orders, I've just finished an exclusive range for a top designer and I've even taken on an assistant to help me. Just think if I'd stayed in that night!

Speaker 2: People often ask me to describe in detail how I've got to be where I am today, thinking that I've spent years earning beer money in local clubs, but the truth is, I'm literally an overnight sensation! I don't mean that arrogantly; it was just one lucky break, all down to being in the right place at the right time. There I was, an absolute nobody, hanging around backstage with Arrowhead, when their lead guitarist tripped over a pile of speakers and broke his arm, five minutes before they were due on stage. I'd been rabbiting on about my brilliant guitar style, so naturally, they all turned to me and said 'Kid, help us out here …' and I did. The place was packed and I can still feel my hands shaking as I picked out that very first solo. It went OK though, and the rest is … history.

Speaker 3: I was in Milan visiting friends, trying to cheer myself up after a dismal few months – my long-term boyfriend and I had broken up, plus I'd left a job without another to go to. My savings were running low and I was planning to leave a few days later. Anyway, my friends suggested that I should take a look at Verona before going back home and told me what time train I could get from Milan. Well, for some reason, I ended up on a slow train going south, without realising my mistake – both trains had left at the same time. I fell asleep in the compartment and woke up in a panic as the train was drawing in to Bologna! I had a wander round and fell in love with the place and knew it was where I wanted to be. Everything just fell into place – I found a teaching job, took a room in a beautiful flat and settled in brilliantly. I lived there for six years and I go back regularly.

Speaker 4: It's funny how you can hit a vicious spiral; you're chugging along quite happily in your life and then, bam, something comes out of the blue and knocks you sideways and then, wham, something else. I'm OK now, but I've had a rocky couple of years. My problem was quite simply that I'd been living beyond my means for a good long time and some debts finally caught up with me. Even then, I thought I'd be OK; I arranged to pay them off little by little from my salary, monthly, you know. But then, <u>the factory where I was working cut back on its workforce, and they 'let me go'</u>. Well, that was it, I was in freefall. I suppose I panicked, I wasn't thinking straight, you know. So I just walked away, got on a train and left. Ended up in London. Got in with a bad crowd, one thing led to another. Awful. It's a miracle my brother ever tracked me down, but he's got me back and sorted, job, roof over my head … but I'll be paying off that money for years yet.

Speaker 5: <u>It could be a story in *True Romance*</u>, but it really happened just like this. Almost twenty years ago to the day, I was waiting for a bus after another mind-numbingly awful day at work, no bus in sight, of course. I was in a rut, my job was going nowhere. Anyway, there I was, staring gloomily at my reflection in a puddle, feeling utterly sorry for myself and thinking: is this really all there is to life? Then I saw two things in that puddle, one imperceptibly after the other. The first was no surprise, huge splashes of rain, as the heavens opened yet again, but then, this enormous red umbrella, appearing behind my head as if by magic! <u>A gorgeous gravelly voice to my left said</u> did I mind, it was big enough for two and he didn't want my hair to get wet. Very fortunately, it was another fifteen minutes before the bus finally turned up and hooray, it didn't stop raining! <u>His name was Terence, though he's been Terry to me ever since</u> – and Dad to our three wonderful children.

Speaker 6: Tennis was kind of my second choice as a kid – I suppose I preferred team sports like football. I'd had lessons, and I always watched the big championships on TV – Wimbledon, Roland Garros, the US Open – but I certainly wasn't competing myself. Then one Easter, there was a talent-spotting week at the local college and, having nothing better to do, I went along with a friend. We were 13 – or maybe 14. It was quite intensive, there were lots of practice sessions first and then a series of matches at the end of the week. <u>I came top in my age group out of forty-six players – I couldn't quite believe it when they presented me with the cup!</u> With that, I earned my place in a coaching squad and I've never looked back since! I make a good living from tennis and I wouldn't have it any other way, though I still try to find time to play football with my mates, when I can.

4 Be careful with word order when using phrasal verbs. The verb and particle cannot be separated:
- when it is a three-part phrasal verb
  I caught up with Jack further down the road.
- if the phrasal verb is used intransitively (without an object)
  All my hard work paid off.
- when the particle is a preposition
  Sally jumped at the chance of visiting Rome.

Answers
hang around
jump at
cut back on, look back
track down
chuck in, draw in, get in with, settle in, stay in
pay off
rabbit on
pick out
break up, catch up with, cheer up, end up, run up, turn up, wake up

5

Answers
a hung back / drew back   **b** broke in on / cut in on
c was cut off   **d** looked down on
e ran off with / had run off with   **f** has taken up with
g draw up   **h** got out of

6

Answers
1 B   **2** C   **3** B   **4** A   **5** C   **6** D

1.2 pages 10–11

1

Answers
1 b   **2** c   **3** d   **4** a

Possible answer
I think the funniest cartoon is the one about the oil slick, because the slick is in the shape of a person who is making a rude gesture.

All four cartoons use a perfect tense: **a** *you'd been* (past perfect); **b** *you've been at sea* (present perfect); **c** *you've come to* (present perfect); **d** *your husband's engaged* (present perfect).

A *quack* (**c**) is a person who pretends to be a doctor but has no actual qualifications. This word is used to show disapproval of someone.

2 Refer to the Grammar folder on pages 180–188 if you are unsure of a point covered in any unit. Even at Proficiency level, you need to spend time studying grammar and you should check your written work for grammatical accuracy. Here is a checklist of things to watch out for:

- subject–verb agreement
- choice of modal verb
- tense in conditional structures
- choice of past/present/future tense
- choice of preposition
- punctuation in relative clauses
- structure with reporting verbs, e.g. *insist on doing, urge someone to.*

3 These sentences were written by past Proficiency candidates and show typical errors with perfect tenses at this level.

> **Answers**
> **a** went to **b** has been used **c** had never seen
> **d** were measured **e** I've been practising,
> (I've been) trying / I've tried **f** you have bought
> **g** they had got married **h** people care

4

> **Answers**
> **a** *has gone* = he is still there
>   *went* = he is no longer there
> **b** *has been suffering* = ongoing situation, i.e. unemployment is still high
>   *was suffering* = continuous situation at unspecified time in the past
> **c** *were given* = one specific instance in the past
>   *have been given* = task is ongoing
> **d** *have been dealing* = continuous action that is not yet completed
>   *have dealt* = action completed, i.e. problem successfully handled
> **e** No difference in meaning
> **f** *I've thought* = focus is on the result, implies that a decision has been taken
>   *I've been thinking* = focus is on the activity, implies that person is still thinking
> **g** *could have done* = past speculation
>   *will have done* = future forecast, e.g. 'I'm writing up our annual report – is there anything else we will have done (by the end of the year)?'
> **h** No difference in meaning, though the future perfect continuous tense is more common, as 'living here' is continuous and ongoing.

5

> **Possible answers**
> **a** I've been learning English for ten years.
> **b** I've never done a course in deep-sea diving, though I would really like to.
> **c** One particular street in the centre has been closed to private cars, which has made traffic in other parts of the town much worse.
> **d** Including Proficiency, which I'll pass first time, I'll have taken five English exams.
> **e** I may have moved to another city for work.

6 The text is a diary entry. It is in fact the concluding entry from the successful book *Adrian Mole: The Cappuccino Years*, written by Sue Townsend.

7

> **Answers**
> **Perfect tenses**
> *Eleanor's burned:* present perfect for recent action
> *had joined:* past perfect for action further back in time
> *had been extinguished; had been arrested; she'd been refused:* past perfect (passive); as above
> *should never have been let out:* modal + perfect passive to express regret about something in the past
> *have often wondered:* present perfect for repeated action that continues
> *will have embellished; (will have) given:* future perfect for action completed by a definite time (by tomorrow)
>
> **Phrasal verbs**
> burn down let out came out of turned out
> tie (you) down grow up stand up

8

> **Suggested answers**
> - The writer, Adrian Mole, is a father of two; all his possessions have been lost in the fire.
> - Eleanor Flood set fire to Adrian's house; she was probably Adrian's former girlfriend and did it as a form of revenge.
> - William is Adrian's son; he used to keep insects.
> - Glenn is 13 and also Adrian's son; he wore trainers; he had started to keep a diary.
> - Andrew is a small furry animal, a pet of some kind.

9

> **Possible answer**
> I would feel relieved that my family was safe, but angry about losing my possessions. I don't entirely agree with Adrian's father, as somewhere to live and possessions give you security in life.

1.3 pages 12–13

1 The pictures show:
- the same maple tree in spring and winter
- two bars of Cadbury's chocolate – one from 1905, showing a dairy churn, and a modern version, showing a glass and a half of milk (the amount that goes into each 200g bar)
- someone using a mobile phone in Shanghai and a row of traditional red telephone boxes (which have now been phased out in Britain).

Background information

The Cadbury's Dairy Milk slogan 'a glass and a half of full cream milk' has remained unchanged since its launch in 1928, due to its phenomenal success in selling this chocolate – the Dairy Milk 'megabrand' has sales of £230 million a year.

Suggested answers

The maple tree shows environmental – or seasonal – change. You might also describe it as a physical change, in that the tree loses its leaves in winter.

The brand updating of the chocolate bar is an example of commercial change.

The change from using telephone boxes to using mobile phones shows both social and technological change.

An example of political change would be a change of party in power.

2

Answers

commerce – ial (drop the 'e' and add 'ial')
technology – ical (drop the 'y' and add 'ical')

Examples of -*ful* and -*less*: *hopeful/hopeless*; *thankful/thankless*

create/desire – 'e' is dropped and suffix added
vary – 'y' is dropped and '-iable' added OR 'y' changes to 'i' and suffix added

3

Answers

a predictable b alternative c hopeful
d philosophical e experimental f speechless
g noticeable h flawless

Adjectives from the remaining words: *admirable, identifiable, massive, successful, understandable*

4 Underlining important information is a vital first step in planning a summary, as it shows which ideas must be included.

Answers

C

Rather than burgers and fries being <u>a product</u> of the <u>social changes</u> seen over the <u>last fifty years in America</u>, the author suggests that <u>fast food</u> brands were to a large extent <u>responsible for these changes</u>, as they profoundly <u>affected both lifestyle and diet</u>.

D

<u>Tiny holes</u> found <u>in human teeth</u> estimated to be <u>over 8000 years old</u> are now believed to be the <u>earliest evidence of dentistry</u>, for when these holes were examined with an electron microscope, researchers found their <u>sides were too perfectly rounded</u> to be caused by bacteria and have therefore proposed that they were <u>drilled by prehistoric dentists</u>.

1 The sentence summarises the general idea that people pick up on things through facial features, but it omits any reference to health and social status, which means it is less clear than the original text.
2 The word *judge* could be replaced with *assess* or *evaluate*.
3 The underlined words in text B that could be replaced are: *produced* (developed, concocted, made); *chance* (accident); *revolutionised* (changed, updated, modernised); *innovations* (new techniques/inventions); *significantly* (notably, importantly). A word like *mauve* or *aspirin* cannot be paraphrased, as it is something very specific.

5

Answers

c is the best choice, as it captures all the important information, uses new words not in the text where possible, is written in a suitably neutral register and is concise (13 words).

Comments on the other sentences:
a Omits reference to Perkin and does not highlight the fact that aspirin was the most significant innovation.
b Unduly informal, with use of phrasal verbs; quite wordy.
d Unnecessary reformulation of *mauve* leads to lack of clarity and wordiness; other words are lifted from the text, e.g. *revolutionary, innovation*; too long a sentence.
e Wrong focus of information (aspirin); incomplete.
f Good attempt at reformulating, but lacks precision due to omission of *mauve*; register slightly too informal – better if sentence started 'Commercially' rather than 'Commercially-speaking'.

> **Suggested answers**
> **C** According to the author, fast food has caused social change recently, by influencing how Americans live and changing their diet. (20 words)
>
> **D** Research has uncovered evidence of prehistoric dentistry, as minute, round holes in 8000-year-old teeth cannot have been caused by bacteria. (20 words)

2.1 pages 16–17

1 The photos are of the Taj Mahal at dawn and the Empire State Building taken from street level.

Exam folder 1

> **Possible answer**
> They are both landmarks. I would like to go to the Taj Mahal because it is so evocative of a past era of romance and elegance. However, I would expect to be disappointed as it is quite near an industrial area and it is suffering from pollution.

Paper 3 Part 1
Open cloze page 14

1 The first photo is of two people watching the 1968 student riots in Paris. It was taken by Henri Cartier-Bresson. The second photo is of Henri Cartier-Bresson.

Read the introductory information very carefully.

> **Answers**
> **1** could/should **2** beneath/beyond **3** wherever
> **4** which **5** must **6** chord **7** itself **8** but **9** So
> **10** less **11** nothing **12** take **13** at/during **14** Despite
> **15** rate

Background information

Taj Mahal
Built in Agra in Uttar Pradesh, India between 1632 and 1654 as a mausoleum for Mumtaz Mahal, the favourite wife of Shah Jahan. It is built of white marble and inlaid with semi-precious stones and mosaic work.

Empire State Building
Built as an office block in Manhattan, New York City between 1930 and 1931. It is 449 metres high, including a 68 metre high TV mast added in 1951. It was the tallest building in the world until 1954.

Paper 3 Part 2
Word formation cloze page 15

2 The first photo is of a young woman with tattoos and piercings. The second is of a young boy with traditional designs painted on his body and face.

> **Answers**
> **1** antiquity **2** dominant **3** customising/izing
> **4** kingdom **5** kinship **6** extraordinary **7** practical
> **8** significance **9** Arguably **10** infinitely

Remember that in the examination you are required to fill in your answer sheet in CAPITAL LETTERS.

2

> **Answers**
> Yes, they were impressed. The following parts of the text tell you the answers.
> A – *They told me that the Taj Mahal is beautiful, and they were right.*
> B – *it's a work of art*

3

> **Answers**
> **1** B **2** A **3** C **4** D
>
> **1** **B** is correct because the writer says that they told him it was white and they were wrong. Therefore he was misinformed. It can't be **A** because he says it was in the spirit of *the betrayal of expectation* that he went there. It can't be **C** because when it is at its best isn't mentioned. **D** is wrong because the writer agrees that the Taj Mahal is beautiful.
> **2** **A** is correct because he writes in a poetic way about the building, singing its praises. **B** is wrong because he makes no criticism of it. **C** and **D** are wrong because there is nothing ironic or sentimental about the writing. Look these words up in an English–English dictionary if you aren't sure of their meanings.

3 C is correct because he says that most people who are from our planet will have seen something about the city. **A** is wrong because there is no mention of it being a good thing. **B** is wrong because, although the police are mentioned, there is nothing about the city being dangerous or otherwise. **D** is wrong because there is no mention of finding out about the city in advance.

4 D is correct because the streets are *jammed*, that is full, of *the little winking toy yellow cabs*. **A** is wrong because there is no mention of a public transport system, i.e. buses or subway. **B** is wrong because the only mention of streets is that they are *jammed* not narrow. **C** is wrong because the drivers are just moving from one lane to another, there is no criticism of their driving.

4 Use an English–English dictionary if there are words you do not know.

Answers
a for luck, i.e. hoping it would be as good as people said
b They are words connected with crime.
c It's worth seeing.
d He talks about it being so fast that people 'have no time to get embarrassed with each other's company'.
e to bring the colour to life / make it more exact

Style extra

A simile is a figurative device in language where something is referred to explicitly to make writing more descriptive or interesting. There are many in English which are fixed expressions. However, writers often make their own similes up to suit their own purposes.

Possible answers
Eyes as green as emeralds / blue as the sea / like deep pools
Hair as soft as silk / golden as the sun / black as night / like spun gold

Rain like bullets / as cold as the Arctic
Snow as crisp as an apple / like fluffy clouds

A hot day – like being in an oven
A cold day – like the inside of a fridge

Some fixed expressions using similes are not always very logical. Compare what is said in English with what is said in your language.

Answers
a like water off a duck's back   b as clean as a whistle
c as deaf as a post   d like chalk and cheese
e like a bat out of hell   f as warm as toast
g as white as a sheet   h like a sieve

5 To me 'eco-tourism' and 'green holidays' mean: bicycles rather than car parks; recyclable/local materials; no commercialisation; no high-rise hotels, etc.

The exercise looks at noun endings. Make a list of as many noun endings as you can. You should end up with a list similar to this one.

-tion	-dom	-ery
-ence	-or	-ess
-ance	-er	-hood
-ness	-ory	-ist
-ity	-th	-ian
-ship	-ment	

Answers
1 appearance   2 awareness   3 realisation   4 operators
5 presence   6 categories   7 wilderness   8 growth
9 movements   10 choice   11 regulation(s)
12 definition

2.2 pages 18–19

1 Refer to the Grammar folder on pages 180–181 if you are unsure about which tense is used to express a particular aspect.

Possible answers
a To talk about arranged plans for this evening; things you have already organised or booked, e.g. a cinema or theatre visit or friends for dinner.
b To talk about plans which are not organised and maybe are just ideas or spur of the moment plans. These could include plans which might change depending on circumstances, e.g. If it rains, I'll watch TV instead of playing tennis.
c To talk about your intentions this evening; something which you are thinking of doing but haven't quite got around to booking/planning in detail.
d Usually used to talk about a specific time in the future, e.g. What will you be doing at 8.00 this evening? I'll be washing my hair.
e To talk about what will have happened by a certain time in the future. You are looking into the future and saying 'this will have happened', e.g. I will have finished all my homework by 10 tonight.
f To talk about plans which have been abandoned for one reason or another, e.g. I was going to play tennis tonight, but now I have to stay in to babysit my little sister.

2

Answers
a is going to cut   b will be   c leaves   d he's going to get   e I'll go   f I'm not going   g will you be doing
h will have landed   i is not allowing   j will do
k will have been painting   l will have finished
m he'll be   n will you do   o is   p am having
q am going to be   r arrive   s will be arriving   t Shall I

3

Possible answers
a I'll be a doctor in 10 years' time. / I'm going to be a doctor in 10 years' time. Note that you can't say *I'll be being a doctor in 10 years' time.*
b It's going to rain.
c It will rain next week.
d I'm having salmon and salad for dinner tonight.
e My government will have found a solution to pollution by the year 2030.
f I'm going to clean my car tomorrow.
g The flight to Athens leaves at 6.00 on Fridays.

4   *To be bound to* expresses a strong feeling of certainty. It is often tested at Proficiency level.

Possible answers
a My life is bound to change as a result of computerisation. I imagine that I will be able to program everything that happens in my house – the temperature of my bath water, the feeding of the cat, when to close the curtains, when the automatic hoovering will take place.
b I am unlikely to have become a millionaire by the middle of the century, but I hope I will be reasonably comfortable. I will certainly have been to university and trained to become a doctor. I am also likely to have married and had three children.
c You can expect to have to work quite hard in this office. The boss is bound to be rude until he gets to know you. You will certainly get rewarded for hard work and you are likely to get a pay rise every year.

5

Possible answers
Lack of rain will leave the Sudan on the verge/brink of a disaster.
I'm about to go to bed.
Some animals are on the verge/brink of extinction.
The country is on the brink of revolution.
The arguments brought her to the brink of leaving home.
She was on the verge of leaving home when she received the news.
I am about to leave home to get the bus.

I'm about to get married.
Scientists are on the brink/verge of a scientific breakthrough.

6   These are paraphrases of the prepositional phrases not explained in the exercise above.
on the grounds (that) – because
in keeping with – appropriate for
in lieu of – instead of
in the region of – about
in vain – without success
on edge – nervous
on the fringe of – on the outside/edge of

Answers
a on the grounds   b in lieu of   c on edge
d in keeping with   e on the brink of   f on the fringe of
g in the region of   h in vain

7   You should learn the construction *have no* + noun as it is often used and frequently appears on the Use of English paper.

Answers
a She seems to have no difficulty (in) learning foreign languages.
b I have no objection to you/your coming camping with us.
c I have no intention of inviting John to the party.
d Sylvia has no interest in package holidays.
e I have no regrets about staying at home this summer.
f Some airlines have no hesitation in/about double booking their seats.
g My mother has no recollection/memory of what she did as a child.
h You have no alternative/choice but to come with me now.

2.3 pages 20–21

1   The illustrations are of:
  • the *Freedom Ship*, the subject of one of the listening extracts
  • Thomas More, who wrote a book about Utopia
  • Mars, also called the Red planet

The subject of the listening extracts is an ideal state.

Try to work out what the words in italics mean from the context they are in. The words are all in the first extract you will hear and it is helpful to have some idea of their meaning before listening.

2 Play the recording twice if necessary. The underlined parts of the tapescript confirm the answers.

Extract 1

The desire for an ideal state, a utopia, is something that has surfaced again and again throughout our history. The word itself, 'utopia', was coined by the English philosopher Sir Thomas More in a work in 1516, from the Greek meaning 'no place'. However, many consider the concept to have been in existence long before More. Plato, in his work *The Republic*, invites philosophers to establish an ideal state, whereas Thomas More merely describes an imaginary society without the inequalities of money and status which characterised his own time.

Nevertheless, the allure of an ideal society is such that various communities based on utopian ideals have been founded, but few of them have been able to withstand the tension between their own ideal principles and the pressures from the unreformed outer world. The problem of how to found a radically new society from scratch, with people who have grown up in existing societies, has been a major problem that has plagued all attempts to establish utopias.

3 Play the recording through once or twice. The underlined parts of the tapescript confirm the answers.

Extract 2

Reporter: Construction is about to start on a new ship, called the *Freedom Ship*, which has been billed as a maritime Utopia sailing the seven seas. Over 15,000 labourers will be working 24 hours a day to get the ship built on time. Already more than fifty of the 20,000 residential units, which cost from £80,000 to £5 million have been sold, with sales averaging £4.7 million pounds a week. US businessmen and engineers behind the project are so confident that they're already planning three more *Freedom Ships*. According to the project's marketing manager it'll be 'a new lifestyle for this new millennium' and promotional literature of the project paints a magnificent picture of a luxurious tax haven. This is, of course, bound to be the most appealing part of the venture. There'll be shops, parks, concert halls, schools, homes and even a university on board and a huge duty-free shopping mall will generate significant revenue. The builders confidently believe that the ship is so big – six times larger than any other vessel ever built – that a 40-metre wave will hardly affect it.

The ship's captain will be in a position to enforce the laws of whichever country's flag the owners decide to sail her under. Although states such as Panama have traditionally provided so called flags of convenience, the management are considering two European Union nations as possibilities.

The ship's private security force of 2,000 will be led by a former FBI agent, in an attempt to make residents toe the line. They can expect to be kept busy, according to sociologists, maritime security experts, criminologists and intelligence experts. The ship will have all the problems of any small city, including crime, outbreaks of disorder, juvenile delinquency and neighbourhood disputes. Residents will be cosmopolitan, and that may not help social cohesion. Experts say that when you create an artificial environment involving people with very different ethical, cultural, political and legal customs and values, the potential for tension is very great. It could well turn out to be more of a dystopia, than a Utopia.

Others, however, are more sanguine about the *Freedom Ship's* prospects.

4 Play the recording once, or twice if necessary. The underlined parts of the tapescript confirm the answers.

Background information

Mars
The fourth planet from the Sun, with a diameter half that of Earth. Two small natural satellites, Phobos and Deimos. A dry, cold planet with a thin, 95% carbon dioxide atmosphere, violent duststorms and canal-like features.

Extract 3

Another searcher after Utopia has been one Dr Zubrin. He has no doubts that humans are on the brink of inhabiting Mars. In his book, *Entering Space: Creating a Spacefaring Civilisation*, he describes how Mars will be made habitable. At present, the temperature can reach more than 100 degrees C below zero, humans cannot breathe unaided because of the dust and the habitat is barren. 'We would need to turn Mars into a viable arena for the development of life. This would involve terraforming,' Dr Zubrin explains in his book. Terraforming is the process where fluorocarbons are injected into the atmosphere to set off the greenhouse effect. As the planet thaws, carbon dioxide is released from the melting snowcaps and soil and would thicken the atmosphere. Add some trees and plants to convert the carbon dioxide into oxygen, and before long humans could be breathing comfortably on a green planet. As Dr Zubrin says, 'Mars is an entire world. It has all the resources needed to support life and civilisation – and some day there will be civilisation on Mars. Mars is an open frontier, as the rules haven't been written yet. The most profound freedom that people can have is the freedom to make their own world.'

Now in the studio to discuss Dr Zubrin's ideas are …

5

> **Possible answers**
> a I plan to go to university and train to be an archaeologist.
> b I would want someone who enjoys life but is realistic about the need for money and is willing to work hard. Also someone who has things in common with me. I like music and travelling.
> c Personally, I am a bit cynical about these sorts of places. I believe that if everyone made their own rules it would be chaos.
> d My priority would be security, followed by creature comforts such as food, warmth, water, etc.
> e For the most part I believe people will eventually colonise Mars because there will soon be too much pressure on Earth from population and industry. I'm in two minds as to whether I would want to go there. On balance I think probably not, as it's a long way and I could be doing more interesting things on Earth.

Pronunciation

6

> **Possible answers**
> a way   How much do you weigh, now you've been on your diet?
> b pairs   I love pears, but I can't stand apples.

> c meet   Meat and two veg is still the standard English meal in some parts of the country.
> d heir   The air is wonderfully clear in Majorca.
> e aisle   I have never visited the Isle of Skye in Scotland.
> f principal   Some people put their principles before common sense.
> g Grate   The new band that played last night were really great.
> h mane   We took what looked like the main road through the town, but still got lost.
> i plaice   This place is great for real Spanish tapas.

Idiom spot

Explain that parts of the body – nouns – are often used in English as verbs with an idiomatic meaning. Ask students to match the verbs on the left with the words or phrases on the right. Make sure they use an English–English dictionary to help them.

> **Answers**
> 1 j to shoulder responsibility
> 2 d to foot the bill
> 3 i to thumb a lift
> 4 k to elbow your way in
> 5 l to table a question
> 6 h to corner a thief
> 7 c to tiptoe into a room
> 8 f to man a ship
> 9 e to coat with paint
> 10 a to cash in on an idea
> 11 b to ship goods
> 12 g to house asylum seekers
>
> 1 to thumb a lift   2 shipped the goods   3 foot the bill
> 4 shoulder (the) responsibility   5 tiptoed into the room
> 6 elbowed her way into

Writing folder 1

Paper 2 Part 1
Letter   pages 22–23

In Paper 2 Writing, you must write in a register that is suitable for the task set. Most Proficiency questions will demand formal or neutral register and it is vital to produce this *consistently*, as inappropriately informal language would have a negative effect on the reader (examiner).

1   The pictures show a part of the Elgin Marbles, originally on the east section of the Parthenon in Athens, and the head of an 11th century Cambodian statue.

It is common for a Part 1 task to include a short text, which is usually there to stimulate ideas on the topic. Read the text carefully and underline key words and phrases. Try to reword these in your own answer where possible.

2   The main views expressed are that ancient statues exhibited in museums around the world should be returned to their former sites and that the current practice of stripping sites of art treasures for commercial gain should be stopped, as it ruins the sites and prevents nations from appreciating their own heritage.

Suggested answers
The article raises the issue of ownership of ancient works of art.
It gives the example of the Elgin Marbles, taken from the Parthenon and brought to England by Lord Elgin in the nineteenth century.
It argues that the Elgin Marbles belong in Greece.
According to the writer, this vandalism continues.
Some strong language is used, such as 'theft' and 'cultural barbarism'.

3   Make a similar paragraph plan before you start writing.

Answers
Para 1 Give the reason for writing this letter
Para 2 Endorse the condemnation of art theft
Para 3 Consider the position of the purchasers
Para 4 Evaluate the action that could be taken

4

Answers
Para 1 very much (really); liaise over (chat about)
Para 2 extremely (dead); steal (nick); damaged beyond repair (completely trashed)
Para 3 someone else (another guy)
Para 4 unite (band together); rich (rolling in money)

5   Use a variety of linkers in your writing and begin your sentences in different ways. This will impress an examiner.

Answers
Para 1 to add my similarly strong views
    At the same time, I do not wish
Para 2 What is extremely serious, in my view,
    Thus, these irreplaceable works of art
Para 3 However, where does this leave the art dealers?
    It is therefore a vicious circle.
Para 4 Naturally, I endorse this view
    nevertheless, I doubt whether
    Indeed, it would probably

6   In the exam, it will not matter if you go a little beyond the word limit – it is much more important to bring a piece of writing to a suitable end.

Sample paragraph
Ancient works of art need to be on view to everyone. Even more importantly, they are part of a nation's heritage. The world's citizens must find a way to keep historical sites intact for future generations.

Yours faithfully

7

Sample answer

Dear Sir or Madam

I have just read Henry Reid-Streebling's letter on family values, in the readers' letters section of your June edition. As I am part of the younger generation referred to by Mr Reid-Streebling, I would like to take issue with some of his criticism, which I feel is unfair and shows teenagers in a bad light.

In the first place, I can vouch for the fact that my classmates and I are not 'lazy'. We have to spend a lot of time studying, not just completing our homework but also reading round the subjects and practising our languages. If we were to do nothing, we would fail our exams!

Secondly, in my experience, many students have part-time jobs at the weekends or in the evenings. They do this work in order to be financially independent of their parents, so quite obviously, they do not 'take everything for granted', as the writer maintains. With respect, Mr Reid-Streebling's letter may say more about the problems within his own family than about trends among today's youth.

Speaking personally, I do not view my parents as servants and I always try to be a helpful member of the family, looking after my younger brothers and sister and assisting with the usual chores. Of course, teenagers have different attitudes and personalities just like adults do, so it is not surprising that some are lazier than others. In the writer's case, perhaps some 're-training' of his grandchildren is necessary – they might well listen to him rather than their parents.

From what my own mother and father have told me, I recognise that their childhood was very different from mine. However, I think they would agree with me that it was not necessarily more difficult. There is a lot of pressure on our generation to succeed, in a world which is far more competitive than it was 40 years ago. I am lucky to have the support and encouragement of my parents and will appreciate them even more, having read Mr Reid-Streebling's letter.

Yours faithfully

Unit 3

3.1 pages 24–25

1 The photograph is of a sunset to show 'red sky at night'.

> **Possible answer**
> I think the one about *red sky at night, shepherd's delight* is true. I've often noticed that if there is a red sky at night the weather the following day is good. It's something to do with the refraction of ice crystals in the atmosphere I think.

2 Read through the questions carefully before you listen. A rain goose is a type of bird. Play the recording twice – first to get an idea of what it is about and secondly to write your answers. The underlined parts of the tapescript confirm the answers.

> **Answers**
> 1 T 2 F 3 F 4 T 5 F 6 T 7 F 8 T 9 T 10 T

Sue: Good morning. Now, the huge growth of interest in environmental issues has led to a careful re-examination of all kinds of traditional lore. Today I have with me Peter Watkins, a lecturer in psychology at the Smithson Institute. He's just written a best-selling book, *The History of Weather Folklore*, which explains country sayings and the role of animals and birds in forecasting the weather. Sayings my granny used to come out with, like *Birds flying low, expect rain and a blow,* <u>which I've always felt rather sceptical about.</u>

Peter: Well, Sue, <u>the way in which animals and birds can apparently predict changes in the weather before we can has always fascinated people and, for that matter, still does.</u> If it didn't, the sayings wouldn't still be in current use, and of course, nowadays the weather is anxiously studied to see if the greenhouse effect is starting to bite.

Sue: But is there any truth in these old sayings? Given that there are so many, apparently 500 at the last count, and they've been around a while, presumably they should be fairly accurate?

Peter: Well, generally, there's a better chance of their being right for short-term weather forecasting rather than long-term. Of course, the most interesting natural weather forecasters are the birds, which is why there are so many sayings involving them. Birds depend on the right weather conditions for flying and, <u>in particular, birds that fly very high like swifts and swallows stand very little chance of survival if they get caught in a bad storm. They are also insect feeders and when the weather is fine the insects are high and the birds will follow them.</u> Insects have good reason to dive for cover if rain is imminent as

they are covered with water-repellent hairs. <u>It actually doesn't take much for them to get completely soaked, so they respond quite rapidly if there's a drop in temperature or a rise in humidity.</u>

Sue: So, there is an element of truth in that one. Now, I used to live off the coast of Scotland and they had a saying on the islands about a bird called the red-throated diver. They used to call this bird the rain goose, and the saying went pretty much like this: *If the rain goose flies to the hill, you can put your boat where you will, but if she flies to the sea you must draw your boat and flee.* I must say that I used to be rather puzzled by this saying, as I didn't understand why it would fly out to sea when the weather was getting worse. Anyway, one time when I was out in a boat the wind started to get up. We tuned in the radio and it said a gale was due from the north. <u>We saw the geese everywhere flying around and heading out to sea. So despite common sense telling you otherwise, the saying of the local people seemed to be true.</u>

Peter: Yes, and we still don't know the reason for its strange behaviour. But you know, not all weather lore is doom and gloom. Some birds can predict when things are about to brighten up. Certain geese set off for their breeding grounds in Iceland when the weather is fine – you just have to wait and watch and then plan your harvesting or house painting!

Sue: Not very practical! However, if there is some truth behind these weather sayings, do they ever have any practical use?

Peter: Obviously, weather lore had a very important application in the farmer's world. Farming and weather are intrinsically linked and the ability to predict, or at least think you could predict, was very important to them, <u>although of course, they weren't the only ones with a vested interest in weather forecasting.</u> One of the things about human beings is that we do not like to feel that things are happening with no purpose whatsoever. Weather lore makes a connection between something that is happening and something that is going to happen – <u>we need to feel we're not simply the victims of chance and circumstance.</u> Although it's very difficult to put dates on these sayings, many of them probably go back thousands of years. Some of them work and some of them don't, and some of them don't even make sense. Many actually negate each other.

Sue: <u>Quite.</u> So, how reliable are sayings which predict the year ahead, if we can't even rely on ones predicting the weather the next day?

Peter: Well, I find it very difficult to believe that you can tell the rest of the winter from the way birds are flying or how your cat behaves in the autumn. By putting our own interpretations on how nature works we can get it completely wrong. For our ancestors the weather was a life and death situation – not just an inconvenience, and I think that had they had anything more reliable, they wouldn't have had to base their predictions on this kind of thing. <u>They were really clutching at straws when they observed animal and bird behaviour and linked it to the weather,</u> but <u>they</u> <u>really</u> <u>had</u> <u>no</u> <u>other</u> <u>choice</u>.

Sue: My thanks to Peter Watkins. Next week we'll …

Idiom spot

> **Answers**
> These were the idioms that needed correcting:
> time and again; fame and fortune; flesh and blood; touch and go; safe and sound; life and soul
>
> **a** thick and thin **b** sixes and sevens
> **c** fame and fortune **d** touch and go
> **e** First and foremost **f** Time and again
> **g** safe and sound **h** give and take **i** life and soul
> **j** flesh and blood **k** high and dry **l** black and white

3 *Quite*, *fairly* and *rather* are often confused. Check in the Grammar folder on pages 184–185 if you need more help.

Read the note about gradable and ungradable adjectives before you listen to the recording.

> **Answers**
> **1** a **2** b **3** a **4** b **5** a

Tapescript

1 You're quite wrong in what you say about her!
2 It's quite a nice dress, but I can't make up my mind whether to buy it or not.
3 Quite!
4 She's quite happy in her new house, but she does still miss her friends.
5 This cake is quite delicious.

4

> **Possible answer**
> I am fairly certain that men are what their mothers made them. I often see mothers saying to their little boys, 'Oh, don't you worry about tidying up, dear, your sister will do it.' I'm rather dubious about the saying that *imagination is more important than knowledge*. I think both are equally important and often being knowledgeable is more useful than just having a good imagination.

5 The article is about animal behaviour and how it may be possible to use it to predict major earthquakes.

You are given the answers here, but in the examination you have to think of them yourself.

> **Answers**
> **1** far **2** yet **3** little **4** the **5** given **6** which
> **7** turn **8** It **9** during **10** make **11** and **12** put
> **13** sort **14** whatever **15** before

3.2 pages 26–27

1

> **Possible answer**
> I'm not sure that the personality of people in a country is influenced by the type of weather they have. They say the British are reserved because it's so cold and rainy, but there are many British people who are quite jolly! Again, not all Latin types are easy-going and lazy. People from hot countries work equally hard and I'm sure worry just as much about life as people from cold countries. I don't agree with reinforcing stereotypes.

2 The sentences are all conditional.

> **Suggested answers**
> **a** there are 50% more traffic accidents and 20% more industrial injuries.
> **b** the air will make you feel invigorated.
> **c** the number of murders would rise.
> **d** if there hadn't been a Santa Ana blowing.
> **e** you leave Switzerland during a Föhn.
> **f** I would go to California if I wanted to murder my husband.

3 You should be able to explain what kind of conditional sentence each is. They are all examples of basic forms. Check in the Grammar folder on page 181 if you have any problems with this.

> **Answers**
> **a** Zero conditional used for general truths.
> **b** First conditional used when something is possible.
> **c** Second conditional used to talk about something that is unreal and is improbable.
> **d** Third conditional to talk about something impossible.
> **e** Zero conditional to talk about a general truth.
> **f** Second conditional to talk about something which is unreal or improbable.

4 This exercise gives examples of other forms of conditional sentences.

Answers

a inverted first conditional to express tentative statements = *If you should happen to …*
b polite use of *would* = first conditional
c parallel conditional – first conditional = *I'll do something if you do something.*
d disguised conditional – *as long as = if*
e inverted third conditional = *If I had known about the weather conditions …*
f disguised first conditional – *provided that = if*
g mixed conditional – second + third using *now* to show past effect on present
h inverted second conditional to express tentative statements = *If the Prime Minister were to announce …*
i first conditional with *unless = if not*

5 This exercise is also an awareness exercise to check that you realise that other words and phrases are possible in a conditional sentence besides *if*.

Answers

a Given that **b** Unless **c** As long as / Provided that
d But for / Without **e** Even if **f** on condition that
g Suppose / Supposing

6 Many of the forms used here, especially the inversions, are quite formal.

Suggested answers

a Should you see her, could you tell her my address? OR Should you happen to see her, could you tell her my address?
b Given that people were dependent on farming for their livelihood, it's not surprising that they used animal behaviour to predict the weather.
c Provided that you take care of it, you can borrow my bike.
d If you'd (like to) take a seat, I'm sure Mr Johnson won't be long.
e If I were you, I'd get another job.
f If I had worked harder to pass my diploma, I would be earning more money now.
g But for my grandmother leaving me some money, I wouldn't have been able to afford to go to university.
h Were climatic changes to occur / Were there to be climatic changes, weather lore would be rendered obsolete.

7

Possible answers

a I will say nothing and be happy for them / try not to look horrified.
b I will try hard not to get too excited / reply immediately giving details of when I'm available / ignore it because one of my friends probably sent it.

c I will go to bed early / light some candles / cook dinner over an open fire.
d I will call the police from a phone booth / buy another one quickly.
e I would hide under a table / pray as hard as I could / go outside the building.
f I would be very upset / think of ways of getting revenge / try to find out why.
g I would keep it if it were less than £5 / take it to the police station / put up a notice saying I had found it.
h I would decline politely / jump at the chance / take a friend with me.
i I would have phoned the police / hidden behind a door / taken down any car registration numbers.
j I would have married them / thought carefully about the situation / tried to forget about them.
k I would have had more opportunities for travel / probably not been much happier than I am now / had a Ferrari for my 18th birthday.
l I would have ended up a spoilt brat / been a very unhappy person / probably taken to a life of crime.

3.3 pages 28–29

1 The photos show two girls in a playground with arms crossed, obviously angry with each other; also a man in a car who is angry with someone in another car.

Possible answer
If someone is angry they have a flushed face / loud voice / strong body language / staring eyes, etc. Women and girls are often silently angry and 'freeze' out the person they are angry with. Men tend to be more aggressive and physical.

2 Try to guess words you don't know from the context. You are not allowed to take a dictionary of any description into the examination. You are bound to come across words you have never seen before during the exam and you should therefore get used to trying to guess the meaning from the surrounding words. It is important to try to get out of the habit of translating every word. Some words defy translation anyway!

Answers
1 A in a magazine or newspaper (style, language, vocabulary – not specialised, neutral register)
2 C
3 On the surface there seems to be no reason for it.
4 **inward:** feeling annoyed/tense/anxious; raised blood pressure
   outward: sweating; averting gaze; hiding; making yourself immobile; hair-pulling; foot-tapping; getting red in the face; leaving

3 Students often find it difficult to find different ways of saying the same thing. Here you are introduced to the use of negative prefixes. You will gain marks if you can show you can manipulate language, either to make a sentence shorter or to show you can paraphrase a sentence.

> **Answers**
> **a** indiscreet   **b** undeniable   **c** illegible   **d** insignificant
> **e** irreplaceable   **f** inexhaustible   **g** unassertive
> **h** misleading

4 You may be asked to do a similar exercise with a partner in Paper 5, the Speaking paper. It is important that both students should contribute equally to the discussion and they must both give reasons for decisions.

The cartoon illustrates the idea of 'noisy neighbours'. 'Clear off' is a way of saying 'Go away'. There are many expressions using 'off' in this way – most of them taboo.

> **Possible answer**
> I think that noisy neighbours is the thing that infuriates me the most, so I would put it top of my list. It doesn't matter how rude people are to you at work or in the street, but when you get home you should be able to relax and not have to worry about noise. My second biggest bugbear is unpunctuality. I think it is very rude if people are continually late for appointments. I think it shows a lack of respect for other people. As for the other things in the list, I think being overtaken by a sports car is the least of my worries!

Exam folder 2

Paper 3 Part 3
Gapped sentences page 30

For this part of the paper you will need to write your answers in CAPITAL LETTERS on your answer sheet in the examination.

1 Read each sentence carefully and don't just put down the answer to the first one. The word should make sense in all the sentences.

> **Answers**
> **1** open   **2** task   **3** turn   **4** strictly
> **5** distinguish   **6** seriously

Paper 3 Part 4
Key word transformations page 31

2 Remember that only between three and eight words are required. A contraction counts as two words. Don't forget to use the key word.

> **Answers**
> **1** was put in jeopardy / was put at risk
> **2** I have (some / a few) reservations about his theories
> **3** sooner had Pete met / did Pete meet Sue than
> **4** friendship with Paula dates back
> **5** responsibility for breaking / having broken
> **6** has finally come to terms with
> **7** no expectation of an upturn
> **8** were given / had no choice/alternative/option but to

Unit 4

4.1 pages 32–33

1 The pictures show:
- a Japanese Tea Ceremony, with a Hideyoshi-Shogun tea master
- an English bride and groom cutting their tiered wedding cake.

Another example of ritual behaviour in eating and drinking is making a toast at an official dinner, where everyone raises a glass and drinks to something or someone.

2 The underlined parts of the tapescript confirm the answers.

> **Answers**
> **Before the meal:** phone calls to relations, preparation of lots of food
>
> **During the meal:** eating, praising the food, family discussion, more general arguments about politics, coffee, senior member leaves, end of event

Unlike many modern families, mine still holds to the tradition of large family meals at times of celebration or crisis. I use the word 'large' of both the group and the amount of food on offer. The pattern is always the same: <u>endless phone calls weeks ahead of the occasion</u> to mobilise distant cousins and elderly aunts; <u>on the eve of the event, the preparation of excessive amounts of food</u> by the host family member, which never fails to be stress-inducing for all concerned; and then <u>on the day itself, we slip into our well-established roles</u>, devouring all that is set before us and expressing the joy and contentment that convention demands. <u>Once the wine has started to flow, the praise of</u>

succulent dishes gives way to another, more sinister part of the ritual: <u>snide comments on family members not present, the surfacing of ancient grudges and petty family rivalries</u>. This in turn leads to the more general but equally predictable <u>debates on politics and the world at large</u>. Manners always prevent us from actual bodily assault, but the verbal gloves are certainly off at this late stage in the proceedings. As the insults start to fly, <u>the host hurries away to prepare coffee, hunting out chocolates and jugs of ice-cold water</u>, in a valiant attempt to restore calm. Ritual behaviour dictates that all hostilities cease at this point and so, finally, peace prevails. <u>After his second cup of coffee</u>, handing down a final blessing to the assembled group, <u>the most senior member takes his leave</u>, signalling that it is time for others to do the same. Another memorable family occasion draws to a close.

Possible answer

In Melbourne last Christmas, I was invited to Christmas lunch with my brother-in-law's Armenian family by marriage. There were over thirty people present, ranging from young children to grandparents. We started off in the garden, eating appetisers and toasting everyone's good health – including the health of the entire Liverpool football team. Eventually we all went inside and sat down together, at the longest table I have ever seen! There were so many succulent things to eat, including huge trays of sliced roast lamb and pork, different types of potato dishes, vegetarian salads and roasted vegetables. The meal was a leisurely affair, punctuated every so often by fresh supplies of warm bread or another bottle of Australian wine. A tempting selection of desserts was then wheeled out and we were allowed to help ourselves and adjourn once more to the garden, where the sun was shining. Later still we came inside again, for the children to be given their presents. It was a truly splendid day.

---

3   The narrator, Triton, is Mister Salgado's cook.

Ⓑackground information

Romesh Gunesekera has been favourably compared to Chekhov and Graham Greene. Much of his writing portrays the dilemma of living in Sri Lanka, a spoiled paradise where violence and political unrest are ever-present. *Reef*, his first novel, was shortlisted for the Booker prize in 1994 and won the Italian Premio Mondello in 1997. His other books include *Monkfish Moon*, a set of short stories, and another novel, *The Sandglass*.

4

Answers

1 B   2 C   3 A   4 D   5 A   6 C

Detailed explanation:

1 The answer, B, can be found in the sentence *He was concerned to make sure there was plenty of time to prepare, even though he acted so nonchalant*. A is ruled out because the narrator says *it had never happened before in his life*. C is wrong as Mr Salgado did give his cook advance warning. D is plausible though the first paragraph shows that Triton has plenty of culinary experience.

2 The answer, C, is supported by the references Triton makes to Miss Nili's manner of eating in the second half of the first paragraph: *she ate like a horse, so hungry-looking* and *I expected her to bulge out as she ate ...* . A, though plausible, is not stated in the text. B is falsely suggested by the words *I don't know where she put it*. As with A, Triton does not pass judgement on Miss Nili, so D is ruled out.

3 The answer, A, is rooted in the whole paragraph that begins *Triton made it*, where Triton talks of his 'coming of age'. B is wrong, as it was *the one phrase Mister Salgado would say ... again and again*. C is ruled out by Miss Nili's words in the next paragraph, where she says that Triton *makes a lovely cake*. D is not suggested by the text, apart from Triton's general comment on *the petrified morass of all our lives*, which is beyond the scope of the tea party.

4 The answer, D, lies in the words *I rode in it like a prince*. A is wrong, as although Triton implies that the taxi is slow, *a black tortoise*, there is no suggestion that he is annoyed by this. B is not suggested by the text and it would be inappropriate for Triton, a servant, to have such feelings. C is wrong, as it is Miss Nili who is helped into the taxi by Mister Salgado.

5 The penultimate paragraph (the one before the final paragraph) shows that Triton feels positive about life when his work goes well: *Suddenly everything becomes possible and the whole world ... pulls together*, so the answer is A. B is the opposite of Triton's view, for he *felt stupid* to need the praise. C is not suggested by the text; in fact Triton appears to prefer being the sole owner of the kitchen. D is not suggested by the paragraph.

6 The answer, C, is rooted in the sentence *It was as if he couldn't believe his eyes, seeing Nili sitting there in front of him*. A is wrong, as, although Mister Salgado drank lots of tea, he ate nothing. There is no evidence in the paragraph for B, as it was Nili who *would murmur her approval*. D, though plausible in view of Mister Salgado's nervousness before her arrival, is not suggested in the paragraph and Triton is the one who orchestrates the delivery of each part of the meal, with the exception of Mister Salgado's words *No, bring the cake now*.

Style extra

Using similes sparingly in your own writing will demonstrate your range, as already highlighted in Unit 2. Another useful device is to replace a standard colour adjective with a noun phrase – for example, instead of 'brown', you could say *coffee-coloured* or *the colour of mud*. You can also supplement the adjective with a noun, to give a more vivid description – for example *mint green, ice blue*.

Answers
The animals associated with Miss Nili are:
a horse *she ate like a horse*
a snake *like a snake swallowing a bird ... one leg coiled under her*
a cow *She made a lowing sound between bites.*

The effect is to accentuate her appetite and unconventional behaviour.

By referring to the taxi as having a *butter-coloured* top, the author brings his own writing to life and also skilfully reminds us that Triton the narrator is also Triton the cook, who sees life through his cooking (see the answer 5A in the multiple-choice questions above).

5 The *Cambridge International Corpus* is a large collection of texts held on computer. The texts come from novels and non-fiction books, journalism, academic writing, everyday speech and other forms of written and spoken English. A powerful computer program allows the corpus 'browser' – in this case, both authors of *Objective Proficiency* – to call up many different examples of a single word, which provides a lot of useful information about common usage. These examples of 'savour' have been chosen to show typically modern uses of the word.

Answers
The noun collocates are: *success, freedom, memories, past, wine*

6

Possible answers
a I savoured the moment when Brad Pitt came up to me and kissed my cheek.
b I don't relish the idea of spending the night in a tent!
c I found it hard to swallow the news that the factory was closing.
d I absolutely devour things like blockbuster novels and trashy love stories in magazines.

4.2 pages 34–35

1 The picture shows a selection of old and new forks, including a serving fork with five prongs and a long-handled toasting fork.

Suggested answer
Over 400 years, forks have slowly become accepted as an important item of cutlery at the meal table. They have changed from being an implement for holding meat in place while it was being carved to being used for eating in their own right. In the nineteenth century, their design was modified to increase the number of prongs from three to four. In the latter part of that century, the English introduced the fashion of holding the fork in the left hand while cutting up food with a knife in the right hand.

2 Read the section in the Grammar folder on page 182 if you are unsure about these tenses.

Answers
a past perfect (*the knife was put down once the food had been cut up*)
b used to; would (*used to use special spoons; people would more often share forks with others*)
c modal verbs (*as well they might have done; scooping with them must have been impossible*)
d present perfect (*have been used for over 2000 years*)

e *is thought **to have been used*** (past passive infinitive)
f ***was being carved*** at table (past continuous passive)
  were satirised** / these **were** now **shortened**... / the fork **was then used** / the knife **was kept (simple past passives)
g ***had been making** forks* (past perfect continuous)
  were** successfully **introducing (past continuous)
  *as we **have been doing** ever since* (present perfect continuous)
h spread (spread); strove (strive); done (do); bore (bear); seen (see); sought (seek).

3 A *tine* is the technical term for the prong of a fork.

Answers
a tools b list c female-like behaviour: used to show disapproval d picking up e fussy or ultra-careful
f sin g still / without moving h spread (widely)
i changing j fashionable

4

Answers
a was thought; had mastered
b have carved; was carried out
c have always insisted; should be torn; arose; is/was dressed; may/could react
d had murdered; was given; ate; drank
e continued; had started / had been starting
f have been supported; have been chosen

5 Use compound adjectives in your writing to show your language range.

Suggested answers
1 a an orphan baby lamb b an undergraduate
  c junior staff

2 a about to be impeached b hyper-inflation
  c desperate for money

3 a a company plaque b a bathroom tap c a pen

4 a to hold it together b to prevent it smelling
  c to keep them hot

5 a ice cream b oranges c some types of yogurt

6 a a tiger **b** a football hooligan **c** a vampire

7 a a dish **b** a recipe
c a jar of baby food (to prevent criminal activity)

8 a silly, not serious
b with perfect features and immaculate clothes
c wise, bright-eyed

4.3 pages 36–37

1 The fruit shown includes raspberries, strawberries, red plums, yellow plums, apples, grapes, two varieties of melon, tangerines, pineapples, kiwi fruit, ruby grapefruit, lemons, a lime, bananas, pears, blood oranges, a star fruit, a mango.

Suggested answers
A mango is fleshy, juicy when ripe, and rather sensuous.
Raspberries are soft, usually sweet, and heavenly with cream!
Lemons can be quite fibrous and are tart, if not sour.

2 The main points below are also underlined in the tapescript. Play the recording twice.

Answers
Ideal temperature for ripening: over 40°C
Chief mango-growing area: to the north of Calcutta (Eastern India)
Facts about the mango tree: up to 60 feet (about 18 metres) tall, has a massive trunk, shiny green leaves
History of mango-growing in India: established by the Moghuls in the 17th century and taken up by the Nawabs, who diversified the varieties grown

For the last two months, across much of India, <u>temperatures have soared daily to over 40 degrees Celsius – perfect ripening weather for the mango</u>, perfect wilting weather for humans. The thing about India, and Calcutta in particular, is that everyone here eats seasonally – there are no supermarkets, there is no option. And mangoes are everywhere – in every home, on every hotel menu, and sold on every street corner. In the markets, they're beautifully arranged, stacked up according to variety on big wide wicker baskets.

<u>The main mango-growing areas are situated to the north of the city.</u> I headed out to an old family estate where they still have a number of the original orchards. This estate, laid out around an old indigo-planter's house, is wonderfully peaceful and the air so clean – a million miles from Calcutta. Against the exotic foliage of the coconut palm and the banana plant, <u>the mango tree looks like a shiny-leaved evergreen oak. It has a massive, gnarled trunk and can easily grow to a height of sixty feet.</u> Many trees were planted over a hundred years ago.

Indians today have <u>the Moghul dynasties of the seventeenth and eighteenth centuries</u> to thank for the amazing diversity of mangoes available now. They <u>established large plantations across the northern states of Uttar Pradesh and Bihar.</u> It was the Muslim leaders – <u>the Nawabs</u> – who <u>cultivated the fruit in Bengal.</u> They were great fruit-loving people and they missed their apricots and their melons and uh … they cross-pollinated the mango, <u>they got 101 varieties</u>, and these are the sophisticated mangoes that grow mainly in eastern India. When the Moghul empire was in its decline, <u>the Nawabs moved southward and here they cultivated their mangoes</u>, planting them according to their different varieties in orchards – they gave them the most romantic and poetic names, names like 'passari', the loved one, 'begum pasan', the Nawab's wife's favourite …

3

Answers
a The speaker uses the word 'perfect' ironically: although the high temperature is perfect for ripening the mango, it causes people to 'wilt', that is, become tired and without energy.
b The mangoes are arranged in piles according to their varieties.
c leaves that grow in the tropics or another faraway place from the speaker's point of view
d the Moghul Empire or royal families
e incredible variety (101 different types)

4

Suggested answer
India is not a big importer of food, so food grown is consumed according to the time of year it is ready. Many countries are locked into importing food by air freight from other parts of the world for sale in supermarkets. Generally, India does not fit this pattern.

5

Answers
a icing; cake **b** apple; eye **c** eggs; basket **d** fish
e breakfast/dinner **f** pinch; salt **g** beans **h** hot cakes **i** egg; face **j** pie **k** fruit(s) **l** holes; cheese

1 There are more holes in this history essay than a Swiss cheese!
OR This history essay is a complete dog's breakfast.
2 I've put all my eggs in one basket work-wise.
3 Harry got egg on his face when Professor Samuels confronted him in the canteen queue.
4 Valentina now has bigger fish to fry in Bologna.
5 Liam is the apple of his mother's eye.
6 I finally got Simon to spill the beans about his wedding.

7 Chocolate is forbidden fruit to Angela while she's on her diet.

8 Maria's earrings are selling like hot cakes on the market stall.

6 The desserts shown are:

   A Summer pudding, a dessert made with white bread and soft fruit (raspberries, blackcurrants, redcurrants, strawberries), garnished with mint.

   B Pineapple boat, filled with different varieties of fruit.

   C Open apricot tart, finished with toasted almonds and cream.

   D Apple cake.

Possible idioms are:

   A/C using mint/almonds – the icing on the cake

   D presentation – a dog's breakfast/dinner

Record yourself talking about the desserts and then play back the piece to check your accuracy and pronunciation. Think of ways to improve what you have said, for example using a wider range of vocabulary.

Possible answer
Well, the apple cake is a complete dog's breakfast, so that has no chance of winning. I also feel the apricot tart is a bit rough around the edges – the pastry is almost burnt and it's a little too thick for my taste. For me, the pineapple boat deserves to be shortlisted because of its visual impact, but I would award the prize to the summer pudding, which looks absolutely luscious – the fruit has a perfect consistency, the juice has soaked through the bread beautifully, and the mint garnish is the icing on the cake.

Writing folder 2

Paper 2 Part 2 Review pages 38–39

If you decide to write a review in Part 2, remember to address the question rather than merely describe what happens in the book or film you are reviewing. Make early reference to the title for clarity.

1 The picture is a 'still' from the end of the film *The Perfect Storm* and shows Mark Wahlberg clinging to wreckage of the fishing boat, in a very heavy sea.

Possible answers
The steel grey sea looks bitterly cold and very sinister.
The huge waves tower menacingly over the poor fisherman.
Such a vast amount of heaving water threatens the sailor's life.

2 The paragraph plan covers all parts of the exam task, including the general aspect at the end.

3

Suggested answers
The review is not very successful. There is only a minimal lead-in. The film is not named. The third paragraph is all plot, most of which should have been omitted. There is insufficient description of the special effects in the fourth paragraph. The evaluation is barely attempted.

To improve the review, the balance of the content needs to be addressed: there should be less plot, more reference to the special effects used, and some expansion of the general evaluation at the end.

4

Answers
a Hollywood blockbuster (film)
b the budget (money spent)
c an interesting sub-plot (part)
d portrayed (acted) by George Clooney
e he heads out (goes) to sea
f the safety of his crew (men)
g through the eye of the storm (worst weather)
h where the special effects kick in (start)
i really outstanding (very good)
j clever use of digital imaging (computers)
k those gigantic (big) waves
l the film also stars (has) Mark Wahlberg
m the film cuts to (shows)
n the girlfriend, scanning the horizon (looking out to sea)
o a prerequisite (essential part) of all films
p its best feature (thing)

5

Corrected and improved answer
As part of the feature on special effects, the film *The Perfect Storm* is a very good example to consider. In one way, it is not a typical Hollywood blockbuster, as there is no happy ending, but in other ways – the actors used, the budget, the special effects – it is.

Why is it 'perfect'? It is actually a weatherman who uses this word. As he tracks the worsening weather out at sea, we see him getting genuinely excited about the unique set of weather conditions. This was an interesting sub-plot for me.

The captain of the fishing boat, portrayed by George Clooney, does not care about the safety of his crew and only wants to find more fish and make money. His irresponsible risk-taking eventually leads the tiny boat into the very eye of the storm, which is brought vividly to the screen by really outstanding use of special effects, including some clever use of digital imaging. When the special effects kick in, you feel as though you are in the boat with the crew, facing those gigantic waves. At the end, the ship goes down and we see one of the sailors – the film also stars Mark Wahlberg – drifting on an empty sea. The huge waves tower menacingly over the poor fisherman. Somewhat unbelievably, he is shown thinking beautiful thoughts about his girlfriend. Then the film cuts to the girlfriend, scanning the horizon with an anxious look on her face.

Are special effects a prerequisite of all films today? In my own opinion, it depends on the type of film – a psychological drama has no need of special effects to heighten the tension between characters. However, most of today's younger cinema-goers choose action films and they do expect special effects to be an integral part of the entertainment. In *The Perfect Storm*, they were probably its best feature.

6 Follow the sample paragraph plan below when writing your review.

Sample plan
Para 1   Introduction to review/advert chosen
Para 2   Brief description of the advert
Para 3   Visual effects
Para 4   Other features – music, actors, voice-over, etc.
Para 5   Assessment of influence adverts have on us

Sample answer
It is true that advertising has become an art form in its own right. Nowadays, some of the very best film directors are employed to produce a visually impressive fifty or sixty seconds of footage that we will remember and associate ever afterwards with the product being sold. My own favourite has to be a recent Guinness advert, which lives up to the high standards set by earlier adverts for this dark beer from Ireland.

The product becomes part of a visual extravaganza, set somewhere in South America or the Caribbean. At the outset, you are unsure what you are witnessing, which cleverly encourages better concentration. Tension is in the air and you realise that a race is about to start – incredibly, a snails' race! Each snail lines up in its own lane, with a number on its shell, and bets are taken on which one will be the winner. Snails being what they are, the race gets off to a slow start, but then, one snail finds its way into an almost-empty glass of Guinness, takes in the necessary sustenance and streaks home, to the wild cheers of the crowd.

One striking image follows another and special effects are judiciously used to accentuate the snail's speed. The film is also shot from unusual angles – a snail's eye view, you might say, where human faces become slightly distorted and more unusual. At the end, we are almost participants in the vibrant celebration, which is fuelled by Guinness and exudes only good humour and love of life.

Characteristically of a Guinness advert, loud music alternates with silence, busy scenes with stillness. There is no need for a voice-over, which would only labour the

point. The overwhelming impression created is that you are watching something utterly unique, a message that you will then associate with the product itself.

In general, I believe adverts have a huge effect on our lifestyle and aspirations. If they didn't, far less money would be spent on them. However, in this particular case, I have to admit that, much as I enjoy every single Guinness advert I see, I am no fan of the beer in question. No doubt there are plenty of other customers who are, though.

Units 1–4 Revision

pages 40–41

This revision unit practises the language covered in Units 1–4, as well as extending the work done on reviews in Writing folder 2. Specific exam practice is provided for Paper 3 Parts 2, 3 and 4. This Use of English section could be done as a timed test of 30 minutes.

1   The picture shows Tiananmen Square, Beijing, as it is today.

Background information

John Simpson is one of the most experienced and respected British journalists. For many years a BBC television reporter, he covered the beginning of the Gulf War from Baghdad and was in Belgrade at the height of the NATO bombing campaign. The text is taken from *A Mad World, My Masters*, the very readable account of his working life. He now lives in Ireland.

Answers
1 authorities   2 problematic   3 imperceptible
4 enduring   5 imitations   6 disillusioned
7 identifiable   8 disheartened/downhearted
9 faceless   10 survivor

2

Answers
1 have no alternative but to ask
2 known there was going to be a delay
3 was made to / had to shoulder the financial burden of
4 he was on the verge of tears/crying
5 you find it necessary / it be necessary to contact me urgently
6 hotel is bound to be good as/because/since Pablo

3

Answers
1 provided   2 features   3 bound   4 swallow
5 pinch   6 jammed

4 The review originally appeared in *The Guardian* newspaper, in a slightly longer version. The writer is fairly negative about the book, dismissing it as 'publishing froth'.

Note that there are some alternatives in the choice of punctuation (see below). In the first and second paragraphs, the dashes could be replaced by commas; in the third and fifth paragraphs, the colons could be replaced by dashes.

Punctuated and paragraphed review

No one has yet written 'Froth: the Trend that Changed History' but *Universal Foam* comes pretty close to being the definitive example of publishing froth. The book blends two recent publishing trends, the newer of which is the wacky science subject. If there is a market for books on cryptography, chronometry or cod – and books on all these subjects have sold well in the last decade – then there is no reason why any subject should seem boring.

Once you have discovered a subject so obscure that no other publisher has come across it before, all that remains is to prove that it holds the key to universal understanding. 'Cod: a Biography of the Fish that Changed the World' is a pretty good example, but 'Universal Foam: the Story of Bubbles from Cappuccino to the Cosmos' outdoes it, since it permeates the universe from the smallest to the largest scale. After all, there aren't any galaxies stretched on the skin of unimaginably vast cod; nor do physicists speak of the world arising from fluctuations in the quantum codfish. So 'The Boys' Bumper Book of Froth' might contain – as every bestseller should – everything you need to know about the universe. Then again, it might contain everything else. That's pretty frothy too.

In fact, 'Universal Foam' runs into another current publishing style: the book of lists. Among the subjects covered here are volcanoes, shaving-foam, champagne, fire-fighting equipment and meringues. Then you list everything you know about everything in the first list: 101 important facts about galaxies; then 20 things you never knew about the cappuccino, and so on.

Finally, all this is wrapped up in the academic style, as old as exams, where you simply cram in all the knowledge that you can possibly get hold of and regurgitate it with the echoing solemnity of a TV anchorman on 'The Simpsons', suggesting a rhetorical question: 'Can everyday foams like milk foam ever be fully understood and controlled?' At which point, there is foam flecking this reviewer's lips.

You can't really blame the author, Sidney Perkowitz, who has worked hard and writes clearly. It is not his fault that he has nothing particular to say after he has got through the bits that particularly interest him: the fairly technical discussions of how to measure foams and describe them mathematically. However, the fact is, there is no sound reason for this book to have been written in the first place.

Crossword

This revises idioms and vocabulary from Units 1–4.

1.T	O	E	2.T	H	E	L	3.I	N	E	■		4.A	5.S
R	■		W	■		R	■		6.O	F	■		P
A	7.F	O	8.O	L	P	R	O	O	F				I
C	O	■	N	■		E	■						L
K	9.O	V	E	R		10.P	R	E	V	11.A	I	L	
D	T	■				L				P			T
O	12.T	O	U	C	H	A	N	D	G	O			H
W	H	■		C	■			13.L	I	E			
N	E		14.L	I	K	E		15.T	O	■			B
	B	■	I	■	A		16.V	O	G	U	E		
	I		V	■	B				E				A
17.I	N	L	I	E	U	L		18.O	U	T			N
N	L		U		19.G	E	T			I			S
			P		O			20.B	A	C	K		

Listening test 1

See page 281 and key on page 287.

Unit 5

5.1 pages 42–43

1

Possible answer

I would probably be a shopaholic if I had enough money. As it is, I do tend to buy too many shoes. I hardly ever wear some of them, so I guess I am wasting my money. Designer labels are important to me as well. I really adore Armani, but it's a little expensive. I think it's important to keep in fashion. I always make a point of complaining if I buy something which has a fault. I take it right back to the Manager and ask for my money back. I never want an exchange. I know my rights and if I had a real problem I would have no hesitation in getting a lawyer in to plead my case.

You may not know *malpractice* (someone's failure to act correctly or legally when doing their job). Other words beginning with *mal* (meaning bad) are: *malnutrition, malfunction, malicious, maltreat, maladministration.*

2 Read the Exam spot carefully before listening to the recording. If you need more information on this part of the exam refer to Exam folder 8 on page 134. Play the recording twice, as in the exam.

Paula: Good morning. On the programme today we have Mike James, a familiar face on television as the champion of consumers' rights. Mike, you've been doing *Pricewise* a long time now, is it something you set out to do?

Mike: Far from it Paula. It all began in 1982 when I was a reporter on a nightly news programme – they wanted a consumer slot, so I took it on. It wasn't until nearly ten years later that it became a programme in its own right. The audience has grown in that time and we regularly get more than ten million viewers.

Paula: Where do the stories you look into come from?

Mike: Well, from you, the public. We get thousands of letters, phone calls and e-mails that tell us about poor service, ridiculous small print, malpractice and the need for information. We actually read all the correspondence and we follow up some stories immediately but most are filed for future use on our database.

Paula: What happens when you get a particularly juicy story?

Mike: We check it out thoroughly of course, and then we contact all the people involved and arrange filming. Then the script is written and our reporters do the necessary interviews, calling to account whoever has led the public astray. Then the film is edited, and of course, it's essential that our lawyers check the script for any problems and then the voice-over is recorded. It's all done to very tight deadlines.

Paula: Do any particular stories stand out in your memory?

Mike: Oh, yes, many. There was one about an advert which promised to make you a lord or lady for anything up to £1,000. One couple, Lord Robert and Lady Tracy de Vere, or Bob and Trace as they are known to many disgruntled members of the public, will sell you a piece of land which allows you to call yourself lord or lady. However, the land only measures 20cms by 20cms. One of the researchers went along and bought a title and tried to find out if having one would help him out in London.

Paula: And did it?

Mike: He went to Harrods, the posh department store, and they were very nice to him, but then they are nice to everyone. He then tried to book a table in a trendy restaurant and he got one – but by the kitchen door! So, really, it won't do you a lot of good having a title nowadays.

Paula: Anything else that comes to mind?

Mike: Well, we did a programme not long ago about shopping by Internet. One of the big supermarkets will deliver to your door for £5 if you order online.

Paula: Now, that's something I've always wanted to try out.

Mike: I think a certain amount of caution is called for. We found that some customers hadn't received quite what they ordered. One poor man had ordered apples and got hairspray! Another customer found that items she'd ordered had been substituted with items which were more expensive. The supermarket was very apologetic when we pointed out these problems and said it was just 'teething trouble'.

Paula: Do you think consumers are more ready to complain these days?

Mike: Oh, yes. Research has been done that shows that attitudes have changed remarkably in the last forty years. It's probably because a lot of purchases no longer qualify as 'needs' so much as 'wants'. Take a well-known brand of trainer. We had a lot of complaints about them squeaking. Now, as they cost upwards of a hundred pounds, people weren't prepared to put up with this, but when they returned them to the shop the shop didn't want to know.

Paula: So they wrote to you for help.

Mike: Yes. We bought a pair of the trainers and sent them to be inspected by an expert. He said that some of the glue inside the shoe had come unstuck. We contacted the manufacturer with evidence of the problem and they were more than happy to back down and refund the money paid by the purchasers. They say that they will look into the manufacturing process and take measures to prevent this happening again.

Paula: Another success then.

Mike: Yes, it's funny how quickly manufacturers and retailers react when they think they might get bad publicity.

Paula: Indeed. It just shows what a good job you're doing. Long may you continue. Our thanks to our guest this week and now next week …

3   The aim of this exercise is to learn phrasal verbs in context, rather than in a list. Write down the whole sentence in your vocabulary notebook.

4   Play the recording and stop it after each of the expressions.

b an interesting story maybe with some scandal/gossip
c to have to get work done for a specific time
d unhappy about something
e problems at the start of something
f to do something to solve a problem

Phrase spot

Use an English–English dictionary to help you with this exercise.

Answers
a By rights **b** as right as rain **c** in the right
d right under their noses **e** the film rights
f right on time **g** within your rights
h makes all the right noises **i** the right way round
j serve Michelle right

5   This text is about the relationship between star signs, personality and shopping. It is not meant to be taken seriously.

Answers
1 A is correct. B, C and D take the preposition *from*.
2 D is correct because *source* collocates with *impeccable*.
3 A is correct. *Seek out* means *to look for* or *concentrate on* in this case.
4 C is correct because it is contrasting what is said in the previous sentence with what is being said now.
5 A is correct. We use *tendency* to talk about people who have an inclination towards doing something.
6 A is correct. It forms the collocation *brand loyalty*.

5.2 pages 44–45

1   Most of the sentences in this exercise contain the type of errors that students make when they write. The importance of knowing whether a noun is countable or uncountable cannot be stressed too highly as it affects the whole grammar of a sentence.

Answers
a Correct. *Scissors* are plural but can be limited by saying *a pair of scissors*.
b How **much** – *luggage* is uncountable. *How many* is used for countable nouns.
c Correct. *Persons* is usually restricted to notices. Use *people* normally. *People* takes a plural verb.
d The news **was**. *News* is uncountable despite ending in *s*.
e *Paper* here is newspaper, so *a paper* is correct; *news* is singular so *news* **is**.
f Correct. *Travels* is used to talk about a very big journey – often to be amusing, e.g. *The little boy set off on his travels down the road to school. Travel* is normally used uncountably, e.g. *Travel by train can be expensive*.

g Correct. *Work* is uncountable when referring to jobs. There are three uses of *works* – *road works*, *works of art* and *works* meaning a factory.
h **Equipment** is uncountable.
i Correct.
j Correct. *People* is normally uncountable (even though it takes a plural verb). *Peoples* refer to races or inhabitants of other lands.
k **Information is** – *information* is uncountable.
l **Fish** – dead fish are uncountable. Live ones are countable.
m Correct.
n **Scenery** is uncountable.
o Correct.
p **Police** is uncountable but takes a plural verb.
q Correct. *Family* can take a singular or plural verb. However, it's more common to use a singular verb when talking about 'the family' as a unit and a plural verb when talking about 'my family'.

2

Answers
a **work** – job; **works** – factory/of art/literature/road
b **iron** – material; **an iron** – machine for smoothing garments
c **a disorder** – an illness; **disorder** – untidiness
d **a speech** – a talk; **speech** – language/noise
e **a room** – a place; **room** – space
f **a language** – German, Greek, etc; **language** – the method of communication
g **home comforts** – a comfortable bed, central heating, etc; **a comfort** – someone or something that gives you sympathy
h **an experience** – something that happened to you; **experience** – what you have learned doing something
i **a capital** – chief city; **capital** – money
j **a coffee** – a cup of coffee; **coffee** – the plant or beans

Suggested answers
a The work I do is confidential.
There are road works on the motorway.
I've never read the *Complete Works of Shakespeare*.
The Tate Modern has some wonderful works of art.
b The box was made of iron.
I used an iron to make the dress look more presentable.
c He is supposed to be suffering from a heart disorder.
Her room is in a terrible state of disorder.
d The Minister made a brilliant election speech.
Her speech was affected by the accident.
e Go to your room at once!
There is no room in our house now we have four children.
f What languages do you speak?
Language is one of the features that sets human beings apart from other animals.
g I love my home comforts like the microwave and jacuzzi.
It is a comfort to know that someone cares about me.

h I had a terrible experience on a train once.
Does she have enough experience for the job?
i The capital of Italy is Rome.
The company had depleted its reserves of capital.
j Would you like a coffee?
Coffee grows in certain places in Brazil.

3 It is not wrong to use *a bit of* or *a piece of*, but more marks can be gained if the right word is used.

Answers
a a burst of applause   b a pane of glass
c a stroke of luck   d a grain of sand   e a gust of wind
f a speck of dust   g a stream of abuse
h a ray of sunshine   i a source of amusement
j an item of clothing/news   k a rumble of thunder
l a puff of smoke   m a state of emergency

4 Spelling is important in all the papers in the examination, but particularly in Paper 3.

Answers
Look around. You're in the midst of a global maelstrom. A swirling mass of converging technologies and new business opportunities unleashed by the Internet. All waiting to be harnessed by companies like Fujitsu – the world's largest IT services provider. 'We've focused our energy and resources on creating technology to solve the unique problems of thousands of individual businesses. Last year alone we invested £2.5 billion of our £31.1 billion global IT and telecommunications revenues on R & D. Innovations that keep your business one step ahead of the Internet. And light years ahead of the competition.'

5 Students are often confused as to how to use the apostrophe s in English. As a result they tend to use *of*, which is often not correct. Use the notes in your book to justify your answers.

Answers
a back seat   b boss's wife / wife's boss – depending on whether the boss is male or female
c corner of a/the room   d pay day
e week's holiday   f wine glass
g moment's delay   h Anne's best friend
i door handle   j sports field

6 Prepositions are often a problem in English for students of all levels. Make sure that you learn which preposition goes with a word when you put it in your vocabulary notebook.

Answers
1 at/in   2 of   3 by   4 next/close/near   5 in   6 of
7 over   8 to   9 to   10 after/for   11 of   12 into/on
13 of   14 with   15 to   16 through   17 without   18 of

5.3 pages 46–47

2 Spend about five minutes reading the two texts and answer the questions.

Answers
• Both texts could be from a newspaper, but different sections. Text A is from the features section, whereas text B is a book review.
• Text A is semi-formal and journalistic. Text B is more formal, apart from the use of *savvy*.

3 Looking for synonyms is a good way of enlarging your vocabulary.

Answers

Text A	Text B
shifting	deferential
rigid	sceptical
integral	doomed
discerning	savvy (informal)
aspirations	daunting

4 This exercise practises the type of question you may be asked in the exam.

Suggested answers
Text A
a putting them into categories / social classes
b You use the expression *tools of the trade* to talk about what you need in order to do your job. Here the tools are abstract and the use of the expression is slightly disapproving.
c They no longer trust companies.
d companies
e asking the consumer what they want and how they feel

Text B
f the age of economy versus the age of affluence
g that some people find in shopping what people once found in religion, e.g. comfort if they are unhappy
h buying and spending money generally
i *shattered* and *fragmented*
j for manufacturers to talk to their customers

5 There will be at least four points in the summary question. They can be 2/2 or 3/1 or 1/3 from texts A and B. Sometimes there may be five points. Always keep the question in mind all the time you are looking for the points.

Suggested answers
The parts underlined are as follows:
1 set on individualism and self-expression /
  free thinking / individualistic / against pigeon-holing /
  increasingly self-opinionated
2 willingness to complain
3 using brands that fit ideas about ourselves that we
  already have
4 sceptical of figures of authority / rocked the stability of
  established institutions
5 exhausted the things they need to purchase

6 Count the number of words you have written. Less than 50 is too short and more than 70/75 is too long and you will be penalised for this. You may find it hard to change some words. Sometimes it isn't possible to change them all, in which case you should spend your time making sure the paragraph reads well and is grammatically correct.

Suggested answer
Consumers today have an independent outlook and are keen to assert their point of view. Not only are they more likely to be mistrustful of authority figures, they also make more complaints than they used to. Given the high levels of prosperity, consumers now are not restricted to buying necessities, they buy goods for pleasure. They also look for brands that reinforce their own idea of themselves. (*67 words*)

7 As you have seen in Unit 3, it is important to be able to manipulate words, both for the summary and for the word formation text on Paper 3.

Answers
a boredom b obsolescence c awareness d pride
e confidence f austerity g generosity
h independence i inefficiency j insecurity
k meanness l individualism, responsibility
m aspirations n scepticism

Exam folder 3

Paper 3 Part 5
Comprehension questions and summary writing task pages 48–49

1 The photo is of Caxton and his printing press.

This part of Paper 3 is the part students often have the most trouble with. You should remember that the four or five summary points can be taken from both texts. There are two questions on each text, but sometimes one question can ask for information from both texts. Practice is needed in writing a summary so that it will have all the necessary information in a well-written, succinct paragraph. Remember that your ideas/opinions are not required and that you should keep your answers relevant to the question.

Answers
1 the book
2 to take a look into someone else's mind without being intrusive
3 It's scary by yourself and difficult to take seriously when you're with friends.
4 when people feel that going to the cinema has few advantages to staying at home

2 This summary contains the key points. However, the following need to be improved:

Answer
It is too long.
The paragraph requires no introduction.
No opinion is asked for.
The linking is poor.
The student has not used his/her own words.

3

Sample summary
Both books and the cinema possess advantages that new technology does not. Not only is a book inexpensive, it is also small enough to be easily carried. In addition, in comparison with a computer screen, a book is both a pleasure to read and is aesthetically pleasing. The cinema is likely to survive because there will always be certain films that require a large screen and also some films are more enjoyable in the company of others. (*77 words*)

Unit 6

6.1 pages 50–51

1 The photos are of two young children learning to play the violin by the Suzuki method and of some buskers – these are street performers who hope people will give them money.

Possible answers
I'm afraid I find it very hard to concentrate if music is playing – it doesn't matter what type it is, I still find it very distracting.
It's quite true that every child should learn to play an instrument, although getting them to practise may be a problem. Learning how to read music is very good.

Pop music can improve my mood, it depends, and sometimes it just makes it worse!

I don't believe that listening to classical music improves your intelligence. There is no proof of this.

I love listening to buskers – I love any kind of live music.

2 This part of the Reading paper is the one students often have the most trouble with. Read all of the base text and then all the extra paragraphs before doing the exercise. Some of the important references have been highlighted in bold as this is the first example of this type of task. They are not in bold in the examination. Read both sides of the gap to make sure you have the right answer. Just reading the paragraph before the gap will not always help.

Background information

Wolfgang Amadeus Mozart 1756–1791. Born in Salzburg, and a child prodigy, he made his first professional tour when he was six. He settled in Vienna and wrote his operas and became court composer to Joseph II in 1787. He composed over 600 pieces of music during his relatively short life.

Answers
1 C The paragraph after 1 refers to more than one person.
2 F **He** is Shaw. **This test** in the following paragraph refers back to the **standard IQ test** mentioned in F.
3 A **This experiment** is **this test** referred to earlier, and **he** in the following paragraph is **Christopher Chabris**.
4 E **Detractor** means **critic**.
5 G **It** in the following paragraph refers to **the Sonata**.
6 H **This vagueness** refers to the question of whether other types of music would work.
7 B The **sequences** refers back to the **sequences** in the preceding paragraph and **finding** in the following paragraph means the same as **results**.

3 This exercise will help you to improve your summary skills.

Answers
Gordon Shaw
He was the first to do a test where the rhythms of the brain were turned into sound. He joined Rauscher in using an IQ test to see if students got better at paper folding after listening to Mozart. He concluded that Mozart's music had helped them do it better.

Frances Rauscher
She was a colleague of Shaw who worked with him on the paper-folding experiment. She also believes other types of music might work as well as Mozart's does.

Christopher Chabris
He couldn't find any proof of the Mozart Effect – he believed the music just made people feel better.

Lois Hetland
She concluded that Mozart's music did work.

Ed Seigel
He wanted to prove the Mozart Effect wrong so he set up a test, but he found that subjects who listened to Mozart did better.

John Hughes
He has studied various compositions by different composers. He found Mozart was in tune with what was happening in the brain.

Phrase spot

Phrases with *take* are often tested in the examination.

Answers
a seriously b notice c place d part e the view
f into account/consideration / account of g issue
h advantage i by surprise j second place
k account of / into account l for granted m a stand
n exception to

6.2 pages 52–53

1 Refer to the Grammar folder on page 183 if you are not clear about the uses of these modal verbs.

2 Take about ten minutes to do this exercise. There may be more than one answer to some questions.

Answers
a A b C c A d A e A f A/B g A h A i B
j A k A/B l A m B n B

3

Possible answers
a It's quite likely that another Mozart will be born. I can't believe that only one musical genius will ever exist.

b I guess an asteroid could hit the Earth, but I'm sure the government will do all in its power to prevent it.

c It's quite possible people will have brain transplants in the future – after all, we have transplants for most parts of the body, don't we?

d I don't think England is dominant in world pop.

e There's no chance of New Zealand winning the football World Cup, not when there are teams from France, Spain, Italy and Brazil.

f It's a foregone conclusion that electric cars are the cars of the future. It stands to reason that oil reserves won't last forever.

4 Try to work out who or what is being talked about in this exercise. You may have different answers to the ones suggested below.

Suggested answers
Example: Death of President J. F. Kennedy
a Neil Armstrong landing on the moon
b the dawning of the Millennium
c Versace
d mobile phones
e the fall of the Berlin Wall

5 Count how many words you have used to complete each sentence. You should also check that you have used the word given and that you haven't changed it in any way.

Answers
1 chances are (that) Alan will be
2 is doubtful whether/that Professor Potts will take
3 bound to get the Head's job if / provided that
4 all likelihood the cause
5 a foregone conclusion that

6 The article is about how bands are often 'manufactured' by people in the music industry for profit.

Answers
a The writer is rather cynical.
b The comparison between groups in the past who got together themselves and what is happening now.
c That music bands are like any other product.

1 Not 2 as 3 out 4 in/to 5 may
6 With 7 who/what 8 far/much
9 Although/While/Though/Whilst/Whereas
10 before 11 having/likely 12 together 13 charge
14 fact/reality 15 any

6.3 pages 54–55

1 Use an English–English dictionary to help you with this exercise if you are unsure of the answers.

Answers

violin	string
piano	keyboard
drum	percussion
flute	woodwind
synthesizer	electronic
trumpet	brass

2

Possible answers
I used to play the piano, very badly. The instrument I would like to play is the saxophone – it has such a brilliant sound, very sexy. I'm sure some instruments are harder to play than others – take the violin – it's hard to make a decent sound on it for ages after you take it up, whereas the flute is much more straightforward.

3 Read through the questions before listening to the recording. Try to predict the answers. Write down what you think the answer is going to be and check whether you were right after you have heard the recording. Play the recording twice, as in the exam. The underlined parts of the tapescript confirm the answers.

Answers
1 fussy 2 cold slopes 3 strength (and) flexibility
4 wastage/waste 5 1.1 to 1.2 mms 6 steamed
7 glued 8 neck 9 mellow 10 200 to 300 years'

Interviewer: Any string player will tell you that no instrument is identical to another. Thirty violins may look the same, but each has a characteristic, however subtle, all of its own. When I went to Middletown College I saw why stringed instruments can be so different. It's here that the college runs a violin-making course for students of all ages. And to see a violin in its stages of development, and especially the intricately carved wood, makes you appreciate why string players are so <u>fussy</u>. The head of the violin school is one of its ex-students, Sue Pearson. I met her in the violin workshop. Sue, before you start to make a violin into the instrument we all know and love, where do you go to find your wood?

Sue: Various places. The pine really needs to come from northern Europe – from fairly <u>cold slopes</u>, as the tree needs to have grown fairly slowly so that it grows straight and we have close, uniform grain lines.

Interviewer: Why is that – that you need such finely grained wood?

Sue: It's all relating to <u>strength and flexibility</u>. We make the front of the violin from pine and the back from maple. These two woods have the qualities we are looking for.

Interviewer: What we've got here are basically just blocks of wood, aren't they? As with any great piece of woodwork, you can never believe for a moment that you could just produce something out of a boring block of wood.

Sue: This piece here is basically a neck block – it just needs to be of sufficient size for us to create the scroll and the neck itself. In any operation in violin making, I think you're looking at 80–85% <u>wastage</u>.

Interviewer: And you've got some other bits as well. Very thin pieces.

Sue: These are the ribs or sides. I mean these are probably one and a half to one and three quarter millimetres thick, and before they can go onto the instrument, they'll be reduced to <u>one point one or one point two millimetres</u>.

Interviewer: Now, a little bit further along the bench you've got something a bit more developed.

Sue: This is actually what we build the instrument around. It's called the inside mould or form, and it's simply a piece of birch plywood shaped to the inside of the instrument. You bend and shape the ribs around it, but first they are <u>steamed</u> to soften them to make them more flexible, and simply by drying the rib out to the shape we want, it will keep it permanently in that position.

Interviewer: We've got the *shape* of the body here. What happens next?

Sue: Basically we shape the top and bottom and then they are <u>glued</u> together. We don't use a machine for this. We've still got the <u>neck</u> to do and this is easily the most elaborate part of the instrument. It's quite intricately carved, and it's always quite difficult for a novice student to undertake. We're really dealing in three dimensions.

Interviewer: There's an instrument that looks finished over there, but it's an unusual colour. Why is that?

Sue: Well, it's not finished yet. It needs a good clean – it can get a bit grubby when it's being made – and then it's ready for varnishing.

Interviewer: Now, that must have an effect on the sound?

Sue: I do think myself that the varnish can take the sharp tones from the violin – it can <u>mellow</u> it slightly.

Interviewer: Some of the greatest violins are fairly old. Are you expecting when you make these instruments that they might still be around a couple of hundred years hence?

Sue: That's one of the things that always interests us. We're all mortal and it would be nice to think one of your instruments was still being played in <u>two to three hundred years</u>.

Style extra

Collocations are often tested in the examination and you can gain more marks if you use them in your compositions.

> **Suggested answers**
> a Michael Jackson is widely believed to have had plastic surgery.
> b She gave her boyfriend a carefully chosen present.
> c CDs are keenly priced at retail outlets across the country.
> d Our seats at the rock concert were staggeringly expensive, but at least we had a good view of the stage.
> e Their new album has been singularly unsuccessful and is unlikely to make number one.

Idiom spot

The idioms here all derive from words to do with music. A fiddle is another word for a violin.

> **Answers**
> a fiddle – to being less important than
> b tune – to be distanced from mentally
> c song – very cheap
> d string – to have another skill
> e score – to get revenge
> f note – to be greeted favourably
> g chord – was understood by in a non-literal sense

4

> **Possible answer**
> (These are ideas for one side of a conversation.)
> The atmosphere young people listen to music in is very important to them. They usually don't want to be sitting in the rarefied atmosphere of a concert hall – they prefer clubs and open-air pop or rock concerts, where you can get up and dance. The sound quality is also of the utmost importance – this is more of a problem at an open-air concert, but it's better now than it used to be. Young people like to be together, yes, it's OK to listen to music at home or on a walkman, but half the fun of listening to music is to be with your friends. Often open-air concerts are a rip off – one I went to was charging £150 for three days. Not many young people can afford that, especially if they are still at college.

5 This exercise looks at contrastive stress. This is particularly important for the modal auxiliaries you have seen in this unit as the meaning can change depending on how they are said.

> **Answers**
> a irritated   b reproachful   c irritated
> d suggesting   e worried   f angry

6

> **Answers**
> a I <u>thought</u> you'd gone home.
>   Yes, she/he has gone home.
> b I thought you'd gone <u>home</u>.
>   No, he's/she's gone somewhere else.
> c She's an <u>English</u> teacher.
>   Yes, she teaches English (not Spanish).
> d She's an English <u>teacher</u>.
>   Yes, she teaches English; she's not a student.
> e I'm not buying a <u>car</u>.
>   No, he's getting a bike, etc.
> f I'm not <u>buying</u> a car.
>   No, she's hiring one.

g She's not <u>pretty</u>.
No, but she's intelligent/friendly, etc. or possibly she's ugly.

h I <u>had</u> wanted to see the paintings.
No, she didn't see them.

i I had <u>wanted</u> to see the paintings.
Yes, he saw them.

Writing folder 3

Paper 2 Part 1 Essay pages 56–57

In the Part 1 essay task, include the information given but also develop relevant ideas of your own. Plan your answer before you start writing, so that your ideas are presented in a logical order.

1 The opening paragraph gives a clear introduction to the essay.

2 A neutral register is appropriate for both the essay and the Part 2 report task.

> **Suggested answers**
> **a** frequent opportunities to play live
> **b** highly competitive, hard
> **c** substantial earnings
> **d** enjoyable

3 Notice that the sentence openers are all impersonal in tone.

> **Possible answers**
> **a** Professional musicians are seen as
> **b** On the question of / Taking the example of
> **c** At the same time / In actual fact / On the other hand
> OR It is true that / It is often said that / The reality is that
> **d** No one would dispute / One argument in favour of this is
> OR Set against this is
> **e** This is not to say that
> **f** It is true that / It is often said that / The reality is that
> **g** No one would dispute
> **h** In contrast to

> **Extra sentences**
> **1** From the classical performer's point of view, it is very hard to find orchestral positions nowadays.
> **2** It is usually the case that you can find live music in small local venues.
> **3** People tend to regard music as a less important part of the school curriculum than mathematics.
> **4** Considering the advantages of listening to music, it is clear that it is both relaxing and enjoyable.

4 The twelve sentences have been added to the paragraph plan below, along with additional notes.

> **1** (Opening paragraph)
>
> **2 General perceptions of the role of music in society**
> The reality is that music is more available to us than ever before.
> *Give examples.*
> It is usually the case that you can find live music in small local venues.
> *Include parties and CD sales here.*
>
> **3 Performers**
> From the classical performer's point of view, it is very hard to find orchestral positions nowadays.
> Professional musicians are seen as highly-skilled individuals, yet their earnings don't always reflect their talent.
> In contrast to this, it should be added that the best performers earn a great deal.
> *Give examples (rock and classical).*
>
> **4 Music in schools**
> *Sentences need reordering!*
> This is not to say that everyone should be able to read music, as it is not a fundamental lifeskill.
> At the same time children who learn music at a young age benefit academically.
> On the question of teaching music in school, not enough is done.
> People tend to regard music as a less important part of the school curriculum than mathematics.
>
> **5 Benefits of music (playing and listening)**
> No one would dispute the fact that it is easier to make your own CD these days.
> No one would dispute the many benefits of listening to music.
> *Add benefits of playing music.*
> Considering the advantages of listening to music, it is clear that it is both relaxing and enjoyable.
> *Say how.*
>
> **6** (Concluding paragraph)

5 Make sure your ideas are in a logical order and are clearly linked.

Sample answer

No one can deny that music features in all our lives. At the same time, I believe that many members of our society undervalue professional musicians and, indeed, the teaching of music. In this essay, I will cover both of these aspects, as well as outlining some of the many benefits of playing and listening to music.

What then is the role of music today? The reality is that music is more available to us than ever before. It is possible to listen to CDs on a walkman wherever you are, and even to download music from the Internet. Furthermore, it is usually the case that you can find live music in small local venues. People often hire bands for parties. Bands like these may never record a CD, or if they do, will earn very little from it.

Professional musicians are seen as highly-skilled individuals, yet their earnings don't always reflect their talent. In contrast to this statement, it should be added that the best known performers – from Madonna to Pavarotti – earn a great deal. From the classical performer's point of view, however, it is very hard to find orchestral positions nowadays. This must be disheartening after so many years of study.

On the question of teaching music in school, not enough is done. People tend to regard music as a less important part of the school curriculum than mathematics. At the same time children who learn music at a young age benefit academically. This is not to say that everyone should be able to read music, as it is not a fundamental lifeskill.

Having said that, it is true that music offers many benefits. Anyone who plays music has a ready-made social life. Most amateur musicians also find making music very creative. Considering the advantages of listening to music, it is clear that it is both relaxing and enjoyable. What is better than putting on a CD at home or dancing the night away to live music?

Perhaps it is time for government policy to change. If more resources were made available to schools and musicians were given financial support, society would benefit enormously.

Unit 7

7.1 pages 58–59

1 The pictures all have an 'eye' in common. They show:

- a detail from a painting by the nineteenth-century French painter Georges Seurat, showing the eyelid of a young woman
- a peacock's eye feather, in close-up
- a cat's eye, the device used on main roads to guide drivers at night
- a macrophoto of the human eye, showing the dark central pupil surrounded by a blue iris

2 As the Exam spot mentions, there are four short extracts in Paper 4 Part 1. In the exam, you will have 15 seconds before each extract to read through the questions. In this time, try to predict what you might hear. Play each extract twice. The underlined parts of the tapescript confirm the answers.

Answers

1 C   2 B   3 C   4 A   5 B   6 A   7 B   8 C

Extract 1

Woman: When Sam was two and a bit, he began to use one of the living room walls, which was unfortunately white at the time, as a drawing surface. It was always the same wall and he appeared to be attempting pictures, as well as showing a definite sense of colour. <u>I had no wish to stifle any artistic genius he might have, so I tended to turn a blind eye to what he was doing</u>, making sure that he was armed with washable felt-tips and cleaning up after him without delay. But one weekend I was out and my husband caught him at it … a boat with two funnels, as I recall, and he hit the roof, both with Sam and with me. In the end we compromised: I bought some huge rolls of white paper and taped it to the wall, all the way along. As soon as Sam completed one magnum opus I would take it down and replace it with a fresh canvas, so to speak. <u>It cost me a fortune, but I've never regretted it, in fact I feel proud of myself, as I believe it helped to make him the way he is.</u> But Sam loves to wind me up about it. You see, he has absolutely no leanings towards art, being heavily into information technology!

Extract 2

Woman: But *is* photography an art form? I can't help feeling there's a world of difference between <u>the structure of, say, a Seurat painting – not to mention his planning in early sketches</u> – and some instant black and white image of cornfields. Where's the skill in that?

Man: Oh come on. You have to judge what's there. And above all, it comes down to having an eye for a good shot – otherwise, I agree, your cornfield is just a snap.

Woman: I don't know, I mean in painting, there's also the choice of materials – the type of paint, the canvas – that's missing in a photograph.

Man: Well, you're wrong there, too! First off, there are many different types of film you can work with. Then, in the dark room, the best photographers maximise the effect they're looking for by going for a particular printing paper. You've just proved my point: there's creativity right through the process.

Woman: Hmm. I don't think we're ever going to quite see eye to eye on this one, are we? Better agree to differ.

Man: Suits me.

Extract 3

Man: Percy Shaw always had an eye for practical solutions. Driving home through the unlit outskirts of Halifax at night, he found the perfect substitute for night vision, following the glint of his headlights in the metal tramlines. But he ran into a problem: no longer in use, these rails were soon taken up for good. With this serious setback, Shaw decided it was time to come up with something that would help him – and others – to steer in the dark. His now ubiquitous invention, modelled on the eye of a cat, consists of a mirror and a spherical lens mounted on a rubber pad. Each time a vehicle runs over it, the assembly is forced into its iron base and the lens is wiped clean by the rubber, which acts like an eyelid. Shaw patented his invention in 1934 when he was only 23 and, thanks to the cat's eye, became a very rich man.

Extract 4

Interviewer: Dr Joanna Walters, your new book *The Complex Eye* has been featured in many newspapers this week. In it, you remind us that the eye is not only a passive receiver of information, but a great communicator too.

Joanna: Erm, I should point out that I collaborated on the book with a leading zoologist – it's the human communication side that's my field.

Interviewer: Sorry, that's journalism for you, I've been misinformed. Anyway, we all remember being told by our mothers that it's rude to stare.

Joanna: Right. Staring is the most aggressive facial expression with which to threaten a rival and in the animal kingdom, those species that can't frighten off their would-be attackers in this way, from moths to fish to birds, have evolved false eye spots, which fulfil the same function.

Interviewer: And you draw parallels with human beings here.

Joanna: Absolutely. Because it's taboo for us to physically stare someone out, other, subtler, strategies are often in play. Look in your rear-view mirror late at night and you may see a pair of dazzling headlights eyeballing you. What do you do?

Interviewer: Let them overtake?

Joanna: That's right, avoid confrontation, especially in these days of road rage. Once we're behind the wheel, those headlights become an extension of our persona, whether aggressively so, or in self-defence.

Idiom spot

The idioms used in the recording are: *turn a blind eye to; see eye to eye with; have an eye for.*

Catch someone's eye means to be noticed because of standing out in some way; there is a related compound adjective: *eye-catching.* (*Catch someone's eye* also means 'get their attention'.)

Cast your eye over or *run your eye over* means to check something.

Possible answers

a The thing that really caught my eye was that pair of orange silk pyjamas hanging out of the school window.

b I shouldn't have turned a blind eye to the child's petty stealing of sweets from the shop counter: he needed to be taught what was right and wrong.

c Could you cast your eye over my essay – I'm sure there are lots of spelling mistakes!

d I've never seen eye to eye with my younger sister, but her decision to quit college is her stupidest yet.

e You definitely have an eye for interesting accessories – I love those earrings.

---

3 Look back at Exam folder 1 on pages 14–15 before doing this word formation task.

B ackground information

Georges Seurat was a highly innovative artist, responsible for the whole Pointillist movement. He was not really appreciated by the Parisian art establishment during his lifetime. His most famous painting is *Un dimanche après-midi a l'île de la Grande Jatte* (Sunday afternoon on the island of Grande Jatte), shown on page 59. This painting took three years to complete (1884–1886) and is now on permanent exhibition in the Art Institute of Chicago, USA. The painting was the subject of a successful musical by Stephen Sondheim, *Sunday in the Park with George.*

Answers
1 classical 2 Hitherto 3 unpredictable 4 intuitively
5 stability 6 scientific 7 incomparable
8 influential 9 interaction 10 systematically

Style extra

Using extended noun phrases is an effective way of varying the beginning of sentences. It would be particularly appropriate to use them in an article or review.

Possible answers
a A highly-regarded and influential film-maker, Wim Wenders has now produced a documentary classic in *Buena Vista Social Club*.
b Best-known for his magnificent novels, Emile Zola also wrote extensively on naturalism, in prefaces to his works and letters to contemporaries.
c Undervalued as an actor until very recently, Johnson is now being offered every part under the sun.
d The youngest of a large family, Serena Williams has made her mark on the tennis circuit and threatens to outplay her older sister Venus.
e Young, rich and famous, River Phoenix suffered an early death through an accidental drug overdose.

7.2 pages 60–61

1 The Hubble Space telescope image shows star formation in the Horsehead nebula.

Possible answer
The image is sensational; the gas clouds are almost flamboyant in their towering grandeur. There is something very inspiring about them.

2 a In the example, *dazzling* is an adjective; *eyeballing* is a participle.

2 b

Answers
i The participle *Driving* is active and refers to Percy Shaw.
ii The participle *modelled* is passive and refers to his invention (the cat's eye); the clause could be rewritten as a defining relative clause: *His invention, which is modelled on the eye of a cat, ...*

2 c

Answers
i The cat is sitting on the roof.
ii The person is sitting on the roof.

3

Suggested answer
In the nineteenth century and earlier, the artistic tradition was to paint the beauty of nature; thus, beauty derived from nature. Now, artists no longer represent nature on canvas, and so their works are not usually described as 'beautiful'.

4 Read the section in the Grammar folder after doing this exercise.

Answers
having viewed: active; previous action
taken: passive; previous action
having been launched: passive; previous action
sending: active; simultaneous action
being (successfully) repaired: passive; simultaneous action
seeing: active; simultaneous action
imitated: passive; previous action
concerned: active; simultaneous action

5

Answers
1c Receiving mixed reactions from members of the public, the exhibition includes some rather shocking images.
2f Often occurring in open landscape, Andy Goldsworthy's sculptures are particularly effective during dramatic weather conditions.
3b Wanting to create order from chaos, physicists are constantly trying to reduce the universe to a set of basic principles.
4e Having taken quite a few warm-up shots, the photographer then caught the model unawares in a more relaxed pose.
5a Coming in from the street for an hour's rest, people don't realise that the beds – and they themselves – are part of an installation.
6d Having bought two previous works by this artist, I am now looking out for a third.

6

Answers
a (being) chosen b shown c sold d made
e being searched f announced g damaged

7.3 pages 62–63

1 The pictures show:
- a hackneyed greeting card, showing a still life
- a kitten with a green bow sitting in a saucer
- one of photographer David Johnston's 'environmental portraits' (see text in exercise 2)

> **Possible answer**
> I find the kitten sitting in the saucer with a bow around its neck the most clichéd image. You see the same thing all the time in magazines and on cards. It's so posed too – when would a kitten sit like that of its own accord?

2

> **Answers**
> paragraph 1 – **c**
> paragraph 2 – **a**
> paragraph 3 – **d**

3 The types of question shown all demand detailed understanding of the text.

4 The most successful is **b**: the answer is concise and meaningful, and does not repeat words from the text.

Comments on the other answers:
a: Rambles and lifts substantially from the text.
c: Although the stylistic intent seems to be recognised, the answer is unclear and inadequate.

5 The number of words used in each answer is given in brackets below. As the answers to **d** and **e** show, it is not always necessary to write a complete sentence.

> **Suggested answers**
> **a** Trophies like these are put on shelves and forgotten, so they gather dust. (13)
> **b** The club members are determined to win the trophy, whatever the cost. (12)
> **c** It means that any photographer who imitates existing ideas will fail. (11)
> **d** David Johnston's stock portrait of two people. (7)
> **e** Innovation – new ideas. (3)

6

> **Suggested answers**
> **Para 1** Relative beauty is subjective while natural beauty is not.
> **Para 2** Beauty in nature is for a biological reason.
> **Para 3** Natural beauty is often reduced to clichéd images.

7 Keep your answers short and avoid repeating words from the text, wherever possible.

> **Suggested answers**
> **a** Beauty is a matter of personal opinion.
> **b** Only a distant relationship to.
> **c** To emphasise how clichés restrict our appreciation of beauty (like swaddled babies, who cannot move).
> **d** Something that is small and ugly.
> **e** Transient.

Exam folder 4

Paper 1 Part 1
Lexical cloze pages 64–65

The photograph is of a fresco by Giovanni Stradano (1523–1603) of the Piazza del Mercato Vecchio in Florence.

You need to get used to organising your vocabulary systematically. This will help when you come to do this type of exercise. It's important to read through the text from beginning to end to get a good idea of what it is about and also the register it is in. Some answers may depend on register rather than meaning.

> **The rhythm of life**
> 1 B *just what the doctor ordered* is an idiom
> 2 A *to make use of something* is a fixed phrase
> 3 C *in the hands of someone* is an idiom
> 4 A *to serve* means here to be used in this way
> 5 D *issue* is more than topic/subject or matter, it also has the idea of something of importance requiring a decision
> 6 C *to turn out* is a phrasal verb which means to result

> **The need for aged buildings**
> 7 B – *badly* often collocates with *need* and means very much
> 8 C – *a state of repair* is a fixed phrase
> 9 A – *although* here is in parenthesis
> 10 C – *rundown* means dilapidated
> 11 A – *limited* takes the preposition *to*
> 12 B – *worn out* is a phrasal verb meaning to become useless

> **Merchant@florence**
> 13 B – *represented* is an example here of semantic precision
> 14 A – *instance* means example here
> 15 C – *to unearth* is literally to find buried underground, but it can also be used figuratively meaning to discover something which is hidden well
> 16 D – *Apparently* is a comment adverb here, giving the idea of 'this is what I have been told'
> 17 B – *to take on* is a phrasal verb, here meaning to acquire
> 18 A – *to enhance* gives the idea of to increase in quality or power

Unit 8

8.1 pages 66–67

1   The pictures show:
   Sydney: the Opera House and harbour
   Tokyo: downtown, at night
   Rome: Piazza della Rotonda and the Pantheon

Possible answer

Obviously a big city has many cultural amenities, such as an opera house, and plenty of night life. Cities often have historical buildings too. There is usually a lively atmosphere, with so many people. On the other hand, big cities are noisy and polluted, and it often takes a long time to travel from one district to another.

Every city should offer people an efficient and cheap public transport system, as well as good public services, such as rubbish collection, recycling facilities and open spaces to relax in.

---

2   There are four short texts in Paper 1 Part 2, each written in a different style. Exam folder 6 on pages 98–101 gives advice on this part and includes a complete task.

   Skimming the texts before you start answering the questions is important as it provides information on style and genre.

Suggested answer

Cool Brazil: magazine article, factual and impersonal
English Journey: personal account, possibly in a book
A Magnificent Failure: specialist magazine article, personal view

---

Background information

Beryl Bainbridge has written several successful novels, including *Sweet William*, *The Bottle Factory Outing*, *Every Man for Himself* (on the Titanic disaster) and *Master Georgie*. *English Journey* is the factual account she wrote on retracing the writer J.B. Priestley's footsteps: in 1933, he took a journey through England and wrote a book by the same name.

---

3   As questions 1–6 show, the multiple-choice questions in Part 2 can take a variety of forms, testing opinion, attitude, tone, purpose, implication, text organisation, main idea or detailed meaning.

Answers

1 D   2 C   3 B   4 B   5 A   6 D

Detailed explanation

1   The answer, D, lies in the phrases *extraordinarily lateral-thinking* and *politically astute*. A is wrong as it is almost the opposite of the answer. There is no evidence for B, as we know they were *extremely cost-effective*. C cannot be true, as although the text mentions other cities, external advice is not suggested and, indeed, Curitiba took a very different decision to Rio and Sao Paulo.

2   The answer, C, is prefaced in *More significantly* and confirmed in the words *in a trice*. A is not possible, even though the buses are longer than average. B is manifestly not the case, as there is heavy traffic. There is no information about cost of tickets to support D.

3   The answer, B, is rooted in two places: 'the original *English Journey*' and 'Fifty years ago'. A is wrong, as Bainbridge talks about the efficiency of the service in the past but concludes that because of high unemployment, a station would not be used now. C goes against the style of the text, which is factually objective rather than a complaint. D is not supported by the text, even if a reader might look at the Priestley version out of curiosity.

4   The answer is B: you can almost hear Bainbridge's disgust in the sentence 'What a farcical piece of planning.' The other three words are used more neutrally.

5   The answer, A, is found in the words 'he bewailed what had happened to it' and in the train of events, whereby it is clear that Calthorpe's plan was abandoned. B is wrong, as the text calls his plan 'visionary' and he is a 'passionate advocate of "New Urbanism"'. C is plausible, in that the writer criticises Laguna West's lack of transport, but it is not why Calthorpe is unhappy. D is not suggested in the text.

6   The answer, D, echoes 'one solitary bus shelter'. The other words do not pick up on an earlier statement: A and C are extra-textual references to shared knowledge about the words; B has no additional reference.

---

4   Were you able to work out the meaning of any of these by looking at the surrounding context?

Answers

Cool Brazil

a place of pilgrimage somewhere that must be visited by those interested in it (a pilgrimage is a religious journey; for example Mecca is the most important place of pilgrimage for Muslims)
a fraction of only a small amount of (fractions in mathematics represent amounts between zero and one)
the main arteries the main routes (an artery is the main carrier of blood round your body from the heart)
in a trice very quickly

English Journey

rigid and wanting inflexible and inadequate
degradation humiliation or shame

A Magnificent Failure
passionate advocate someone who believes strongly in
   something and recommends it
bewailed complained bitterly about – a literary word,
   which serves to underline Calthorpe's unhappiness, as
   the reader is surprised by its use
in contravention of going against, breaking

Phrase spot

Answers
far-sighted, far-thinking
poorly-constructed, poorly-fitting, poorly-thought-
   through
long-running
short-sighted
blown-down, blown-out, blown-up

Examples of noun collocations
a far-sighted plan
a poorly-constructed office block
a long-running play
a short-sighted mathematician
blown-down trees

Style extra

Possible answer
These short sentences have a powerful effect on me –
they make the scene very real. The almost chatty style
makes it feel as though Bainbridge is talking directly to
me. The style also supports the factual nature of the
account, by giving hard-hitting and immediate
observations.

The use of 'dumped' is derogatory and conveys a lack of
planning and thought – whereas 'landscaped' would convey
the opposite. 'Set' is a more neutral word.

Possible answers
Author's note: I have taken all these examples from the
Cambridge International Corpus – my favourite one is the
sentence about Graham Anderson, which is a
wonderfully vivid description! The collocations are
underlined.
True to a sport in which <u>chauvinistic traditions</u> die hard,
every player's wife or girlfriend is expected to help
prepare sandwiches and brew tea in the cricket pavilion
twice a season.
She put out one arm towards Tom, looking up at him
piteously with her helpless, <u>childish</u> blue <u>eyes</u>.
Hard Bop has acquired a <u>reputation</u> of being <u>clichéd</u> and
samey.

There were days of ferocious stress and excitement, when
Kevin started to yell into the phone, impatient with
buyers <u>raising fatuous objections</u>.
Graham Anderson was a very red man: ginger hair, <u>florid</u>
<u>complexion</u>, bow-tie in unvarying pink, flame-striped
shirt and scarlet braces.
What I've just said to you is <u>a load of garbage</u>!
I cannot be absolutely sure that there is no mention of
Idso in the book because of its other <u>glaring omission</u> –
there is no index.
I found myself uttering the <u>hackneyed words</u> 'How long
does she have?'
Hall, far from performing any embarrassing ritual, was
wandering around like a <u>vacuous tourist</u>.

8.2 pages 68–69

1   Both examples use inversion. Read the section in the
    Grammar folder on page 183.

2

Possible answers
a Never before have I felt as contented as I do now.
b Only once in my life have I regretted taking a trip.
c Scarcely had the clock struck midnight when the lights
   went out.
d No sooner had I put my raincoat on than the sun came
   out again.
e Hardly a moment had passed before someone else
   hammered on the door.
f Not until last month did I feel in control of my
   workload.
g Seldom do any birds visit the garden, due to the
   number of cats around.
h Rarely will there be an opportunity for proper
   discussion.

See the Grammar folder for further examples of
prepositional phrases.

3

Answers
1 stood   2 sat   3 hung   4 had   5 stretched
6 were   7 did

4

Answers
1 once did the train run on time / on/to schedule
2 had Brian and Sue met when/before
3 no circumstances are you to
4 sooner had they left their car than/before/when
5 one postcard did Kerry send us while
6 had the bus company put their prices up

8.3 pages 70–71

1 The meaning of *The grass is always greener …* is that there always appears to be a better situation than your own.

2 Sally is Meg's daughter and they currently live in Wales. Kevin works in London but is disenchanted with the rat race and plans to swap living accommodation with Meg and Sally temporarily.

Interviewer: OK, well there are three people sitting in the studio with me now – Sally, Meg and Kevin – who are about to embark on a rather unusual 'lifeplan' as they call it, something that will bring about a change of gear for all three of them. By way of introduction, we need to go through some recent history, and I'm going to start with you, Sally, because it's your discontent about where you're living now that has played a large part in all this. Sally, tell us where you and Meg call home at the moment.

Sally: It's a tiny village in the Welsh hills, which no one will have heard of. Last November we quit London and headed for the border. Mum and Dad decided to go their separate ways, you see – I think Mum took this literally, she wanted to get as far away as possible from Dad at the time.

Meg: It wasn't quite like that, but yes, the divorce had a lot to do with needing to get out of the city and start again.

Interviewer: So out of the blue you chose a remote Welsh village?

Meg: Not quite, I had good friends there …

Sally: Who have since left.

Meg: Yes, but, well anyway, as Sally will tell you, it hasn't quite worked out for her, though for me at the beginning, winding down was a godsend, it gave me the chance to rethink my life and decide on priorities.

Interviewer: So Sally, why has it been less than perfect for you?

Sally: I'm 15 now and I left really good friends behind me, some I'd known my whole life. Plus I've had to learn Welsh to even function at school and that's been hard. And as you can imagine, there isn't exactly a lot to do where we are – most people of my age just hang around the village green or go to each others' houses. It's not that great. Fortunately, I've been staying some weekends at my Dad's place – so I can meet up with some of my old friends, go to clubs, you know.

Interviewer: Mmm … so the country idyll, not such good news for you, but for you, Meg, you're content with your life there?

Meg: Yes and no-o. I have to confess that once the honeymoon period was over (a rather unfortunate term in my case) well, you know after a while I woke up and realised that this wasn't right for me either. It's hard to pin down exactly why – I don't suffer from boredom, and I still get a rush out of the sheer beauty and calm that surrounds us, but I … I feel that I'm missing out too, that I should be working, socialising more, going to exhibitions, all those things I used to take for granted, but which are totally out of the frame at the moment.

Interviewer: And that's where Kevin comes in …

Kevin: One lucky break all round …

Sally: Well, it's pretty flukey. Basically Mum and I sat down one night and agreed we had to get back somehow … but we realised that there was no way we could expect to move back to London as easily as we'd left.

Meg: Selling the cottage wouldn't be easy, and nor would finding somewhere in our price range in London.

Sally: Mum had this real brainwave, she decided to look for anyone who might be interested in changing places, house swaps, that sort of thing.

Kevin: And thanks to the power of the Internet, they tracked me down.

Interviewer: And everything's fallen into place. But what's in it for you, Kevin? You've already told me you have a large flat in a very desirable part of London, a good job, …

Kevin: What I've got is a nice flat I hardly ever see, a high-profile, high-stress job in share-dealing, no girlfriend, 'cos she dumped me a month ago, so life's not exactly a bed of roses. But I've been very successful and can afford to negotiate my future. Well, I want to get out for a while but not burn my boats completely, so Meg's proposal is perfect.

Interviewer: And how is this lifeplan going to unfold now?

Meg: In a nutshell, we've agreed to change places for three months initially, swapping everything – we leave the car, the furniture, the tins of soup in the kitchen …

Kevin: Not the clothes though!

Meg: If we're all happy, then we'll extend to a year, which will give Sally and I a wonderful base in London and Kevin some peace and quiet to realise his dream.

Interviewer: Which is?

Kevin: I've got an idea for the next bestseller, a racy paperback on city slickers.

Interviewer: Plenty of first-hand experience to draw on – sounds promising. And Sally, you'll get back your social life, but isn't it potentially disruptive, to your schooling and so on?

Sally: We're going to be moving at the start of a new school year, so there's a natural break anyway. And if things don't pan out, I can always move in with Dad.

Meg: But I think we're all quietly confident that it *will* work out.

Kevin: Yeah, 'cos it's what we all want deep down. And if I

make it as a writer, well it might end up a permanent
arrangement, you know, six months on, six off, <u>the best
of both worlds.</u>

Interviewer: Well, they say *the grass is always greener*, but
you seem to have things pretty much sorted out. Meg,
Sally, Kevin, the very best of luck.

All: Thank you.

3

> **Possible answer**
> It does sound very unusual. I suppose the success of the
> lifeplan will depend on how well the three of them get
> on – and on how well they look after each other's
> properties. It does give Kevin an escape from city living
> and gives Sally and Meg more flexibility. The downside is
> that they will all lack a permanent base and it might be
> difficult to make long-term plans.

4 The idioms are underlined in the tapescript in 2 above.

> **Answers**
> a 5 b 4 c 6 d 3 e 2 f 1

Idiom spot

The key word is *burn*.

> **Answers**
> a burn a hole in your pocket – have money that you want
>   to spend
> b burn the midnight oil – work late into the night
> c get your fingers burnt – have something go wrong
> d someone's ears are burning – a person is being talked
>   about in their absence
> e have money to burn – have lots of money
> f burn your bridges – take action which you cannot reverse

5 As the Exam spot says the three ideas on the Part 3
prompt card are there to help you, but you do not need
to cover them. Look back over Unit 8 for ideas about
the question. Decide whether you think there are more
benefits or more drawbacks to living in a city nowadays.

6

> **Answers**
> a B b B c D d E e B f D
> g E h D i E j D k B l E

Record your answer, speaking for about two minutes
and including some of the phrases given above.

7 Play back the recording and look for ways to improve it,
for example by including additional ideas or a greater
variety of vocabulary.

9

> **Answers**
> 1 raw 2 band 3 burn 4 low 5 loose

Writing folder 4

Paper 2 Part 2 Proposal pages 72–73

Writing folder 7 on pages 126–7 covers Part 1 Proposals.

1 The genres required are: **a** and **c** are proposals, **b** is a
report.

3 It is important to write with conviction and adopt a
positive tone in a proposal. The asterisked examples
below appear in exercise 4.

> **Possible answers**
> Manchester is of particular significance because of its
> excellent sports provision.
> Of equal merit is its thriving nightlife.*
> Not only can we provide excellent transport, but we can
> also offer a wide variety of reasonably-priced hotel
> accommodation.
> Above all the city is easy to get to, with good road and
> rail links and an international airport.*
> It is widely recognised that people living here are the
> friendliest in the country.
> The city's good reputation for live music and theatre
> makes it eminently suitable.
> We would like to underline our total commitment to this
> project.
> We believe wholeheartedly in our ability to get the
> details right.

4

> **Suggested answer**
> The city boasts over 30,000 hotel rooms to suit every
> taste and price. In addition, not only could the university
> provide ample accommodation on its beautifully
> landscaped campus, but there is also a purpose-built
> conference centre, which is conveniently situated close to
> the motorway.

5 Any of these conclusions would work, depending on the
earlier text. However, the use of the first person singular
in the third example is slightly inappropriate and the
sentence reads more like the ending of a letter.

6 Before you start writing your answer, make a paragraph
plan. Then write your proposal, following the advice
given on page 73.

Sample answer

We understand that you plan to hold your major five-day annual conference in our country in 2005 and we would therefore like to propose Norbridge as the perfect venue for your organisation. Norbridge is tailor-made for a large conference of this kind and has hosted similar events in the last ten years.

It is beyond dispute that our state-of-the-art transport system is second to none. The regular fast transit monorail service operating from the airport can move up to two hundred thousand passengers per hour. Transport within the city is cheap and reliable, with an extensive tram network and efficient bus service, which even operates through the night.

Not only can we offer comfortable student accommodation on our prestigious university parkland site, but Norbridge has recently unveiled a brand-new conference centre, which is located within five minutes of the university itself. These twin venues should more than cover your requirements, but should some delegates wish to stay in hotels, Norbridge's are second to none in terms of quality and service.

We would also like to take this opportunity to introduce you to our many entertainment facilities, including two multiplex cinemas, which attract visitors from the whole region. Of equal merit is our theatre, which regularly has productions direct from the London stage and boasts a consistently good record for offering enjoyable shows of the highest calibre. In addition, there is a popular leisure and sports centre, complete with 50-metre swimming pool, in the vicinity of the university.

As the above information has no doubt shown, Norbridge is unique in terms of what it can offer. We believe wholeheartedly that our city is the best choice for you and would like to invite you to visit us at your earliest opportunity, so that we may personally introduce you to Norbridge's countless attractions.

Units 5–8 Revision

pages 74–75

This revision unit focuses on the language covered in Units 5–8 and supports the work done in Writing folder 3 on essays. Specific exam practice is provided on Reading Part 1 and Use of English Parts 3 and 4. These Paper 1 and Paper 3 tasks could be done as a timed test of 30 minutes.

1 The picture shows someone wearing a Tommy Hilfiger sweatshirt.

> **Answers**
> 1 B 2 A 3 C 4 D 5 B 6 C

2

> **Answers**
> 1 a widespread belief that having your/a photo
> 2 can't have set off yet
> 3 takes great pride in
> 4 did we know at the time what a
> 5 had I returned from the supermarket than
> 6 the time you've come to mind

3

> **Answers**
> 1 fit 2 notice 3 high 4 peak 5 strikes 6 bar

4 The picture shows a sculpture by Andy Goldsworthy set in the Lake District, Cumbria.

> **Answers**
> 1 C 2 A 3 E 4 B 5 D

Crossword

This revises idioms and vocabulary which you have encountered up to Unit 8.

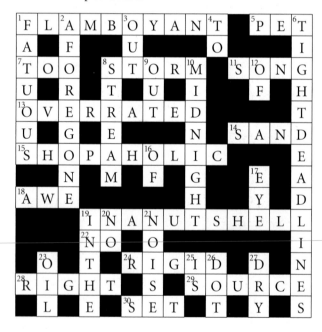

Listening test 2

See pages 282–283 and key on page 287.

Unit 9

9.1 pages 76–77

1 The photos are of:
- a wedding – formal attire – hats for women and morning suits for men
- a business executive
- a model in a designer outfit
- soldiers in uniform
- a streetwise teenager.

Possible answer
These people are wearing these particular clothes because that is what is expected of them, i.e. the wedding guests are wearing their best outfits, the soldiers are wearing their uniform and the executive is wearing smart business clothes and carrying a state-of-the-art briefcase. The model is being paid to wear her designer clothes and the teenager is very fashionable and would want to keep up with the latest trends.

2

Possible answer
I would wear something quite smart but comfortable to a birthday party. Maybe something a little glitzy.
For a long distance plane trip a track suit is the most comfortable as you tend to swell at altitude. Slippers are also more comfortable than shoes.
On a first date it's really difficult. Perhaps something that reflects what your date was wearing when you first met? Definitely not jeans. Possibly chinos and trainers. Ties are out generally – you get so hot in clubs.
A very smart suit, absolutely. Polished shoes, new haircut and briefcase.

3 This exercise will help you to understand some of the vocabulary in the listening task. Use an English–English dictionary to help you with any words you have trouble with.

Answers
a snap b down c code d paramount e speaks
f tip g laid h harboured i foster j constrained
k detrimental l nines

4 Refer to the Exam spots then play the recording to get a general idea of what the discussion is about.

Answers
Colin is against wearing suits at work.
Sue is in favour.

5 The aim of this question is to show you exactly how an answer is arrived at. When attempting this type of question, you should listen carefully for double negatives, words like *quite, indeed, well, it depends, I can see your point but,* and the way that the speaker says *um, ah,* etc. These words and phrases all convey attitude.

Read through all the questions and then play the recording again. The underlined parts of the tapescript confirm the answers.

Answers
1 B 2 S 3 B 4 C 5 C

Presenter: Do suits make for a better workplace? One well-known firm of accountants seems not to think so and this week dropped its requirement for staff to wear suits from its dress code. With me I have Colin Frome, who works in a large advertising agency, and Sue Turner, a senior buyer with a large department store. So, Sue, what do you think about this development?

Sue: I disagree with it, not surprisingly, you may think, but I think most people would feel the same. The effort we take in our own personal appearance and style of dress is, rightly or wrongly, always used by others as an initial indication of our character.

Colin: Well, only fools think that first impressions aren't paramount, but come off it, Sue, the company is saying, 'Look, guys, we're not starchy, we're not stiff – we're in the ideas business here. We're creative people.'

Sue: Well, I'm not arguing for the introduction of office uniforms – the colour and style of a suit should, clearly, be as individual as the wearer – but a professional appearance speaks volumes about the attitude of an individual and that individual's company.

Colin: But just take a look at some of today's big business men. They're in jeans and jumpers – something a little more personal. If someone wore a suit where I work it would be because someone's just died. It's not just us who feel that way, it's a lot of our clients too.

Sue: I don't doubt the professional abilities of today's business moguls, but aren't they just the ones at the tip of the business iceberg? We are not all blessed with equal amounts of charisma: some people will be fantastically successful, regardless of the clothes they wear. But most of us need all the help we can get, and dressing smartly and with style each morning can only bring a little extra confidence, which makes us happier and more effective in everything we do.

Colin: So, what you're saying is that people should wear suits because they're too dumb to think of anything else suitable to wear?

Sue: I wouldn't put it quite like that, but you must admit there's a grain of truth in it.

Colin: Umm, I'm not sure about that one. But I think there's no stopping the trend. This laid-back style is becoming more prevalent not just in businesses like mine, but in more 'serious' enterprises like accountancy firms and law firms.

Sue: It could be that changes in our working environment are leading to less personal contact, which can fool us into thinking that, since everything can be done with computers and telephones, there's no need to look good any more.

Colin: The 'nobody can see me, so why bother' idea. Well, you've got a point there, but perhaps even stronger is the growing antipathy towards men in suits. Chaps in suits can damage the environment that commerce is currently trying to foster.

Sue: That's one way of looking at it, I suppose.

Colin: Let me come clean with you. I do have a couple of suits and they are a pleasure to wear. Both were made for the weddings of close friends. They helped to make each event more important and acted as a sign of respect to my friends. On rare occasions, I'll put one on for work, especially if I want to show who's boss. But I'd far rather look and feel approachable and open-minded. Being dressed up to the nines, however satisfying, doesn't deliver this. Business shouldn't be a battle and there can be a thin line between panache and posturing.

Sue: Well, my company sells suits to some of the most charismatic and free-spirited individuals anyone could hope to meet – people who would never let themselves be constrained by a suit.

Colin: It's just that wearing clothes you feel at ease in allows some people to work better.

Sue: Oh, and since when have suits stopped you feeling that? Colin, we're all motivated to succeed, whatever our business: don't you think that if wearing a smart suit were detrimental to free thought and fresh ideas, we'd have discovered this a little earlier?

Presenter: Unfortunately, we must finish there. My thanks to Colin and Sue for that frank discussion and next week we have …

Phrase spot

Expressions with *come* are often tested in the examination.

Answers
a come to terms with b come across
c came out in sympathy with d come up with
e came to blows f first come, first served
g comes up with the goods h come true
i come down in the world j come forward

9.2 pages 78–79

1 This first exercise aims to review some key points about verb patterns. Refer to the Grammar folder on page 184 if you have problems with this.

Answers
a wearing b to wear c you to wear
d wearing / to wear e him to shave
f her buy / her buying g her wear

2 This exercise looks at common mistakes which are made with gerunds and infinitives.

Answers
a I would have helped her find / to find the right wedding dress.
b We shouldn't spend so much time trying to find bargains in the sales.
c I suggest you use a plaster if you have a blister on your foot.
d The old uniforms in the museum are worth seeing.
e We enjoy ourselves laughing at the stars at the Oscars.
f My new glasses enable me to read more easily.
g We should let them enjoy themselves while they are young.
h I missed talking to my sister when I was away from home.
i I convinced him to apply to the Editor of the magazine.
j You aren't allowed to come into the hotel without wearing a tie.

3 These verbs often cause problems.

Answers
a I mean to = I intend to
b It will mean = It will involve
c We regret to inform you = We are sorry to have to tell you
d I regret wearing = I wish I hadn't worn
e The first thing that happened is the walk, now I remember it.
f First remember, then buy the milk.
g First not forget, then post the letter.
h First meeting boyfriend, then not forgetting.
i Try to = Make an attempt
j Try doing = Experiment with
k First he talks about one subject, then another
l goes on talking = continues talking
m After a period of time he accepted this
n A way of moving, describing the action
o I heard him once
p I heard them regularly

4 This exercise gives practice in the type of transformation found in Part 4 of the Use of English paper.

5 The woman is talking about the uniform she had to wear when she was at school and how she felt about it. The underlined parts of the tapescript confirm the answers.

Suggested answer
The uniform was bottle green for the girls with a shirt and tie. The boys wore grey trousers and a black jacket. Some teachers were friendlier than others. The French teacher was awful, but the English teacher was inspirational and wore interesting clothes.

Woman: What do I remember about being at school? Well, it was some time ago now – in the 1960s in fact. I do remember the uniform – it was bottle green, rather dingy, and all the girls had to wear a shirt and tie, which was a pain, I can tell you. The boys got off lightly. They had grey trousers and a black jacket, but ours was really uncomfortable.
The girls' skirts had to be the right length – this was the sixties remember, the era of the mini-skirt, and of course we all wanted to look as trendy as the next person. Anyway, if one of the teachers thought you were wearing a skirt which was too short then they'd make you kneel down and measure the length from the hem of the skirt to your knees. You had to go home and change if it was too short. Some teachers were worse than others of course.
There was one really ancient teacher – she taught French – she hit me once because I was talking in the corridor. Others were much more amenable. The English teacher, in particular, really gave me the inspiration to read. She gave us a book list once and said: 'Read these.' The books were brilliant, not fuddy-duddy at all. I used to go to the library every Saturday and hunt them out. This English teacher used to wear the most amazing clothes – red swirly skirts and purple and silver shoes. She had blonde hair tied back in a pony tail and large glasses, which she

could peer over the top of at you. I guess she brought a bit of colour.

Possible answer
I didn't have to wear a uniform at school, but I suppose wearing jeans and a T-shirt was some sort of uniform. Many of the girls wore dresses but I never did. We only had school in the morning – we started at 7.00 and finished at 1.00 because in the afternoon it got too hot for class. I remember going home and spending about an hour doing homework and then going to the swimming pool to meet my friends. Once a week I had dance class and also my piano lessons.

6

Answers
a refers to person talking – conscious of themselves
b wrongly heard
c going against something, not productive
d for something, in favour
e too much of something
f under/below
g more than – here it is more than human
h against something
i before – arranged before
j to do more in the sense of competition here
k less – the idea that something isn't given its true worth

7 It is important to know how prefixes are used, although you will never be asked to form a word in the Use of English paper which has a hyphen. Take care, as dictionaries often do not agree on the use of hyphens. Use the prefixes you looked at in exercise 6 to complete this exercise.

Answers
a self-contained b sub-tropical c has outlived
d underestimate e misunderstanding f pre-packed
g super-concentrated h anti-lock i overcooked
j counter-argument k pro-American

8

Answers
We have become more informal and less rigid in both what we wear and when we wear it.

1 would 2 intents 3 time 4 tell 5 between
6 say 7 our 8 into 9 come 10 such
11 ourselves 12 out 13 being 14 when 15 do

Possible answer
I think what we wear is a reflection of our personality and someone who looks scruffy and untidy is unlikely to be a very good receptionist – they would give a bad impression to customers for a start. Social workers, for example, have to be careful what they wear. They mustn't look scruffy, but equally they mustn't dress too smartly, because that would alienate them from their clients, who usually can't afford smart clothes.

9.3 pages 80–81

1 The photos are of a very messy teenager's room and a very neat room.

Possible answer
My room is like the one with clothes all over the place. I do hang some up, but I must admit I also leave things on the floor before I go to bed. I'm usually just too tired to hang them up.

2 Write out a sentence to show that you have understood how the word is used.

Answers

immaculate	person/place
manicured	person/place
houseproud	person
smart	person/place
spick and span	place
bedraggled	person
cluttered	place
in disarray	person/place
dishevelled	person
messy	person/place
scruffy	person/place
unkempt	person
windswept	person/place
orderly	person/place

You should also think about whether the word is formal, informal or neutral as this will help you in the writing papers.

Answers

immaculate	F
manicured	F
houseproud	N
smart	N
spick and span	N
bedraggled	F
cluttered	F
in disarray	F
dishevelled	F
messy	I
scruffy	I
unkempt	F
windswept	F
orderly	F

3 The two texts are about tidiness, looked at from two slightly different angles. Try to guess words you don't know rather than open a translation dictionary. There are more questions here than there would be in the exam to give more practice at this part of Paper 3 Part 5. Notice that the answers are not in full sentences.

Answers
1 weaning
2 They are doing a social service, or, it is not they who are obsessive, but everyone else who is lazy.
3 One meaning is of being tidy and the other is of being good/great.
4 irksome
5 the home/house
6 hoarding and minimalism
7 Arguments may develop. / The relationship will suffer.

4 Refer to the Exam spot before beginning to write the summary.

Possible answer
A person who is compulsively tidy or insists on having their own way regarding house decoration is probably a victim of stress. It is possible to keep this problem in check. Firstly, one could suggest not putting away clothes. Additionally, moving objects a millimetre from their usual place on a daily basis and lastly trying to make greater use of discussion and compromise all might help to modify the individual's behaviour.
(71 words)

5 It's a good idea to increase your range of vocabulary so that you don't repeat the same word when you write or speak.

Answers
a correct
b wrong – they have a lot to say on every subject, whether they know what they are talking about or not
c correct
d wrong – they are lively and excitable
e wrong – they hoard things
f correct
g wrong – they have good taste
h wrong – they see no need for change even if needed
i wrong – they like to remain in the background
j wrong – they are shallow and not given to analysis
k wrong – they try to control people
l correct

Exam folder 5

Paper 1 Part 3 Gapped text pages 82–83

This type of reading comprehension requires the reader to understand what is happening both in terms of content and also in terms of reference. Sometimes the links between the paragraphs are not obvious and it will require some skill to sort them out. Read the base text first and then the gapped paragraphs. Think about the scenario, i.e. what the passage is about. Are there any references, e.g. *it/she/they* or *moreover/secondly/however* which might give a clue?

This text on lying has some clues to help you with the first few questions.

Answers
1 E **2** B **3** F **4** A this sort of background (i.e. university qualifications) – a smooth-talking lawyer and consummate liar – lying in corporate culture **5** C body language – visual clues – shifty eyes **6** H more reliable than body movements **7** D doesn't take too much mental planning … make up a story about something they know well

Unit 10

10.1 pages 84–85

1

Answers
The languages (in the same order as in the SB) are:
Chinese Turkish
Hungarian Bulgarian
Greek Polish

There about 6,000 languages in the world.
A language dies about every two weeks.
The language spoken more than any other is Chinese.

Possible answer
I think my language, Portuguese, is definitely worth learning. It really helps you to understand your own language if you learn another one. Also Portuguese is a beautiful language and is spoken in Brazil as well as Portugal.

2 Scan the text to find the answers to the questions.

Answers
a It is a pun (play on words). A 'death sentence' is the words used by a judge to condemn someone to death. The use of the word 'sentence', which is connected with language, also relates to the topic of the article, the death of languages.
b He seems ambivalent/undecided. (*Or so they think.*)

3 Ignore the words in italics when you read through the article at this stage.

4 Reference devices are often tested both in Part 4 of the Reading paper and Part 5 of the Use of English paper.

Answers
a the death of a language **b** Kasabe **c** the 6,000 languages **d** The fact that half are going to die out **e** languages **f** language death **g** language death **h** what we learn from a language **i** some people

5 These questions are similar to the ones found in Part 5 of the Use of English paper.

Answers
a made an impact / been considered a matter of some importance
b People start out by being forced to speak the majority language. Then there is a period when both languages are spoken and finally the old language is totally forgotten and the majority language takes over.
c You need to have a wide range of species of animals for a healthy environment. The same is true of different cultures.
d If you lose a language you lose more than just a method of communication.
e medical treatments, early civilisations, new ideas about language itself
f One language is not enough to hold all human/world knowledge.

6 The cartoon is someone asking in Esperanto if the shop accepts credit cards.

Possible answer
I think Esperanto never became popular because it was based on European languages. It is quite an easy language to learn, but only if you already speak a romance language. People from Japan, for example, would have as much difficulty with it as they do with German or Spanish. My language, Hungarian, could never be a world language because so few people speak it.

Background information

Esperanto is the best known of the world's auxiliary languages and was invented by Ludwig Zamenhof in 1887. It was designed to overcome problems of international communication. Newspapers and journals are published in Esperanto, together with the Bible and the Koran. It is also taught as a school subject in many countries.

7 This text is taken from an encyclopaedia. It is written in an impersonal and informative style.

Answers

1 B is correct. A is used for a piece of guesswork; C is also used with *between* but in the sense of two things having something in common; D is for a person who you only know slightly.
2 D is correct. A, B and C all have the idea of *come from*. An idea can *stem from* or *spring from*. A declaration is *issued*.
3 A is correct. B takes the preposition *from* and C and D don't collocate with the idea of language.
4 D is correct. Only D collocates with *rely on*.
5 C is correct. *Once* here has the meaning of *when*.
6 B is correct. A language may *expand*; feet *swell* when they are hot; you can *enlarge* a photograph and *increase* is a general word which can't be used here.

10.2 pages 86–87

1 This extract is from an English newspaper and is a true story.

Suggested answers

I wish they wouldn't look so embarrassed.
I wish I could speak to them.
I wish the interpreter were here.
I wish this meal would end.
I wish someone would say something.

2 and 3 These exercises should act as a review of the structures. Refer to the Grammar folder on page 184 if you have problems with them.

Answers

a the past simple
b the past perfect
c *would* – be careful with this, it can't be used when the subject is repeated, i.e. you can't say *I wish I would …*

If only and *I wish* have more or less the same meaning. Some people believe *If only* is slightly stronger / more formal in tone.

4

Answers

a I hope you have a nice time
b I wish I could
c She wishes she were / could be
d I hope you like
e I hope you have
f they had allowed us
g he could remember / he remembered
h I hope I have some luck
i her children were
j they would stop smoking
k I wish there could always be / I hope there will always be
l I hope I live / I wish I could live

5

Possible answers

For my family, there is nothing more I could wish for – we are all quite happy as we are. However, for my studies, I wish I could concentrate in class more and also that I had a photographic memory. I wish my country had a better public transport system and also that everyone went to a State school and we had a fully Socialist system. I wish the world were a happier place and that poverty had been eradicated, along with wars and disasters.

6 *It's about time* and *It's high time* are slightly stronger than *It's time*. Note that *I'd rather* is **never** used with *prefer* as in *I'd rather prefer*.

Answers

a to go b you went c spend d left / had left
e had given f he did g she took

7 The sentence transformations practise the structures reviewed in this unit.

Answers

1 you stood up for your rights / for yourself
2 you stopped behaving as though you were
3 they carried out
4 would/'d rather all students wrote
5 to fill in
6 he had let us/me know
7 she were/was aware of the strength / she had been aware of the strength
8 would rather you took off / you didn't wear

Phrase spot

Some of these phrases are easy to guess, e.g. *to turn as red as a beetroot*. Others are more difficult, e.g. *a turn-up for the book*. Use an English–English dictionary to help you.

Answers

a Well, there's a turn-up for the book – I never thought he'd get a girlfriend.
b He has a nice turn of phrase.
c He turned as red as a beetroot when …
d You can't turn back the clock, however …
e I didn't know which way to turn when the airline …
f I tossed and turned all last night.
g The head teacher turned a blind eye for once when the boy was late.
h Muriel didn't turn a hair when …
i Now, everyone must take it in turns to have a go …

10.3 pages 88–89

1 The photos are of:
   - people in Niger, Africa, using a solar powered TV set
   - a young boy eating a hamburger
   - Disneyworld Tokyo
   - a McDonald's Internet café in Costa Rica

Possible answer
I think it's hard to tell where the photos were taken because they all show people doing things they do now all over the world.

2 The photos are supposed to reinforce the idea that things are global and that everyone nowadays sees/eats/enjoys similar things.

Possible answer
I've got mixed feelings about the impact of a global culture on my country. Many of the small restaurants and bars in the part of the old city where I live are fast disappearing as there is now too much competition from the large fast food chains – McDonald's, Burger King, Kentucky Fried Chicken, etc. Young people seem to think it's cool and you even find members of the older generation going there occasionally too.
Many people now have satellite TV and so have become part of the global audience that watches programmes like *Friends* or the *Simpsons*. I'm not sure this is so bad really. Our own TV programmes are not always very interesting and certainly not very amusing! And of course, everyone watches MTV!

3 Allow about five minutes to read through the questions. *Tampering* means altering; *a dumping ground* is another expression for a tip / a place where you put things you don't want.
The three extracts are from one speech.

Play the recording twice, as in the exam. The parts underlined in the tapescript confirm the answers.

Answers
1 C   2 B   3 A   4 B   5 C   6 C

Extract 1

A friend of mine studies village life in central Africa. A few years ago, she paid her first visit to a remote area where she was to carry out her fieldwork. The night she got there, she was invited to a local home for an evening's entertainment. She expected to find out about the traditional pastimes of this isolated community. Instead, the evening turned out to be a viewing of the film *Basic Instinct* on video. The film at that point hadn't even reached the cinemas in London. <u>This appears to be the norm these days and such vignettes reveal something about our world</u>. And what they reveal isn't trivial. It isn't just a matter of people adding modern paraphernalia – videos, TVs, computers – to their traditional ways of life. We live in a world of transformations, affecting almost every aspect of what we do. For better or worse, we are being propelled into a global order that no one fully understands, but which is making its effects felt on all of us.

Globalisation: the term may not be particularly attractive or elegant. <u>But absolutely no one who wants to understand our prospects and possibilities can ignore it. I travel a lot. I haven't been to a single country recently where globalisation isn't being intensively discussed</u>.

The global spread of the term is evidence of the very developments to which it refers. <u>Every business guru talks about it. No political speech is complete without it.</u> Yet as little as 10 years ago, the term was hardly used, either in the academic literature or in everyday language. It has come from nowhere to be almost everywhere.

Different thinkers have taken almost completely opposite views about globalisation in debates that have sprung up over the past few years. Some dispute the whole thing. I'll call them the sceptics. According to the sceptics, all the talk about globalisation is only that – just talk. Whatever its benefits, its trials and tribulations, the global economy isn't especially different from that which existed at previous periods. The world carries on much the same as it has done for many years.

Others take a very different position. I'll label them the radicals; they argue that not only is globalisation very real, but that its consequences can be felt everywhere. The global marketplace, they say, is much more developed than even two or three decades ago, and is indifferent to national borders. Nations have lost most of the sovereignty they once had, and politicians have lost most of their capability to influence events.

Extract 2

It is wrong to think of globalisation as just concerning the big systems, like the world financial order. Globalisation isn't only about what is 'out there', remote and far away from the individual. It is an 'in here' phenomenon too, influencing intimate and personal aspects of our lives. The debate about family values, for example, that is going on in many countries, might seem far removed from globalising influences. It isn't. <u>Traditional family systems are becoming transformed, or are under strain, in many parts of the world, particularly as women stake claim to greater equality</u>. There has never before been a society, so far as we know from the historical record, in which women have been even approximately equal to men. This is a truly global revolution in everyday life, whose consequences are being felt around the world in spheres from work to politics.

Globalisation thus is a complex set of processes, not a single one. And these operate in contradictory or oppositional fashion. Most people think of globalisation as simply 'pulling away' power or influence from local communities and nations into the global arena. And indeed nations have lost much of the economic power they once had. Yet it also has an opposite effect. Globalisation is the reason for the revival of local cultural identities in different parts of the world. If one asks, for example, why the Scots want more independence in the UK, or why there is a strong separatist movement in Quebec, the answer is not to be found only in their local cultural history. Local nationalisms spring up as a response to globalising tendencies, as the hold of older nation-states weakens.

Extract 3

Globalisation is not a benign force, however. It creates, some argue, a world of winners and losers. And indeed the statistics are daunting. The share of the poorest fifth of the world's population in global income has dropped from 2.3 per cent to 1.4 per cent over the past 10 years. The proportion taken by the richest fifth, on the other hand, has risen. In many less developed countries, safety and environmental regulations are low or virtually non-existent. Some transnational companies sell goods there that are controlled or banned in the industrial countries – poor quality medical drugs, destructive pesticides or high tar-and-nicotine content cigarettes.

As one writer put it recently, rather than a global village, this is more like global *pillage*. Along with ecological risk, to which it is related, expanding inequality is the most serious problem facing world society. It will not do, however, merely to blame it on the wealthy. Globalisation today is only partly Westernisation. Globalisation is becoming increasingly decentred – not under the control of any group of nations and still less of the large corporations. Its effects are felt as much in Western countries as elsewhere.

This is true of the global financial system and of changes affecting the nature of government itself. What one could call 'reverse colonisation' is becoming more and more common. Reverse colonisation means that non-Western countries influence developments in the West. Examples abound – such as the Latinising of Los Angeles, the emergence of a globally oriented hi-tech sector in India, or the selling of Brazilian TV programmes to Portugal.

4   Noun + noun usually has the stress on the first word. Adjective + noun usually has the stress on the second word.

Some extra words can be made with *red* and *old* but not all are included here.

Answers

park bench   red carpet   horse race   racehorse
sheep dog   tea bag   boat house   house boat
road sign   back seat   seat back   glasshouse
old woman   red wine

---

5   Prefixes might be tested here as well as suffixes. Always read the passage carefully before you do the exercise.

Answers
1 meaningful   2 singular   3 scholarly   4 replace / displace   5 literary   6 obsession   7 response   8 conception   9 unsatisfactory   10 spectacle

---

Writing folder 5

Paper 2 Part 1   Article   pages 90–91

1   The logos shown are: MTV Europe, Yahoo.UK.com (both off the Internet), Pepsi Cola and Mercedes Benz (shown on a car bonnet).

Answers
a Yahoo.UK.com   b Pepsi Cola   c MTV
d Mercedes Benz

2   Remember to include a title when you write an article.

Answers
The best title is c.
Title a doesn't reflect the argument expressed; b is uninformative; c is catchy and in the spirit of the article.

4   Try to use some of these expressions in your writing, as they offer further ways of linking and reinforcing ideas. However, it would be inappropriate to use them in an essay, due to their journalistic style. They are best used in articles, reviews and letters (to newspapers).

Answers
a end   b all   c come   d cold/clear   e all

5   Rhetorical questions are appropriate to both articles and essays (they were used in the essay on art in Units 5–8 Revision on SB page 75).

Possible answers
a Don't American products impose a way of life on us that many regard as alien at the end of the day?
b All things considered, mightn't globalisation bring more equality to the world?

c When you come to think of it, isn't it rather depressing to find a McDonald's in every town?

1 All in all, is it so disastrous that everyone can link up to the Internet?

2 In the cold light of day, won't these transnational companies bring much-needed investment to poorer countries?

3 Do we all want to wear the same branded clothes, in the final analysis?

6 When you write your article, follow the advice given on page 91.

Sample answer

Are we living in one big, happy global village? Or are we currently witnessing, as one journalist so neatly put it, 'global pillage'? Globalisation is a complex issue, but one thing is certain: it is irreversible. Many transnational corporations are now more powerful than national governments; they will not give up their dominance, as too much is at stake economically.

Yet at the same time, the decline of the centralised nation-state is allowing more independence at local level. Regions (which were often countries in their own right formerly) are re-asserting themselves, from Scotland and Wales to Catalunya and Macedonia. Far from mourning the loss of tradition, these parts of the world are strengthening their cultural identities. Take the speaking of Catalan in north-east Spain, for example. Banned for decades, it has re-surfaced stronger than ever in the last 25 years, and is now the medium of instruction in schools, the language of local government and often of business too.

However, in the cold light of day, it cannot be denied that global pillage is going on. Doesn't every town boast a McDonald's? Isn't everyone dressed in Nike trainers and Tommy Hilfiger sweatshirts? Companies such as these have made huge profits from our desire to conform. Nevertheless, if people want to make those choices, that is their decision.

My own reaction to globalisation is to take it with a pinch of salt. I do not see any evidence of regional differences dying out and, as I have argued above, the opposite is actually true. There are many positive aspects to the new world order. Not least of these is the Internet, which has revolutionised communication and encourages a political openness that may serve to prevent world war rather than instigate it. All in all, we have much to look forward to in the 21st century, if we concentrate on dealing with the real threat to our individual survival: environmental change.

Unit 11

11.1 pages 92–93

1

Possible answer
Three different relationships are shown in the picture. The couple on the left seem to be arguing about something and the man looks very aggressive. The man shown top right is reading a letter, but it can't be a love letter, as he looks rather distraught. His girlfriend must have dumped him. The third relationship is complicated: the boy and girl gazing a each other seem very much in love, but another woman is looking very jealous, so she must have something to do with them.

---

2 Play the recording twice, as in the exam. The underlined parts of the tapescript confirm the answers.

Answers
1 D 2 A 3 B 4 B 5 C

Interviewer: Last week, Steve came into the studio to prove to us that life still has some happy endings. Here's his story … So, Steve, your relationship with Abby has been through some ups and downs but is definitely on a high now?

Steve: That's right, and we're finally tying the knot next month. Just over five years ago, I met this bubbly little lady – Abby. We went out, shared some laughs, and pretty soon, I knew she was the one for me.

Interviewer: And was it love at first sight for her too?

Steve: She was happy enough to spend lots of time with me, but treated me more like a big brother, if anything – she even told me about another guy she was hoping to get together with. At which point, realising I would get nowhere romantically, I decided I'd better cast my net elsewhere. I met a nice girl called Samantha, very down-to-earth – the opposite of Abby – and we started seeing each other once in a while. We had well-paid jobs and money to burn. After a good holiday in Spain, we decided to move in together. I think we both understood that it wasn't true love, but we rubbed along fairly well. Unfortunately, quite soon after that, Abby made up her mind that I was Mr Right after all, and made this very plain to me, though not to Samantha.

Interviewer: How did you take this bolt f…

Steve: It was baffling. I actuall… joking, she used to do that,… wouldn't pull that trick any … whipping up a fleeting fantas… hands, as she'd been fired fro… own a lot – her then current b…

Interviewer: And there were displays of obvious jealousy, weren't there?

Steve: Yeah, we'd be at the same pubs and that, and there would be anguished looks from Abby across the room, deep sighs if she was ever standing next to me at the bar, that sort of thing – I misread the situation for ages – she's always had a streak of theatricality.

Interviewer: What was your reaction once you realised it was genuine?

Steve: Well, it dawned on me that I was calling the tune now; if I wanted it, Abby and I would have a life together – otherwise, things would stay the same. It wasn't straightforward, there was Samantha to consider. She'd always been very supportive and loyal. For a while, I couldn't decide what to do. To fend off the problem, I threw myself into my job.

Interviewer: And did colleagues at work pick up on anything different about you?

Steve: Very much so – I'd never been that keen and efficient before! Although my daily routine was much the same, I was glad to get to work, because it distracted me – but I made sure I kept my private life out of our usual conversations. As time went on, there was growing pressure on me to do something – for all I knew, Abby might give up in disgust.

Interviewer: Then, one summer's day …

Steve: Yes, one beautiful morning last June, I couldn't keep up the pretence any longer. I sat Samantha down at the kitchen table and blurted everything out. She was terrific, far from holding back tears, she didn't seem even mildly phased by the revelation that I'd been carrying a torch for someone else and it was over. Just rolled up her sleeves and started sorting out my life for me: phoned my office to say that I was at death's door and wouldn't be coming in, then told me to get round to Abby's place pronto, preferably with a big bunch of flowers – she let me buy those myself.

Interviewer: And so Samantha walked out of your life and Abby walked in.

Steve: Yeah. Abby and I rented a cottage out in the country. Last summer was idyllic, and, well, it matched our mood. We got to know each other properly, spent every evening gazing into each other's eyes at sunset and … well, I'm sure you can picture the rest.

Interviewer: Absolute rapture, straight out of *True Romance* … how wonderfully slushy! So when did you finally pop the question, Steve?

Steve: I was at a big family wedding, one of my cousins, and Abby hadn't come, I think she had 'flu. Anyway everything seemed to fall into place at that event. I managed to sit down with my mother and talk about [...] – Mum'd been giving me the cold shoulder, as she'd [...]ked Samantha and, social norms being what they [...] [s]een her as a prospective daughter-in-law.

Anyway, she came round after our heart-to-heart and I went off to offer a lift to my cousin's old schoolfriend, who lives in the States – I hadn't seen him for five years. Well, he looked me between the eyes and said, 'You've always loved Abby, so how come you're not married yet – get a grip, Steve.' So I did, leapt in the car without him, drove back and proposed. It's funny though, it had taken someone at one stage removed from my life to state the obvious.

Interviewer: Well, Steve, I wish you and Abby every happiness – you certainly deserve it.

Steve: Thank you.

3

> **Possible answer**
> It's got as good a chance as any marriage. At least Abby knows what she really wants now, and Steve seems pretty keen.

4

> **Answers**
> Steve means that Abby sometimes likes to behave in a dramatic way.
> Some collocations with *streak* can be positive, e.g. *romantic*.
>
> **1** first sight   **2** streak   **3** slushy
> **4** displays   **5** one   **6** popped

Idiom spot

If necessary, play the recording again and stop after each idiom.

> **Answers**
> **a** tying the knot – getting married
> **b** cast my net – look around for someone else
> **c** bolt from the blue – a total surprise
> **d** time on her hands – plenty of free time
> **e** calling the tune – in charge
> **f** carrying a torch for – in love with
> **g** rolled up her sleeves – behaved very practically
> **h** at death's door – very ill
> **i** giving me the cold shoulder – ignoring me
> **j** get a grip – take charge, get in control
>
> **k** hands   **l** grip   **m** sleeve   **n** clutching
> **o** grasp   **p** grips   **q** hands   **r** grabs

5 Both examples contain phrasal verbs (with noun collocations).

Suggested answers
blurt out a problem, a secret
bottle up a problem, emotions
choke back tears, emotions
fend off criticism, a problem, blows, accusations
keep up appearances
shoot down an argument, accusations
sweep aside an argument, accusations, criticism
tease out a problem, a secret
tone down criticism, accusations
whip up rage, emotions

The sentences should include:

a bottle up / blurt out a secret
b tone down criticism
c whip up emotions
d fend off blows
e choke back tears / bottle up emotions
f shoot down an argument

11.2 pages 94–95

1 The picture shows Tom Hanks in the film *You've got mail*.

Possible answer
I send some personal emails but most of my friends text me back. I must admit I prefer sending text messages myself, as I have my mobile with me all the time. I do have one e-pal in Sweden, who emails me about once a fortnight. As for chat rooms, I've visited a few, but they can be a bit of a time-waster. My brother's on the Internet every evening visiting some chat room or other and I'm sure half the time he doesn't know who he's chatting to! That's the main disadvantage, I suppose: you don't know who you're actually in touch with. It could be dangerous if you made arrangements to meet the person somewhere.

2 Richard and Cindy met through an Internet chat room.

Answers
1 since/from **2** as **3** anything **4** a
5 hardly/barely/scarcely **6** Having **7** so **8** who
9 Within **10** making/in **11** most **12** sooner
13 over **14** whose **15** and/where

3 No – you cannot say 'completely affectionate', as 'affectionate' is a gradable adjective; conversely, 'devastating' is an ungradable adjective, so you cannot say 'extremely devastating'.

Answers
Gradable adjectives (*deeply, fairly, immensely, rather, very*) go with A; ungradable adjectives (*absolutely, entirely, utterly*) with B. *Pretty, quite, really* go with both but there are register restrictions.

4

Answers
a pretty lonely **b** deeply disappointed **c** really dreadful **d** absolutely amazing **e** rather envious
Suggested answers
f James is being utterly stubborn on the matter and won't give in.
g Shouting in the street like that was a quite disreputable performance, if you ask me.
h At the moment, Ellen is fairly laid-back about tomorrow's race.

5

Answers
b and **c** are gradable uses.

Gradable adjectives can be quantified – you can say how far it is true. So you can use adverbs like *extremely* or *fairly*. This cannot ordinarily happen with an ungradable adjective, but you can use an adverb like *completely* or *utterly* for emphasis.

6

Answers
a alternative **b** cautionary **c** collapsible
d detestable **e** honorary, honourable **f** laborious
g loathsome **h** mendacious **i** philosophical
j repulsive **k** tenacious **l** theatrical **m** virtuous
n voluntary

7

Answers
1 massive **2** indeterminate **3** setting **4** relationships
5 significant **6** alliance **7** crucial **8** ratings
9 bullish **10** inroads

11.3 pages 96–97

1

> **Possible answers**
>
> People conform in society by wearing similar clothes, having similar tastes in entertainment and leisure activities and by behaving in the same way. Being part of a group offers security and the feeling of belonging, rather than being an outsider. People may join a sports club to play sport, but they often want to make new friendships too. Being accepted into a gang is also a form of conformism.
>
> When Groucho Marx said he wouldn't want to belong to any club that would have him as a member, he was presumably denigrating himself and thinking that such a club would have rather suspect members!

The picture shows Groucho Marx.

Background information

Groucho Marx was one of the four famous Marx Brothers, who appeared in many American comedy films. These include *Duck Soup* and *A Night at the Opera*.

2 The overlap in the two texts is in the area of belonging to a group.

3 The question in 3 is a typical one – the words *mistaken belief that the group is invincible* in text A echo the phrase *illusion of invulnerability* in text B.

4 Reformulation is an important part of the summary task; you will lose marks in the exam if you stick to the wording of the texts.

> **Answers**
>
> 1 a 2 a 3 b 4 b 5 a

5

> **Suggested answers**
>
> a groups often lack caution / throw caution to the wind
> b pinpoints a trio of important characteristics
> c the inclination to regard the group as better than it is
> d the natural decency/honesty/goodness of the group
> e blinkered thinking
> f suppression of individual views
> g those who disagree being forced to toe the line
> h the pressure for common accord
> i earlier catalysts for groupthink
> j aggravating circumstances

6

> **Possible answer**
>
> Both texts identify a trend of excessive boldness, leading to undue risk-taking. Surprisingly, decisions are often polarised and do not reflect the middle ground. Total agreement is of paramount importance. According to Janis, self-belief is ingrained and for this reason, a group becomes blinkered and fails to seek external advice, which is a key factor in poor decisions.
> (58 words)

Exam folder 6

Paper 1 Part 2 Themed texts pages 98–101

The first question has been done for you, so that you can see how a multiple-choice question works. You need to read the question very carefully to make sure you choose the right option or answer. Some of the other options may sound plausible or may even be true, but they either don't answer the question or do so only in part.

> **Answers**
>
> **2** **B** is correct because the text says that most modern humour theories subscribe to Aristotle's belief that jokes are based on a 'reaction to incongruity, when the punchline is nonsense'. **A** is wrong because Kant and Freud are not present-day psychoanalysts. **C** is wrong because although 'we revel in the misfortune of others', the text says nothing about insulting rivals. **D** is wrong because the text says 'we revel in the misfortune of others' and gives no indication of whether this is right or wrong.
>
> **3** **B** is correct because of the pun (get a grip) and the rhetorical questions at the beginning. **A** is wrong because there is nothing to suggest he is suspicious. **C** is wrong because he is not disapproving, more slightly superior in tone. **D** is wrong because offhand means not really interested and he obviously is.
>
> **4** **D** is correct because the text says that open and liberal-minded men have weaker handshakes, which leave a lukewarm first impression. **A** is wrong because the text only implies that you should practise, it doesn't say you should. **B** is wrong because it only talks about the impression created by intellectual (clever) *women*, not clever men. **C** is wrong because it does say that it is borne out by personality tests.
>
> **5** **C** is correct because it isn't necessary for a post office clerk to be perfect whereas an actor does need to try hard. **A** is wrong because the writer says that a sitcom is different, thus requiring different skills. **B** is wrong because he implies that because of the repetitive nature of the job of post office clerk, it isn't necessary to work hard at it. **D** is wrong because although he says working in a post office is tedious – a treadmill of repetition – this isn't the point of his remark.

6 A is correct because the writer refers to them as 'trite and formulaic'. **B** is wrong because, although it is probably true, the text doesn't say so; instead it says that 'nobody needs a sitcom'. **C** is wrong because it says that people won't like sitcoms if they are the same every week. **D** is wrong because, although the writer says that writers will be out of a job if they don't do the job well, he or she doesn't suggest that this is poor treatment.

7 C is correct because the writer doesn't agree with the narrow-minded world of physics. He or she is quite critical and refers to 'the worship of measurement for its own sake', a rather scornful comment. **A**, **B** and **D** are therefore wrong.

8 C is correct – 'wisdom lies somewhere between compulsion and revulsion'. **A**, **B** and **D** aren't stated but the writer would probably agree with them.

Unit 12

12.1 pages 102–103

1 The three questions are typical ways in which an examiner might ask you to extend topic discussion with the other candidate after the individual long turns in Paper 5 Part 3.

> **Possible answers**
> Ordinary people have greater life expectancy due to improvements in medicine. DNA analysis has led to better crime detection and conviction of criminals.
>
> This area of genetics and biotechnology is bound to give rise to new discoveries, as further work is done on the human genome.
>
> Multinational companies are very powerful and the attempt to introduce GM (genetically modified) food illustrates that government ministers need to keep a close eye on what they are doing. Current legislation and governmental controls may be inadequate.

2 The photo shows the minuscule guitar from Cornell University that is referred to in the opening sentence of the text.

> **Suggested answer**
> The writer has tried to simplify the difficult subject matter by referring to things from the real world – parts of cells are likened to scissors, motors, pipes, and so on, and the DNA helix is compared to a ladder. Atoms and molecules become busy commuters, rushing around the body.

3 You must spend enough time reading the text and missing paragraphs, in order to work out the links involved. In the exam, underline key phrases in both as you read.

The parts of the text which link to the underlined phrases in paragraphs A–H are given alongside the answers below. Notice that there isn't always a link both before and after a gap.

> **Answers**
> 1 D before gap: *tweezers, scissors*, etc;
>   after gap: *collectively*
> 2 H after gap: *urban environment, commuting*
> 3 A before gap: *no overseer supervises their activities*;
>   after gap: *nowadays, convincing explanation*
> 4 F before gap: *they say*
> 5 C before gap: *more than the sum of its parts, the job of explaining life*;
>   after gap: *with the discovery of DNA, early 1950s*
> 6 G before gap: *handrails, rungs*
>   after gap: *A, T, C, G*
> 7 B before gap: *slot together snugly, complementary projecting arms*;
>   after gap: *this is guaranteed to be identical to the original*

4

> **Answers**
> a a pump   b valves   c (a pair of) scissors
> d (some) tweezers   e a chain

Idiom spot

> **Answers**
> a nail – something that has finally caused failure
> b spade ... spade – to speak directly
> c tubes – to fail
> d chain – unreliable part of something, usually used of people
> e fuse – to lose your temper
> f strings – unconditional
> g wires – to misunderstand
> h bolt – to fail
> i gear – to start to deal with something effectively
> j knife – to deliberately make someone feel worse

12.2 pages 104–105

1

> **B**ackground information
>
> Edwin Hubble, an American, did a lot of pioneering work on galaxies in the 1920s, detecting spiral galaxies similar to our own. Hubble's Law about the expanding universe is one of the most important in astronomy.

Suggested answers
1 In 1929, proof was found that the universe is expanding.
2 Cosmic microwave radiation was detected by Penzias and Wilson in 1965. The Big Bang theory is supported by this discovery.
3 Photos of Neptune were transmitted back to earth when the *Voyager* spacecraft flew past in 1989.
4 The Hubble Space Telescope, named in honour of Edwin Hubble, was launched in 1990.
5 Rock on the surface of Mars was analysed by the *Sojourner* rover vehicle.

2

Answers
a Marie Curie was given the Nobel Prize for Chemistry for her discovery of radium.
b Ten previously unknown moons were detected by *Voyager 2* as it flew past Uranus in 1986.
c 'Dark matter' has been said to exist in the universe, but has not been detected as yet.
d Meteorites have been found in Antarctica which are believed to have come from the Moon.
e Other galaxies were shown to exist by Edwin Hubble, who calculated accurate distances for them.
f These spiral nebulae had already been observed by earlier astronomers, but they had been assumed to be part of our own Milky Way galaxy.

3 Use of the passive will make your writing appropriately neutral and impersonal in tone.

Answers
a Lunch cannot / must not be brought into the lab.
b More missions to Mars are going to be sent.
c The miracle drug was found to have unpleasant side effects.
d It is hoped that the new building will be opened by Bill Gates.
e Homes in and around the city have been severely affected by power cuts.
f Further tests are being carried out by three research students.
g No photographs may be taken inside this museum.
h Infra-red equipment will be used today to search for further survivors.

4

Answers
a be reminded   b being delayed   c being damaged
d to have been invited   e having been asked / being asked   f be discovered   g that an announcement would be made (by the hospital)

Answers
1 was discovered   2 has shown   3 could not have been caused   4 was detected / had been detected (specific to one research project) OR has been detected (traces of iridium continue to be found there)   5 must have been formed   6 would have been thrown   7 to be blotted out   8 were eaten   9 would have been killed

6

Answers
1 for a probe to be landed
2 will need/have to be worn for the duration
3 be seen with the naked eye
4 increasing number of planets have been found
5 to be on the brink of
6 being / having been advised against physics

12.3 pages 106–107

1 Remember that the prompt card is there to help you in the exam, rather than to restrict your ideas.

Possible answers
career opportunities – more now than ever before
commercial interests – very strong, may go against government policy
moral issues – tampering with nature

2 The recording lasts the full two minutes.

Interlocutor: Now, in this part of the test you're each going to talk on your own for about two minutes. You need to listen while your partner is speaking because you'll be asked to comment afterwards.
So Jana, I'm going to give you a card with a question written on it and I'd like you to tell us what you think. There are also some ideas on the card for you to use if you like.
All right? Here is your card, and a copy for you, Erik.

Jana: Well, I don't have a scientific background, but I think science is something that affects us all nowadays. You can't afford to ignore what's going on in advanced science. There's a lot of media interest right now in the latest developments in, say, genetics and DNA profiling. Erm, I do think it's worrying how genetic testing will be used, actually. In fact, it's already happening. For example, if you're found to have a genetic disorder of some kind, you may not be able to take out life insurance … or get a job even. But then, on the other hand, we know that DNA analysis is now helping to solve crimes, and that's good for society, so it's good and bad, I suppose.
The main problem centres around information. I mean, the majority of the public don't know much about any of

this and so naturally they're worried. So what is needed is more information in simple language for everyone to understand … and perhaps this needs to come from the government or even internationally, not be given to us by so-called scientific institutions. Because I think the biggest worry of all is that the whole area of genetics is being driven by the business world. It's obvious that a lot of the research going on today is backed by big companies – drugs co…, pharma… pharmaceutical companies and so on – and they're going to want something back from their investment. Which means that the research is not being done just as research, it's not pure, not independent. … I think too, that they're not controlling this research. It's high time the government got involved. It must set the ball rolling, and not just in terms of regulation. The public needs to be properly informed. There are potential benefits, yes, but we must be told what's happening and why. You know, things are being pushed ahead at such an alarming rate and … I don't know, it seems to me, it's maybe not always going to be helpful for ordinary people.

Interlocutor: Thank you. Erik, is there anything you would like to add?

Erik: It's a big, big subject. Jana's raised a lot of questions and they're important questions. But, what to add … well, just on the aspect of career opportunities. I'm actually in the final year of a biology degree so I can comment on that personally. We're always being told by our lecturers that more progress will be made in biology in the next five to ten years than has occurred in the last fifty. It's a fast-moving field. As Jana said, there are many new companies … biotech companies springing up, so yes, job prospects are good for someone like me, I think, plenty of different directions to go in. So it's not all doom and gloom, far from it.

3 The meaning of the expressions is given below.

Answers
a at the forefront of
b with both advantages and disadvantages
c someone without a scientific background
d because of that and for no other reason
e effectively controlled (by the government / international law)
f for the good of society at large

Notice how Jana stresses important points (underlined in the tapescript below) and pauses for emphasis (shown by … in the tapescript).

a You can't <u>afford</u> to … <u>ignore</u> what's going on in the <u>vanguard</u> of science.
b So it's … a <u>double-edged sword</u>, I suppose.
c So what is needed … is more <u>information</u> in <u>simple</u> language … for the <u>lay</u> person to understand.

d Which means that the research is not being done for its <u>own sake</u> … it's not <u>pure</u> … not <u>independent</u>.
e I think too, that the research is … not subject to <u>enough regulations</u>.
f It's maybe <u>not</u> always going to be for … the greater good.

4 Practise building up these phrases, repeating aloud after the speaker.

a concern
   cause for concern
   considerable cause for concern
   There's considerable cause for concern in the whole area.

b duty
   duty bound to
   Governments are duty bound to regulate the industry.

c repercussions
   possible repercussions
   There are a number of possible repercussions.

d significance
   the social significance
   The social significance of biotechnology should not be underestimated.

e cusp
   on the cusp of
   We're on the cusp of completely new forms of treatment.

f reservations
   extreme reservations
   I have extreme reservations about the confidentiality of all this information.

Phrase spot

Answers (clockwise)
set the wheels in motion, set the scene, set out your stall, set your heart on, set the record straight, set the world on fire, set a dangerous precedent, set in stone, set your teeth on edge

The other verbs are *pull* and *run*:
pull your socks up – improve your behaviour or work
pull out all the stops – do everything possible to make something happen (there are 'stops' on an organ, which, when pulled, increase the volume of the music)
Pull the other one! – if you use this expression, it means you don't believe what someone has just said to you. Also: *Pull the other one, it's got bells on it.*
pull the strings – control people or an organisation
pull a fast one – trick someone
run rings round – beat or do better than someone
run the gauntlet – suffer unpleasant behaviour in order to achieve something
run a tight ship – manage something efficiently

5

> **Answers**
> a Jenny set her heart on having the new gadget.
> b The consultant set out her stall to the whole department.
> c Allowing her teenage son to stay out late has set a dangerous precedent.
> d Nothing is set in stone as yet.
> e The vivid description of the Martian landscapes sets the scene at the beginning of the book.
> f The sound of a young child attempting to play the violin really sets my teeth on edge.
> g A leading biotech company immediately set the wheels in motion to recruit the young scientist.
> h Carla's a good singer, but she's never going to set the world on fire.

6

> **Answers**
> 1 hooked   2 code   3 scratch   4 seize   5 matter

Writing folder 6

Paper 2 Part 2 Report pages 108–109

1   The work you have done on passive structures in Unit 12 can now be used in your writing. Notice how passives are used in the report.

> This report aims to summarise the current career opportunities for new science graduates, drawing largely on the experiences of past and present students. Many final year students have already been invited to interviews and some have even been offered jobs, conditional on their graduation in June.
>
> **A broad scope of employment**
> The first point that should be stressed is that many interesting opportunities exist outside the specialist scientific fields. This is dealt with in the final section of the report.
>
> **Academic research**
> Returning to pure science, it has been estimated that there will be over a thousand post-graduate posts available for the next academic year, throughout the country. Students should consult their tutor for advice in the first instance.
>
> High-achievers should contemplate applying for scholarships to the U.S.A, where much of the research is at the cutting edge. Should students wish to follow up on specific research possibilities in the States, they are advised to consult Professor Grimbleton.
>
> **Exciting new opportunities**
> The fast-moving developments in biotechnology and genetics look set to provide many job opportunities for graduates, as many recently-formed companies are being expanded in their bids to become a market leader. Four local companies have specifically requested graduate trainees from this college. They are:
>
> - Bio-futures
> - Genotech
> - PJF Seed Research
> - Railton Systems.
>
> Application forms can be obtained from the Administration Secretary.
>
> **Education as a career**
> Many of our past students have opted for jobs in teaching and it is recommended that anyone considering such a career should attend one of the information days planned by this department. At this event, it will not only be possible to meet Head Teachers and Science Coordinators from schools in the region, but also to talk to former college students who are now qualified and practising teachers.
>
> **A more unconventional path**
> As indicated above, any report on current opportunities would be incomplete without mentioning some of the other non-scientific jobs that past students have taken up with relish. While none of these jobs can be said to demand the recall of actual scientific learning, the generic skills that students have been given through their undergraduate science courses are directly relevant.
>
> Here are some of the more unusual career moves:
> - accountancy
> - stockmarket brokering
> - counselling
> - air-traffic control
> - casino management.
>
> **Next steps**
> More details on all the areas mentioned in this report can be found on the student website. A booklet is also in preparation.

2   Other examples of signposting are given below.

> **Answers**
> This report aims to summarise
> The first point
> This is dealt with in the final section
> Returning to pure science
> Here are
>
> Referring forward: c, e, g
> Referring back: a, b, d, f, h, i, j

3

> **Answers**
> a high-achievers
> b fast-moving, recently-formed

c un- (unconventional), post- (post-graduate),
  non- (non-scientific)
d -al (unconventional, conditional), -ally (specifically),
  -ist (specialist), -ship (scholarship)
e at the cutting edge, career move

4 Do you find spider diagrams helpful? There are many
  other ways of making notes, so use the one you prefer
  when planning your report.

5 Write your report, following the advice given on page 109.

Sample answer
KELVINGTON FILM CLUB ANNUAL REPORT

Following another successful year, the club is in a strong
position and able to make ambitious plans for the
coming twelve months. This report will summarise its
current financial situation, review recent events, and
outline future plans.

Financial affairs
The club has seen a slight rise in expenses: film rental
costs were increased last July and mailing costs have also
risen, due to a notable increase in membership. In the
last year, 32 new members have joined and their fees
have contributed to the club's healthy bank balance.
Moreover, in March last year, the club was awarded a
grant of £500 from the Princefield Film Institute, due to
the impressive bid submitted by the Chair.

Main events
The highlights of last year's programme are given below:

• Welcome for new members, February
• Short season of Bertolucci's films, March
• Talk by screenwriter Todd Grafton, April
• Visit to the Cannes Film Festival, June
• Summer barbecue and party, August
• Lecture series on animation techniques, October
• Annual club dinner, December

Of these, the Cannes visit was particularly popular and
thanks must be given to Joy Wellman for organising
everything so well. In contrast, the lecture series in
October was poorly attended, and enrolments barely
covered the costs of the venue and speaker. It would be
appreciated if members could give the committee
feedback about the timing and subject matter of the
event, so that the same mistakes are not repeated.

Future plans
As always, the film programme is defined largely by
members' requests. While the booking secretary already
has a potential list of screenings, it is not too late for
further films to be proposed.

One exciting development is the imminent setting up of
a video library, which has been requested by many
members. The scheme will allow members to rent up to
two films at a time, for periods of three to five days.

Finally, the club is proud to confirm that the Canadian

director Brad Eastwood has accepted the invitation to
give a talk to members in May, date to be confirmed. This
event promises to be both informative and exciting, as
Brad is known to be a lively and controversial speaker.

Units 9–12 Revision

pages 110–111

This revision unit practises the language covered in Units
9–12 (and earlier units), as well as extending the work done
on reports in Writing folder 6. Specific exam practice is
provided for Paper 3 Parts 1, 3 and 4. This Use of English
section could be done as a timed test of 30 minutes.

1 This text comes from a magazine.

Answers
1 with 2 us/readers 3 Not 4 but 5 come
6 nothing 7 all 8 gives 9 among/perhaps/possibly
10 although 11 go/date 12 better 13 everyone
14 When 15 might/could

2

Answers
1 tip 2 turn 3 smart 4 tone 5 matter 6 habit

3

Answers
1 agreed to take it in turns to tidy
2 went on to discuss
3 Peter had put on a suit for
4 is remembered for always having
5 not/never lose sight of the fact that luck
6 as friendship is concerned, I'd rather have

4 Using compound adjectives in your writing will show
  your range of language.

Answer
Here is my report on our club's recent exchange visit to
Australia. Without exception, members who participated
in this trip were highly appreciative of the **meticulously-
planned** itinerary, not to mention the warm welcome
extended by our **easy-going** Australian hosts. This **long-
standing** relationship continues to flourish and we will be
hosting a **record-breaking** number of visitors this
summer (see below).

Travel
The **inter-continental** flights went smoothly and we
arrived in Melbourne on schedule. A coach had been
organised to transport us to the civic reception, where

our individual hosts awaited us. Travel within Australia was mostly by plane – unfortunately, our visit coincided with the grounding of much of the Ansett fleet, so our transfers were not entirely **trouble-free**.

Trips
The highpoint was the Great Barrier Reef, where two exhilarating days were spent **deep-sea** diving. Those members who chose not to dive were given the alternative of a **half-day** cruise in a **glass-bottomed** boat, which was said to be very enjoyable for all concerned.

Some members have suggested that the visit to the Kakadu National Park could have been extended, as it was rather rushed. In subsequent years, it might also be more informative to visit during the dry season, which would allow **wider-ranging** access to the park.

Return visit
There will be 48 visitors to us in July, including six families with young children. In view of this, it will be necessary to find extra hosts. Strategies for achieving this should be agreed at the next club meeting. In anticipation, could the following suggestions be tabled:
- advertising in relevant journals
- feature in local newspaper
- posters in public places, e.g. library
- mailshot to schools and colleges
- interview on KJY radio
- club website?

Perhaps other members should be asked for further suggestions in advance of the meeting.

Crossword

This revises idioms and vocabulary which you have encountered up to Unit 12.

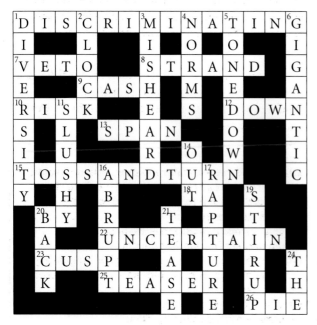

Listening test 3

See page 283 and key on page 287.

Unit 13

13.1 pages 112–113

1 The photos are of:
- floods over a large area
- children in a Third World country on a rubbish heap
- a motorway in Bangkok, with smog.

> **Possible answer**
> I would try to halt global warming by curbing the use of cars and reducing emissions of carbon into the atmosphere. Using energy from renewable resources – solar/wave/wind power – would also be a good idea.

2

> **Possible changes:**
> Recycle glass, paper and cans.
> Don't carry shopping in plastic carrier bags.
> Don't use disposable containers or cups.
> Turn off lights / switch off computers and TV.
> Turn down the thermostat in your room.
> Plant a tree.
> Ride a bike to work/college.
> Use recycled stationery/toilet paper.
> If you use a car go electric and share car space.
> Use energy efficient light bulbs.
> Volunteer to help in local environmental programmes.
> Fix any dripping taps.
> Always use biodegradable products.
> Don't use herbicides or insecticides in your garden.
> Use paper carefully.
> Turn off the tap when you clean your teeth.
> Use dishwashers and washing machines that use less water.

3 Read through the questions before you play the recording. Play each extract twice. The underlined parts of the tapescript confirm the answers.

> **Answers**
> 1 B   2 B   3 A   4 B   5 C   6 B   7 A   8 C

Extract 1
Speaker: Kids love it when I say I talk rubbish for a living, but it's the truth. As a recycling officer, I'm pretty obsessed with cutting down on consumption and waste. People come into this field from a medley of backgrounds. Mine is teaching, which is ideal, and most days during term time I'll have some contact with

schools. <u>Kids are very receptive to the 'save the planet' message and they're actually natural collectors of everything from bottle tops to newspapers, which is useful.</u> If it's a keen school, I'll ask questions and they'll bombard me with questions of their own, which is great. But if I ask, 'What's recycling?' and someone answers 'Riding your bike' I know I've got a long morning ahead of me. Usually they're rapt, they've a rough idea of what the local 'dump' is, but with a video and descriptions and the occasional trip, I can really spell out what landfill means. The cost of burying rubbish is enormous. <u>Even taking into account the rollercoaster changes in price for recycled plastics, glass and paper, it's still worth recycling, and children are receptive to that. What really gets me is the lack of local initiatives – there is often no direct link between policy and action.</u>

Extract 2

Interviewer: A huge chunk of the famous cliff at Beachy Head near Eastbourne in Sussex crashed into the sea in a massive landslide today. The rock fall can be seen from five kilometres out to sea. Ray Kent is a spokesperson for the Environment Agency and is on the phone from Eastbourne. Ray, what exactly happened?

Ray: This was a massive fall, hundreds of thousands of tonnes have fallen away from the cliff face and it has caused very significant damage to Beachy Head. It is basically down to climate change. The level of the sea is rising, so bigger waves are hitting against the cliff base, causing bigger vibrations to reverberate up the cliff. <u>This was combined with 12 days of extremely wet weather during December.</u> The chalk was absolutely sodden so the combination has caused the rock to fall away. <u>Unfortunately, it could be the shape of things to come.</u>

Interviewer: Thank you, Ray. <u>Freezing temperatures are believed to have expanded the water which seeped into the chalk, causing it to crumble and sheer off.</u> Coastguards have warned people to stay away from the edge of the cliff, as experts try to establish whether further falls could be expected.

Extract 3

Speaker: I remember once I was high up on the moors early one morning. The mist was very thick since the sun had only just risen and hadn't gained sufficient strength to disperse it. Shivering in the dew-drenched heather, I could hear the stags around me roaring their fierce belligerent cries. It was very frustrating to hear them but not see them. Then, very close at hand, I heard one stag's challenge answered by another and through the mist came the clatter and rattle of antlers and they started to fight. <u>I started to creep carefully</u> forward and, as luck would have it, a slight breeze blew up at that moment and parted the veils of mist to reveal two magnificent stags locked in battle. <u>You could see (as in many other animals that have contests like this) that they weren't bent on mutual destruction but were involved in a test of skill and strength.</u> Unfortunately, after I'd been watching them for about two minutes the wretched mist came down again and blotted out the deer and moorland as well. It was a beautiful sight, and the memory of it brings home to me, more than anything else, the need for constant vigilance against the ever-encroaching hand of so-called progress.

Extract 4

Presenter: With me to talk about environmental issues today is Dr Jane Dove, of the University of Melchester. Welcome, Jane.

Woman: Good morning.

Presenter: Today we're discussing the Gaia hypothesis, a theory about the Earth put forward in 1965 by James Lovelock. Now Lovelock was a scientist outside the British establishment. <u>He took issue with the accepted view</u> that the Earth was just a passive host to millions of species of plants and animals, and that these living organisms simply adapted to the environment they found themselves in. Jane, <u>nowadays Lovelock's theory that denuding forests will ravage delicate ecosystems is generally accepted, isn't it?</u>

Woman: Indeed, but you know, even in the 1960s he was thought of as a tree-hugger – someone who goes around hugging and worshipping trees. <u>A bit of a weirdo really.</u> Of course, it didn't help that he abandoned the formal title of his idea and replaced it with the earthier name, Gaia.

Presenter: <u>Yes, in fact this name, after the Greek goddess of the Earth, pushed Lovelock even further away from his peers.</u>

Woman: <u>I guess to them it seemed to represent the very opposite of rigid scientific enquiry.</u>

Presenter: True, more a 'holistic' view of the earth as a whole rather than its individual components. He wasn't an amateur though, and his ideas have since gained acceptance.

4   Play the recording again and decide which register each extract is. You need to get some idea of register in English because you are often tested on it in different parts of the exam.

Answers
Extract 1: informal – 'to talk rubbish' is a play on words; quite a few words are informal: *pretty, kids, cutting down, spell out, a rough idea*; use of *bombard* – exaggeration for effect
Extract 2: formal news report – use of passive; enumeration of events; impersonal
Extract 3: fairly formal – highly descriptive language; just at the end becomes more informal – use of *wretched* and *blotted out*.
Extract 4: man uses fairly formal speech; woman more informal – *a bit of a weirdo, I guess*

5 These words are all from the *Cambridge Learner Corpus*.

Answers

a *people* is neutral; *persons* is used in notices and government handouts
b *amelioration* is formal; *improvement* is neutral
c *bloke* is informal; *man* is neutral
d *narrate* is formal; *tell* is neutral
e *frequented* is formal; *went to* is neutral
f *reckon* is informal; *think* is neutral
g *boozing* is very informal/slang; *drinking* is neutral
h *mates* is informal; *friends* is neutral
i *fellow* is rather dated informal; *guy* is modern informal
j *snaps* is informal; *photographs* is neutral
k *pluses* is informal; *advantages* is neutral
l *lousy* is informal; *terrible* is neutral
m *prudent* is formal; *careful* is neutral
n *guts* is informal; *courage* is neutral
o *becoming* is formal; *attractive* is neutral

6 Although it's a good idea to look for synonyms, you should also be aware that there might be usage differences.

Answers

a broke (*destitute* is a formal, literary word)
b skinny (*skinny* is more negative in tone than *slender*)
c enemies (*opponents* is mainly used in sport)
d sneaking (*tiptoeing* is being quiet; *sneaking* has the idea of doing something underhand)
e yelling (a baby can't really shout)
f ravaged (*ravaged* is much stronger than *destroyed*; it emphasises how long it will take to recover)
g struck (this is much stronger than *hit*)
h trickling (*trickling* is for water that is moving slowly; *leaking* is used more for pipes and taps that have a hole in them)

7

Answers

1 D is correct. A collocates with *plan*; B means *at the beginning*; C means *result*.
2 A is correct. B takes *to* as a preposition; C takes *for* and D takes *of*.
3 B is correct. *Wane* is used to talk about the moon and fortunes; houses *depreciate* and power can be *curtailed*.
4 A is correct. The only word here that means have a limited life is A. The others all have the idea of limited movement or growth.
5 C is correct. The expression is *to give way to*.
6 B is correct. *To bring about* is to make something happen.

8

Possible answer

Good afternoon. I'm here today to propose some changes to the town's square. It's been obvious to most residents for some time that, since the computer factory closed five years ago, there has been high unemployment in our town. The town itself is both of some architectural merit and of historical importance, and our priority is to attract more tourists. By increasing the attractiveness of the centre, more money would be brought into the town in the form of tourist pounds.

We are going to instigate a daily rubbish removal programme and have decided to get rid of the unsightly car park in the town square and plant trees and put benches in their shade instead. If we have the opportunity, we plan to introduce a new bus service, which will run every half-hour from the car park on the town's outskirts into the town centre. More pedestrianised areas will be introduced as well. A bicycle loan programme will begin in high season and tourists will be encouraged to cycle along the new cycle path around the town.

Businesses around the square will be encouraged to plant tubs of flowers and cafés will have permission for chairs, tables and umbrellas outside their premises.

It's our belief that by making these, admittedly small, changes, tourists will find our town even more attractive. Now, if anyone has any comment on what I've said, I'll be pleased to take your questions. Thank you.

13.2 pages 114–115

1 The illustration is of a blue whale, an Ascension frigate bird, a gorilla, an American bison and a giant panda. The bison is the only one which is no longer endangered, thanks to a special breeding programme carried out in the USA.

2 This listening task is aimed at introducing reported speech. Play the recording once or twice and make notes. The underlined parts of the tapescript confirm the answers.

Answers

1 southern Africa   2 desert landscape
3 collect plants and paint   4 (rhino) footprint
5 geologists   6 media   7 thriving / doing well

Presenter: Nowadays we're all aware of the need for biodiversity. Without a range of animals and plants our planet would be a poorer place. Well, I've recently been to <u>southern Africa</u>, which is the last truly wild home of endangered black rhinos. Here something is being done, albeit in a small way, to encourage biodiversity. In most other places black rhinos live either in fenced enclosures or under armed guard. But here in this out of the way desert landscape they are completely free to roam. And yet the fact that any rhinos survive in that part of the world at all is partly due to our guest today, Susan Newhall. Susan, how did you come to get involved?

Susan N: I was in the desert collecting plants and painting and I came across a rhino footprint. That was how I first found out that there were rhinos in the area. I didn't realise that this was unusual until I met up with geologists who were working there, and they said there was a terrible slaughter going on and showed me places where dead rhinos were lying around. So I launched ahead and used the media tremendously to help me expose what was going on.

Presenter: It's amazing to think that if you hadn't found that footprint, things could've been different.

Susan N: Yes, that's right. It's extraordinary you know. Thanks to one rhino which I didn't even see.

Presenter: That was back in 1980, and after her discovery Susan got together with a group of other people to help form an organisation to help the rhinos. At the time, poaching in the region was so rife it seemed unlikely the rhinos could be saved, but Susan and her dedicated supporters refused to admit defeat and today rhinos are not just surviving in their harsh desert home, they're positively thriving.

3   Use your notes to report what was said. Refer to the Grammar folder if you are unclear about how sentences in reported speech are formed. The reporting doesn't have to be word for word as long as the gist of what is said is there.

Suggested answers

Southern Africa is the last truly wild home of endangered black rhinos. In most other places they live in either fenced enclosures or under armed guard. The man said that in the desert they are/were completely free to roam. He stated that rhinos were helped to survive in southern Africa because of Susan Newhall.

She said she had had no previous knowledge of rhino being in the desert and that when she had been looking for plants and doing some painting she had come across a rhino footprint. She had eventually met up with geologists who had been working in the area and they had told her about the terrible slaughter and had taken her to see the dead bodies. As a result she had used the media to expose what had been going on.

The man congratulated her on finding the footprint, as things would have turned out differently if she hadn't found it. She agreed and said that it was an amazing story, especially as she hadn't actually seen a rhino.

The man went on to say that Susan had got together with some friends and started an organisation to protect the rhino. He said that poaching in the country had been rife and if it hadn't been for Susan there wouldn't be any rhinos today.

---

4   Refer to the notes above before you do the exercise, which contains some examples of unusual patterns. More information on these forms can be found in the Grammar folder.

Answers

a She said that her grandmother had been able to walk / could walk to school without worrying about traffic.

b She said that it would be good if I came to tea sometime / that I must come to tea sometime.

c She said that I had to remember to recycle the rubbish.

d She said that I mustn't smoke in the restaurant.

e She said that companies which pollute rivers must be fined.

f She said that if she had been mayor, she would have made public transport free.

g She said that if the children picked up the rubbish regularly, she would pay them.

---

5   Read the notes at the bottom of page 114 before you do this exercise.

Answers

a Tina suggested going to Crete this year for their/our holiday.

b Fred declared that he would always love Daphne. / Fred declared his undying love for Daphne.

c Colin decided to take the job.

d My mother sighed and forgave me for breaking it.

e The old man objected to the window being opened.

f Rose claimed that I had her book in my school bag.

g My brother insisted on going out.

h Lucy refused to go by train.

---

6   This exercise shows how using an adverb can enliven a reported sentence.

Answers

a Tina tentatively suggested …

b Fred declared passionately that …

c Colin reluctantly decided …

d My mother sighed resignedly …

e The old man peevishly objected …

f Rose confidently claimed …

g My brother stubbornly insisted …

h Lucy categorically refused …

---

7   Remember to write in direct speech for this exercise, not reported speech.

Possible answers

a 'You'll pay for that broken jar!' the shopkeeper said angrily.

b 'Well, you've blocked that exit very nicely with your car, sir,' the policeman said sarcastically.

c 'No, Patricia, a colon, not a dash,' the teacher said pedantically.

---

d 'Now, where are my glasses?' my grandfather said absent-mindedly.

e 'I think I'll go shopping this afternoon,' Theresa said decisively.

f 'What did you say your name was?' the doctor said blankly.

g 'Don't let your children near my house,' my neighbour said rudely.

h 'Well now, I'll have to think about a pay rise,' his boss said cautiously.

8 This text is about how man began to study nature.

Answers
1 as 2 having 3 turned/gave 4 way/style
5 up 6 not 7 sake 8 common
9 hardly/scarcely NOT rarely 10 such 11 more
12 without 13 because/since 14 it 15 keep

9

Possible answer
I believe that animals shouldn't be kept in zoos. The best way to preserve endangered species is to have a sperm bank and then to try to organise national parks in the animal's country of origin with the aim of reintroducing native species back into their own habitat.

13.3 pages 116–117

1 and 2 Refer to the Exam spot, which gives some example questions and advice that you need to follow.

Read each text in turn and answer the questions on each part. The texts are about species which are not native to an area and the effect they can have. In these exercises the questions follow the relevant text. In the examination you may need to use information from both texts to answer a question.

The photo is of Hanauma Bay on Oahu in Hawaii.

Answers
A
1 They are both newcomers to the island.
2 Because the scientists are isolated and far from home. Intrepid means adventurous.
3 to take revenge on each other
4 They have been taken for a reason or have gone there accidentally.

B
1 predators, parasites and diseases (it isn't always necessary to paraphrase)
2 by flying/swimming/walking, etc. or being swept there in a storm or wind
3 stowaways

3

Suggested answer
Firstly people have taken a species to a new environment because they needed to use it, in the case of pigs or yams, for food, or in the case of dingoes, to help them look for food. Secondly people have imported decorative plants in order to take pleasure in their beauty. Lastly, some species have been introduced, for example, reptiles, because some people want to have an unusual pet. (69 words)

4

Background information

The rat came to Europe from India on board merchant ships. It brought with it the Black Death, which wiped out a large percentage of the population of Europe in the fourteenth century.
Terrapins were bought by parents as pets for their children. The children had seen a film called *Mutant Ninja Turtles* and to own a terrapin was very fashionable. Unfortunately, terrapins can be vicious when they are full-grown and do not make very good pets. Parents released the terrapins into the wild and they have killed many native river species as a result.
Tobacco was also introduced into Europe by Raleigh. Whether this was a good idea or not is debatable.
The rabbit was introduced into Australia by European settlers. It did so well that it was necessary to introduce a disease – myxomatosis – in the middle of the 20th century in order to try to keep the numbers down.
The potato was introduced into Europe by Sir Walter Raleigh, an English adventurer, in the seventeenth century. It has prospered and had few ill effects.

Possible answer
I have chosen chocolate. This is, unlike a tree or an animal, not a species which has been transplanted here, more of a dietary change which has been introduced. Chocolate was introduced into this country in the 16th century. It became popular first as a drink for wealthy people. I believe it has had a beneficial effect on people, although it does have a tendency to be addictive. Chocolate contains cocoa fat and caffeine, both of which are not good for our health. It also contains a compound which affects mood. Despite those rather negative points, I believe chocolate has given such pleasure to so many people that we should be pleased it was introduced.

Exam folder 7

Paper 1 Part 4
Multiple-choice text pages 118–119

This text is about what happens to computers when people no longer want them – maybe because the technology is old or they are broken.

Students often worry too much about vocabulary they do not know, instead of trying to guess the meaning from the context. Sometimes, it is difficult to guess the meaning, but it is always worth a try. You are not allowed to take a dictionary into the examination with you.

> **Answers**
> The part of the text which contains the answer is mentioned together with the answer.
>
> 1 C – they just leach heavy metals into our drinking water – that's the worst case scenario anyway
> 2 B – doing very nicely out of it
> 3 A – a weird kind of culture shock
> 4 D – computers aren't a cash-rich scrap purchase
> 5 C – And they won't be able to pass the cost on to the consumer – or not in any obvious way, at least
> 6 B – where the rules about what you may or may not stuff in a hole in the ground are non-existent
> 7 C – one which, if ignored for too much longer, will eventually come to haunt us

Unit 14

14.1 pages 120–121

1 One photo is of a 114-year-old woman from China and a child. The other photo is of a woman exercising in her living room.

> **Suggested answers**
> a false – Depends on what your daily routine is. If you work on a building site then you probably don't need so much as someone who sits at a desk all day.
> b false – You need to keep active to keep your bones and muscles healthy.
> c true – They're carbohydrates, good sources of energy.
> d true – It will be digested much more easily than a large evening meal.
> e false – It is just one form of exercise. It is best in combination with other types of exercise.
> f false – The only known way of living longer is to live on a very low calorie diet.

2

> # **B**ackground information
>
> Mark Twain – pseudonym of Samuel Langhorne Clemens (1835–1910). American writer who wrote *Tom Sawyer* and *Huckleberry Finn*.

> **Suggested answer**
> Mark Twain seems to be a sociable, rather contrary person who likes breaking the rules. A bit of a rebel.
>
> The writer in B seems to be someone who likes a challenge and is now so obsessed by running that he wants to talk about it all the time.

3 This exercise gives more practice in Paper 1 Part 2.

> **Answers**
> **Text A**
> 1 B is the answer – 'these rules are often flouted'. A is wrong because there is no other mention of people's attitudes. C is wrong because a healthy lifestyle is mentioned, but not in relation to people's attitudes. D isn't mentioned.
> 2 A is the answer – 'it will not slow down the ageing process. Nor yet … would any of the patent remedies'. B is plausible but wrong because there is no mention of the treatments often not being approved. C is wrong for the same reason. D is wrong because any comparison he makes is negative.
>
> **Text B**
> 3 B is the answer – 'being palpably unsuited for such a pursuit, I feel the need to discuss my training regime with anyone who crosses my path'. A is wrong because he says 'I'm not suggesting that marathon runners as a group are dull'. C is wrong – although he mentions friends, he doesn't mention whether they are dull. D is wrong but plausible. He isn't doing anything else but he doesn't blame being boring on this.
> 4 B is the answer – 'the anticipated sense of achievement in finding a whole new facet to my character' i.e. discovering whether he has the guts to do it. A is wrong because he says he hasn't got 'an innate desire to win'. C is wrong because although he does want to show he can do it, it is for himself not other people. D is wrong because he talks about 'the sheer ghastliness of it all'.

Style extra

The aim of this exercise is twofold – firstly, to analyse what makes a text formal or informal and secondly, to increase your awareness of a literary device that could make your writing more interesting. It also may be something you will come across in Paper 1 or Paper 3 Part 5.

> **Suggested answers**
> Text B is more informal in tone. The vocabulary here is not particularly informal, but the way it is written, with brackets and rhetorical questions, is. The tone is quite chatty – the writer is talking directly to the reader. The linking is also quite informal – *so, but*.
>
> The alliteration used here evokes the type of weather found in winter, making the image of winter more vivid.

4   This exercise gives more practice in register. Having a wide vocabulary, which can be used appropriately, will mean that you gain higher marks on the Writing paper.

Answers
a harangued – much stronger than *lecture*
b resolved – much more formal than *decided*
c swear – more formal than *promise* and stronger
d scrounge – more informal than *borrow*
e craved – stronger than *wanted*
f was seething – stronger than *angry*
g yank – stronger and more informal than *pull*
h unearthed – stronger than *found* and more formal
i loathes – much stronger than *doesn't like* and more formal

Phrase spot

Check that you are keeping expressions and idioms in some sort of ordered way in your vocabulary notebook.

Answers
a lived it up   b learn to live with
c lived up to our expectations   d live down
e live in clover   f live by their wits

14.2 pages 122–123

1   This exercise should throw up any problems you have with articles. Articles are a constant problem for students of English and you should regularly revise your knowledge of them. Refer to the Grammar folder on pages 185–6 for greater clarification.

Answers
1 Indonesia, Berlin, Europe, Oxford University
2 European, university, one-day ticket, household, union
Hotel is used with both *a* and *an*, but more often with *a*.
3
a i   Ken's job is as a personal trainer. Article needed before jobs.
b Both are correct. *The* gym – we all know which one. *A* gym – the first time it's been mentioned or one of many.
c i
d Both are correct. You use an article when you are referring to something in particular, no article if it is more general.
e ii   With nationality words of this type you need an article.

f Both could be correct. Generally you don't use an article with meals. The exception is for public events, e.g. *the rugby club dinner*.
g ii   *I play violin* is American usage. British usage is an article before an instrument.
h i   No article with sports.
i i   *I want a drink of water* is more usual. *I want one drink of water* emphasises how many. You can say *I want one more drink of water*.
j i   You always use *the* unless you are using an *attributive* adjective, e.g. The weather often affects people's moods.
We won't go out if the weather's bad. BUT Fishing boats don't go out in bad weather.
k ii   We use the possessive rather than an article for parts of the body unless they are referred to generally in a medical context.
l Both are correct. No article if you are talking about the purpose for which the bed exists, i.e. to sleep in. You use *the* if you are talking about the piece of furniture. Similarly you use an article with *prison/hospital/school* if you are just referring to the building, but no article if you are referring to the building's purpose.

2   Read through the article quickly to find out what it is about. There may be more than one answer, depending on meaning.

Answers
1 The   2 the   3 the/–   4 the   5 the   6 the   7 the
8 the/–   9 –   10 a   11 a   12 –   13 –   14 a
15 a/the/–   16 the   17 –   18 the   19 the   20 –
21 the   22 –

3   These idioms can be grouped together as nouns which don't take an article when they are part of an idiom. This may help you to remember them. The meaning of the idioms is given in brackets.

Possible answers
a All the orders were given by word of mouth to avoid leaving written evidence which might be later discovered. (by speaking only)
b The child lay face downwards in the sand and screamed. (on its stomach)
c Man first set foot on the island in the nineteenth century. (landed)
d My mother took me aside and suggested we have a heart to heart about my new boyfriend. (a good chat)
e They walked down the street hand in hand. (holding hands)
f Phil and I strolled arm in arm along the beach. (with arms linked)
g Traffic is nose to tail every morning on the road into the city centre. (bumper to bumper)
h Liz came face to face with Roger at the party. (met unexpectedly someone she didn't want to meet)

i His family lived from hand to mouth while he was growing up because his father was unemployed. (they were very poor)

j All our pottery is made by hand. (not by machine)

k The MP fought tooth and nail to get the bill through Parliament. (to fight very hard)

l I'm finding it increasingly difficult to see eye to eye with my boss. (to agree with)

4

Answers
a in **b** to **c** at **d** to/at **e** about/of **f** at/near
g to **h** of **i** on/against/for **j** on **k** on **l** for **m** on

5 This exercise gives practice in using prepositions accurately. It also illustrates weak forms. Some words in English – prepositions, pronouns, conjunctions, article and auxiliary verbs – have two pronunciations: one is used when they are stressed, and the other when they are not. Prepositions are stressed when they come at the end of a question.
For example:
What did he apply for? *strong* for /fɔ:/
He applied for a grant. *weak* for /fə/

Possible answers
a Who did he rely on? He relied on his parents.
b What does she take pride in? She takes pride in her appearance.
c What are they looking forward to? They are looking forward to their holiday.
d What are they prohibited from? They are prohibited from smoking in the classroom.
e Who does the group consist of? It consists of three teachers and six students.
f What did he interfere in? He interfered in my plans for the party.
g What do you admire her for? I admire her for her strong opinions.
h Who did she apologise to? She apologised to my brother. What did she apologise for? She apologised for being rude.
i What are they accused of? They are accused of arson.
j What do you believe in? I believe in truth and justice.

6 This exercise links word formation with the texts in 14.1. You need to be able to say exactly what part of speech a word is. The main forms are listed. There may be one or two which are not in this list.

Answers
Text A
tolerable (adjective)
  tolerate, intolerant, tolerant, tolerably, tolerantly

sense (noun)
  sensible, sensibly, nonsense
moderation (noun)
  moderate, immoderate, moderately, immoderately
regular (adjective)
  regulate, regularity, irregular, regulation/s, irregularity
survival (noun)
  survive, survivor

Text B
bore (noun)
  boredom, bored, boring, boringly
known (adjective)
  know, knowledge, knowingly, unknown
personally (adverb)
  person, personable, personalise, impersonal, impersonally
resolved (verb)
  resolution, unresolved
unsuited (adjective)
  suitable, unsuitable, suit, suitably
suspect (noun and verb)
  suspicious, suspicion, unsuspected, suspiciously

7 Use an appropriate form to complete the sentences. This can be quite difficult if a prefix is involved, for example d.

Answers
a knowledge **b** survivor **c** tolerant
d nonsense **e** resolution **f** suspicions

8 Key word transformations often test word formation.

Answers
1 is showing / shows signs of (some/an) improvement
2 am full of admiration for
3 has the reputation of inspiring / of being an inspiration to
4 for Professor McDougal's kind assistance / the kind assistance of Professor McDougal

14.3 pages 124–125

1 A health scare is when the public is made aware of a possible health hazard. However, more often than not, there is no good basis for the story.

2 This is not an exam-type listening task. It gives practice in deciding if a statement is made or not. It doesn't matter by whom, just that the statement is made. Play the recording twice – once for general understanding and the second time to pick up on detail.

The underlined parts of the tapescript confirm the answers.

Alice: Health scares – don't they make you sick! Or do they challenge your complacency? Every few days a new story appears in the newspaper about, first of all, butter is bad for you, then butter is good for you. Salt is bad for us, salt is good for us. You just have to pick up a cup of coffee and you're engaged in a health debate. With me today to discuss this issue is Professor Robert Atkins. Robert, what do you think about all this?

Robert: Personally, <u>I'd rather have ten false health scares and one of them prove to be serious – then it leads to action</u>, than the cynical sense that somehow all this is just a media confection. That's what I really object to.

Alice: But how often do health scares come true?

Robert: There are random events in which microbes do emerge. They can be extraordinarily lethal and these account for massive epidemics that have occurred in the past in human history and I think we would be arrogant in the extreme to think that such things may not occur again in the future.

Alice: You're thinking of bubonic plague, of course. But nowadays it seems is the best of times and the worst of times if you want to be healthy. This is a paradox, because, on the one hand, we live in a relatively healthy society. Our longevity is unprecedented. By historical standards communicable lethal disease is exceptionally controlled. Yet we seem to be getting better, but feeling worse. Why, if we're so healthy, are we so easily spooked?

Robert: If you were living two or three hundred years ago, you were in the hands of God or Fate and if you were struck down by a mortal disease you thought you'd been sinful, but you also had your beliefs to console you – you'd go to paradise or heaven or whatever. Nowadays, we have tremendously high expectations about long healthy life continuing and some of us no longer have an expectation of an afterlife. It's partly a matter of a crisis of rising expectations.

Alice: Umm, so our health anxiety is like a big eater's gluttony or a rich man's miserliness. <u>Health excites expectations of perfection. It's also a disease spread by commercial interests</u>, isn't it?

Robert: Indeed. The margarine industry, for example, is actually now a very powerful instrument in pushing the line that butter is bad for you and actually there's a strong industrial lobby that has an interest in making sure that we are all anxious and worried about our health.

Alice: And they're not the only interested players. <u>If health scares sell pills they also sell papers.</u> And what about the research community which keeps the health scare industry supplied with stories?

Robert: Health is always in the news. <u>Sometimes it's the doctors themselves who are maybe responsible. In every branch of life there are people who like a touch of publicity and enjoy the turbulence. Others are often so convinced by their findings that they ignore the critical views of other doctors and have this urge to promulgate their ideas when it may not be appropriate to do so.</u> If I wanted to avoid heart disease I'd be taking aspirins, reducing my weight, I would probably frequent my local gym a bit more. I would drink more red wine. I would eat this, that and the other and so on. Then there might be another disease I might get. What do I do then?

Alice: How much difference would it make to you if you made all those changes? Should you just discount what you read and hear?

Robert: Who knows? Some health scares can actually seriously damage your health – they lead to stress, deprive us of the comfort of eating chocolate and clog up doctors' waiting rooms. There is clearly an information overload and unfortunately, when the real risk comes along, people might have difficulty distinguishing it from all the background noise.

Alice: And of course it's difficult to disprove something once a claim has been made, however fallacious that risk is. Thank you, Professor Robert Atkins.

Pronunciation

3   The general rule is that when the word is used as a verb the stress is on the last part of the word; when it is used as a noun then the stress is on the first part of the word.

Alice and Robert say: ob<u>ject</u>   fre<u>quent</u>   dis<u>count</u>
This is because these three words are being used as verbs in the listening extract.
invalid – noun stress on **in**; adjective stress on **val**
alternate – verb stress on **alt**; adjective stress on **ter**

Possible answers
I frequented the same places as Hemingway did in the 50s.
He's a frequent visitor to the club.

The entrance to the hall is via the side door.
She was entrancing in the part of Ophelia.

I was incensed to find my car had been vandalised.
I can't stand the smell of incense.

Your visa is invalid, I'm afraid.
Her aunt has been an invalid for over ten years.

Is everyone present?
I bought a present for my father.
Can I present Mr Delgado to you?

Students receive a discount on entry prices.
Don't discount everything she says just because she's a child.

The stall was covered in local produce.
The factory produces 5,000 components every year.

I can see you on alternate mornings only.
You will have to alternate with Fred over who uses the room.

4   This section gives more practice in Paper 5 Part 2. You should remember not just to describe the photos but to talk about the lifestyles of the people and make comments or give opinions on them. Make sure you time this activity so you get used to being concise and not spending too much time thinking.

The photos are of two girls smoking, possibly at school and of a young woman running, looking very fit.

Possible answer
The young people in this photo are probably at school and smoking illegally. They probably still think it's cool to smoke and spend any money they can get on cigarettes. The fact that cigarettes can kill you probably doesn't enter their heads.
I think that the fit young woman probably gets up fairly early in the morning, doesn't drink, eats moderately healthily, but probably does eat junk food, and takes her training very seriously. She probably doesn't socialise as much as she would like and goes to bed early on nights before an athletics meeting. It's not a lifestyle I would consider personally.

5   It might be useful to go through the unit underlining vocabulary connected with health and fitness, and then try to incorporate it into your talk.

Possible answer
Possibly a poster campaign would have the greatest impact. I always remember the campaign for teenage pregnancy with a man looking pregnant. That had a great impact. The posters could be distributed around schools, youth clubs and even in bus shelters – anywhere where young people congregate. I think cigarette smoking and drinking alcohol should be highlighted because of the rising number of teenage girls who smoke and also the problem with under-age drinking in this country.

Writing folder 7

Paper 2 Part 1 Proposal pages 126–127

Writing folder 4 on pages 72–73 covered Part 2 proposals.

1   This type of visual presentation could come up on Paper 2 Part 1. The graphs/charts show that the best course of action is B.

2   Read the exam task carefully and underline key information.

3   Look back at page 73 and the advice given. It is very important to write in a consistently appropriate register and tone.

Improved answer

Following the rather negative external report on our sports facilities, we would like you to reconsider your position and give students increased access. Barring students from using the pool and the hall at certain times is a little unfair. And as the report points out, this public-oriented policy is adversely affecting our basketball and swimming teams, both of which have hitherto represented the college at the highest levels of competition and won many events.

It has come to our notice that funding is available nationally, which we would be in a good position to apply for. Perhaps you are aware of this already? We would like to support you in submitting a bid for this money, which would enable the college to carry out much-needed repairs to the sports hall, such as the replacement of the substandard flooring and major improvements to the lighting. Regarding the latter, no doubt you appreciate the difficulties faced by users, being a squash player yourself. We estimate that the money would also allow for an extension of the present changing facilities, whereby separate 'wet' and 'dry' areas could be introduced, to service the pool and hall respectively. This would be extremely popular with all users of the facilities, not least the general public, who are often critical of the present arrangements.

If this work were to go ahead, we believe that the college would profit by it, as fees for external use of the facilities could be raised. At the same time, we would again ask you to reconsider the extent to which these college facilities are out of action for students and possibly reduce the number of hours allocated to the public. We are not against public use of the facilities, which strengthen the links between the college and the town, but we feel the number of hours involved is inappropriate. Perhaps public access could be restricted mainly to the mornings, when fewer students use the facilities?

We share your desire to maintain the good reputation of the college and would therefore urge you to implement the recommendations made in the external report.

4   Use some of these expressions when you write a proposal.

Answers
a A b A c B d A e C (or B) f B g A
h C i A j C

5   Write your proposal, following the advice given on page 73. See also the answer in exercise 3 above.

Unit 15

15.1 pages 128–129

1 The contrasting jobs in the pictures show colleagues at a creative meeting (perhaps in advertising or design) and a glassblower.

> **Possible answers**
> I may stay in the same career, but I'm likely to move around.
> Perhaps the workplace will become even more automated and computerised, with more mundane jobs being done by robots.
> I don't expect to stay with the same company, though I believe there will always be opportunities in my field.

2 Before you listen to the recording, read through the questions and check anything you are unsure of. You will have one minute in Part 3 of the exam to look through the multiple-choice questions. Play the recording twice, as in the exam. The underlined parts of the tapescript confirm the answers.

> **Answers**
> 1 B 2 B 3 D 4 C 5 A

Interviewer: Diane Webber, you've switched careers more than once during your own working life, and you now run a highly regarded employment agency for media high-fliers, where, above all, you advise your clients, both companies and applicants, to be fully flexible. You seem to see this as a fundamental principle, if your agency slogan – Keeping your options open – is anything to go by. Is that a fair assessment of how you operate?

Diane Webber: Absolutely. I know that not so very long ago we used to see jobs for life as the norm, with unquestioning company loyalty, and a golden handshake at the end of it all – which, nine times out of ten, probably wasn't in actual fact deserved – but things are very different now. And yes, there does seem to be something positive in all this, despite the obvious question mark over security. Successful players in the current job market cut their teeth in one firm, and are willing to step sideways more than once to gain fresh experience. Unlike their predecessors, they may only progress up the rungs when they land their third or fourth job, or even later in their career. This increased movement brings benefits, not just for them, but for the companies they work for, too.

Interviewer: In spite of the instability? Surely it's important to have some continuity?

Diane Webber: Well actually, it's a mixed blessing. Individuals can get terribly stale if they stick in one place for too long, especially if they report to managers who fail to challenge them. That implies a hierarchy riddled with complacency and under-achievement, which can no longer be tolerated in today's fast-moving, dog-eat-dog world. Also, much of today's work consists of fixed-term projects, done in teams, and if one or two members drop out along the way, it really doesn't matter, provided that the team remains an entity. The one exception to this is the team leaders themselves, who are not only the driving force, but the guardians of the project, who hold important historical detail in their heads, so yes, continuity is important there. But even then it's a clearly defined cycle. We're frequently approached by highly-experienced team leaders who, having completed one project, decide they can't face even the slightest whiff of repetition and so come to us seeking fresh challenges.

Interviewer: And they manage to find work?

Diane Webber: Oh, they're snapped up! Because generally speaking, a project-based job can easily demonstrate a track record, it's there in the successful completion of the project.

Interviewer: And these people would have no problem getting references from the employers they're essentially walking out on? I would have thought that that could be an issue …

Diane Webber: Employers don't view it like that at all. Their mindset is different now, as I said earlier, and companies actually take steps to foster a more dynamic environment, as they feel this yields better productivity, though the jury's still out on this, in my view. Nevertheless, with a flow of people, there's a quantum leap in terms of the ideas generated, not to mention the chance of new ways of problem-solving imported from elsewhere. These effects are tangible and they're often very attractive because they're perceived as lean and efficient, instant solutions, even if they generally turn out to be only quick fixes which later have to be reversed.

Interviewer: Ah, but isn't that the nub of it all, that this shifting and fragmented approach leads to poor decisions? Of course, the perpetrators are never taken to task, as they've already made a quick exit and are knocking on your door for another job!

Diane Webber: That's a bit unfair! For one thing, there have always been bad decisions. No company can rely on its personnel to make the right choices one hundred per cent of the time – even with the help of highly-paid outside consultants, staff will continue to get it wrong from time to time. However, I'd argue that it's the mediocre employees, who just want to keep their heads down, who are far more likely to cause problems than the risk-takers, who, don't forget, are only as employable as their last success.

Interviewer: Ruthless …

Diane Webber: Pragmatic!

Interviewer: Which brings us neatly back to your slogan, doesn't it? Keeping your options open. How far do you encourage people to go in this?

Diane Webber: With new opportunities opening up all the time, the sky's the limit really. It's certainly never too late to contemplate a move, and so the maxim has to be, don't rule *anything* in or out.

Interviewer: We'll end on that positive note. Diane Webber, thank you.

Diane Webber: It's been a pleasure.

3

> **Answers**
> a financial reward for long service
> b get experience
> c climb the career ladder
> d good and bad
> e fiercely competitive
> f a tiny bit of
> g recruited immediately
> h evidence of previous success
> i way of thinking
> j people haven't decided
> k huge improvement
> l apparently simple and instant solutions (which don't succeed)
> m concentrate on their work

4

> **Answers**
> a something quick to eat
> b the quickest but most competitive route to success (original meaning: the outside overtaking lane of a motorway)
> c (earn) money fast
> d the quickest line in e.g. airport check-in
> e a quick swim
> f not moving ahead, undynamic
> g answering quickly
> h brief sleep, usually during daytime

Idiom spot

Many new expressions are entering the language, particularly in the areas of business and journalism.

> **Answers**
> 1 the jury's still out   2 a quantum leap
> 3 the slightest whiff of   4 quick fixes
> 5 track record   6 a mixed blessing
>
> a red ink   b green shoots   c blue chips
> d white goods   e golden hello   f white knight

15.2 pages 130–131

1

> **Possible answer**
> Although there are male and female secretaries in an office environment, the men see themselves as more important, often spending time on the phone networking.

2

> **Answers**
> 1 so   2 what   3 be   4 no   5 since   6 from   7 as
> 8 on   9 into   10 while/though/although   11 their
> 12 rather   13 whose   14 up   15 every/the

3

> **Possible answers**
> Sales rep working on commission (to Sales Manager)
> Copy writer (to Publicity Manager)
> Administrative assistant (to Office Manager)

4 It is a purpose clause. Turn to the Grammar folder on page 186 and read the paragraphs on purpose clauses and reason clauses.

5 The two most formal linkers are *for fear that* and *lest*. Both are used in literary texts and are slightly old-fashioned.

Remember that the other linkers used in reason clauses are *as, because, since*.

> **Answers**
> a for fear that   b so as not to / in order not to
> c in order to / so as to   d in case   e so that
> f so as not to / in order not to   g in case   h lest

6

> **Possible answers**
> a I would like to work abroad at some point, in order to broaden my experience.
> b When I'm older, I won't stay in the same job for more than two years, so as not to get stale.
> c I want to continue my English studies, in order to get a better job.
> d It would be useful for me to have my own website, so that I could promote my products.
> e I want to find work that I can do from home, in order to be able to spend more time with the children.

Style extra

A good dictionary will give you information on usage restrictions.

Answers
Nouns
used of men
bounder (old-fashioned), buffer (informal, slightly old-fashioned), charmer (old-fashioned, slightly derogatory), geek (informal), lout, Neanderthal (informal), nerd, patriarch (formal), thug
used of women
bag (offensive), bimbo (offensive), vamp (old-fashioned)
used of both
actor, chairman, freshman, gofer (informal), mate (informal), partner, sibling, spouse (old-fashioned), whizz kid

Adjectives
used of men only
chivalrous, effeminate
used of both
bullish, doting (but see Possible answers below), laddish, lanky (but usually of men and boys), prickly, wimpy

---

When you write your example sentences, you can use any suitable noun. The possible answers below have been taken from the *Cambridge International Corpus* – the type of source is given in brackets. Additional usage notes reflect the corpus evidence.

Possible answers

I think you're the most chivalrous man I've ever met. (popular novel)

Beckham is such a doting dad that he's just had Brooklyn's name tattooed on his back. (tabloid newspaper – referring to the Manchester United footballer David Beckham) *Note: although the adjective can be used of men and women, there were notably more examples of 'doting dad' and 'doting father'.*

A pale, delicate, effeminate boy, who might have been taken for my master's brother... (novel: *Wuthering Heights* by Emily Brontë) *Note: most corpus lines are from literary sources and the use appears to be slightly old-fashioned.*

As Jon and I are the newest of new men, this insinuation of laddish sexism cuts very deeply. (Varsity website) *Note: the example contrasts a laddish attitude with the now slightly old-fashioned expression 'new man' (a man who is sensitive and caring, and takes responsibility for childcare and traditionally female chores).*

The lanky centre forward found himself rushing towards a head-on collision with the goalkeeper. (sports report) *Note: there are many similar examples in the corpus relating to sports players.*

Most of the officers were personally chosen by Mr Noriega or his equally prickly predecessor. (*The Economist* magazine)

Beautiful men are a bit vain and wimpy. (tabloid newspaper)

15.3 pages 132–133

1

Suggested answers
a decisiveness, forthrightness, vision
b determination, good humour, stamina
c decisiveness, intuition, stamina

Other characteristics:
ambitious, able to articulate ideas, good public speaker, charismatic

---

2

Background information

The first text is taken from Sir John Harvey-Jones' autobiography *Making it Happen*. Sir John was Chairman of one of Britain's largest companies, ICI, and was forced to make some tough management decisions when the company faced problems. He subsequently became a consultant, offering companies in trouble his sound advice.

Suggested answers
1 sufficient updating / passing on of relevant background information
2 determination; vision
3 one that doesn't challenge or discuss
4 Their sharing of responsibilities earlier on doesn't equate with Gates' public image (as a nerd).
5 Members of management were originally technical experts.

---

3   Look back at Unit 9, page 81.

Answers
At the same time   Conversely   Instead
On the contrary   On the other hand

---

5   You will lose marks if your answer is longer than the word limits. Underline the sentences in the answer where A–D are dealt with. You will be left with one sentence that is not underlined.

Answers
A The first text talks about the need for concrete outcomes from discussions with board members. The second describes long meetings where decisions were taken.

B The writer of the first text sees strong leadership as essential, while the second shows that a looser partnership worked in a young company.

C The first text highlights the enormous amount of responsibility that goes with the job.

D The first text says that you need to learn how to do the job once you have taken over as chairman. The second one refers to how people in charge of a young company had to learn as they went along.

You should not have underlined the sentence below.

In the second text the individuals had to work long hours and expected this of others.

It is unnecessary in the summary to mention that Gates and Allen worked long hours, although this has informed sentence C. Their expectations of others is irrelevant to the task (which asks you to summarise the characteristics of the top jobs).

6 The correct order is D, B, A, C.

> **Sample summary**
> Both texts refer to top people experiencing a learning curve when running a company and highlight the importance of conclusive discussions with decision-makers. The first argues for strong leadership, but conversely, the second describes a less-clearly defined partnership. In each case, total commitment to the job is taken for granted.
> (50 words)

Exam folder 8

Paper 4 Part 2
Sentence completion page 134

Read through the advice carefully. Then look at the questions and try to predict what the answer will be. Time spent looking carefully at the question paper is never wasted, and you have 45 seconds to do this. It is important to read ahead when listening so that, if something is missed, there is no sense of disorientation. There is no need to panic, as the piece will be played again.

Play the recording twice to simulate exam conditions. The underlined parts of the tapescript confirm the key.

> **Answers**
> 1 polite and respectful   2 refresher course
> 3 roundabouts   4 (thick) mud   5 long-term rental(s)
> 6 test drive   7 handbrake   8 best interests
> 9 hand controls

Part 2

You will hear a man talking about his job working for a car hire company. For questions 1 to 9, complete the sentences with a word or a short phrase. You now have 45 seconds in which to look at Part 2.

Presenter: Dealing with the general public can be a tricky business, and none more so than the job of reservations manager with a car hire company. As John Farrant knows only too well!

John: Even when you can't quite believe that someone is being serious, it's part of our job to be <u>polite and respectful</u> and remember the customer is always right. Sometimes it can be difficult. When taking a booking, we have to ask certain questions, one of which is: 'Do you possess a clean driving licence?' To which one man snapped at me, 'Of course I do. I keep it in a plastic wallet!'
Sometimes we can hardly believe it's not a hoax. We had an elderly gentleman enquire about a car to go to Paris the following morning. We went through the questions and he said he was 69, and it turned out that, although he had a full driver's licence, he hadn't driven for years. He said, 'Is there any way you could give me a <u>refresher course</u> over the phone?' We suggested he let his friend drive.
Travel doesn't always bring out the adventurer in people, though. We had an American tourist ask for a car from Gatwick airport to drive to Glasgow, and who said: 'How many circles are there between Gatwick and Glasgow?' After some questioning, I realised he meant <u>roundabouts</u>. There's only one in the whole of America, in Washington, and he'd only ever driven on motorways here before. He only wanted me to work out a route for him!
Then we had one client from Birmingham book a car for a fortnight. A week later I received a call from him in Israel, saying he was just about to drop off the car. I said, 'Sorry, sir, where are you?' He said, 'Tel Aviv.' I asked if he'd told the reservations clerk he intended to go abroad with the car, and he said no, really unconcerned. Presumably he didn't realise, or maybe even care, that he hadn't been covered by insurance. I spoke to the supplier afterwards. He said when they got the car back it was so thick with <u>mud</u> it took two days for them to valet it and now it's unrentable.
A similar scenario happened when we had a client who said, 'Do you do <u>long-term rentals</u>, like for six months?' The reservations clerk said, 'Of course we do,' cheerfully rubbing his hands together because the booking was worth loads of money. The client asked if he could drop off the car in East London. The clerk said that wasn't a problem, not realising until the customer called months later, that he meant East London, South Africa.
We had one gentleman who had a medical condition that meant that he was on drugs that made him semi-drowsy, but he had a certificate from his doctor saying that he could drive. I got a call from the depot manager saying,

'I'm not giving him a car. He can hardly stand up.' We decided he should give the customer a test drive round the block. This guy pulled out of the depot and there was a car coming towards them. He didn't even see it. The depot manager had to pull on the handbrake. The manager said he'd never been so scared in his life. Other people refuse to believe you're genuinely concerned about their best interests. I remember it once took me 15 minutes to persuade a customer that it really wasn't worth hiring a Seat Marbella, a fairly small car, to go through the Alps. He'd just get stuck and it would ruin his holiday. He simply refused to accept that this type of car wouldn't be up to the job. What d'you do?

We can solve most problems though. We had a gentleman who wanted car hire in Miami. Everything was fine until he suddenly said, 'By the way, I've only got one arm.' I had to call in a few favours, but one of my suppliers managed to get me a car with hand controls.

So, although it may not be straightforward, I enjoy my job on the whole – I guess it's the challenge – every day is different after all!

Paper 4 Part 4
Three-way matching page 135

In this part of the exam it is necessary to listen carefully for evidence of whether the speakers express the stated opinion. The speakers will both mention the topic and it is important to listen to see if they agree with each of the phrases. Sometimes only one will agree and sometimes both will. Play the recording twice, as in the exam. The underlined parts of the tapescript confirm the answers.

Answers					
1 E	2 M	3 B	4 B	5 M	6 E

Part 4

You will hear two people, Monica and Edward, talking about the use of the Internet by businesses. For questions 1 to 6, decide whether the opinions are expressed by only one of the speakers or whether the speakers agree.
Write M for Monica, E for Edward, or B for Both, where they agree. You now have 30 seconds in which to look at Part 4.

Presenter: Today we'll be talking about the use of the Internet in British business. With me to discuss this is Monica Jones, visiting professor at City College, and Edward Morley, Editor of *Internet* magazine. Monica, the Prime Minister recently chastised our captains of industry for being ostriches over e-commerce. Did you agree with him?

Monica: Well, we must be careful here I think. IT systems don't come cheap, and e-commerce systems certainly don't. E-commerce is wrongly being seen as a panacea for what are potentially much deeper business and organisational problems.

Edward: Umm … I think we should get to the nitty-gritty here. Most companies are moving to the net because of the biggest business problem a company can ever have: falling revenues, or the threat of them. They're moving to the net because there's a financial imperative, not because it's a quick fix.

Monica: But, to me, the question is: where does the Internet fit in? What products are better suited to being sold through this medium? Take for example the recent launch of an interactive Internet service for stamp collectors. Customers will be able to purchase stamps via the Internet – but aren't stamps one of those commodities that you need to see before you purchase them?

Edward: Four years ago, I had the same doubts as you – but every week the net advances, and it never ceases to amaze me what people buy online. Now it's possible to buy houses, cars, mortgages, insurance policies – anything and everything.

Monica: And then there's still the issue of security in paying; many, including myself, remain sceptical.

Edward: Mm, but you wouldn't be seeing the growth we're having now if it was still true.

Monica: OK, but for many people it's the social contact involved in shopping in the High Street that they love. Meeting friends and exchanging gossip is an integral part of the shopping process, and serves a social need in more ways than one.

Edward: But don't forget that not everyone lives near a High Street. I'm sure people in far-flung communities and those without access to good transport love the choice and immediacy that the net brings them. And let's not forget that newsgroups, chatrooms and online book reviews can all provide a place for people to get together to chat and compare purchases.

Monica: But to return to what I was saying earlier. Underlying all this is a far deeper problem within British industry. The most critical factor is the lack of boardroom experience and awareness of the potential value and pitfalls associated with IT. Sadly, while the majority of top executives say they are keen to become inclusive members of the e-business world, few show signs of crossing the threshold.

Edward: I think you're approaching the problem from the wrong end. In my experience, board-level management are too high up to appreciate anything that happens on the shop floor.

Monica: Yes, but …

Edward: Sorry, can I just finish? At the moment the e-commerce revolution is being competently led by a small band of footsoldiers at the important end of the company: the salespeople, marketing people and small companies up and down the land. Compare this week's marketing job adverts to those of a year ago and you'll see that practically everyone wants e-commerce and new media experts and this is how it should be.

Monica: But given the serious shortage …

Edward: It is these people, not chief executives, whom you should be training to use the net effectively. Putting your IT director in charge of a website is like putting an electrician in charge of your shop window dressing. By all means let them provide your network, but for God's sake don't let them sell anything.

Unit 16

16.1 pages 136–137

1   This unit is all about literature and the printed word. As is often the case in the exam, this Paper 1 Part 4 task is taken from a short story.

> **Possible answers**
> A short story has few pages and so there is little space to develop characters or plot. The writing must be succinct and 'lean'.
>
> In a novel it is easier to use flashback and other time reference devices. There is much more scope to include long descriptions and/or sub-plots.

2   The significance of the title is that Elizabeth's behaviour and that of her parents shows nothing new or different from previous generations. It is predictable.

Background information

Laurie Colwin wrote five novels and three collections of short stories before she died in 1992. This story appears in her second collection *The Lone Pilgrim*, a book that includes many stories to do with early experiences of adult life.

3

> **Answers**
> 1 C 2 B 3 B 4 A 5 D 6 C 7 D
>
> **Detailed explanation:**
> 1   The answer (C) is in the words 'was extraordinarily pretty, and such children are never called difficult'. A is wrong, as the text only refers to one child who was older, Nelson Rodker. B is not suggested: the use of 'original' does not imply great intelligence. D is ruled out as there is no evidence of 'painstaking preparation' and only one relationship is referred to (her parents hoped Nelson and Elizabeth might marry).
> 2   The answer (B) lies in the final sentence of the second paragraph. There is no evidence that she had a 'sense of

duty' (A), in fact the reverse is true. C is ruled out as it was Elizabeth who hated the Rodkers, not the other way round. Although it is true that Elizabeth did hide her true feelings ('she learned to turn a cheerful face'), there is no evidence to suggest she disliked doing this (D).
> 3   The answer (B) is rooted in 'none of her friends wanted to entertain at home'. A is ruled out because the careers weren't always successful ('blacklisted movie producers'). There is no evidence to support C; Holly was the only friend who came home and Elizabeth's mother approved of her, so she would have been unlikely to feel uncomfortable. D is not suggested by the text.
> 4   The answer (A) lies in the words 'manure was not on her mother's mind' and 'she was much relieved' – presumably her mother had been imagining an illicit relationship with a man at the stables. There is no evidence that Elizabeth's mother begrudged spending the money on the jodhpurs (B). C, though plausible, is not true: her parents 'who felt riding once a week was quite enough' were mildly interested and the mother did arrange the purchase of the jodhpurs. D is likely, but not stated in the text.
> 5   The answer (D) lies in the final sentence of the fifth paragraph. A is insufficiently rooted in the text: although it implies her parents believed in moderation in reading, we do not know how she was brought up. B is wrong, as Elizabeth's appearance didn't change (only her behaviour at college did). C is wrong as it was other students who 'went wild', while Elizabeth spent time alone in her room.
> 6   The answer (C) lies in the words 'wanted to enjoy it finally on her own terms' and 'refusing to take a cent of their money'. A is wrong, as she used the bracelet 'as collateral' to borrow money – that is, she didn't sell it but named it as an asset that could be set against the loan if she defaulted on her payments. B is not stated, even if implied by the fact that the daughters of her parents' friends were getting engaged. D is wrong as Elizabeth had always loved New York.
> 7   The answer (D) is in the final two sentences of the text. A and C are not supported by the reality in the text. B is wrong, as both Nelson and Elizabeth had a good education and in her case, the text shows us it led to other things.

4

> **Answers**
> a Elizabeth's mother forced herself to sound positive.
> b Elizabeth pretended to be happy when really she loathed the Rodkers and her parents.
> c Beautiful daughters like Elizabeth are over-protected.
> d It might have adversely affected Elizabeth's social life.
> e Elizabeth's parents regarded 'adult behavior' as important.

5

> **Answers**
> Nelson is conventional, spineless and apathetic.
>
> **Suggested opposites for the other words**
> articulate / inarticulate
> brazen / modest
> callous / compassionate
> fickle /steadfast
> flawed / impeccable
> loquacious / taciturn
> trustworthy / treacherous
> unflappable / panicky

16.2 pages 138–139

1   Do you see anything odd about the poem by Bud Weiser? Look carefully: the poet's name, if put together as one word, is the name of a make of beer, which echoes the content of the final line. The poem is a joke!

Background information

Spike Milligan is perhaps best known for his collaboration with Harry Secombe and Peter Sellers in the BBC radio comedy series *The Goons*, which has influenced many other comedians' work. Gary Snyder is an American poet who was part of the 'Beat Generation' and a friend of the writer Jack Kerouac.

2   If you are interested in poetry, it is worth buying a bilingual edition of a poet you enjoy and comparing the original version with its translation.

> **Suggested answers**
> Poetry can be translated, but demands additional skills on the part of the translator. It is sometimes impossible to preserve the original rhyme or rhythm. For this reason, a translator should be able to 'take liberties' that the translator of a novel wouldn't contemplate. The first poem contains some idiomatic language (switch off your face, put your love into neutral) that might be difficult to translate within the same rhythm. The first two poems have tightly defined rhythm and some lines rhyme, so perhaps the free verse of Gary Snyder would be easier to translate. On the other hand, some of its nuances are personal to the poet and might be difficult to understand fully and/or get across in another language.

3

> **Answers**
> 1 analysis   2 scholars   3 mistrusted   4 supposedly
> 5 imperial   6 imprisons   7 Familiar   8 unexpected
> 9 enigmatic   10 nevertheless

Style extra

Two of the occurrences of *as* are in the same example.

> **Answers**
> *as* the poet Robert Frost once claimed
> *As* a result
> Familiar *as/though* I was with
> *As* remote *as*
>
> The change in word order adds emphasis to the fact that it is unlikely.

Turn to page 186 of the Grammar folder after completing the exercise (**c** and **d** do not contain concessive clauses).

> **Suggested answers**
> a Greatly acclaimed though his novel is, I find it rather disappointing.
> b As entertaining as the play is, it is lightweight in comparison with his earlier works.
> c As well as being a writer, Romano was a painter.
> d As Robert Frost said, 'A poem begins in delight and ends in wisdom.'
> e Gripping though the storyline of the novel undoubtedly is, its characters lack development.
> f Much as I have tried to get into the book, it remains impenetrable.

4

> **Answers**
> a In spite of / Despite the nice atmosphere ...
>   OR Although the atmosphere is nice ...
> b ... despite the fact that ...
>   OR despite my knowing only ...
> c Although it is not easy ...
> d Despite what she felt ...
> e Although one could see ...
> f In spite of that / Despite that ...
> g Even though I was wrong ...
> h ... in spite of writing ...

5

> **Answers**
> 1 even if its/the rhyme is/gets lost OR even if he/she loses the rhyme
> 2 my hand at (writing) short stories, poetry is
> 3 enjoy/like poetry readings, I sometimes take exception to
> 4 as/though the biographer's progress was / had been initially
> 5 strike it lucky with/by creating a bestseller, though/but/whereas

16.3 pages 140–141

1 The different genres shown are: novels, science fiction, detective fiction, travel writing, poetry, plays, biographies.

2 The extracts are fairly short, like those in Paper 4 Part 1. Play them twice if necessary.

Answers
The Dumas Club (detective story)
Congo Journey (travel writing)

Qualities:
The Dumas Club: subtle plot (two strands, apparently interlinked), compelling, makes the reader come up with links and suppositions
Congo Journey: more than straight description, brilliant insights into a remote region, meticulous detail on wildlife, superb use of dialogue, funny, moving

Speaker 1: If I had to single out one book from the many I read last year, it would be *The Dumas Club*, by Arturo Pérez-Reverte – that's in translation from the original Spanish. Although I read the opening couple of chapters quite slowly, I soon got completely immersed in the subtleties of the plot, so much so that I quite literally could not put the book down until I had finished it. Some books have this compelling effect on me, and not just detective stories like this one. What is so skilful about the way *The Dumas Club* has been constructed is that there are two strands to the plot, and as a reader you assume these are interwoven and all the time you're engaging with the text on this basis, making links and suppositions of your own. Well, without giving anything away, there is a masterful twist, which makes this an exceptional book.

Speaker 2: I read loads of travel writing, partly because I have a penchant for travelling myself. That said, I do expect a lot more than straight description and first-hand observation from a truly great travel book. Redmond O'Hanlon's masterpiece *Congo Journey* does not disappoint! Will Self – the author – named it as one of his books of the year and said he felt like starting it again the minute he'd finished it, which is praise indeed. I'll certainly re-read it at some point. It's got brilliant insights into what is a really remote region of our planet. There's meticulous detail on its wildlife … and superb use of dialogue. Brings the whole thing to life. And then much more besides – it's funny, moving – so you're reading it on many different levels. Above all, though, you marvel at his sheer guts in enduring such a difficult and dangerous journey. Epic stuff.

3

Answers
a immersed **b** compelling **c** assume **d** suppositions
e masterpiece **f** insights **g** meticulous **h** guts

4 *Subtleties* has a silent 'b'. The silent consonants are underlined in the tapescript.
know̲ledge
w̲retched
rust̲le
r̲hythm
h̲eir
cou̲p
indeb̲ted
ex̲hilarating
denouemen̲t
p̲seudonym
doub̲t
m̲nemonic
condem̲n
apropo̲s
penchan̲t

5 The silent consonant is 'b'.

Answers
```
1   A P R O P O S
2               C O U P
3 M N E M O N I C
4           P E N C H A N T
5           P S E U D O N Y M
6   D E N O U E M E N T
7       I N D E B T E D
```

6 Remember that in Paper 5 Part 3 you need not cover all the prompts on the card in the exam.

Answers
a technological alternatives OR practical advantages
b technological alternatives
c practical advantages

7 Plan your talk, working through the checklist. Record the talk and then analyse it, referring to the checklist.

8

Answers
1 parts **2** token **3** plot **4** body **5** tip

Writing folder 8

Paper 2 Part 2 Set text question pages 142–143

Avoid writing at length about the whole plot in the exam – all set text questions ask something fairly specific about the book you have read.

1 Underline the key parts of the question as you read it.

2

> **Answers**
> 1 G 2 F 3 B 4 D 5 A 6 C

3

> **Answers**
> a B b C c B d E e C f B g E h B
> i E j B k E
>
> **Possible sentences**
> By and large, the author is successful in his portrayal of
>   female characters.
> In much the same way, memories of the past are included
>   as flashbacks.
> As it turns out, Prentice could not have witnessed the
>   event.
> Within a matter of hours, her condition had worsened
>   and she died the following day.
> By the same token, nobody should have been working
>   that day.
> On balance, this is an ambitious first novel, which
>   promises much for this talented young writer's future.

4   Use some of the collocations in your own review later.

> **Possible collocations**
> utterly impressive characterisation
> zealously detailed chronicle
> painstakingly accurate depiction
> utterly enigmatic hero
> hauntingly moving images
> intensely compelling narrative
> ingeniously woven plot
> subtly realistic portrayal
> annoyingly pompous protagonist
> exquisitely intricate storyline

5   Write the review, following the advice given on page 143.

Units 13–16 Revision

pages 144–145

The aim of this revision unit is to focus on the language
covered in Units 13–16, and earlier, as well as extending the
work done on proposals in Writing folder 7. Specific exam
practice is provided for Paper 3 Parts 2, 3 and 4. This Use of
English section could be done as a timed test of 40 minutes.

1

> **Answers**
> 1 unacceptable 2 scientific 3 likelihood

> 4 unobserved 5 patchy 6 complementary
> 7 necessarily 8 maximise/maximize 9 overlapping
> 10 recommendations

2

> **Answers**
> 1 form 2 issue 3 heavy 4 deal 5 rude 6 set

3

> **Answers**
> 1 the outset the man (had) denied
> 2 never saw eye to eye when it
> 3 as I sympathise with the line
> 4 as it may seem / seems (to you)
> 5 is setting / sets great / a lot of store on
> 6 came as (something of) a surprise (to us)

4   The draft proposal has been written as a joke – the date
is 1 April, which is otherwise known as April Fool's Day.

Background information

On April Fool's Day, people in Britain play tricks on their friends
and work colleagues. Newspapers often carry 'spoof' articles –
ones that aren't true. The joke has to be done before midday.

> **Sample answer**
> To the Managing Director   1 April
>
>   As conscientious members of the IT department, we
> would like to propose a few amendments to our working
> conditions. You are aware of our expertise in dealing with
> computing problems company-wide. Indeed, we think it is
> fair to say that we are indispensable. To guarantee a rapid
> response, we have always been willing to work long hours
> whenever necessary. However, we are not prepared to
> continue working in this way unless you can put
> something extra on the table. We would like to suggest
> the following:
>   Firstly, it is unreasonable to expect us to travel in on
> public transport, given that we start very early and stay
> late. Could we perhaps suggest that the company invests
> in some stretch limousines (five should be adequate), to
> cover door-to-door transport. This would clearly lead to
> better productivity and goodwill.
>   Secondly, we are rather disappointed with the
> restaurant downstairs and suggest that it would be more
> convenient if we had our own chef and facility on this
> floor. We feel an extended lunchbreak would be only
> reasonable, as we work so late into the evenings.
>   Thirdly, we regret to tell you that the salaries paid by
> this company are derisory. It would be appropriate for you
> to offer us a little more at this point, particularly given

our track record.

Could you possibly give us some form of response before midday?

With thanks,
Frank McGeek
IT Department

Crossword

This revises idioms and vocabulary which you have encountered up to Unit 16.

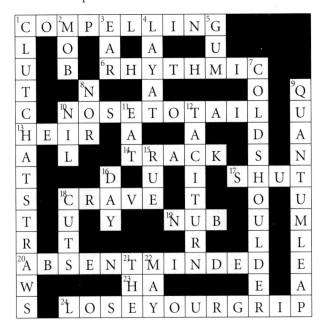

Listening test 4

See page 285 and key on page 287.

Unit 17

17.1 pages 146–147

1 The pictures show:
- a father with his newborn child
- a young couple on a beach
- a man sitting on a remote mountainside
- some young people enjoying a water fight
- a girl reading a book in a hammock.

2

Answers
bliss, ecstasy, idyll
contagious, infectious, virulent
ephemeral, fleeting, transient
foster, nurture, sustain

3 Before playing the recording, spend thirty seconds (the time you will have in Part 4 of the exam) reading the statements. Listen to the recording twice to replicate exam conditions. The underlined parts of the tapescript confirm the answers.

Answers
1 M 2 I 3 M 4 B 5 I 6 B

Miriam: OK, Ian, so we have to try and define happiness, express what it means to us.

Ian: Uh huh, a personal view …

Miriam: That's right. Well, I suppose I would bring to mind certain snapshots in my life, fleeting moments when I was on cloud nine – the birth of each of my children, or, more recently, a forest walk on a beautiful spring morning with the birds singing their hearts out – at times like these, you sort of step outside yourself and think, yes, this is as good as it gets.

Ian: For me it's not transient, I tend to recall whole periods of my life when things were basically going right and I was very content. I suppose I can't have been in the same state of ecstasy from dawn till dusk and for months at a time, but it feels that way – looking back through rose-tinted spectacles, no doubt …

Miriam: But you are a very positive person, so that's probably true for you. At any rate, happiness is not something that lasts forever.

Ian: Sadly not, but I think it can be sustained. Your forest walk, you were alone, I take it?

Miriam: Yeah, my experiences of extreme happiness often come on me that way, take me by surprise when there's no one around to witness the fact.

Ian: Whereas in my case, nine times out of ten it's all to do with those around me – positive vibes fostered by goodwill, like infectious laughter rippling through a bunch of friends.

Miriam: And what about home life, does that have a bearing too?

Ian: Absolutely fundamental, yeah – being in a stable relationship, sharing a good bottle of wine in front of the fire.

Miriam: Mmm, I'm actually enjoying being a household of one right now, but if you're talking crackling logs, well, that's the bee's knees! Happiness is being curled up on the sofa with a long book while the wind's howling outside. So the aspects of comfort and security are key ingredients to happiness, aren't they?

Ian: I'm not convinced they are prerequisites. Sometimes I have felt a surge of joy in the midst of a truly perilous situation, say scaling a difficult peak with a fellow-climber. You put yourself on the line and achieve the impossible through teamwork. That's something which also brings about happiness.

Miriam: In any event, <u>you wouldn't take issue with this, er, that there's an identifiable element that tips the balance</u> – be it my forest birds or your craggy summit?

Ian: <u>Sure, that's normally the case</u>, isn't it? Oh wait, I'm getting a vivid image now of another special time, this was real lotus-eating, the classic desert island idyll …

Miriam: Holiday?

Ian: Work, in fact. I was studying marine activity on a coral reef, part of a close-knit research team on this otherwise unpopulated island.

Miriam: Sounds bliss.

Ian: Utter and complete. Anyway, there was one day when I'd done three separate dives, the last at night, and I was so exhilarated I couldn't turn in. Unusually for me I was alone – I lay on the ghostly white sand listening to the ocean, transfixed by the canopy of stars above me, with *A Kind of Blue* on the headphones, to nurture the well-being!

Miriam: Music, always useful for maximising the experience …

Ian: Whether it's jazz or classical …

Miriam: Solo piano or opera …

Ian: Uh, <u>no vocals for me, that just trivialises the whole thing</u>.

Miriam: Beg to differ there, it's definitely 'play on' in my book, whatever the genre.

Ian: Fair enough. So, music, good company, the natural world, <u>is there anything else that acts as a catalyst</u>?

Miriam: <u>Bodily sustenance</u>! A delicate, creamy bowl of pasta with wild mushrooms on an empty stomach …

Ian: <u>The perfect omelette, plenty of fresh bread</u>, washed down with an exquisite glass of red.

Miriam: Mmm, food for thought – it doesn't always take much to achieve happiness, does it?

Ian: And yet, and yet, it may be an old cliché, but it's true, you can't buy it, not at any price.

Idiom spot

Find and underline the idioms in the tapescript above.

Answers
a be extremely happy
b a tendency to view everything positively
c just right
d commit yourself, stand up for what you believe in
e sway (an argument) in one direction
f enjoying oneself doing nothing, usually in an exotic (holiday) setting
g according to my way of thinking
h worth thinking about

Suggested answers
1 In the roomful of people, Jack was the only one to put himself on the line and challenge the speaker.

2 After the U2 concert, Sheena was on cloud nine.
3 In my book, children should show respect for their elders.
4 The fact that the sun was shining tipped the balance and they took the day off.

Style extra

Some use of metaphor in Paper 2 (and Paper 5, if the tasks are suitable) will impress the examiner.

4

Suggested answers
bruised egos
contagious criticism
fatal dose of scepticism, flaw in the argument
feverish state of activity
healthy bank balance, criticism, dose of scepticism, turnout of voters
jaundiced criticism, sense of humour
sick sense of humour, bank balance
sore loser

5 Metaphors may be easier to learn by topic. An excellent book on this area for learners of English is the *Collins Cobuild English Guide 7: Metaphor* by Alice Deignan (HarperCollins), also *Meanings and Metaphors: Activities to practise figurative language* by Gillian Lazar (Cambridge University Press).

Answers
a growth/plants   b water/liquid   c fire
d bad weather/storms   e light   f cooking

6 Be careful not to mix your metaphors (see second answer below).

Possible answers
The recent wave of violent protests against globalisation have caused many injuries.
There's a whirlwind of activity at our house just before we go away on holiday. (Note: *feverish* has been deleted, as this would be a 'mixed' metaphor.)

7

Background information

Gerald Durrell, younger brother of the writer Lawrence Durrell, grew up on the Greek island of Corfu, which is where his interest in the natural world began.

> **Answers**
> 1 B 2 C 3 C 4 D 5 A 6 B

8

> **Answers**
> **Similes** as gently and clingingly as pollen
>   glossy and colourful as a child's transfer
> **Metaphor** the dark skin of night would peel off
>   barred with gold

17.2 pages 148–149

1 The picture shows a marble bust of the ancient Greek philosopher Epicurus. The word 'natural' in the three headings means that it is understandable for a human being to want such things.

2

> **Answers**
> 1 of 2 odds 3 What 4 other/previous/earlier
> 5 its/the/an 6 Few 7 not 8 whose 9 despite
> 10 further/far 11 to 12 rather/more 13 Such/These
> 14 reached/drawn 15 however

3 Add extra words in front of the comparative adjectives to vary the answers (see below).

> **Suggested answers**
> a I would be much more glad to hear that a friend had recovered than to be offered a free trip to New York.
> b As delighted as I would be to win a competition, I would be far more delighted to have found something special that I had lost.
> c I would feel a great deal more content after a bar of chocolate on an empty stomach than after a meal with some boring relation!

5 Statements a–h exemplify other comparative structures. See the Grammar folder on page 186.

> **Possible answers**
> a I'm actually happier now than I was then.
> b I agree, it's often more enjoyable to eat good food at home in good company.
> c I disagree!
> d Obviously the most important thing to anyone is to be in good health.
> e It depends – sometimes it is easier to hear the songs at home, though it is definitely more exciting to be there on the spot.
> f I disagree, it is far better to watch than play, especially during the winter.

> g It is a remedy, but the best one is to meet someone else who you care for.
> h I'd have to agree with this one – it's not nearly as comfortable being out in a snowstorm as being inside by the fire.

6

> **Answers**
> 1 pulled out all the stops to
> 2 changed his tune / sang a different tune
> 3 keep a straight face in such
> 4 on cloud nine at winning/gaining/getting first
>   OR on cloud nine when she won/got/gained first
> 5 nowhere near as much
> 6 living in clover but since being / since he was / since he has been OR living in clover but on being

17.3 pages 150–151

1 The pictures show:
- a healthy-looking woman riding a horse
- a large house with a swimming pool
- a fit and active family running along a beach.

2 Unit 17 and Unit 19 have complete Paper 3 Part 5 tasks. Remember to write concise answers for questions 1–4. In this unit, the summary task comes after exercise 3, an exercise on synonyms, which should help you when you write your summary.

> **Suggested answers**
> 1 because they are concerned with the welfare of our environment, which affects how we feel
> 2 the fundamental drive to reproduce and thus maintain a species
> 3 they moved because their lives were adversely affected by their pressurised city lifestyle
> 4 death (often personified as a black figure carrying a scythe)

3 Before choosing the best synonyms look back at the text in order to see how each word was used.

> **Answers**
> a surroundings b dispositions c result
> d remunerative e nominal f constraints g flimsy

4

> **Sample answer**
> Four aspects that promote happiness and well-being are identified. Both texts consider physical surroundings important, whether in terms of quality of housing or a

beautiful landscape. Good health and a positive mental disposition are also singled out as pre-conditions. Finally, the individual needs a lifestyle not tied to remuneration and requiring only nominal outside commitments, to allow for 'quality time', exemplified in the second text by family life and hill-walking.

(70 words)

Idiom spot

The idiom *make ends meet* means manage on very little money.

> **Answers**
> **a** feel the pinch   **b** tighten your belt
> **c** keep you head above water   **d** cut corners
>
> *cut corners* – save time, money or effort by not following the usual procedure
> *down and out* – without hope and usually without a job or place to live
> *keep your head above water* – struggle to survive, usually under pressure
> *feel the pinch* – have less money than previously and suffer as a result
> *in the red* – overdrawn at the bank
> *do something on a shoestring* – do something with very little money
> *on your uppers* – having very little money
> *tighten your belt* – economise

Exam folder 9

Paper 4 Part 1
Multiple-choice questions   page 152

1   In the examination there are four different extracts. Here, there are only two because of lack of space. Play each extract twice. The underlined parts of the tapescript confirm the answers.

> **Answers**
> **1** A   **2** B   **3** C   **4** A

Part 1.
You will hear two different extracts. For questions 1–4, choose the answer (A, B or C) which fits best according to what you hear. There are two questions for each extract.

Extract 1

Man: From what I can tell from this current CD, apparently the singer Ellen Gray is on cloud nine and now leaning towards pop music.

Woman: Yes, it'll probably come as a surprise to some people; it might not appeal to many, but she has always been full of surprises and contradictions.

Man: Mm …, interesting isn't it – the alternative artist who has always refused to conform to mainstream notions of musical genres, but who has just made a commercial album which looks set to be a hit. Why do you think that is?

Woman: It looks as if she has now found a kind of fulfilment, after years of swimming against the tide. And with that fulfilment has come a looser, more relaxed approach to both her singing and the way she deals with fame, I guess. After hits like *Needing You* and *Crying Out*, Gray seemed hardly likely to make an album celebrating happiness in love. But with her new album, that is exactly what she has done.

Man: Well, she certainly seems to have got over her aversion to pop and with this new album she has definitely proved that she can do it.

Extract 2 (extracted from an article by Simon Pooley first published in The Independent on Sunday 8 April 2001)

Critic: The artist Kate Schermerhorn claims to view her native culture with affection, but the fact that she left her homeland and has lived in London since 1995 suggests that what might be *America's Idea of a Good Time* – the title to her show – isn't necessarily hers. Her images depict a largely blue-collar collection of Americans amusing themselves in ways that only a nation hopelessly committed to the pursuit of personal happiness could devise. *Largest Waterslide Park West of Mississippi* gives an overhead view of a gaggle of day-trippers aimlessly drifting along the artificial waterway in their inflatable doughnuts. In *Demolition Derby Winner with local beauty Queen* we find the most unlikely pair of champions: the check-shirted and bushy-bearded Derby victor and a vapid-looking beauty queen. As with most of the characters in Schermerhorn's aberrant parade of hedonists, their quest for enjoyment is rendered inconsequential and naive or perhaps, at worst, even vulgar and trashy. The restrained documentary style in which the photographs depict their subject matter contrives sardonically to offer the recreational kinks of these diverse individuals for our amusement, rather than suggesting a sentimental reaction to such eccentricity.

Paper 4 Part 3
Multiple choice questions   page 153

2   This is a complete Part 3 question. Play it twice. The underlined parts of the tapescript confirm the answers.

> **Answers**
> **1** D   **2** B   **3** D   **4** C   **5** A

Part 3.

You will hear an interview with Darren Roberts, who recently decided to give up his well-paid job in the City of London in order to do voluntary work. For questions 1–5, choose the answer (A, B, C or D) which fits best according to what you hear.

You now have one minute in which to look at Part 3.

Interviewer: After eight years, working in his high-powered job in the City of London, Darren Roberts decided that he no longer cared about his job or his clients and wasn't even bothered about getting his annual bonus. Darren, how did this all come about?

Darren: Well, having loathed my job for a year, I mean just sitting in my office made me tense and irritable, my performance was pretty poor. People told me it was just a temporary thing, but in my heart I knew my career there was over. <u>Yet what else could I possibly do?</u> The job I did provided few transferable skills and basically nothing else paid nearly as well. Though that wasn't much of a problem as I had a tidy sum in the bank. Really, the only thing stopping me was myself.

Interviewer: So that was when you started applying for other jobs?

Darren: Um … Not really. Well, I didn't know what I wanted to do; I only knew what I didn't. More months passed with me stuck in my rut until another friend got drunk and told me to 'go and do voluntary work or something'.

Interviewer: How did you react to that advice?

Darren: Strangely enough, pretty well. I decided to take some time off and volunteer for a charity. I reckoned that if I guaranteed them six months, during that time I would be bound to find a proper job, you know a paid one! It wasn't quite as easy as I thought, though. I decided to apply to 12 well-known charities, ranging from overseas aid to homelessness. I put in my applications, <u>but I guess my lack of real conviction and experience was pretty obvious, and they saw straight through me.</u> They didn't even bother to reply.

Interviewer: Presumably things did improve?

Darren: Yeah – I got a lucky break. A friend of a friend had a contact with one of the charities I had applied to. She gave me a name, Anna Rogers, and within days Anna had come back with a proposal. Now, I'm a history graduate and I'd spent eight years on a trading floor in the city so most of her spiel on government research papers went straight over my head, but I did manage to make out that she wanted me to find out about schemes that prevented or alleviated homelessness. <u>I jumped at the chance and handed in my notice straightaway.</u> My colleagues told me they'd thought I'd never really do it – they had no idea how desperate I was.

Interviewer: And how did the new job go?

Darren: Well, I actually found it a bit on the quiet side, but that was OK. I could hear the tapping of keyboards and conversations on the phone. Even the people were different – they spoke in whole sentences, without the 'yeah, yeah, right, right, offer this, bid that, done' tempo I was used to. I was expecting a collection of meek do-gooders, and I was surprised to find they were OK, and <u>I just got on with things.</u> They were a nice bunch and were only mildly curious as to why I had given up a well-paid job. The biggest surprise, however, was me. Being a bit of a cynic about these things, I never expected to enjoy it so much.

Interviewer: And I believe you stayed on longer than you anticipated?

Darren: It took five months to complete the project. That done, I had no real desire to leave and volunteered for another couple of months, writing bits and pieces, even stuffing envelopes. It was novel to be working 14-hour days without moaning for what I once regarded as a pittance. I don't think the City is an easy life. There are too many egos, too many targets to achieve for it ever to be a breeze. Equally, <u>it's not that tough; it just wasn't right for me, while this is.</u> I feel pretty stupid that it took me so long to figure that out. I'm just glad I got there in the end and I can now look back on it as the best year of my life!

Unit 18

18.1 pages 154–155

1 Think about the bulleted points in relation to all parts of the world.

> **Possible answers**
> - Slavery exists in different parts of the world, for example in West Africa.
> - There are many repressive regimes around the world where people suffer these infringements on their personal liberty.
> - I suppose everyone has a nationality, though not always the one they would like – perhaps their country is under the control of another.
> - Religious intolerance is prevalent in many societies; freedom of thought is not always possible under a dictatorship.

2 The picture shows the tearing down of the Berlin Wall in 1989, which signalled the end of the 'Cold War' and led to the re-unification of Germany.

Carry out the gapped text task, following the advice given in Exam folder 5 on page 83. Remember to underline key words and phrases in both the base text and the paragraphs.

Answers
1 E 2 H 3 B 4 F 5 D 6 A 7 G

4

Answers
a in limbo   b a rather faltering endeavour
c a loosening of the reins   d a (soft) sideshow
e dealing a blow to   f remit

5

Answers
a have a lot of influence
b expansion (in the number of)
c made people more aware of
d auspicious, favourable
e violate, encroach on
f confirmed in
g put forward by
h under the direction of

18.2 pages 156–157

1 The poster is by the British Union for the Abolition of Vivisection and shows a dog that is used for animal experiments.

2 The speaker is against animal testing.

Two and a half million animals are used in Australian medical research every year, half a million in Victoria alone. They justify the obscene waste of life like this. Animals must be used in order to trial new drugs and treatments safely. But, a growing number of doctors and scientists have challenged this line, saying that in fact, animal research is counterproductive. It could in fact be damaging to human health. This is because animals are not like us – their bodies are different, they suffer from different diseases and obviously their reactions to drugs are also different. So animals cannot be used to find cures for humans.
Why does animal testing continue? Answer, it's a huge industry. There are many, many vested interests in animal research, from the big pharmaceutical companies themselves to the manufacturers of the cages that these poor dumb animals end up in. Then, apart from those obvious commercial interests, there are the many scientists who have chosen to base their careers on animal experiments. They would lose their jobs tomorrow if animal testing was stopped, wouldn't they?
Basically, animal research is the ultimate quick fix. You generally need many years to monitor the progression of a human disease. Obviously laboratory animals, with their

shorter lifespans, tend to decline more rapidly. This means that research projects can be wrapped up quickly. Papers presented, trials successfully concluded, bam, new drugs hit the market. It can't be scientifically sound. But what *should* have been done – full-scale controlled monitoring within a human population – is ruled out as uneconomic. The hard truth is that just about every medical advance has come about either independently from or despite animal research. You shouldn't believe everything you hear, right?

3

Answers
a can be kept ... must have
b must be changed
c ought to have been / should have been
d (correct)
e can't have been
f wouldn't have bought
g could live
h wouldn't

4

Answers
a shouldn't have   b might have   c must have
d needn't   e don't have to   f shouldn't   g Ought
h Would

5

Answers
1 to have put in more
2 have been less humane prior to the establishment
3 put themselves / their job on the line
4 have let us know (about) Lisa's / let us in on Lisa's
5 the record straight about how
6 raise any objections to my

6

Background information

The text comes from the book *The New Existentialism* by Colin Wilson, a British philosopher whose most famous book *The Outsider* was written when he was only 24.

Answers
1 insignificant   2 evolutionary   3 sufficient
4 interminable   5 consciousness   6 submissively
7 empower   8 resourceful   9 footing   10 natural

18.3 pages 158–159

1 The pictures show:
   - children working in a carpet factory
   - someone making a speech at Speaker's Corner in Hyde Park, London
   - a demonstration being broken up violently by the police.

2 Look at the pictures as you listen to the first part of the recording. Notice how the man keeps interrupting the woman and doesn't allow her to give her own opinions. He also challenges what she says quite aggressively, which is rather unfair in an interview situation.

Interlocutor: Now, in this part of the test you're going to do something together. Here are some pictures on the theme of freedom. First, I'd like you to look at pictures A and C and talk together about what might have happened just after these photos were taken. You have about a minute for this, so don't worry if I interrupt you.

Man: Shall I start?

Woman: Sure, go ahead.

Man: Well, I'll choose the easier of the two – it's nowhere near as difficult to speculate about picture C as picture A! So, if we consider what C shows, it's some kind of demonstration which may have started off peacefully but has obviously turned sour. It could be one of the anti-globalisation protests, they're quite violent. The police are in there, there'll obviously be lots of arrests, and maybe worse, physical abuse of some kind …

Woman: The … there's a doctor or someone with a medical training there, the armband has a red cross, it doesn't look good …

Man: Yes, yes. The police might take away banners, too, that's what often happens in situations like this.

Woman: To … trying to suppress the message, but they probably won't win in the …

Man: We can't say that. It all depends on how … on the crowd control. Anyway, what about picture A? What might have happened after that photo was taken?

Woman: Well, I'm sure the owners of the factory weren't too happy with the photographer, so perhaps they tried to confiscate the film.

Man: But we're looking at the photo, so what you suggest can't be true!

Woman: I didn't say they succeeded. Yes, obviously the photographer …

Man: Perhaps it was taken in secret? That's what that kind of investigative journalist often does, take in a camera under the jacket and, you know, trigger it by scratching their arm or coughing or something.

Woman: Uh-huh.

Man: Thank you.

3 Play the second part. The candidates decide to include additional photos to do with education and animal rights.

Interlocutor: Now, I'd like you to look at all three pictures. I'd like you to imagine that they are all going to be used in a book about freedom. Talk together about the aspects of freedom that are shown. Then suggest two other aspects of freedom that you feel should be included in the book.
You have about three minutes to talk about this.

Woman: Well, we've already identified political freedom and the rights of children, haven't we? Looking at picture B, I suppose it's illustrating the rights of the individual, isn't it?

Man: Mmm, yes. It's taken in Hyde Park in London, the place is called Speaker's Corner and every Sunday …

Woman: I didn't know that. Anyway, the man is holding forth to the crowd about something, so it's all about free speech. He's rather unusually dressed, he's got a mortar board on his head like teachers used to wear, and look, he's wearing a real dog's collar! That's underlining the message of personal liberty – in a liberal society, you can wear what you want.

Man: Yes, that's an important point, you don't have that freedom of choice everywhere. Well, we have to suggest other aspects of freedom to include in this book.

Woman: Speaking purely for myself, I'd want to include something on education. It's a basic human right. I suppose it's linked to those girls in the factory, they're being deprived of what they should be doing at that age, going to school and learning. If they can't read and write, they'll be trapped for the rest of their lives.

Man: That's true. But how would you select a photo to show this type of freedom? If you just show a class of school children, it wouldn't make the point, education's something we take for granted.

Woman: Right, well fortunately, we don't have to worry about which photo is actually chosen, but I do think the book should focus on education.

Man: Oh yes, yes, I agree. And then, something else? Freedom of the press maybe, that's part of political freedom, but also the book could focus on how the paparazzi chase after famous people, you'd get a good photo of that!

Woman: I'm not sure that's strictly about freedom, though. And it seems rather flippant, after we've been considering basic human rights like education and freedom of speech. What about including animal rights? It's an important element – we're not the only species on the planet, after all.

Man: But now I'm beginning to wonder what the focus of this book is. I mean, you can't just call it 'Freedom' and put everything in it – there would have to be some limits?

Woman: I don't see why. It would be very interesting. Perhaps a bit long.

Man: Just a little! … Well, OK, we'll include animal rights. But in my humble opinion, the book will become very unwieldy, an editor's nightmare.
Woman: Maybe …
Interlocutor: Thank you.

4   Read the Exam spot and then listen to utterances a–f, which have been recorded separately. Repeat after the speaker, paying particular attention to your stress and intonation.

Tapescript

a   Anyway what about picture A? What might have happened after that photo was taken?
b   I didn't say they succeeded.
c   Looking at picture B, I suppose it's illustrating the rights of the individual, isn't it?
d   Yes, that's an important point, you don't have that freedom of choice everywhere.
e   Speaking purely for myself, I'd want to include something on education.
f   I'm not sure that's strictly about freedom, though.

5   Read the task and spend just a few seconds thinking about your ideas – you won't have longer in the exam!

6

> **Answers**
> **1** rally   **2** dipped   **3** drift   **4** quarters
> **5** supporting   **6** bill

Writing folder 9

Paper 2 Part 1 Essay pages 160–161

1   Before reading the task, look back at the advice given in writing folder 3 on page 57.

2   The sample answer would not receive a good mark in the exam.

3   Tick the boxes that apply to the answer.

> **Answers**
> The script shows the following features:
> Limited range
> Some attempt at organisation
> Inadequate development of topic
> Errors sometimes impede communication
>
> The answer is also too short (about 230 words).

4

> **Corrected and improved paragraph 1**
> In order to review the status of civil liberty in the 21st century, it is necessary to assess the human rights provided under the legal system. A criminal may believe that he or she has personal freedom, but anything that goes against the social code will be punished. This essay will also look at the issue of prejudice, assess whether every world citizen enjoys the same rights and whether everyone is permitted to transfer from one place to another, or is confined in some way.

5   Remember to show range and variety of expression in the exam.

> **Possible answers**
> | Paragraph 1 | you need to encompass freedom within the law
This essay considers both sides |
> | --- | --- |
> | Paragraph 3 | On the other hand, in my view, we must be tolerant of others and what they believe |
> | Paragraph 4 | Of course it cannot be denied that
Other countries should investigate this |
> | Paragraph 5 | In my book, freedom is an illusion |

6   As paragraph 2 contains two separate ideas, it should be split into two paragraphs (see below).

> **Sample answers**
>
> **Paragraph 2**
> It goes without saying that every society needs a legal system, which people must observe and adhere to. In the absence of laws, people will not be aware of what code they must abide by and the result would be total anarchy.
> *(New paragraph needed here)*
> In some parts of the world, people do not have freedom of worship or, if they feel intimidated, they choose not to practise their religion. Even in multicultural societies this can be a problem and is an affront to basic human rights.
>
> **Paragraph 4**
> Of course it cannot be denied that equal rights for every citizen is a fundamental principle, but we have not yet achieved this. Slavery still exists in some parts of the world, with children as young as four being sold by their families and forced to work in richer countries against their will. This is an infringement of their rights and other countries should investigate this practice and campaign for an end to such a barbaric trade.

7 In Paragraph 3, the final sentence shows some misunderstanding of the question: freedom of movement has been misinterpreted. The tone is unduly personal here (you/I) and the register inconsistent, with inappropriately informal language.

8 Look back at Units 17 and 18 for ideas and relevant vocabulary.

Sample concluding paragraph
Although in many respects we have come a long way since the end of the Second World War, contemporary society is still not as enlightened as it should be. The tireless work done by Amnesty International and similar organisations shows that there is a long way to go. In my book, freedom is an illusion – the battle has not yet been won.

9

Sample answer
In order to review the status of civil liberty in the 21st century, it is necessary to assess the human rights provided under the legal system. A criminal may believe that he or she has personal freedom, but anything that goes against the social code will be punished. This essay will also look at the issue of prejudice, assess whether every world citizen enjoys the same rights and whether everyone is permitted to transfer from one place to another, or is confined in some way.

It goes without saying that every society needs a legal system, which people must observe and adhere to. In the absence of laws, people will not be aware of what code they must abide by and the result would be total anarchy.

In some parts of the world, people do not have freedom of worship or, if they feel intimidated, they choose not to practise their religion. Even in multicultural societies this can be a problem and is an affront to basic human rights.

Freedom of movement is sometimes denied, especially in countries whose regimes are oppressive. Before the Berlin Wall came down and Germany was unified, for example, it was impossible for people in East Berlin to visit their relatives in West Berlin. In my view this is an intolerable way to treat ordinary people, who have suffered because of a political decision.

Of course it cannot be denied that equal rights for every citizen is a fundamental principle, but we have not yet achieved this. Slavery still exists in some parts of the world, with children as young as four being sold by their families and forced to work in richer countries against their will. This is an infringement of their rights and other countries should investigate this practice and campaign for an end to such a barbaric trade.

Although in many respects we have come a long way since the end of the Second World War, contemporary society is still not as enlightened as it should be. The tireless work done by Amnesty International and similar organisations shows that there is a long way to go. In my book, freedom is an illusion – the battle has not yet been won.

Unit 19

19.1 pages 162–163

1 The photo is of the Treasurer's House in York, a city in the north-east of England. The story you will hear is true.

Possible answer
I don't believe in ghosts, I think they are the product of people's imaginations. I'd take a torch and maybe a good book to read as I'm sure I wouldn't see or hear anything. On the other hand, maybe I would also take some garlic to ward off the devil and evil spirits, just in case!

2 The adjectives refer to personality. Use an English–English dictionary if necessary to find the odd one out.

Answers
a sceptical The other words all have the idea of 'easy to mislead or deceive'. *Sceptical* means 'doesn't believe things easily'.
b derisive The other words all mean 'easy to deceive'. *Derisive* means 'not worth taking seriously'.
c apathetic The others all have an active meaning. *Apathetic* is passive.
d sensible The other words have the meaning of being aware of things. *Sensible* means 'having common sense – knowing what to do'.
e temperamental The other words refer to people who are 'down to earth'. *Temperamental* is the opposite of this.
f upright It is a positive word, the others are all negative.

Suggested answer
Someone who believes in ghosts is gullible, naïve, credulous and impressionable.

3 Read through the questions and try to predict the answers. Play the recording twice. The underlined parts of the tapescript confirm the answers.

Answers
1 chains 2 burial 3 crisis apparition 4 a patch of mist / some mist 5 a/an (apprentice) plumber 6 a ladder 7 waist 8 a wash and shave 9 an over-sized dagger

Presenter: Good morning. Today we're going to talk about one aspect of the supernatural – ghosts. Now, ghosts have always been with us and are as much of a mystery now as they were in the first century AD, when Athenodorus, a hard-up philosopher, rented a house in Athens which was cheap because of its eerie reputation. Sitting working late at night, Athenodorus heard the rattling of chains and, suddenly, the horrifying figure of an old man appeared before him. It beckoned to him and, although Athenodorus tried to ignore it and get on with his work, it refused to let him. So Athenodorus followed the ghost into the garden, where it pointed to a spot on the ground and disappeared. Next day, a hole was dug at the place indicated by the ghost and a human skeleton was discovered. After the remains were given a proper burial and the house purified, the haunting ceased.

This was clearly a ghost with a purpose, but usually the reason for haunting is not clear. There have been a few modern cases where ghosts seemed to have a message, such as a 'crisis apparition' of a person, seen by close friends and relatives at the time of his or her death, an event unknown to them until confirmation came later. However, in many ghost sightings, there seems to be no purpose and the ghost's identity remains unknown. Some people are sceptical and do not believe in the existence of ghosts. It is indeed likely that some witnesses who claim to have seen ghosts out of doors have, in fact, mistaken a patch of mist for a human figure, especially if they have been alone and the place was eerie. Other people may have vivid imaginations and 'see' externally something that is really only in their mind.

One of the most vivid apparitions on record was that seen in 1953 by 18-year-old Harry Martindale. Now retired, but an apprentice plumber at the time of the sighting, Martindale was working in the Treasurer's House in York. One day he was at work in the cellar, when to his astonishment and fright he saw a Roman soldier step out of the wall. He instantly dropped his tools. What he did not know at the time was that he had put his ladder on the course of an old Roman road. He later described in detail what he had witnessed.

Harry: I heard a sound – the only way I can describe it is the sound of a musical note. At the same time, a figure came out of the wall. And the head of the figure was in line with my waist, with a shining helmet. I was terrified. I got out of the way and scrambled into the corner. And from there, I got a bird's eye view of what it was. It was the head of a Roman soldier. He crossed the room and disappeared into a pillar. Then another soldier on horseback came by, followed by soldiers walking in pairs, side by side.

You couldn't see through them. They were all about one metre five, in want of a good wash and shave. Nothing smart about them. They all had the same helmets on, with the plume coming out of the back, down the neck. They all carried a short sword on the right-hand side. I used to think that Roman soldiers carried a long sword, but this was similar to an over-sized dagger. And they went as quick as they came. When they were in the centre of the cellar, I could hear a murmuring – no speech, just a murmuring.

Presenter: When the museum curator found the terrified boy collapsed at the top of the cellar steps, he immediately knew what had happened because he had seen the soldiers himself seven years before. And he knew the plumber didn't know that the soldiers' legs were missing because they were walking on the course of the old Roman road, which was beneath the cellar floor.

4

> **Possible answer**
> I think that Harry's experience was probably the result of drinking beer at lunchtime or maybe overwork. I can't believe this actually happened.

Style extra

Using onomatopoeic words will help give life to your writing.

> **Suggested answers**
> Chains were described as 'rattling' and the Roman soldiers as 'murmuring'.
> creak – wooden floors
> hiss – steam, a snake
> crunch – gravel or crisp snow when walked on
> peal – bells, laughter
> click – door lock
> rumble – thunder, train on track
> drip – a tap
> slam – a door
> squelch – mud
> screech – parrot, brakes
> slap – waves on the beach, hand against face.
> tinkle – a bell; broken glass
> growl – angry dog, people
> slash – an angry person cutting cloth viciously with a knife
> slither – snake moving smoothly, person sliding down or across something smooth
>
> **a** creaked **b** squelched **c** slashed **d** slithered
> **e** crunches **f** dripping **g** tinkled **h** hissed
>
> **Possible answer**
> I was lying in bed at home one night – all alone, except for my dog, as, for once, my family had gone out for the evening to a concert. It was a cold, rainy evening and the shutters had begun to bang against the side of the bedroom wall. I could hear the wind getting up and it howling down the chimney. Suddenly, I heard something

tinkle, like glass breaking, then a crunch. I turned over, determined not to be spooked by this. Then, there was a creak. This is when I began to get worried, as I knew the third stair from the bottom always creaked. Betsy began to growl softly and then I knew that something was really wrong. I reached for my mobile phone.

5 Read through the text, which explains what a poltergeist is.

Answers
1 B is correct. A is when something is written in stone or metal; C is written in a meeting; D is for a course or in school.
2 A is correct because the text goes on to give the translation of the word.
3 C is correct. *Turned over* means 'being put upside down'.
4 D is correct because it is the only verb here that is reflexive.
5 B is correct because it collocates with 'rules'.
6 A is correct because it gives the meaning of 'started'. B, C and D need the preposition 'from'.

19.2 pages 164–165

1 Refer to the Grammar folder on page 187. The examples given cover most of the basic word order rules. Some words can change order depending on what you want to emphasise.

Answers
a Yesterday I went home on foot. OR I went home on foot yesterday.
b Later she briskly walked up the hill to where, luckily, another coach was waiting.
c Last night I was hardly in the mood to go swimming. OR I was hardly in the mood to go swimming last night.
d Of course he is still lying. OR He is still lying, of course. OR (with the meaning of not moving) Of course he is lying still.
e In fact, Stephen spoke to me in a friendly way the other day.
f Strangely enough, it rained heavily non-stop all day. OR It rained heavily non-stop all day, strangely enough.
g Apparently, people rarely hide things of value in the attic.
h She performed the dance far too slowly.
i To be honest, I think you should get out of the house more often.
j I saw the comet in the sky only yesterday. OR Only yesterday, I saw the comet in the sky.

2 Make sure you pay attention to punctuation when you do this exercise.

B ackground information

Ayers Rock or Uluru (its Aboriginal name) is a huge red rock in SW Northern Territory, Australia, 450 km SW of Alice Springs. It rises from the desert to a height of 348 metres. It is the largest monolith in the world.

Answers
a Another tells how after a terrible battle …
b One legend states that Uluru was originally a lake.
c that has been sacred to the Aboriginal people for hundreds of years.
d Many aboriginal paintings tell important Earth stories.
e the time when the world was created.
f the Earth rose up in revolt at the bloodshed to form the great blood-coloured rock.
g They believe that it was made by spirits in the 'Dreamtime' …

The order is c, g, e, d, b, a, f

3 Refer to the notes about adverbs and adjectives.

hard means difficult or not soft; *hardly* means not very much
short means not tall; *shortly* means soon
right and *rightly* mean correctly; *right* is only used after verbs and is informal
high is similar to tall; *highly* means a great deal
late is the opposite of early; *lately* means recently
wrong can be used informally after a verb

Answers
a hardly b highly c wrongly/rightly d hard
e shortly f wrong (also possibly wrongly or right)
g lately h right i short

4 This text gives background information on how to carry out a ghost hunt.

Answers
1 deal 2 before 3 carry 4 of 5 addition 6 on
7 a 8 As 9 and 10 may/might/could/would/can
11 at 12 taken 13 all
14 while/whilst/though/although 15 finding

19.3 pages 166–167

1 The pictures are of things which are supposed to bring good luck.

The four-leaf clover is popular in the UK, the little bag in Mexico, the St Christopher in Catholic countries, the white heather in Scotland and the evil eye in Greece.

2 These are common expressions.

> **Answers**
> Talk of the devil! – said when you mention someone and they then appear
> to have a guardian angel – said about the feeling that there is someone you can't see who protects you
> It's a small world. – said about a coincidence involving people known to both speakers
> to have second sight – to be able to know what will happen in the future
> female intuition – a feeling about something that might happen that women are supposed to have
> a feeling of déjà vu – a feeling of being in a place you've visited before or of experiencing something that has happened before

3 Refer to the advice in Exam folder 3. This is a complete Part 5 question.

> **Answers**
> 1 that they were in touch with the paranormal as they had no reason to believe anything was wrong
> 2 the correlation between the dreams etc. and something happening
> 3 mundane
> 4 not afraid of the unknown / not superstitious / not imagining things which can't be seen
> 5 The summary needs to contain the following points: People who have experience of the paranormal …
> … want to remain anonymous
> … may experience physical symptoms
> … are embarrassed/worried/puzzled by the experience
> … may act impulsively.
>
> People who have no experience of the paranormal…
> … are cynical/rude about the people involved.
>
> **Summary answer**
> People with experience of the paranormal often worry or are embarrassed by the experience. They may think that other people will think they are crazy so they try to keep their experience quiet to avoid ridicule. Additionally, they might have physical symptoms or act impulsively or even try to remain anonymous. However, people with no experience of it often dismiss it out of hand.
> (64 words)

4 Look through the texts again in order to find the words and describe which part of speech they are.

> **Answers**
> imagery (noun) image, imagination, imaginative, imagine, unimaginative, unimaginatively
> conscious (adj) unconscious, subconscious, consciousness
> impression (noun) impress, impressive, unimpressive, impressively, impressionable
> impulse (noun) impulsive, impulsively

> psychical (adj) psychiatrist, psychologist, psychologically, psychological, psychic
> dismissed (past participle) dismiss, dismissive, dismissal
> coincidences (noun) coincidental, coincide, coincidentally
> speak out (phrasal verb) outspoken
> anonymity (noun) anonymous, anonymously
> childhood (noun) childish, childlike
> disturbing (adj) disturb, disturbance, undisturbed, disturbed, disturbingly

5

> **Answers**
> **a** outspoken **b** dismissive **c** anonymous
> **d** childish **e** disturbance **f** impressionable
> **g** psychiatrists/psychologists **h** subconscious

Exam folder 10

Paper 5 Speaking pages 168–169

In the examination there will be two or three students and two examiners. For the purpose of this test you should try to find someone to play the part of another student or the examiner.

Make sure that the timing is correct: Part 1 – 3 minutes, Part 2 – 4 minutes and Part 3 – 12 minutes. There can be anything from one to seven pictures/visuals in the examination. Here there are five photographs.

The photographs for Part 2 are as follows:
A a Ford Ka
B an iMac computer
C a book
D a clock
E a refrigerator

Unit 20

20.1 pages 170–171

1 Scan the text to find out what impression Bill Bryson gives of life in the USA.

> **Possible answer**
> He gives the impression of someone who is fairly happy to be back in his own country, but with reservations. He is enjoying playing with new toys.

2

Answers

1 **D** is correct because he talks about her enjoying simple pleasures like iced water and she thinks the waitress is just being nice to *her*, not everybody she meets. **A** is wrong because although he mentions food he doesn't say anything about it. **B** is wrong because she does get things for nothing, but nothing suggests that she might not be happy if she didn't. **C** is wrong because he says she is 'slavishly uncritical'.

2 **A** is correct because he thinks a National Health Service is more important. **B** is wrong because he doesn't mention money. **C** is wrong because he doesn't criticise the way things are done. **D** is wrong because he doesn't imply that it is a waste of time, just rather pointless.

3 **A** is correct because it does everything it is supposed to do. **B** is wrong because he doesn't mention anything about free time. **C** is wrong because there is no comparison made between what he thought it would be like and what it is like. **D** is wrong because there is a bit of a fuss when you put in chopsticks and coffee grounds.

4 **C** is correct because he talks about his wife being out of the house. **A** is wrong because he isn't irritated so much as horrified. **B** is wrong because he isn't mending the machine for his wife, but because he himself has been playing with it. **D** is wrong because, although he tries a wider variety of garbage, he doesn't say it should take it.

5 **D** is correct because Bryson's use of 'every', as in 'every basement' and 'every dad', gives the impression that he knows what happens across the United States. **A** is wrong because he doesn't comment on their popularity. **B** is wrong because he just *implies* they should be better used, he doesn't actually say so. **C** is wrong because he doesn't mention their design.

6 **A** is correct because they make children feel intimidated. **B** is wrong because the incidents do not actually happen. **C** is wrong because there is no competition. **D** is wrong because there is no mention of real arguments.

7 **B** is correct because effusive means enthusiastic. **A** is wrong because he isn't critical of his home. **C** is wrong because nostalgic means thinking fondly about the past and he is talking about the present. **D** is wrong because he isn't angry about anything.

3 Some of these phrases are put in for humorous effect.

Answers
a I don't want to start being too serious here
b a volcano-like eruption
c a small stream of water coming from who knows where
d presumably now dead and a skeleton
e so enormously useless – exaggerating for effect here
f some young dynamic father

g other good things about American household life that are taken for granted
h I'll let you know what happens

20.2 pages 172–173

1 Cartoons which play on words are popular in English.

Answer
tow / *toe* same pronunciation – it's a play on words.
   To give someone a tow means to tow their car for them, i.e. pull it using a rope or chain.
   A *toe* is what you have on your foot. A chiropodist is someone who looks after feet.
The first driver doesn't want to mend the vehicle himself.

2 You should be familiar with the construction *have/get something done*, so this should be revision.

Answers
a have   b get   c got   d had   e has/gets   f get

3 *Go* is often tested in Paper 3.

Answers
a down with   b in for   c on   d over   e for   f out
g off   h with   i without   j off

be spent on = go on
ebb = go out
fetch = go for
enter (a competition) = go in for
become ill with = go down with
explode = go off
match = go with
go sour = go off
examine = go over
manage without = go without

4 Remember to count the number of words you write. It must be between three and eight words.

Answers
1 promotion has gone to Penny Stone's
2 went over and over (again) (in his mind)
3 went on record as saying
4 was (ever) allowed to go to waste / (ever) went to waste
5 didn't (always) go off at a tangent

5 This exercise is error correction. The sentences contain common student errors. Refer to the appropriate Grammar folder if you need further help.

Answers
a As it was a wet evening, I stayed at home.
b We would like to know everything that has happened.
c He is already here.
d Only by listening intently, will you hear it singing.
e It would be easier to decide if my son were here.
f I have passed my exam this summer.
g It's worth being alive on such a lovely day.
h My family consists of six people.
i That is a mistake I often make.
j Your hair badly needs cutting.
k I suggest doing it immediately.
l This team is the better of the two.
m correct
n My information isn't up to date.
o I have been wanting / wanted to meet you for a long time.
p I congratulate you on having got / on getting married.
q I wish it would stop raining.
r You can eat as soon as dinner is ready.
s It's a five-mile journey.
t A man came into the compartment to check the tickets.

6 Remember to read the whole text before you do the answers.

Answers
1 sooner   2 adjacent/next   3 it   4 must   5 off
6 into   7 before   8 terms   9 Another   10 no
11 nowhere   12 turned/came   13 There   14 All
15 which/that

7

Possible answer
I remember once sitting on a bus on my way to a party. The girl sitting opposite me was dressed rather strangely and I remember staring and thinking that she looked pretty terrible. When I got to the party, there was the girl – she was my friend's new girlfriend. I was embarrassed because I had stared at her rather critically all through the journey.

20.3 pages 174–175

1

Possible answer
I think someone who is eccentric acts differently from other people. They live by a different code. They can be extraordinarily kind and imaginative people and I would like to be an eccentric if I wasn't so normal! I don't really know anyone very eccentric. I think most people have some eccentric traits.

I would find the man who played the practical jokes very irritating.

2 Read through the questions. You will need to answer True or False. Play the recording twice. The underlined parts of the tapescript confirm the answers.

Answers
1 T   2 F   3 F   4 T   5 T   6 F   7 F

Presenter: In the studio today I have Marion Fielding, whose new book on *The Role of the Eccentric in Society* has just been published. Now Marion, I'm sure most of us know, or maybe think we know, someone who is eccentric, but how do you define eccentricity?

Marion: Well, when we begin to work out what constitutes eccentricity, we might advance the obvious premise that eccentrics are not normal. Human behaviour ranges from absolute conformity, at the normal end of the spectrum, to utterly bizarre non-conformity at the opposite end. So a man who wears pink socks every day of the year, regardless of whether he is wearing a business suit or Bermuda shorts, demonstrates behaviour towards the eccentric end of the scale. <u>Exactly how much deviation from the norm it takes to qualify as a true eccentric is a vexed issue.</u>

Presenter: So, are we all eccentrics then to a greater or lesser extent?

Marion: That seems to be right. The question of what constitutes normality is quite subjective. We have all had the experience of talking with a friend who tells us that he has just met someone with the most bizarre or risqué habit – only to hear described something which we ourselves routinely do or might wish to do.

Presenter: I expect that where you live also comes into the equation?

Marion: Indeed. Social factors are quite potent. Even in the global village, what is normal in New York or London will seem very strange to the Tahitian or the Nigerian and vice versa. Moreover, there is a wide variation in the spectrum of deviations that society will tolerate. In Japan a greater degree of conformity is expected than in the USA or UK. <u>While in a pre-industrial society, such as that of the Inuit or the Indians of the South American rain forests, virtually every aspect of human behaviour follows a rigid pattern.</u>

Presenter: Yes, I suppose that the same thing happens in our society as well; the reason places like New York or San Francisco have become known as havens for nonconformists is because they are more tolerant of such behaviour than are the small towns of America. In your experience, how does the man in the street react to eccentricity?

Marion: <u>We all love eccentrics and yet we are profoundly ambivalent about them.</u> Our collective imagination, is piqued by the bizarre behaviour of someone like, for example, Howard Hughes, the richest man in the world, who lived the last days of his life like a mystical hermit. <u>Eccentrics have thrown off the constraints of normal life to let themselves do exactly as they please – and anyone who doesn't like it be damned.</u>

Presenter: What qualities would you say the average eccentric possesses?

Marion: There are about five common characteristics: being non-conforming; creative; <u>strongly motivated by curiosity</u>; idealistic and obsessed by one or more hobbyhorses. Nonconformity is the principal defining trait.

Presenter: One stereotype we all seem to share is that of the eccentric woman as an old lady in a big house with a hundred cats. Is this true at all?

Marion: Interestingly, one lady I found out about was the Countess of Eglintoune. She kept hundreds of *rats* rather than cats, summoning them to the dining room at meal times by tapping on an oak panel. <u>At her cue</u>, a dozen of· her favourites would appear out of the woodwork and join her at the table. After dinner, at a quiet word of command, the rats would retire in an orderly fashion.

Presenter: There must be some male eccentrics you've come across?

Marion: Indeed there are. Another eighteenth century aristocrat with a love of animals was Jack Myers. He was expelled from two schools and then spent about half a million pounds on alcohol in 17 years.

Presenter: Quite a lot of money for those days.

Marion: That's right. <u>One time havoc broke loose at one of his dinner parties, when he appeared in full hunting costume, mounted on his bear.</u> In the ensuing panic, while his friends jumped out of windows or clambered behind chairs, Myers called out 'Tally-ho' and spurred his mount which turned impatient and ate part of his leg.

Presenter: Well, thank you, Marion, for coming in and sharing your eccentrics with us. Now, next week …

3 You may come across some of the many words English has borrowed from other languages. The ones mentioned here are the most common.

Answers	
in lieu of	instead of
ad infinitum	to infinity / without end
ad nauseam	continually so as to bore someone
par excellence	pre-eminently
quid pro quo	something in return
faux pas	a mistake
prima facie	at first sight
niche	sector, suitable place
risqué	racy – usually jokes
protégé	someone you have under your wing / a follower
fracas	disturbance

cul-de-sac	street open at one end only
clique	small group of people not welcoming to outsiders
nom de plume	pseudonym used when writing
bête noire	something you dislike
tête á tête	friendly, confiding conversation
hoi polloi	the ordinary people
coup de grâce	finishing stroke

4

a faux pas **b** in lieu **c** nom de plume **d** risqué
e tête à tête **f** ad nauseam **g** cul de sac
h bête noire

5

Answers
1 grounds 2 seriously 3 turned 4 coming

6 Read the information in your book. Hesitating, as long as it is in English, is acceptable, as long as it isn't for too long! Time yourself when you do the activity. You have two minutes each on your subject.

Possible answer – Task A
Personally speaking, I think it is better to conform, as this will help your life go more smoothly. I really admire people who try to be different, who maybe don't get married, but live together, who wear weird clothes or have strange hobbies, but in general you have fewer problems if you conform. If you want to be different, then it's better to live in a large city, like London or San Francisco. There, people don't seem to mind so much that your behaviour may be a little eccentric. If you live in a small village, then everyone will comment on what you do and what you wear and you might end up ostracised by the villagers. This is no way to live your life as you need as many friends as you can get. Having a strange hobby is probably not so much of a problem as not getting married or wearing funny clothes. As long, that is, as you haven't got an anti-social hobby like keeping rats or twenty killer dogs!

Writing folder 10

Paper 2 Part 2 Articles and Letters
pages 176–177

1 In the exam, read each question carefully, to decide what style and tone to use.

Answers

Functions
A factual description; speculation; narrative
B factual description; opinion
C opinion; comparison; speculation
D evaluation; opinion
E description; opinion; evaluation

Style and tone
A should be light-hearted, as this is requested.
B should be fairly serious.
C (letter) should be formal; could be fairly light (anecdotal) or more serious.
D could be either, depending on the set book.
E (letter) should be formal and polite.

---

2   This activity should remind you of some of the vocabulary you have learned during the course, which might be relevant to these tasks.

Suggested answers

A adventure, exhilarating, expansion, far-flung, historic, likelihood, multiplicity, unknown, venture
B emissions, expansion, global warming, impinge, judicious, multiplicity, perspective, tendency, trend, wipe out
C birthrate, bread-winner, code, domesticity, historic, likelihood, morals, patriarch, rules, stress, trend, unemployment
D code, denouement, exhilarating, judicious, morals, perspective, plot, rules, tendency, trend, unmistakable
E context, denouement, judicious, plot, unmistakable

---

3   You will not have time in the exam to write a rough copy first. Always make a paragraph plan before you start writing your answer.

4   Choose one of the tasks on page 176 and follow the instructions on timing and all the other advice given on page 177.

Units 17–20 Revision

pages 178–179

The aim of this revision unit is to focus on the language covered in Units 17–20, and earlier, and to provide support for the Part 2 letter (see Writing folder 10). Specific exam practice is provided on Reading Part 1 and Use of English Parts 3 and 4. These Paper 1 and Paper 3 tasks could be done as a timed test of 30 minutes.

1

Answers
1 A   2 D   3 B   4 A   5 C   6 A

2

Answers
1 mustn't/shouldn't/can't allow the rumours to carry on/let the rumours carry on
2 needn't have helped us do/with
3 come when/whenever he likes as far as I'm
4 to preserve her anonymity, I had the press
5 her sore throat/having a sore throat, Eliza excelled herself
6 other than / but a full apology would be acceptable

3

Answers
1 fair   2 hold   3 rights   4 question   5 state
6 account

4

Sample answer
A strange being stood stock still in the middle of the road. There was mist swirling around and it was impossible to make out who or what it was, but I swear I could see horns on its head and a pair of evil, red eyes. As I rammed on the brakes, the radio crackled and went dead. I sat there for a moment, staring in the gloom, trying to work out what was ahead. Then, steeling myself, I sounded the car horn repeatedly and drove towards the ghastly creature, which thankfully bounded off.

Crossword

¹F	O	²O	D	³F	O	R	T	⁴H	O	⁵U	G	H	T
E		O		R				I		U			
E		⁶Z	E	A	L	O	U	S		⁷P	L	U	⁸S
L		E		C			⁹S	O	U	L			U
¹⁰T	O			A		¹¹F				¹²N	I	N	E
H		¹³D	E	S	T	I	N	Y		B			
E		A		S		S			¹⁴F	L	A	N	
¹⁵P	E	R	C	E	¹⁶P	T	¹⁷I	V	E		E		
I		K		R		R	N		¹⁸Y		¹⁹A	²⁰S	
N		E		O		²¹S		O			H		
²²C	O	²³N	T	²⁴E	²⁵M	P	T	U	O	U	²⁶S		R
H		H		²⁷P	U	R	R		²⁸O	W	E		
	²⁹U	U		³⁰T	R	I	G	G	E	R			W
³¹S	P	A	D	E		R		E		³²E	N	D	

Listening Test 5

See page 286 and key on page 287.

Listening test 1

Paper 4 Part 2

You will hear a man talking about Agnes Marshall, a famous nineteenth-century chef and writer. For questions **1–9**, complete the sentences with a word or short phrase.

Agnes Marshall ran a [**1**] in London.

She had a special reputation for her ices and [**2**]

She was the inventor of the [**3**]

She went to lectures on [**4**] in order to develop new techniques.

In her magazine in 1901, she suggested adding [**5**] at the dinner table.

Earlier in the nineteenth century, the demand for ice had been encouraged by the arrival of [**6**], among them culinary experts.

In Norway, the ice was taken from [**7**]

The two things which moved in Nancy Johnson's machine were the [**8**]

Agnes Marshall's 'ice cave' had an [**9**] packed with ice and salt.

© Cambridge University Press, 2002

Listening test 2

Paper 4 Part 1

You will hear four different extracts. For questions **1–8**, choose the answer (**A**, **B** or **C**) which fits best according to what you hear. There are two questions for each extract.

Extract 1

You hear two friends discussing customer loyalty cards.

1   Which phrase summarises the woman's reaction to loyalty cards?

    A a profitable source of discounts
    B a ridiculous waste of time
    C an unnecessary extra stage

1

2   According to the man, stores value loyalty cards because

    A they have stimulated consumption.
    B they are appreciated by shoppers.
    C they can provide essential data.

2

Extract 2

You hear a man reviewing some music CDs on the radio.

3   What does the speaker say with regard to the Chamber Concerto?

    A The composer's own recording of it is preferable.
    B John Adams' playing in it is masterly throughout.
    C The Ensemble Modern has interpreted it well.

3

4   According to the speaker, which recording is considered to be overlong by some people?

    A Sian Edwards'
    B Herman Kretzschmar's
    C Gloria Cheng-Cochran's

4

Extract 3

You hear a woman giving a lecture on the photographer Arnold Newman.

5 Which part of Arnold Newman's work displays innovation, according to the speaker?

   A his artistic compositions
   B his professional assignments
   C his environmental portraits

	5

6 What is Arnold Newman's particular skill in portrait photography?

   A knowing exactly when to take the shot
   B directing each session painstakingly
   C capturing the full character of his subject

	6

Extract 4

You hear two people talking about a city they know well.

7 What has changed significantly in the city since the woman's last visit?

   A the amenities provided by the city
   B the number of new buildings
   C the volume of traffic

	7

8 How has the man's lifestyle improved recently?

   A He spends less time commuting than he used to.
   B He attends more concerts now there is a new venue.
   C He has started leaving the city at the weekend.

	8

Listening test 3

Paper 4 Part 4

You will hear two students, Jerry and Maria, talking about genetic modification (GM). For questions **1–6**, decide whether the opinions are expressed by only one of the speakers, or whether the speakers agree.

Write **J** for Jerry,

    M for Maria, or

    B for both, where they agree.

1   Scientific experts are all too often working in the dark. | 1 |

2   GM research is funded by sources other than the public sector. | 2 |

3   To claim that GM is being used primarily for cosmetic improvements to crops is nonsense. | 3 |

4   It is vital to improve the amounts harvested in order to deal with world hunger. | 4 |

5   Organic farming methods represent a viable alternative to the use of pesticides. | 5 |

6   Scientists' plans to genetically modify mosquitoes are ethically sound. | 6 |

Listening test 4

Paper 4 Part 3

You will hear an interview with Keith McLaren, in which he reviews a new book by Beryl Bainbridge. For questions **1–5**, choose the answer (**A, B, C** or **D**) which fits best according to what you hear.

1 Prior to actually reading *According to Queeney*, Keith McLaren

   A anticipated another book by his favourite author with relish.
   B believed Bainbridge had already written too many historical novels.
   C worried that the book would not live up to his expectations.
   D found the choice of Dr Johnson as subject matter interesting.

2 What does McLaren say about this book in relation to her previous novels?

   A The standard of writing is better.
   B The subject matter is closer to home.
   C It has a longer timescale.
   D It focuses more on bad luck.

3 With regard to the historical dimension, McLaren feels that Bainbridge

   A manages to bring the period to life.
   B has included too many small details.
   C keeps her portrayals in character.
   D could have done more research.

4 McLaren praises Bainbridge's written style for its

   A skilful understatement.
   B contrasting voices.
   C comic originality.
   D marked sensitivity.

5 Bainbridge has chosen to depict Dr Johnson as

   A an unswervingly enlightened scholar.
   B someone who is often misunderstood.
   C a cantankerous old madman.
   D a man of many contradictions.

© Cambridge University Press, 2002

Listening test 5

Paper 4 Part 2

You will hear a woman talking about a NASA employee, George Aldrich, whose job is to detect unusual odours. For questions **1–9**, complete the sentences with a word or short phrase.

George's laboratory is located in | **1**

Anyone wanting to work on George's team must be free of | **2** and have no breathing difficulties.

The ten-bottle test includes three | **3**

Personal items that have been rejected by George's team include | **4**

Following a period of being heated in a container, material is screened for its | **5**

The third level of the 0–4 scale is referred to as | **6** by the Odour Panel.

If George's team had failed to reject the ink, | **7** would have caused problems on a space mission.

Occasionally, the identification is imprecise, such as when the smell was compared to | **8**

George also assesses | **9** at an event near his home.

LISTENING TESTS Key

LISTENING TEST 1

Paper 4 Part 2

1 cookery school
2 sorbets
3 ice cream cone
4 low-temperature chemistry
5 liquid air
6 Italian immigrants
7 lakes and glaciers
8 paddle and handle
9 outer sleeve

LISTENING TEST 2

Paper 4 Part 1

1 B 2 C 3 C 4 B 5 C 6 A 7 B 8 A

LISTENING TEST 3

Paper 4 Part 4

1 M 2 B 3 J 4 B 5 M 6 J

LISTENING TEST 4

Paper 4 Part 3

1 C 2 B 3 A 4 A 5 D

LISTENING TEST 5

Paper 4 Part 2

1 (the) New Mexico (desert) / a/the desert
2 allergies
3 blanks
4 mascara
5 toxicity
6 objectionable
7 (printed) flight plans
8 (an) onion
9 footwear/sneakers/trainers

Acknowledgements

The authors would like to thank Alyson Maskell for her meticulous editorial support.

The authors and publishers would like to thank the teachers and students who trialled and commented on the material:

France: Josephine Rudland; Germany: Caroline Mears; Greece: Christine Barton, Maria Martopoulos; Italy/USA: Gregory Manin; Italy: Sarah Ellis; Poland: Monika Galbarczyk; Portugal: Mark Appleby, Tony Hilzbrich, Neil Mason; Spain: Elizabeth Bridges, Henny Burke; Switzerland: Karyl Müller-Pringle, Anne Weber; UK: Sue Ashcroft, Mike Gutteridge, Roger Scott, Clare West

The authors and publishers are grateful to the authors, publishers and others who have given permission for the use of copyright material identified in the text. It has not been possible to identify the sources of all the material used and in such cases the publishers would welcome information from copyright owners. Apologies are expressed for any omissions.

Text p.11 from Adrian Mole: *The Cappuccino Years* by Sue Townsend (Michale Joseph, 1999) copyright © Sue Townsend, 1999; Text p.14 Henri Cartier Bresson, reprinted with permission from the *Encyclopaedia Britannica* © 2002 Britannica.com, Inc; © Bernard Levin/Times Newspapers Ltd for article p.16, *Born to shop* 3rd February 1978; © The Observer for article by Phil Hogan on p.16, 4th July 1999; Steve Watkins for article p.17, *It's ecological* from Geographical Magazine; © The Observer for article by Jason Burke on p.20, *Freedom ship* 28th May 2000; Julie Cohen for article p.20, *Mars in their eyes* from Geographical Magazine; US Geological Survey for text p.25; Little Brown & Co for text p.26, *Weird weather* by Paul Simons; © The Guardian for text p.28, *Keep your distance* by Oliver Burkeman 14th September 1999; For text p.34 from *Rituals of dinner* by Margaret Visser (Viking, 1992) copyright © Margaret Visser, 1991; John Simpson for text p.40 from *A mad world, my masters*, reproduced by permission of Macmillan, London, UK; © Andrew Brown for text p.41, *Froth* from The Guardian 21st April 2001; © Times Newspapers Limited for text p.43, *Some people are born to shop* by Jonathan Leake 14th September 1997; Douglas Rushkoff for text p.45, *I don't know which of these trainers is me* from *Coercion* published by Little Brown & Co; Meg Carter for text p.46, *Are you in the mood* from The Guardian 10th July 2000; John Thornhill for text p.46, *The new consumer is always right* from The Financial Times 21st August 2000; © Simon Jenkins/Times Newspapers Limited for text p.48 *The book – still precious lifeblood of a master spirit*, 1st January 2000; © Adam Mars Jones/Times Newspapers Limited for text p.49 *Cinema*, 1st January 2000; © Gary Kliewer for text p.50, *Rock me Amadeus* from The Guardian 12th November 2000; BBC Radio 3 for listening exercise p.54, from *Music Machine* originally broadcast 26th January 1999; © The Guardian for listening exercise p.58, *Percy Shaw* by David Newman 8th November 1997; Robert Hughes for text p.59, from *The shock of the new* published by Thames & Hudson Ltd. 1991; Bernard Venables for text p.63, *Beauty, a force for life* from Birds Magazine Summer 2000; June Boyce Tillmann for text p.65, *The rhythm of life* from Classic FM magazine August 2000; Jane Jacobs for text p.65, *The need for aged buildings. The death and life of American cities* Pelican/Cape 1962; © Philip Willan for text p.65 Merchant@florence from The Guardian 31st July 2001; Town and Country Planning Magazine for text p.66, *Cool Brazil* July/August 2000; Town and Country Planning Magazine for text p.67, *Lessons from a magnificent failure* June 2000; For text p.74, from *No Logo: Taking aim at the brand bullies* (Picador (USA), 2000). Copyright Naomi Klein © 2000. With the permission of the author, and also of HarperCollins Publishers Ltd in the UK; © Alan Young and Thomas Mahon for the listening exercise p.77, *Is it time to consign the suit to history?* from The Guardian 29th January 2000; Text p.80, *Are you a domestic tyrant* courtesy of Good Housekeeping Magazine © National Magazine Company February 1999; David Crystal for text p.84, *Death sentence* from The Guardian 25th October 1999; © Jane Bolton/Times Newspapers Limited, for the text on p.86, *Wise up think global* 24th November 1999; Anthony Giddens for the text p.88, *New world without end* from the 1999 Reith Lectures as seen in The Guardian 11th April 1999; © Ian Sansom for the text p.89, *The whole whack* from The Guardian 11th

November 2000; Text p.94, *Love on the internet* by kind permission of Woman Magazine © 15th January 2000; Text p.95, *You buzzing at me?* Reproduced with permission from New Scientist magazine, the global authority on science and technology news © RBI 2000 www.NewScientist.com; Constable & Robinson Ltd for text p.97, *Irrationality: the enemy within* by Stuart Sutherland; Text p.98 from Comic relief reproduced with permission from New Scientist magazine, the global authority on science and technology news © RBI 2000 www.NewScientist.com; Anjana Ahuja for text p.99, *Why it pays to avoid the wet fish* © Times Newspapers Limited, 10th July 2000; © David Lodge for text p.100 from *Therapy* published by Martin Secker & Warburg 1995. Reprinted by permission of The Random House Group Ltd; and Curtis Brown; George A Miller for text p.101 from *Psychology* published by Routledge 1962; Penguin Books Ltd for text p.102 from *The Fifth Miracle* by Paul Davies; Text p.110 from *The joy of socks* reproduced with permission from New Scientist magazine, the global authority on science and technology news © RBI 2000 www.NewScientist.com; BBC Wildlife Magazine for listening exercise p.112 from *My kind of life* by Sue Beenstock, January 2001; Listening exercise p.112 from *The amateur naturalist* reproduced with permission of Curtis Brown Ltd, London on behalf of the Estate of Gerald Durrell. Copyright Gerald Durrell; Listening exercise p.112 from *Glad to be Gaia* by Anjana Ahuja © Times Newspapers Ltd, 15th May 2000; Text p.115 from *The First Naturalists* reproduced with permission of Curtis Brown Ltd, London on behalf of the Estate of Gerald Durrell. Copyright Gerald Durrell; Text p.116 *New flora and fauna for old* © The Economist Newspaper Ltd, London 23rd December 2000; Text p.118 adapted from an article by Matthew Sweet *Into the silicon valley of death* first published in The Independent, 29th October 2000; Text p.120 *Longer health, not just longer life* © The Economist Newspaper Ltd, London 23rd December 2000; Alex Dolbey for text p.120 *Diary of a runner* first published in *The Sticks* magazine, January 2001; © Helen Foster for text p.122 *Gym won't fix it* from The Observer Magazine, 21st January 2001; © Kate Hilpern for text p.130 *Eyes wide shut* from The Guardian, 26th February 2001; Sir John Harvey-Jones for text p.132 *Making it happen* published by HarperCollins Publishers Ltd 1988; Text p.133 *Bill Gates* © 2000 Dorling Kindersley Ltd, text copyright © Robert Heller; Listening exercise p.134 *As others see us* © Susan D'Arcy/Times Newspapers limited, 9th November 1997; Marcus Austin and Monica Seely for listening exercise p.135 *Is e-commerce the only future for British business?* from The Guardian 18th September 1999; Text p.136 from *The lone pilgrim* by Laurie Colwin, copyright © 1981 by Laurie Colwin. Used by permission of Alfred A Knopf, a division of Random House, Inc; Poem p.138 *New members welcome* by Spike Milligan from *Small dreams of a scorpion* by permission of Spike Milligan Productions Ltd; Text p.138 from *Review of Collected Poems of Montale* copyright © 1999 by Nicholas Jenkins. First appeared in the *New York Times Book Review*. Reprinted by permission of Melanie Jackson Agency, L.L.C; Text p.144 from *Mapping biodiversity* © The Economist Newspaper Ltd, London 23rd December 2000; Text p.147 from *My family and other animals* by Gerald Durrell reproduced with permission of Curtis Brown Ltd, London, on behalf of the Estate of Gerald Durrell. Copyright Gerald Durrell 1956; Text p.148 from *The consolations of philosophy* by Alain de Botton (Viking, 2000) copyright © Alain de Botton, 2000. Reproduced by permission of Penguin Books Limited; the dictionary definitions on p.149 are from the Cambridge International Dictionary of English (Cambridge University Press, 1995); © Eddi Fingel for listening exercise p.152 *Love letters straight from the heart* from The Guardian, 13th October 2000; Listening exercise p.152 extracted from an article by Simon Pooley *A nation in hopeless pursuit of happiness* first published in The Independent on Sunday on Sunday 8th April 2001; © Bruce Robinson for listening exercise p.153 *Why I dumped the city job with the six-figure salary* first published in The Guardian 3rd April 2001; Text p.154 from *Values for a Godless age: The story of the United Kingdom's new bill of rights* by Francesca Klug (Penguin, 2000) copyright © Francesca Klug, 2000. Reproduced by permission of Penguin Books Limited; Text p.162 from *The world of the unexplained* by Janet and Colin Bord, published by Cassell & Co 1998; Text p.164 from *The unexplained mysteries of the universe* by Colin Wilson (Dorling Kindersley 1997) copyright © Dorling Kindersley Ltd, text copyright © 1997 Colin Wilson; Text p.166 from the postscript by Renée